THE ANNALS OF
THE KING'S ROYAL RIFLE CORPS

THE ANNALS OF THE
KING'S ROYAL RIFLE CORPS

Vol. I. ' The Royal Americans '
By Lt.-Col. Lewis Butler.

Vol. II. ' The Green Jacket '
By Lt.-Col. Lewis Butler.

Vol. III. ' The 60th : The K.R.R.C.'
By Lt.-Col. Lewis Butler.

Vol. IV. ' The 60th : The K.R.R.C.'
By Major-General Sir Steuart Hare.

APPENDIX, Dealing with Uniform, Armament and Equipment. By Maj.-Gen. Astley Terry and S. M. Milne.

KING'S ROYAL RIFLE CORPS
Regimental Chronicle for 1917.

LIEUT.-GENERAL FRANCIS, BARON DE ROTHENBURG, K.C.H.

From a miniature. By kind permission of his granddaughter, Mrs. W. H. Paget, O.B.E., and of the Editor of the "Journal of the Argyll and Sutherland Highland Regiment."

[Frontispiece

THE ANNALS OF THE KING'S ROYAL RIFLE CORPS

BY
MAJOR-GENERAL SIR STEUART HARE,
K.C.M.G., C.B.

VOLUME V

THE GREAT WAR

WITH FRONTISPIECE AND MAPS

PREFACE

TO

THE FIFTH VOLUME

This work cannot claim to be anything approaching a complete history of the King's Royal Rifle Corps in the Great War. To follow the vicissitudes of all the battalions of the Regiment which took part in it in any detail would require a volume for each battalion, and there were sixteen of them overseas. To attempt to recount the movements of all these battalions, their changes of command, their casualties, and the honours and rewards gained by their members would be to give a mere list of names and dates. The author's difficulty has not been to find material, but to eliminate it; he has therefore been compelled to give accounts of the chief events only in which battalions of the Regiment took part; and even these only in outline. No one can feel more than he does the lack of human interest in his work. Deeds of gallantry were constantly being performed, which would have been worth a V.C. in any other war, to which he has not room even to refer, much less adequately to describe. He has willingly abstained from dwelling on the hardships and horrors of the war, having no desire to make his readers' flesh creep. As Colonel Downes has well said in his history of the Australian Medical Services in the war: 'If victory can be attained at the expense of much individual suffering while it cannot be attained without it, then it must be pursued and the price paid'; and it is not the soldier who complains.

Though short of space, the author has thought it necessary to give some account of the war as a whole, and some explanations of events leading up to the actions in which our battalions took part. Not to do so would make the book a tale of a series of disconnected and purposeless tactical operations. Quite enough of the operations in the war were disconnected and purposeless without letting it appear that they were all so. It would be a fair criticism to say: 'If the author is so short of space, why does he take up so much of it in airing his own views, instead of sticking to facts?' He can only plead 'mitigating circumstances.' How is an author to get any fun out of all his drudgery if he is not allowed, at times, to give his own opinions?

The author's thanks are due, firstly, to the Staff of the Historical Section of the Committee of Imperial Defence, whose kindness and patience to amateur historians is beyond measure; secondly, to the editors of the Regimental 'Chronicle' during the war years; and, indirectly, to those officers who supplied the 'Chronicle' with the individual records of battalions. His thanks are also due to those friends who have supplied him with private diaries and letters of which, from want of space, he regrets not having been able to make more use.

NOTE.—Obituary notices of the majority of the officers of the Regiment killed in the war may be found in the Regimental 'Chronicle' of the King's Royal Rifle Corps for the years 1914–18, copies of which may be obtained from the Editor, Rifle Depot, Winchester.

CONTENTS

CONTENTS

THE FRONTISPIECE

Francis, Baron de Rothenburg, was born at Dantzig on November 4, 1757. *The story of his early youth is unknown, but in March* 1782 *he received a commission in the French Army, where, as we learn from the records of the French War Office, he acquired a reputation as an 'officier exact et intelligent.' He quitted the French Service in* 1791, *and we next find him in command of a regiment of Polish Infantry. He served under Kosciusko in the war with Russia till the defeat of that great patriot in* 1794. *He next joined, as a major, a regiment of German Hussars in British pay, raised by Count Carl von Hompesch, and, on the departure of that corps to the West Indies in* 1796, *remained in Europe to assist Ferdinand von Hompesch to raise a regiment consisting partly of* Chasseurs à pied, *partly of Mounted Infantry. This regiment was merged in our* 5*th Battalion on its formation in* 1798 *and de Rothenburg was given command of the new Battalion. He served with it against the Irish rebels in* 1798 *and took it to the West Indies in the following year, where he commanded it in the expedition to Surinam. He was promoted to Brigadier-General just as the Battalion was about to sail for Portugal in May* 1808. *He commanded in Montreal as a Major-General during the American War of* 1812, *and died at Portsmouth in* 1832.

De Rothenburg—his name was spelt Rotenburg when in the French Army and, usually, Rottenburg in the British Service—became a naturalised British subject when in our Regiment. He was the author of a work entitled 'Regulations for the exercise of Riflemen and Light Infantry,' which Sir John Moore acknowledged as the groundwork of his training of the Light Division. We may rightly claim him as the father of British Riflemen.

LIST OF ILLUSTRATIONS

PORTRAIT

SKETCHES

MAPS

Note.—In all the above Maps and Sketches the North is at the top.

COLONELS COMMANDANT OF 'THE KING'S ROYAL RIFLE CORPS,' 1914—1918

COLONEL-IN-CHIEF

THE KING

COLONELS-COMMANDANT

NAME.

1ST BN. FIELD-MARSHAL THE RT. HON. F. W. LORD GRENFELL, P.C., G.C.B., G.C.M.G.

2ND BN. LIEUT.-GENERAL SIR EDWARD T. H. HUTTON, K.C.B., K.C.M.G.

3RD BN. MAJOR-GENERAL SIR CROMER ASHBURNHAM, K.C.B. (ob. 1917).

4TH BN. MAJOR-GENERAL SIR WYKEHAM LEIGH PEMBERTON, K.C.B. (ob. 1918).

3RD BN. MAJOR-GENERAL R. S. R. FETHERSTONHAUGH, C.B.

4TH BN. LIEUT.-GENERAL SIR WILLIAM PITCAIRN CAMPBELL, K.C.B.

ROLL OF OFFICERS OF THE KING'S ROYAL RIFLE CORPS, AUGUST 1914

LIEUT.-COLONELS

E. NORTHEY.
C. GOSLING, k. in a., 12/4/17.
E. PEARCE SEROCOLD.
HON. C. J. SACKVILLE-WEST.

MAJORS

L. F. PHILIPS.
H. C. WARRE, D.S.O.
H. R. BLORE.

MAJORS—*continued*

G. C. Shakerley, D.S.O., k. in a., 15/5/15.
W. J. Long.
G. V. Hordern.
H. C. R. Green.
W. F. G. Wyndham, M.V.O.
R. G. Jelf.
G. A. P. Rennie, D.S.O.
B. F. Widdrington.
G. A. Armytage.
H. F. F. B. Foljambe, k. in a., 14/9/14.
B. J. Majendie.
H. F. W. Bircham, d. of w., 23/7/16.
J. H. Davidson, D.S.O.

CAPTAINS

W. A. I. Kay, k. in a., 4/10/18.
A. E. Cathcart, k. in a., 14/9/14.
H. Wake, D.S.O.
H. C. Johnson, D.S O., d. of w., 1/1/15.
C. H. N. Seymour.
L. A. E. Price-Davies, V.C., D.S.O.
G. K. Priaulx, k. in a., 24/3/18.
A. D. Legard.
G. Makins, M.V.O., d. of w., 23/8/15.
S. F. McI. Lomer.
H. B. P. L. Kennedy.
G. H. Martin.
G. J. Acland Troyte.
A. R. Leith.
C. F. Hawley, k. in a., 2/11/14.
R. E. Crichton.
F. G. Willan.
G. Culme-Seymour, k. in a., 7/5/15.
A. F. C. Maclachlan, D.S.O., k. in a., 22/3/18.
W. S. W. Parker-Jervis.
E. A. Bradford.
C. A. Howard.
G. H. Barnett.

CAPTAINS—*continued*

G. C. Kelly.
B. J. Curling.
B. Seymour.
J. E. N. Heseltine.
R. H. Seymour.
F. V. Yeats Brown.
G. T. Lee.
F. L. Pardoe.
T. G. Dalby.
R. N. Abadie, k. in a., 10/7/17.
H. A. Vernon.
F. W. L. Edwards.
C. V. L. Poë, k. in a., 3/3/15.
H. W. M. Watson.
G. Wynne Finch.
E. B. Denison.
Sir G. A. H. Beaumont, Bt.
C. J. T. R. Wingfield, d. of w., 29/4/15.
A. A. Soames.
G. J. Jackson.
A. J. Hunter.
W. D. Barber.
M. L. S. Clements.

LIEUTENANTS

H. C. M. Porter.
W. H. Deedes.
A. P. Evans.
G. M. Atkinson.
W. J. Davis, k. in a., 30/7/15.
R. H. Willan.
R. H. Bond, k. in a., 14/9/14.
J. F. R. Hope.
A. C. Oppenheim.
H. J. Flower.
W. L. Clinton, d. 22/11/18.
H. C. Ponsonby.
J. S. Mellor.
M. F. Blake, k. in a., 14/9/14.

LIEUTENANTS—*continued*

J. F. B. Pearse, k. in a., 29/4/15.
F. W. Parish.
L. G. Moore.
Hon. E. E. M. J. Upton, k. in a., 9/5/15.
A. M. Wakefield-Saunders.
R. H. Woods.
W. A. C. Saunders-Knox-Gore.
Hon. J. N. Bigge, k. in a., 15/5/15.
R. J. H. Purcell.
J. F. P. Butler, d. of w., 5/9/16.
J. F. Franks, d. of w., 22/9/15.
A. L. Bonham-Carter.
J. V. E. Lees.
P. G. Chaworth-Musters, d. of w., 12/1/15.
G. V. H. Gough.
J. E. Pleydell-Bouverie, d. of w., 1/11/14.
A. D. Thursby, k. in a., 15/2/15.
C. C. Grattan-Bellew.
J. H. S. Dimmer, k. in a., 21/3/18.
S. H. Ferrand.
H. O. Curtis.
H. M. B. de Sales La Terriere.
F. W. Cavendish-Bentinck.
C. T. Ellison.
E. G. W. Bourke, k. in a., 16/6/15.
B. W. Jackson, k. in a., 14/9/14.
E. R. H. Herbert.
A. E. Lawrence.
E. D. Shafto.
G. S. Oxley.
P. J. R. Currie.
A. H. Brocklehurst, d. of w., 29/7/16.
G. R. Dubs.
C. W. Fladgate.
D. J. Mitchell.
H.H. Prince Maurice V. D. of Battenberg, K.C.V.O., k. in a., 27/10/14.
M. K. Mackenzie, k. in a., 1/2/16.
N. C. H. Macdonald-Moreton, k. in a., 13/10/15.

SECOND LIEUTENANTS

R. V. C. Bodley.
J. S. Alston.
M. S. Ormrod.
R. A. Banon.
C. G. E. Clowes, d. of w., 18/2/15.
R. C. Fetherstonhaugh, d. of w., 14/5/15.
G. S. R. Thompson, k. in a., 14/9/14.
C. S. Price-Davies.
Hon. W. A. M. Eden, k. in a., 3/3/15.
G. Walmsley.
E. H. Barker.
J. Forster, k. in a., 14/9/14.
H. C. Lloyd.
L. H. St. A. King, k. in a., 8/5/15.
E. F. Campbell.
O. H. C. Balfour.
W. R. M. Crossman, k. in a., 2/11/14.
S. Davison, k. in a., 14/9/14.
W. P. Bristowe.
R. Pennefather.
H.H. Prince Leopold A. L. of Battenberg, K.C.V.O.
E. V. Tindall, d. of w., 12/9/14.
R. H. M. Barclay, k. in a., 14/9/14.

ADJUTANTS

	Name.
1st Bn.	Lieutenant R. H. Woods.
4th Bn.	Lieutenant H. C. Ponsonby.
2nd Bn.	Lieutenant Hon. E. Upton.
3rd Bn.	Lieutenant J. F. Franks.

QUARTERMASTERS

	Name.
6th Special Reserve.	Hon. Captain W. Judge.
3rd Bn.	Hon. Lieutenant A. C. Watkins.
1st Bn.	Hon. Lieutenant A. Harman.
2nd Bn.	Hon. Lieutenant A. Robinson.
4th Bn.	Hon. Lieutenant T. Jones.
5th Special Reserve.	Hon. Lieutenant E. Scott.

THE KING'S ROYAL RIFLE CORPS

CHAPTER I

'France and Flanders, 1914–18,' 'Italy, 1917–18,' 'Macedonia, 1916–18'

The Great War in Brief[1]

The German invasion of Belgium having solved the question of whether or not the British Empire should come

Addenda slips for Vols. I, II, and III are to be found at the end of this Volume between pages 450 and 451.

I Corps (1st and 2nd Divisions) were under Sir D. Haig. The II Corps (3rd and 5th Divisions) had just been taken over by Sir Horace Smith-Dorrien, in succession to Sir James Grierson, who died suddenly in the train on his way to the Front.

So far everything had gone well for the Germans. They had successfully overrun Belgium, though they had met with more opposition than they expected, and most of what was left of the Belgian Army was bottled up in Antwerp. A great French offensive in Lorraine had failed, and had done nothing to interfere with the German encircling move-

[1] See Map VIII.

ment through Belgium. The Allied left was in the air and opposed to a greatly superior force.

The French Fifth Army, immediately on the British right, was attacked, and fell back on the 22nd. No news of this movement reached Sir John French, and on the 23rd he found himself holding a front of twenty-five miles with four divisions, and about to be attacked by more than double his numbers. The Germans opened their attack about midday along the whole front, but could make no impression against the superior rifle-fire of the British troops, and it was only the arrival of the information that the French had retired on his right the day before, and the consequent prospect of having both his flanks turned, that caused French to start his retreat at daylight next morning.

The I Corps started its retreat at 4 a.m. on the 24th, and fell back without interference from the enemy to the line Feignies–Bavai. The II Corps, which had been attacked all day on the 23rd and was attacked again at daylight, only got back to the line Bavai–St. Waast–Bermeries after heavy fighting. Touch had not yet been obtained with the French on the right, so both flanks were still in the air. The retreat was resumed on the 25th, the I Corps passing east of the Forêt de Mormal, again without interference; the II Corps to the west of it. The II Corps, and the Cavalry Division farther west, were fighting all the way. The Germans, having realised that the British were now in full retreat, began to press the pursuit vigorously, and to try to get round the western flank of the British.

On the morning of the 26th Smith-Dorrien, at Le Cateau, judged that the only way to check the pursuit was to stand and fight. This he did all day—reinforced by the 4th Division, which had just reached the front—with such success that the German advance was stayed for the time, and he was able to withdraw his badly shattered divisions after dark.

Next day touch was obtained by the I Corps with the French Fifth Army on their right, and by the II Corps and Cavalry Division with a new French Sixth Army, which was being formed under Manoury on the Somme, on their left. By the 28th the whole British force was back in line on the Oise. The danger to the British Expeditionary Force of having either flank turned was over, but there was an immediate prospect of their being cut off from the Channel ports, and the base was hurriedly changed from Boulogne and Dieppe to St. Nazaire, at the mouth of the Loire.

The retreat continued all along the Allied front from near Verdun, which formed the pivot of the backward wheel.

On September 3 the British Expeditionary Force reached the Marne, and by the 5th they were behind the Grand Morin.

This was the limit of the retreat; in spite of heavy losses in men and still heavier in material, the front had remained unbroken.

The disappointment of continual retreat, instead of the expected great battle in defence of the frontier, had not affected the morale of either force. French and British were ready to turn and strike back as soon as the order should be given.

On September 4 Joffre, the French Commander-in-Chief, decided that the time was ripe.

The German plan had been that, while their right was pressing back, outflanking, and enveloping the Allied left, their left was to break through between Metz and the Vosges. Then both flanks were to press on, rolling up the Allied flanks as they went, thus producing a Sedan on a gigantic scale which would eliminate France, and the only army Britain had worth mentioning, from the war, leaving Russia to be dealt with at leisure.

The plan failed, and the chance of Germany winning the war in the first round went with it.

The attempt to break the French line east of the Moselle had begun on August 23, but had been checked, and by September 4 Joffre could look to the security of his right with some confidence.

On August 31 Von Kluck, commanding on the extreme German right, began his wheel to the south-west, which was to roll up the left of the Allied line, but he—or his superiors for him—misjudged the situation.

He appears to have thought that he had already accounted for the French Sixth Army and the British Expeditionary Force, and could afford to neglect them. He regarded the French Fifth Army as the left of the Allied line, and in his march south-west to outflank it offered his own right to be outflanked in turn.

Now was Joffre's great moment. The German forces had weakened as they advanced, or had at any rate become no stronger; expected reinforcements having been switched off to repel the Russian attack on East Prussia. The French force, on the other hand, had become stronger as it retired. In addition to Manoury's Sixth Army, a new Ninth Army had been formed under Foch, and come into line on the right of the Fifth.

The battle of the Marne began on September 6 with an advance by Manoury, quickly followed by that of the British Expeditionary Force on his right. The Germans tried to hold off Manoury, and at the same time to break the Allied line farther east, while the efforts to break the French right were renewed. The battle developed along the whole line. Von Kluck was gradually pushed back, the German attack on the left centre failed, and the Allies began to counter-attack all along their line.

The Germans could only escape disaster by falling back. This they did along their whole line, but in good order, and without any great losses in either guns or prisoners. By September 13 the pursuing Allies were confronted by a fresh and unbroken German line running, roughly, from Compiègne along the line of the Aisne, behind Verdun and Nancy to the Swiss frontier.

The German invasion had ended in failure, but by no means in disaster. The retreat was the result of their plan having miscarried, and did not amount to more than a necessary readjustment of their line.

The inevitable sequel to the retreat from the Marne was the battle of the Aisne. When the Germans ceased to retire and took up their position behind that river, the Allies could only find out by the process of trial and error that they were not still opposed by a mere rearguard. After several days of hard fighting with no great advantage to either side, Manoury began to overlap the German right. Joffre then took steps to exploit this move on a big scale by forming two new armies from troops taken from his centre, and with them prolonging his line to the left at an angle, running almost due north.

The Germans, though occupied at the same time in trying, unsuccessfully, to break the French front on both sides of Verdun, yet found enough troops to reply by correspondingly extending their right.

The result was a competition as to which side would outflank the other. It soon became apparent that neither would do so, and the only question to be decided was where the opposing lines would reach the sea.

An important feature in this race to the sea was the withdrawal of the British Expeditionary Force from their place in line on the Aisne, where they had several French armies on their left—causing considerable crossing of lines of communication—and whence they were brought up into the line again on the extreme left.

Ever since the German occupation of Brussels the remains of the Belgian Army had held out in Antwerp, and it remained to be seen whether the Allied left could be extended far enough to join hands with them there—thus keeping the Germans back from the coast of Belgium—or the Germans would be able to drive the Allies back far enough to deny the use of the Channel ports as a base to the British Expeditionary Force.

The Belgians in Antwerp put up a splendid defence, which was probably prolonged for a few days by the arrival of our hastily raised Naval Division; but the German heavy artillery was too much for them, and by October 10 the garrison had evacuated the fortress, to make the best of their way between the Germans and the Dutch frontier, till they could join themselves to the left of the Allies in Flanders.

It took the British Expeditionary Force a fortnight to withdraw from the Aisne and come into the line again in Flanders, and during that fortnight—the first half of October—the French had very hard work to retain their position in the neighbourhood of what was later to be the battlefield of the Somme.

The first British troops to arrive on the French left were Smith-Dorrien's II Corps, which reached the La Bassée Canal on October 11, and attacked La Bassée next day. Failing to take it they pushed on, farther to the north, with some success.

The III Corps (Pulteney)—on the arrival of the 6th Division the British Expeditionary Force had been formed into three Corps—joined in on the 13th.

A force under Rawlinson, consisting of the 7th Division and a Cavalry Division, had landed at Zeebrugge and Ostend on October 6.

The original object in sending them there may have been to help to prolong the Allied line till it joined hands with the Belgians in Antwerp, but their mission soon resolved itself into that of covering the retreat of the Antwerp garrison. By the 17th Rawlinson was back on a line facing south of east, with his right at Zandvoorde, to the south-east of Ypres. Thus he was separated by a gap of twelve miles from Pulteney's left, which on that day reached Bois Grenier, two and a half miles due south of Armentières.

The Belgians had meanwhile been driven back to the left bank of the Yser, where an Eighth French Army joined them in completing the Allied line from Bixschoote to the sea.

Ignorant of the German strength, Allied Headquarters were still hoping for a successful outflanking movement, and Rawlinson was ordered to advance; the I Corps, which was now arriving, being intended to come up on his left. It was very soon clear that, so far from making any progress round or through the German right, it was going to take the Allies all their time to prevent the enemy breaking through their all too thin line.

For a month the Germans again and again renewed their attacks on all parts of the line from La Bassée to the sea. The British were reinforced by the Indian Corps in the last days of October, and the extreme left at Nieuport was covered by the guns of British monitors. A large area between Dixmude and the sea was made impassable by flooding, thus releasing a considerable part of the French Eighth Army to come to the aid of the British and Belgians where they were most needed. By the middle of November the German attacks died down, and with them their second chance of an immediate success on the Western Front—the Allied hopes were dead a month earlier. The opposing lines now faced each other from the Alps to the sea in such equality of strength, both for defence and offence, that more than three years were to go by before either side was even to look like gaining a complete victory.

The next few months introduced the troops on both sides to the miseries of trench warfare. Though there was no serious move made on either side during the winter, there were occasional small attacks by one side or the other to improve its position, and the daily artillery fire and sniping kept up a perpetual stream of casualties.

The British Expeditionary Force was gradually growing. Though the original force which had crossed the Channel in the autumn was almost wiped out by the end of the First Battle of Ypres, the casualties had been replaced, and reinforcements were at hand. The Indian Army Corps and a few selected Territorial units had arrived in time to take part in that battle; three more Regular Divisions (7th, 27th, and 28th) were formed from units which had been on foreign stations when the war began; some of the Territorial Divisions were considered to be sufficiently advanced in their training to be sent to France before the winter was over; the Canadians were arriving in England before the end of October, and, as will be seen, were across the Channel in time to bear the brunt of the first German attack in the spring campaign; the New Armies were expected to be ready for use early in the summer; the Germans were known to be sending troops from the Western Front to the East, and there were great hopes of a successful Allied offensive in 1915.

The German plan for 1915 was an offensive against Russia, reducing the force on the Western Front to the minimum for safety. This plan was forced upon them by the threat of a Russian invasion, even before the First Battle of Ypres was over.

The plan of the Allies was a big offensive on the Western Front as soon as they could be ready for it, which could not be expected till well on in the summer. Long before the time arrived for the Allies' offensive in France their chances of success had been to some extent discounted by their having embarked on another big operation elsewhere.

Originally intended as an answer to a request by the Russians for action by the Allies to distract the Turks, its other advantages, if successful, were so obvious that the scheme for forcing the Dardanelles was persevered with, although the cause of its original inception had passed with Enver's failure on the Caucasus front.

Whether it would have been better to drop the idea of any offensive action in France in 1915 and concentrate on the Dardanelles, or vice versa, need not be discussed here; but it is quite certain that trying to conduct two major operations at the same time with inadequate resources is not the best way to reach decisive results.

The Allies began the season of 1915 by two simultaneous but widely separated attacks in the middle of March. Neither was on a scale big enough to produce any direct result in the way of shattering the German line. They may have been launched with the idea of making the Germans think there was something bigger to follow, and so preventing them from further reinforcing their Eastern Front, but were more probably only intended as an experiment.

The British attack was made against Neuve Chapelle, and was a foretaste of what was to happen again and again during the next three years: a rapid success where the bombardment had been effective; a costly failure where it had not; a little ground gained; a failure to get any farther as soon as the enemy's reserves came up; and heavy losses, about equal on both sides.

The next move came from the Germans, who, attacking in front of Ypres on April 22, introduced a new horror into war in the shape of poison gas.

The Canadians, the first British troops to encounter this unexpected weapon, saved the situation, and a month's fighting (Second Ypres) ended with no more advantage to the Germans than a slight blunting of the famous salient, and a good credit balance in casualties. The Allies countered with an attack launched on May 9 and lasting till the 16th, in which the French regained a considerable amount of ground north of Arras. The British gains, in the same neighbourhood as that of their March attack but on a broader front, were negligible.

A purely local affair, but of interest to us, as it led to the useless sacrifice of three of our new battalions in a hopeless counter-attack, was the German attack at Hooge, near Ypres, on July 1.

In September the great offensive in France, which had been the obstacle to single-minded concentration on the part of the Allies on the Dardanelles adventure, was launched.

It would be going too far to say that the efforts expended on the Dardanelles would have brought success in France, or vice versa. In neither theatre did success come near enough for this to be said with certainty. The only thing one can say with confidence is that the distribution of effort over the two operations ensured failure in both. However, that is being wise after the event. Joffre, though he had all through protested against a single man or round of ammunition being deflected from the Western

Front, was still confident that he could go through when he liked and where he liked.

The plan was for a big attack northward by the French in Champagne and a lesser one eastward by British and French on a front extending from Arras to La Bassée. Complete success in these two attacks would result in the cutting off of all the German forces between them should they not fall back. The Allies therefore hoped at least to see the enemy back on a straight line between Verdun and Ypres, with the prospect of better things to follow.

Both attacks were launched on September 25, after two days' bombardment. That in Champagne met with tremendous success at first, the greater part of the first line and parts of the second being taken, with great captures in men and guns. After the first day it followed what soon came to be looked on as the almost inevitable course—slight further successes; gradual stiffening of the defence; renewed attacks with less success; counter-attacks; loss of some of the gains; gradual exhaustion, and a net result of a few square miles of devastated ground regained, with losses fairly evenly balanced. Fighting died down at the end of October.

On the La Bassée–Arras front, though the fighting had more ups and downs, the final result was much the same.

The Western Front then settled down for the winter. The Central Powers had certainly a credit balance to show on the year, but victory did not seem to be appreciably nearer to one side than the other.

The position on the Western Front was unchanged. The Allied attack had failed to produce the results expected of it, but had probably reacted on the Russian front, where the German thrust, having carried all before it throughout the summer, died out in the autumn, leaving the Russian Army, in spite of its enormous losses and desperate shortage of material, still capable of mischief.

The Dardanelles expedition having done no more than neutralise—where it had not destroyed—the best troops of the Turkish Army, the Entente towards the end of the year drifted into another expedition in the Near East—in Macedonia. Troops for it were drawn from the Dardanelles and France. This force—though in the end it played a prominent part, their opponents being the first of Germany's allies to crack—for years did little more than prevent the Bulgarian Army and a certain number of Germans from being used elsewhere.

By the end of 1915 it had become evident that the opposing sides were too evenly matched for the war to be won at a blow. In 1915 this might have been done by the Allies if the Dardanelles could have been opened and kept open, thereby ensuring a new and short line by which Russia could have been supplied with the munitions of war of which she was so sadly in need; at the same time depriving the Central Powers of the help of Turkey and Bulgaria. It might have been done by the Central Powers if their success against Russia had been complete enough to force that Power to make a separate peace. With the failure of both these projects it was plain that a decided result would only come with the exhaustion of one side or the other. The efforts of both sides, from now till the spring of 1918, did not aim at any great and immediate strategical result, but at hastening the exhaustion of the other side and deferring that of their own.

The first to begin in 1916 were the Russians, who returned to the charge undismayed by their defeats of the previous year. They had even begun to counter-attack before the end of 1915, and their offensive lasted almost continuously till the autumn. Though meeting with great success at times, they achieved no very great results on their own front, but their efforts were invaluable to their allies in the west, as they drew off German troops from France just when they were most wanted.

The Germans began their great attack on Verdun in February. What their object was in making it is not self-evident, but it seems likely that, expecting a big Allied offensive, they wished to get in the first blow and give the Allies something else to think about.

Verdun was well chosen as their point of attack; firstly, because it had for the Germans the tactical advantage of being the most pronounced salient in the Allied line; secondly, it had the moral advantage of being a place which the French were likely to feel compelled, for their prestige, to concentrate all their energies on holding, thus distracting them from any offensive scheme which they might have in contemplation.

The Germans did not take Verdun. After four months of what was perhaps the most heroic struggle of the whole war, the Allies launched their attack on the Somme, and the German efforts against Verdun slackened. The fighting still went on, and in October the French began their counter-attack. By the middle of December the Germans were back very nearly to the line they started from in February.

The losses on both sides had been appalling and fairly equally divided. The French had gained the moral advantage of beating off an attack into which the enemy had thrown all his weight, but if the Germans' object had been to throw the plans of the Allies out of gear, they had achieved it. The Allied offensive was not launched till July 1. Its success was gradual but persistent, and was only stopped by the winter mud. It is fair to assume that if it had begun two months earlier it would have gone much farther. If Verdun was the cause of the delay, the Germans had some reason for self-congratulation.

For the 1916 'round' the Entente may be said to have been slightly ahead 'on points.' The Central Powers had something to show in minor theatres. In Mesopotamia, Kut had fallen—a heavy blow to British prestige in the East; but even here the end of the year saw the British 'doing all the leading.' Roumania had been almost entirely overrun—a valuable source of supply to the Central Powers—but in the main theatres things looked well for the Entente.

Russia, on the surface, seemed to be growing in strength, while in France the Germans had made up their minds that the battle of the Somme should not be resumed in the spring where it left off, and were about to fall back on to the Hindenburg Line—a wise precaution, as it would entail long preparation on the part of the Allies before they could close up to it and attack it; but still, a definite acceptance of the defensive rôle.

The year 1917 opened full of promise for the Allies. The Germans were obviously on the defensive in France. Their retirement to the Hindenburg Line made a renewal of the battle of the Somme difficult, but apparently it only remained to the Allies to select a more suitable point of attack.

The revolution in Russia was at first expected to enhance her value as an ally. In Mesopotamia Maude was well on the way to wipe out the stain of Kut. No longer was the defence of Egypt to entail the immobilisation of a large force, but was to be secured by an invasion of Palestine. On the Macedonian front the Allies were gradually gaining in strength. Everywhere, in fact, they seemed to have reacquired the initiative.

In April America came in, and however long it might

be before American armies would be fighting in France, America as an ally instead of a neutral meant the removal of all political obstacles to a rigorous blockade.

The year's campaign, except in one or two minor theatres, was one long series of failures and disappointments.

The first movement of the year was the gradual withdrawal of the Germans on to the Hindenburg Line, followed up slowly by the Allies. The opponents on this part of the front had settled down into their new positions early in April. This movement had no particular strategical result, except in so far as it strengthened the German line, as the Allies had already made their plan for their next offensive.

This plan was for a great attack by the French in Champagne, on a fifty-mile front, under the new Commander-in-Chief, General Nivelle; great things being expected for him and by him. At the same time the British were to attack in Artois.

The British attack began on April 9 with the famous capture of the Vimy Ridge by the Canadians under Sir Julian Byng, but Vimy was not the only success. In three days the British troops under Allenby had advanced to a depth of anything up to five miles, from near Bullecourt on the right to the outskirts of Lens on the left, with a capture of 12,000 prisoners and 150 guns.

The French attack was delivered on April 16, and, though at first partially successful, it failed, with enormous losses, to effect more than an insignificant fraction of what had been expected of it. The disappointment had a demoralising effect on a considerable portion of the French Army and on a part of the nation as well. *Défaitisme* was in the air, and on May 15 Pétain was brought in as Commander-in-Chief; his first task being to restore the confidence of the French Army. In this he achieved complete success, but it took time, and it was the middle of August before the French took any further serious part in the fighting.

Meanwhile, though the hope of a great Allied success in 1917 had gone, Haig was obliged to go on attacking so as to keep the enemy employed. The battle of Arras was renewed and went on till near the end of May, by which time the captures had increased to 20,000 prisoners.

A fresh offensive was next opened farther north. The Ypres salient was the scene of the new attack, and the fighting went on almost incessantly from June to November. Any chance of a complete success was destroyed by the weather, which for three or four months turned all Flanders into a buffalo wallow. There had been a scheme for landing a force on the coast of Belgium which, together with a thrust along the coast, was to turn the Germans' right flank and at the same time deprive them of their most effective submarine bases; but this never came off. The autumn fighting of 1917 must have been the hardest trial to which the British troops were put throughout the war. Division after division went up into the line, fought there under the most appalling conditions till it was decimated, and was then withdrawn and sent into the back areas to reorganise. All this without any apparent gain. It is only by reading the accounts of the enemy's commanders that one realises how much this incessant attack did to wear down the enemy, in numbers and morale, in this war of attrition.

From the end of August to the beginning of November Pétain was having a successful campaign, and took a good deal of ground all along the front where Nivelle had failed in the spring.

The fighting in front of Ypres died down early in

November, but Haig had one more try for a big success. Byng, who had succeeded Allenby in command of the Third Army, attacked on a ten-mile front on November 20, opposite Cambrai. His attack was supported by tanks in greater numbers than had ever been used before, and there was no preliminary bombardment. Tanks had been a failure in Flanders owing to the mud, and colossal bombardments had been found to break up the ground so much as to make it impassable for transport and guns; the consequence being that an attack could never penetrate beyond its first objective. The attack to start with was a brilliant success, but it only made a dent in the German line without making a hole in it. German reinforcements were quicker on the scene than ours. The German Commander put in a well-organised counter-attack on the 30th, and by December 7 our front line was not very much in front of, and in one place actually behind, where it had been on November 20.

The fighting in France for 1917 had ended with honours about easy. The losses of the Allies were probably considerably in excess of those of the enemy, but they could afford them better. The time was approaching when, with the arrival of the Americans, the advantage in men-power would be definitely on the side of the Allies.

Meanwhile, Russia had gone out of the war. So far from the Revolution putting fresh life into the Russian Army, it was the beginning of the end. Discipline disappeared and the Army faded away. Kerensky, the War Minister of the Moderate Government, did his best to keep Russia in the war. A final effort was made with the best troops that could be got together early in July and met with some success, but at the first check the Army collapsed. With the entry into power of the Bolsheviks in November all resistance ceased and peace negotiations were begun in December.

In October the Allies received another blow in the Italian rout at Caporetto. Six German divisions had been sent to the Italian front. On October 24 they attacked the left of the Italian line on the Isonzo, and in a few days the Italians were back on the Piave, with a loss of a quarter of a million prisoners and 1,800 guns.

British and French reinforcements were rushed off to ease the situation, as it was feared that Italy might go out of the war. The Germans, having achieved their object in making the Allies withdraw troops from France, where every man would be wanted to meet the obviously impending attack in the spring, left the Austrians to do the best they could on the new front.

The end of 1917 found the situation on the Western Front very much where it was at the beginning—that is, with neither side strong enough to deal a knock-out blow; but it was evident that it could not remain so for long. The defection of Russia had liberated the greater part of the forces that had been opposed to her for service elsewhere. On the other hand, these reinforcements would be as nothing, so far as numbers went, to what America could produce if given time. The question was whether the Germans could win the war before the Americans could arrive with sufficient numbers sufficiently trained, to turn the scale.

It was evident that unless the Germans intended tamely to await the arrival of the Americans—in which case they would certainly lose the war—they must launch an overwhelming attack in France as soon as they were sufficiently reinforced from the East.

No one doubted which alternative they would choose.

The imminence of the German attack did not produce

any very satisfactory preparations for meeting it. The two Commanders-in-Chief, Pétain and Haig, were not in agreement as to the probable point of attack. Each one expected that his own front was that on which the blow would fall. The British Government accepted the French view, and persuaded Haig, against his better judgment, to take over a considerable portion of the French line, thereby proportionally weakening his powers of defence.

Little was done to remedy this weakness. Not only had our Government been trifling with the question of man-power, but, appalled by our losses of the summer and autumn, they seem to have had at the back of their minds that to send Haig more men meant that he would throw their lives away in fresh attacks, and that the safest thing to do with any reserves they had was to keep them at home. Consequently, the losses of 1917 had been most inadequately replaced.

It had become increasingly evident throughout the war how difficult it is for allies to co-operate in the field unless either the two commanders are in complete accord, or one is made subordinate to the other. Consequently, the question of unity of command had from time to time been mooted, and Haig had even been put under Nivelle's orders for the campaign of 1917. The difficulties of unity of command had, however, been recognised. Real unity of command between allies in the field, though an excellent idea, is a practical impossibility. However much one Commander-in-Chief may be put under the orders of another, he still remains responsible to his own Government. To have unity of command in the field one would require also to have it among the Governments, and this is out of the question between allies of anything like equal calibre. It is possible only to a Napoleon or a Xerxes dragging half a continent at his heels. The Central

Powers had something like it, as Germany was sufficiently the predominant partner to be able to bully her allies into complying with her wishes. With the Entente it was out of the question, and their Grand Strategy throughout the war had to be arranged by conferences, which is probably the chief reason that the war lasted as long as it did. As a substitute for unity of command the Allied statesmen hit on a compromise: that device so necessary in politics, so fatal in war. They evolved a scheme of having a General Reserve, independent of the two Commanders-in-Chief, and managed by a committee. On being asked for the troops to supply his quota of the Reserve, Haig replied that he had none to spare, and that was the end of that.

If this committee, or council, had been composed of the chief military advisers of the different Governments, and had been put in command of the whole Allied forces, it might have been a success, and would have been the nearest possible approach to unity of command, especially if any one member of the committee had, by his outstanding personality, been able to enlist the entire confidence of his coadjutors and so act as a leader among them. The idea of having a committee to command a General Reserve to two allied forces, with the committee and the commanders of those forces mutually independent, is too fatuous to require comment.

The British Premier, Mr. Lloyd George, despairing of winning the war in France after the experiences of 1916–17, began exploring the possibility of doing so in Syria by lending large reinforcements to Allenby, who had just taken Jerusalem, with a view to a winter campaign. In this, I fear, he had encouragement from some military source—certainly not from his C.I.G.S., his rightful adviser in such matters—but one can always get the expert advice one wants if one goes far enough afield for it.

However, it was pointed out to him in time, firstly, that success in Syria, however complete, would not bring the end of the war appreciably nearer; secondly, that the transference of the reinforcements would take so long that the first arrivals would be due to start on the return journey to France some time before the last of them had completed the outward journey.

In February 1918 the Prime Minister, who regarded his C.I.G.S., Sir William Robertson, much as Ahab did Micaiah, the son of Imlah, and for the same reason, got rid of him.

Time—and a very short time—was to show which of them was in the right. A month later, when the blow fell, the Versailles Council faded into insignificance, and Allenby was called on to send every man he could spare to France.

The great German attack was launched on March 21, 1918, and the victims were Gough's Fifth Army, which, with fourteen divisions, was opposed to forty-two. On Gough's right was the French Third Army and on his left was the British Third Army (Byng). Both of these got their share of the attack, but neither was outnumbered to anything like the extent to which was the Fifth Army. The attack, which was preceded by only a brief bombardment, was greatly helped by a thick fog. It was by far the most successful offensive that had been delivered so far on the Western Front. Day after day Gough's men were driven back; day after day the French on the right and Byng on the left, if not driven back, had to fall back to maintain contact with Gough. By March 26 the Allies were, roughly, on the line held by them before the battle of the Somme began.

Henceforth the line held from Albert northwards; to the south it continued to be forced back.

The crisis arrived, not only as regards the battle, but as regards the whole campaign and possibly the war, when, on the night of March 24, Pétain, the French Commander-in-Chief, warned Haig that if the enemy's attack went on he would be obliged to fall back south-westwards to cover Paris, which of course meant the separation of the Allied armies and their probable defeat in detail.

The result was the appointment of Foch as Generalissimo. There has been a great deal said and written about Unity of Command. It is claimed that it won the war, and people wonder why it was not introduced sooner, forgetting that it had been experimented with, without any very happy results, in the case of Nivelle. The truth is, that there never was Unity of Command, nor ever could be under similar conditions. What Haig wanted when he asked for Foch as Generalissimo was not someone put over his head who would give him orders, which he would have to carry out whether he agreed with them or not. He wanted someone put over the French Army who would think, as he did, that the one thing needful was that the union of the two armies should remain unbroken, and that separation would be fatal. He had hitherto got on well with Pétain, but now they had disagreed over a matter which Haig considered vital. Our Government could not ask the French to supersede Pétain because he did not see eye to eye with Haig. Haig wanted Foch because he knew his views, and the only way to get him was to ask that he should be put over both him and Pétain.

On the 28th a German attack on Arras was definitely held up. Slight progress was still made south of the Somme, but by the first week in April the great German advance between the Scarpe and the Oise had reached its limit. They had taken 90,000 prisoners and 1,300 guns, and the British Fifth Army had practically ceased to exist, but they had failed to force the Allied armies apart, their line had assumed the shape of a prominent salient, and the country between the line from which they had started and that at which they had arrived was so cut up that the bringing up of reinforcements and supplies to their front line was a work of great difficulty.

This was really the turning-point of the year's campaign. The Germans' attack had not yet reached high-water mark, but they had made the greatest effort of which they were capable without obtaining decisive results. American troops were arriving in France in ever-increasing numbers, and the German submarine campaign seemed to be helpless to prevent them. It was obvious that in a very short time the Germans would lose their numerical superiority caused by the defection of Russia. It must by this time have been pretty evident to the rulers of the Central Powers that they could not win. However, for a nation to go on fighting till it is beaten instead of giving in when it sees that it must be beaten can only command our admiration.

Their next attack was on the Flanders section of the British line. They may have hoped for decisive results in this quarter, but one theory is that the attack was intended as a diversion, preliminary to the greater effort against the French, and that an unexpected success caused them to make a bigger thing of it than had been intended; thus wasting power which would have been better reserved for the offensive against Paris.

The Germans started a heavy bombardment on the selected front on April 8 and launched their attack next day, catching the British relieving two Portuguese divisions, between the Lys and La Bassée, with troops that had recently been through the terrible experience of the March attack.

The German advance was as rapid—though on a much narrower front—as that of March 21. Givenchy held out and formed the southern limit of ground gained by the Germans, the northern being the River Yser. As in the March attack, the advance lost speed as it proceeded, but by the 16th the Germans had gained a great deal more ground than they had lost in the autumn of '17. They had not thereby increased the tactical strength of their position, as they now occupied a very pronounced salient. Reinforcements—French and British—were coming up, and resistance was daily increasing; nevertheless, the Germans, either in hopes of a greater success or as a defensive measure to straighten their line, made one more effort. They gained nothing more on their right or left, but, on the 25th, they reached high-water mark in the capture of Mont Kemmel. They persisted in their attacks till the 29th, after which date the battle died down. Spasmodic attacks occurred along the British front all through May, but were probably only intended to distract attention from what was being planned elsewhere, and they had no definite results either way. The British front was not attacked again throughout the campaign.

Their first two attacks—that of March, with the object of separating the Allies, and that of April, presumably with the object of capturing the Channel ports—having failed to produce any decisive results, the Germans now prepared for a final effort against the French front—presumably with the occupation of Paris in view—as the last chance of patching up a favourable peace before the influx of American troops should put them in a state of numerical inferiority.

The first objective of the attack, which was launched on May 27 and appears to have come as a complete surprise to the French, who were expecting a renewal of the attack on the British line, was the Chemin des Dames. The German success was more rapid than in either of the two previous attacks. The first day the French were back behind the Aisne and on the second behind the Vêsle. The line was partly held by some British divisions which had been sent to this part of the line for a rest, after their rough treatment in March and April. There seems to have been an adverse fate at this time which ensured that any of our divisions sent away for a rest always went to the next point to be attacked. The British divisions made a very fine stand, but when they held their ground they very soon had their flanks exposed by retirements on their right and left, and they were compelled to conform. On the 29th the Germans took Soissons and on the 30th they reached the Marne, not far short of Château-Thierry. Their front had rapidly assumed the form of a very prominent salient. It may be that this was a part of Foch's plan, that by holding on in front of Rheims and Compiègne and letting go in the middle, he was inviting the German line to assume the shape best suited for the counter-attack he was preparing. This would account for the seeming weakness of the French resistance, but to those not in Foch's confidence the situation looked alarming.

However, the history of the March and April attacks repeated itself and, just as the advance had been more rapid than in either of them, so much the sooner did it reach its limit.

Reinforcements were arriving, and on June 4 and 5 American troops were successfully counter-attacking near Château-Thierry, as were the British next day south-west of Rheims.

On June 9 the Germans launched an attack southward between Montdidier and Noyon, which would, if successful, have turned the flank of the French line which formed the western face of the new German salient. Little ground was gained, and the attack was brought to a standstill by a counter-attack against its right. Another attack on Rheims on the 18th met with no success.

Nearly a month was now spent in preparing for one more last attack, but the German higher command must have already foreseen the inevitable end. The Americans were pouring into France at a rate of over a quarter of a million a month, and numerical superiority was already on the side of the Allies.

The point of this last attack was the salient in the line of the Allies at Rheims. There were two separate attacks, one on each side of Rheims.

The attack east of Rheims made no progress whatsoever; that to the south-west gained some success at first, but it was only momentary, and on the 17th the Allies were counter-attacking. On the 18th Foch launched his great counter-attack, destined to develop into an advance along the whole Allied line which was only to end with the war.

He attacked along the whole twenty-seven miles of the German front between the Marne and the Aisne. Progress, though persistent, never achieved the pace of the German attacks. Château-Thierry was not abandoned till the 21st, and Soissons was not retaken till August 2. By the 3rd the Germans were behind the Vêsle, but it had taken seventeen days to drive them back a less distance than they had advanced in four. They were now, however, definitely on the defensive, and that along the whole line. All through July the Allies had been nibbling at the German line, the points of the salients caused by the March and April attacks being the localities that received attention.

On August 8 the British came in on the grand scale.

Haig attacked with Rawlinson's Fourth Army on a twenty-mile front to the east of Amiens, gaining seven miles of ground on the first day. Seven thousand prisoners and 100 guns were taken by 3 p.m., and the captures rose to 24,000 prisoners and over 200 guns on the 9th. Two French armies were operating on the right with similar success. By the 11th the salient had been flattened out from Bray, on the Somme, to Ribecourt, near the Oise. There were further Allied gains in the salient on the River Lys and between the Oise and the Aisne, but the next great blow was struck by Byng's Third Army between Albert and Arras. The attack began on August 21 on a ten-mile front, which widened from day to day till it reached from the Somme to the Scarpe. By the end of August the Germans were back on a line which corresponded roughly with that which they had held before the March offensive, though there was still a considerable bulge south of the Aisne, and it was not till well into October that the French recovered the Chemin des Dames.

During September the pace of the Allied advance died down, but progress was continuous all along the line. The Germans were back on their reserve line known to the Allies as the Hindenburg Line. The Allies soon proved that it was not impregnable, by the capture by British and Canadian forces of a part of it, known as the Drocourt–Quéant line, on September 2.

The Americans who, owing to the pressure on the Allies during the German advance, had consented, contrary to their intentions, to put in a division here and a division there under French and British Army commanders, now took over their own bit of the line east of Verdun, and on September 12 delivered the first attack they had all to themselves. This was against the St. Mihiel salient, which the Germans had held since 1914. The salient was completely flattened out, 15,000 prisoners and 200 guns being taken. The month ended with the crossing of the Canal du Nord by the British First, Third, and Fourth Armies, causing a loss to the enemy of 26,500 prisoners and 340 guns, and the collapse of the Hindenburg Line.

Meanwhile, everything was going well for the Allies in other theatres of the war, the Germans being too much occupied in France to give any assistance.

On the Macedonian front the Allies started their attack on September 15, meeting with such success that on the 25th the Bulgars asked for an armistice, which came into force on the 30th. The defection of Bulgaria opened communication between the Allies and Roumania, and Turkey found herself cut off from the Central Powers.

On September 19 Allenby attacked in Palestine, and in a few days the Turkish armies opposed to him had practically ceased to exist. During October his pursuit was merely a problem in time and space. By the end of the month Marshall had almost cleared the Turks out of Mesopotamia ; but what must have brought their isolation home to the Turks even more than their disasters in comparatively distant fields was the presence of Milne's troops from Macedonia outside Adrianople. On October 30 an armistice was signed, which opened to the Allies the Dardanelles and Bosporus.

In France, October was a repetition of September, in that there was continual progress at one part or another of the Allied front. The last few days of September and beginning of October saw a big advance by the Americans and French between the Moselle and the Suippe, while at the same time on the opposite flank the Belgians were carrying all before them between Ypres and the sea.

Another week's fighting by the Third and Fourth Armies pushed the Germans back behind the Selle, and Le Cateau fell on the 10th.

On the 14th began another great thrust in Flanders by Plumer's Second Army on the right, with French and Belgians on the left, on a front reaching from the Lys to the sea. The fall of Ostend on the 17th was followed by that of Zeebrugge and Bruges on the 19th. By the 21st the Second and Fifth Armies were on the Scheldt, in line with the First, Third, and Fourth on the Selle.

These armies had renewed their attack on the 17th, and by the 25th, though the distance advanced had not been great, they had captured another 21,000 prisoners and 450 guns. The French had all the time been steadily progressing between the Aisne and the Oise and less rapidly in the Argonne. Progress had been slowest on the American front.

Meanwhile, Germany was losing her last ally. On the night of October 23–24 the Italians, who had since their disaster in the autumn of 1917 been supported by French and British troops, attacked the Austrians on the Piave. On the 27th the defence collapsed, and an armistice was arranged on November 3.

During the greater part of October the Americans had been held up by difficulties of transport, but by the end of the month these had been solved, and on November 1 they began a rapid advance down both sides of the Meuse. By the 7th they had reached Sedan.

Haig advanced again on November 1, forcing the line of the Rhonelle. On the 4th the First, Third, and Fourth Armies attacked on a thirty-mile front, the French prolonging the line to the right. Landrecies and Le Quesnoy were taken on the 4th, Bavai on the 7th, Condé on the 8th, Maubeuge on the 9th. On the same day Tournai was taken, and the Scheldt crossed by the Second Army. Early on the 11th Mons was entered, and the British troops were back on the line on which the Old Contemptibles had begun the war.

At 11 a.m. that day the armistice was signed, and the war was over.

CHAPTER II[1]

'**MONS**,' 'RETREAT FROM MONS,' '**MARNE**, 1914,' 'AISNE, 1914'

AT the outbreak of war our 1st Battalion was quartered in Salamanca Barracks, Aldershot, and was in the 6th Infantry Brigade, 2nd Division. The 2nd Battalion was at Blackdown, in the 2nd Infantry Brigade, 1st Division. The 1st Battalion was commanded by Lieutenant-Colonel E. Northey, the 2nd by Lieutenant-Colonel E. Pearce-Serocold.

The order to 'mobilise' was received on the afternoon of August 4. The 1st Battalion left Aldershot in the small hours of August 12, embarked at Southampton, and reached Rouen, where it disembarked, next day.

The 6th Brigade (Brigadier-General R. H. Davies, C.B., New Zealand Staff Corps), consisting of the 1st King's, 2nd South Stafford, 1st Berkshire, 1st K.R.R.C., concentrated at Hannappes, and after a wait of six days set out on its march into Belgium, in very hot weather, on the 21st.

Hard marching brought them to Givry, three miles south-east of Mons, by 11.30 a.m. on the 23rd. They went straight up into the line and dug in, but all the fighting at Mons was done by the II Corps, farther west, and the retreat began next morning without the Battalion having come under fire.

The 2nd Battalion had also left their station on the 12th, and disembarked at Havre on the 13th. Entraining on the 15th, they reached Le Nouvion at 10 p.m., and next morning went into the outpost line. On the 21st their

[1] Map VIII.

Brigade (Brigadier-General E. S. Bulfin), consisting of 2nd Royal Sussex, 1st Loyal North Lancs., 1st Northamptonshire, 2nd K.R.R.C., joined their division on the march. They reached Rouveroy in the small hours of the 23rd, and spent the day listening to the guns of Mons.

In the evening they were sent up to reinforce the 6th Brigade, where, like the 1st Battalion, they dug themselves in, but had no part in the battle.

The Retreat from Mons

The retreat from Mons began on the 24th, and only ended on September 5. Both battalions had their share of long marches, followed by short halts, which were chiefly spent in digging. Neither battalion saw much fighting during the retreat. The first mention of casualties in the 1st Battalion is that on September 1 they lost 1 officer, Lieutenant P. G. Chaworth-Musters, and 12 other ranks wounded, 2 Riflemen missing, of whom 1 rejoined. The 2nd Battalion do not seem to have fired a shot during the retreat, except at a few stray Uhlans. By September 5 they had covered one hundred and eighty miles in thirteen days, during one of which they halted. This means an average of fifteen miles per marching day, which is a very great performance for a large force with never less than one division, and sometimes two, on one road, in constant touch with the enemy, and much of the time when halted spent in digging.

The Marne

On September 6 both battalions found themselves marching towards the enemy instead of away from him, and all their troubles were forgotten. Both battalions had received their first reinforcements of about a hundred of all ranks. Except for the moral effect of advancing instead of retiring, the marching in pursuit was not much less severe than in retreat, and both battalions were soon to come in for hard fighting.

On September 10 the 6th Infantry Brigade formed the advanced guard of the 2nd Division when it came upon a German rearguard in position. The fight which followed is best described in the words of Lieut.-Colonel E. Northey, commanding the 1st Battalion as related by him in the 'Chronicle' of 1915:

'This Battalion, at that time 1,150 strong, was part of a force which suddenly in the grey morning of September 10 came upon a German rearguard of about 1,200 infantry, with a battery of field guns. The leading battalion of the British Brigade, the Berkshires, was detailed to remain on the north-east side of the village of Hautesvesnes, where it had just arrived, and guard the right flank from another German force reported in that direction. The 1st Battalion of the 60th, which was the second battalion in the column, was ordered at once to attack the enemy, who had now halted in a very good fire position along a winding, sunken road, about three-quarters of a mile north-west of the village of Hautesvesnes. From behind the village the Battalion was very quickly deployed; C Company, Captain Willan, was the first.

'A battery of artillery was brought into action west of the village, and C Company deployed in front and to the right of the battery, immediately coming under a very heavy rifle and machine-gun fire, as well as getting most of the German shrapnel, aimed at our artillery, but short. The advance had to be made across open stubble fields with no cover at all, the first platoon (Lieutenant Bonham-Carter's) deployed, losing 4 killed and 11 wounded, including its officer.

'At this time the enemy's fire had not been got under at all, but very soon B Company, Captain Maclachlan, D.S.O., was deployed from a sunken road to the right of C Company, with A Company on the left, under Captain Makins, M.V.O. After an hour the effect of our fire began to tell, and the three companies advanced most gallantly from 1,100 yards to 700 yards from the enemy, gaining complete superiority of fire. D Company, Captain Bradford, was put in to thicken up our line, and with half a battalion of the South Staffords coming up on our left and half the King's Liverpool Regiment on the right, the Germans, who had already shown some signs of surrendering, put up white flags all along the line. Colonel Northey ordered the whole line to advance to the assault, and the enemy surrendered. This fight was an extraordinary proof of the good results of our careful training in fire direction, orders, control, and discipline. Our Riflemen shot steadily, when and where they were told, with such effective results that we killed or wounded about 150 Germans and captured 550. About 500 others got over the ridge behind, and were taken by another of our columns moving parallel with us.

'The co-operation between the Riflemen and the Artillery was splendid. The senior German officer, when asked why they had surrendered when they still had plenty of ammunition, told us that our fire was so accurate that they could not move up or down the road nor off it, nor could they put up their heads to aim their fire: thus indeed the object of all our training, to keep the enemy's heads down, was achieved with most valuable results.

'The losses to the Battalion, who in this fight so well lived up to their glorious traditions, were 4 officers wounded, 10 N.C.O.s and Riflemen killed, and 60 wounded, not a great price to pay for the annihilation of a whole enemy's battalion.

'The fire fight, in which we obtained complete superiority in an hour and a half, was between about equal forces, a battalion and a battery on each side, but our battery had six guns to the Germans' four. The enemy was so pinned to their ground by the accuracy of our fire that when we advanced they were powerless. Such episodes as this went a long way to give our army that feeling of absolute ascendancy, arm for arm, over the Germans, whose only advantages over us from the beginning have accrued from their greater numbers and superiority in guns of large calibre.'

The casualties of the Battalion in this action were: killed, 10 other ranks; wounded, 4 officers, Lieutenant and Adjutant R. H. Woods, Lieutenant A. L. Bonham-Carter, 2nd Lieutenants H. W. Butler and R. A. Banon, 60 other ranks; missing, 5 other ranks.

This was a proud day for the 1st Battalion, and a proud

day for their Commanding Officer. There is no greater moment in a soldier's life than when what he has learnt, and still more what he has thought out for himself, in peace-time training, is put to the proof and stands the test. For once he is the Happy Warrior, who :

> ' Through the heat of conflict, keeps the law
> ' In calmness made, and *sees what he foresaw.*'

While the 1st Battalion was engaged at Hautesvesnes the 2nd Brigade was having an advanced-guard action near Courchamps, a few miles to the north-east. Though our 2nd Battalion was in reserve all day, it lost 2nd Lieutenant E. V. Tindall and 4 Riflemen wounded. 2nd Lieutenant Tindall died of his wounds a few days later.

THE AISNE [1]

During the German retreat from the Marne there had all the time been a gap between their First and Second Armies. This gap had to be filled before they could stop their retreat and make a stand. The necessary troops were found and brought up just in time, not altogether to prevent the crossing of the Aisne by the Allies, but in time to make a stand on the high ground immediately to the north of that river.

On September 12, as the British forces approached the Aisne, the I Corps came opposite the gap between the German armies, which was so far only filled by cavalry. Troops from a hastily formed Seventh Army were, however, being rapidly brought up. This move was unknown to the Allied commanders, unfavourable weather having prevented any effective air reconnaissance.

On the far side of the Aisne, and about four miles from it, runs a flat-topped ridge some 200 feet above the river

[1] Sketch Map I, opposite p. 42.

with numerous spurs running from it right down to the river. Along this ridge from east to west runs the now well-known Chemin des Dames.

The I Corps, preceded by cavalry, had orders to cross on a front extending from Bourg to Chavonne.

A broad canal runs alongside of the river on the south side, but at Bourg a branch of this canal is carried over the river on an aqueduct, and then runs north-west, going under the ridge by a tunnel at Braye.

The cavalry advancing at dawn of a wet morning (13th) found all the road bridges over the Aisne destroyed, but not those over the canal. The aqueduct, moreover, was only slightly damaged.

The cavalry were held up here for some time, but on the approach of our 2nd Battalion, which was advanced guard to the 2nd Brigade, the enemy fell back, and the cavalry crossed, followed by the 2nd Battalion. C and D Companies were sent to occupy the spur immediately north of Bourg, while the rest of the Brigade moved up the road towards Vendresse. The cavalry, which had pushed on to Moulins, found the enemy in position at Troyon, and reported more of them advancing from Chivy. More still were reported by the Flying Corps farther north. The remainder of the Division were hurried over the river, and directed to move up on the right of the 2nd Brigade. By 6 p.m. all were across.

It was still not clear that the enemy had stopped retreating, or that more resistance was to be expected next day than that of a rearguard.

For the 14th the Chemin des Dames was the first objective of the I Corps, and the 1st Division was ordered to occupy the section from Cerny to Courteçon. With this in view Brigadier-General Bulfin was ordered, with his brigade and a brigade of artillery, to seize, before daybreak, the top of the ridge from Cerny to a road junction a mile to the west of it.

The Brigade, except for a few companies on outpost duty, one of which was C Company of the 2nd Battalion, had been billeted for the night in Moulins.

The following account of the battle that ensued is taken from the 'Official History of the War':

'At 3 a.m., amid heavy rain and dense mist, General Bulfin's force moved by Vendresse upon Troyon, the 2nd K.R.R.C. leading, followed by the 2nd Royal Sussex. The Commanding Officer of the former, Lieutenant-Colonel Pearce-Serocold, had orders from General Bulfin to seize the high ground above Troyon and secure it for the passage of the advanced guard of the 1st Division [1st (Guards) Brigade, etc.], while Lieutenant-Colonel Montresor of the Sussex was to keep his battalion in support at Vendresse until needed. The leading company of the K.R.R.C. [D Company, Captain A. E. Cathcart] with a party of the 9th Lancers, on reaching the top of the hill, surprised, about 4.45 a.m., a German piquet, but could not progress much farther, so that Colonel Serocold sent up two more companies to extend his line. The din of rifle fire now gradually increased, although there was a marked absence of artillery fire, and by 5.30 it had become a roar. It was evident that the Germans were in strength, and Colonel Serocold called upon the Royal Sussex, who meantime had been brought up closer in anticipation that they would be required; by 6.30 a.m. they were deployed on his left, each battalion covering nearly 800 yards of front. At the same time General Bulfin threw out the Northamptons to the spur next to the eastward to protect the right flank. The two leading companies of the Sussex, finding that the fire came from trenches some 300 yards to the north of them, moved westward so as to take the defenders in flank. For a brief space there was a sharp interchange of rifle fire; and then large numbers of Germans threw up their hands in token of surrender. Some of the Sussex rose to their feet to bring their prisoners in, upon which other Germans in rear opened fire indiscriminately upon friend and foe; but, none the less, some three hundred of the enemy were captured and sent to the rear. Continuing the fight, the left half-company of the Sussex succeeded in overlapping the western flank of the Germans, who, astride the road from Troyon, north-west to the sugar factory, were opposing the progress of the K.R.R.C., and the British marksmanships was so accurate that here also numbers of Germans threw up their hands. Thereupon two German batteries, entrenched east of the factory, opened fire upon their unhappy comrades, who, between the German shells from the east and British bullets from the south and west, were quickly exterminated. Teams then appeared near the two batteries, but in a very short time every driver, horse, and gunner were shot down by the British rifles; and twelve guns remained silent and derelict upon the plateau.

'It was now nearly 7 a.m. The head of the 1st (Guards) Brigade [1st Coldstream, 1st Scots Guards, 1st Black Watch, 1st Cameron Highlanders] had reached Vendresse, where General Maxse decided to advance and prolong the line of the 2nd to the left. The 3rd Infantry Brigade was in reserve on the right rear of the 2nd at Moulins, less the Queen's, which was on its way farther east to the plateau of Paissy (two miles east of Vendresse) to act as right flank guard and escort to the portion of the divisional artillery in readiness there. The 1st and 4th Cavalry Brigades were in observation near Paissy itself, and the 2nd Cavalry Brigade in the neighbourhood of Vendresse, to which position it had fallen back after General Bulfin's force had passed through it. The 2nd Division was not ready to move, the 6th Infantry Brigade having not yet finished the passage of the Aisne. The two batteries also assigned to General Bulfin's force had not yet joined him, nor was there the slightest prospect, in the fog that prevailed, that they could find a target when they did arrive.

'After 7 a.m. the fusillade upon the ridge of the Chemin des Dames increased, and by 8 a.m. Major-General Lomax (1st Division) was satisfied that a strong German attack was developing upon the front of his 2nd Brigade, and despatched a message to the Cavalry Division at Paissy asking that his right flank should be protected. Between 8 and 9 a.m. the combat rapidly became more intense. The 1st (Guards) Brigade, led by the 1st Coldstream, was approaching the left of the 2nd Infantry Brigade, but General Lomax sent orders to Brigadier-General Bulfin not to push on after he had secured the high ground. Meanwhile, the Loyal North Lancashire were sent up by General Bulfin from Brigade Reserve to support the K.R.R.C. and the Sussex in the attack upon the factory; and all three battalions advanced, and succeeded in occupying the buildings, and entrenching on the flat top of the ridge beyond. They actually passed through the two abandoned German batteries; but, though they clung to the position which they had taken up, they were unable to make further headway against the enemy, entrenched with field guns and machine guns to the north and east of the factory. He, on his side, made repeated counter-attacks, which were steadily repulsed. During the whole day the fight surged to and fro across some 300 yards of ground, the fresh units which arrived as reinforcements being thrust in where they seemed most required.'

To condense the account in the 'Official History' of the remainder of the day's fighting: the 1st (Guards) Brigade now began to come into the line on the left of the 2nd Brigade. The 1st Coldstream had been delayed by having to pass through a patch of thick wood, and their Commanding Officer, Colonel Ponsonby, brought them up to fill a gap between the left of the 2nd Brigade and the Black Watch and Cameron Highlanders, who were already in the line. Here they suffered severely from artillery fire. Colonel Ponsonby then, with the equivalent of about a company, advanced and rushed the village of Cerny well within the German line. The rest of his battalion worked its way to the east, and came into line on the right of the K.R.R.C. At the same time the 1st Queen's, detached from the 3rd Infantry Brigade as a right flank guard, pushed well into the German line a mile to the east of Cerny. Meanwhile, battalions of the 3rd Infantry Brigade had occupied the Beaulne Ridge, and in doing so had checked the advance of a German brigade which was counter-attacking south-eastward towards Vendresse.

About 1 p.m. the Germans launched a counter-attack against the entire front of the 2nd and 1st (Guards) Brigades. The 2nd Infantry Brigade were first driven back through the derelict German batteries to the position they had held earlier in the day. This uncovered the right flank of the Cameron Highlanders, who came under a devastating machine-gun fire, and were almost wiped out. Further German advance was stopped by the two companies of the 1st Gloucestershire, in Brigade Reserve, being thrown into the fight; but the line from Troyon now ran back through Chivy to the Beaulne spur, facing north-west.

By this time all the infantry of the 1st Division was in the front line except for two companies of the 1st Gloucestershire, in Divisional Reserve. For two hours the Germans continued to make counter-attacks at different points in the line, which were all repulsed, and about 3 p.m. the fight died down.

Now, to turn to the part that the 1st Battalion was taking in this battle: on the night of the 13th the only troops of the 2nd Division across the Aisne were the 5th Infantry Brigade, which was occupying the Beaulne spur immediately to the left of the 2nd Infantry Brigade.

The orders for the 2nd Division for the 14th were for the 6th Infantry Brigade, as advanced guard, with a brigade of artillery, to cross by a pontoon bridge at Pont Arcy, and advance northward through the 5th Brigade, who were to follow them. The 4th (Guards) Brigade were to cross behind the 6th Brigade, and advance north-westward. It must be remembered that when these orders were issued it was believed that there was only a rearguard to deal with.

The crossing began at 5 a.m., but it was 8 a.m. before the whole brigade was across and ready to move. The 1st Berkshire then started to advance up the valley towards Braye, with two companies 1st K.R.R.C. as flank guards on the spurs on the right and left [B and C to the right, A and D to the left]. About 9 a.m. the Berkshire were checked by heavy shell and rifle fire from the north of Braye. The 1st King's were brought up between their right, and the two companies K.R.R.C. on the right flank. At 10 a.m. two field batteries of the advanced guard artillery, after themselves being heavily shelled in coming to the Front, came into action on the Moussy spur. At 10.30 a.m. the Brigade started its attack: two companies K.R.R.C. on the right advancing along the Beaulne spur, two companies up the La Bovette spur, with the King's and Berkshire in between. These two regiments advanced till they reached the foot of the steep slopes leading up to the Chemin des Dames plateau, when they were held up by tiers of trenches to their front, and were at the same time heavily enfiladed from their right.

An effort to clear the trenches from which the enfilade fire was coming was made with the help of the 2nd Worcestershire (5th Brigade), but without success. To quote again, verbatim, from the 'Official History':

> 'Still farther to the east, the two companies of the 1st K.R.R.C. pushed on to a wood, where they were counter-attacked by infantry in front, and enfiladed by machine guns from a flank. They fought vigorously, and inflicted heavy losses on the enemy, but were finally forced back to the top of the spur above Moussy; but the K.R.R.C., having been reinforced by the 2nd Worcestershire and the Highland Light Infantry, were able to stem the German onslaught until, by the aid of the 46th and 113th Batteries and of the 3rd Infantry Brigade, which had advanced on their right, as already described, they finally repulsed the enemy with very heavy loss.'

Meanwhile, A and D Companies were taking part in a fight on their side of the valley. The 2nd Connaught Rangers, from the 5th Brigade, had been sent out early to Cour de Soupir. When they first arrived all was clear for a mile in front of them, but at 10.30 a.m they were heavily attacked; the enemy trying to turn their flank by way of the La Bovette spur, which A and D Companies had not yet reached. However, before long, the 4th (Guards) Brigade came up to reinforce the Connaught Rangers, our two companies checked the turning movement, and the German attack was held up.

Later in the day attempts to resume the advance were made by both the 1st and 2nd Divisions, but little ground was gained; the I Corps had firmly established themselves north of the river, but farther west things had not gone so well, and there were wide gaps in the line on each side of the 3rd Division watched by cavalry only. The fact was that the British Expeditionary Force had been fighting all day against considerably superior numbers, and to have gained a footing, such as it was, on the north side of the river was a very great feat of arms.

Casualties had been very heavy, the I Corps having 3,500, of which our 2nd Battalion lost over 300 in killed and wounded, including 8 officers killed: Major H. F. F. B. Foljambe; Captain A. E. Cathcart; Lieutenants R. H. Bond, F. M. Blake, B. W. Jackson; 2nd Lieutenants J. Forster, G. S. R. Thompson, S. Davison, R. H. M. Barclay. The 1st Battalion lost 168 killed and wounded on the 14th and few following days, including Captains A. F. C. Maclachlan, D.S.O., and G. Makins, M.V.O.; Lieutenant J. S. Alston; 2nd Lieutenant H. C. Lloyd, wounded.

The next day various efforts were made to improve the British position, but without success. The Germans also did their share of attacking, but were everywhere repulsed.

For the next few days the Germans were constantly attacking and being beaten off with heavy loss. Their object was, probably, the strategic one of pinning the Allies to their defences, and preventing them from detaching troops to take part in the mutual outflanking competition

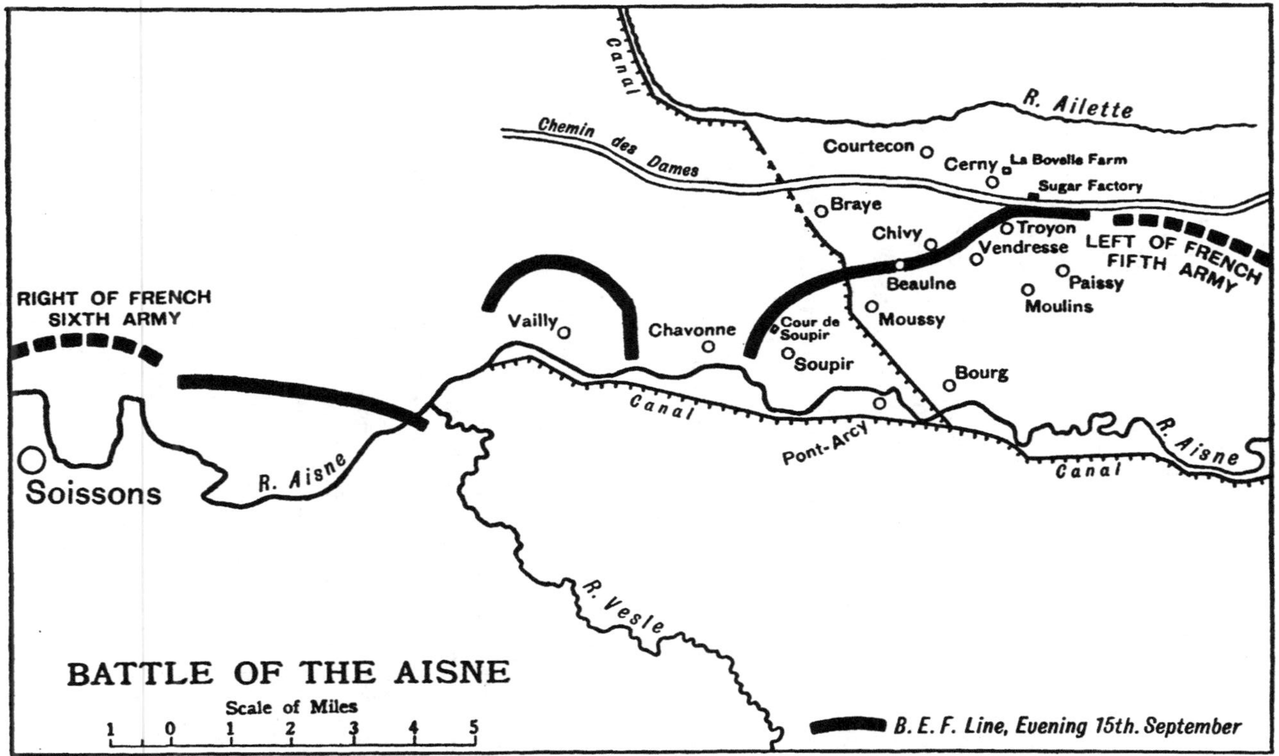

Emery Walker Ltd. sc.

towards the north-west which now began. But for these attacks the Allies would have been having very much the worst of the exchange in casualties, as they were suffering constant losses from the enemy's artillery fire, which had a definite superiority in weight of metal, ranging power and, owing to the topographical situation, in powers of observation.

The general result was that neither side was able to advance, and both settled down to trench warfare, for which, as regards *matériel,* the Germans were very much better equipped.

In one of the German attacks, above-mentioned, which took place on September 17—to quote from the 'Official History,' which, after recounting how the enemy had occupied an abandoned trench, whence they could enfilade the British line, goes on:

'The Northamptons and Queen's, supported by the 2nd K.R.R.C., were ordered to turn the enemy out; and the Northamptons, creeping up unperceived, with a single rush recaptured the trench.

'Shortly afterwards a party of Germans, headed by two officers, advanced towards the 2nd K.R.R.C. with their rifles slung and their hands up. An officer went out to meet them and the men stood up in their trenches, whereupon the Germans opened fire from the hip, wounding several.

'The trick was not forgotten by the K.R.R.C. Almost immediately after this incident another body of three or four hundred Germans repeated the same stratagem against the Northamptons, actually driving them back a few yards in the first surprise. But the machine-gun officer of the 2nd K.R.R.C. [Lieutenant R. J. H. Purcell], who had a gun trained on this second body, mowed them down almost, if not absolutely, to a man. Both sides then made efforts to advance; first the British, who were checked by the German guns, and then in turn the Germans, who were stopped by the rifles and machine guns of the Queen's and the 2nd K.R.R.C. Finally, the enemy fell back, leaving behind him 40 prisoners and a large number of dead. The loss of the 2nd Infantry Brigade in the affair was about 200 of all ranks.'

Ypres[1]

From the moment that the Germans stopped and turned to fight, both sides had started to try to outflank the other on the only side on which it was possible to do so—that is, the Allied left and German right.

The first movements to this end do not concern us here, but towards the end of September it was arranged, for various reasons, chiefly to avoid crossing of lines of communication and to shorten its own, that the British Expeditionary Force should resume its old place on the left of the Allied line.

The movement began on the night of October 1/2 by the relief in the line of the II Corps by the I and III Corps. The III Corps was relieved by the French on the night of the 6th/7th, and the I Corps on the night of the 12th/13th. Each corps marched to the neighbourhood of Compiègne, and trained thence to Flanders. On the 19th the I Corps detrained at Hazebrouck, and moved on Ypres, and the transfer was complete.

On October 20, on the arrival of the I Corps in the Flanders theatre, the disposition of the Allied forces, from the La Bassée Canal, where the British Expeditionary Force right joined with the French left, to the sea was as follows: II Corps (5th and 3rd Divisions), La Bassée Canal to Aubers; III Corps (6th and 4th Divisions), to just east of Ploegsteert—a short gap between the II Corps and III Corps was filled by General Conneau's French Cavalry Corps, to be relieved by the 19th Infantry Brigade, a separate formation made up of battalions which did not, in the original mobilisation scheme, form a part of the

[1] Maps I and VIII.

Expeditionary Force; the Cavalry Corps (1st and 2nd Cavalry Divisions), from the left of III Corps to Zandvoorde; thence to Langemarck was filled by Rawlinson's IV Corps (7th Division and 3rd Cavalry Division), which, as related in Chapter I, had been covering the retirement of the Belgians from Antwerp. On Rawlinson's left came a French force under Foch, which joined up with the Belgians, who held the line of the Yser to the sea near Nieuport. The 2nd Division was at this date just north of Ypres, and the 1st Division about Poperinghe. The Indian Corps had disembarked at Marseilles, and was on its way to the Front.

The race to the sea had ended in a dead-heat, in so far that neither side had succeeded in anticipating the other so as to overlap and turn its flank. There being now no way of getting round, the question to be decided was whether either side was strong enough to break through at any point and roll up the other's flank. This matter was fought out, so far as the British Expeditionary Force was concerned, in what is known as the First Battle of Ypres, which may be said to have begun with the arrival of the II Corps near Béthune on October 11, and did not die down till near the end of November.

Each side started full of hope that it would roll up the flank of the other, but the Germans were all the time being reinforced and acquiring an ever-increasing numerical superiority, and many a time during those months, perhaps the most critical of the whole war, it looked as if the Germans must break through and have another chance of bringing off the encircling movement in which they had so narrowly failed in August.

As mentioned above, General Foch was in command of the French force which connected the British Expeditionary Force with the Belgian Army. It is interesting to hear what our official historian has to say about his influence on the Allied operations when he was only the coadjutor of the Allied commanders on each side of him and not their Commander-in-Chief.

'There were troops of three nations defending Flanders, but no arrangements whatever for unity of command. General Foch, "commandant le groupe des Armées du Nord," was charged by General Joffre with the direction of the French forces in the north. Nominally he had no command over the Belgian and British armies operating there, and officially he could do no more than forward to their commanders copies of the orders issued to his own troops, and make suggestions for co-operation. As a matter of fact, his influence was considerable; and his proposals, so far as means allowed, were carried out by the Allied armies without waste of time and without friction of any kind. French and Belgians, and French and British, as circumstances required—and as far as difference of training, war material, and language permitted—fought side by side, and sometimes as one army.'

From all this, one is inclined to deduce that unity of action among allies is obtained more by finding the man whose personality is such that he can carry his colleagues with him, than by taking any one man of the allied commanders and labelling him Generalissimo or any other high-sounding and meaningless title.

CHAPTER III[1]

'YPRES, 1914,' 'LANGEMARCK, 1914,' 'GHELUVELT,' 'NONNE BOSSCHEN.'

FIRST BATTLE OF YPRES

ON October 18 the 2nd Battalion reached Cassel, where it halted during the 19th. On that date the IV Corps started to attack towards Menin, but was stopped by the advance of the German Fourth Army. The German III *Reserve Corps* and XXII *Reserve Corps* attacked the Belgians, whose line remained practically intact. The German XXIII and part of the XXVI *Reserve Corps* pressed back the French cavalry to the line Passchendaele–Houthulst. The British I Corps was ordered to attack the next day, Sir John French having totally underestimated the enemy's strength.

On the 20th there was hard fighting, all along the line. The I Corps arrived in the vicinity of Ypres. The III Corps was very heavily attacked all day by greatly superior numbers, and lost some ground. The Cavalry Corps was attacked, and withdrew its outpost line to its main position.

Early in the day the 7th Division tried to advance, but was quickly stopped. It was then heavily attacked, but maintained its ground.

The 3rd Cavalry Division beat off an attack, but had to throw back its left to comply with the retirement of De Mitry's Cavalry Corps. The 2nd Division advanced from the neighbourhood of Poperinghe; the 4th Brigade through Ypres, 5th through Elverdinghe, 6th in reserve.

[1] Map I.

Our 1st Battalion went into billets in Ypres. The 1st Division advanced from Hazebrouck, through Poperinghe, towards the left of the 2nd Division. Two battalions of the 4th Brigade took over part of the 3rd Cavalry Division front; the rest of the Division being billeted in rear of the 3rd Cavalry Division. The 1st Division was billeted about Elverdinghe and Poperinghe, our 2nd Battalion marching from Cassel to billets in Elverdinghe. The Belgian line, attacked at both extremities, remained practically intact. The French 42nd Division arrived in reserve, behind the Belgian left.

French still misjudging the situation, his orders for the 21st were for the II and III Corps and the 7th Division to stand fast and entrench; the I Corps to advance in the direction of Thourout (twelve miles to the north-east), with the 3rd Cavalry Division on their right and the French cavalry on their left.

The Germans attacked all along the line.

The 19th Infantry Brigade lost some ground. The Cavalry Corps, two divisions—attacked all day by six German cavalry divisions—almost held their ground, but a partial retirement by the 2nd Cavalry Division imperilled the right of the 7th Division.

Langemarck

The 7th Division was attacked and held its ground, but had to use the 3rd Cavalry Division to reinforce first its left and then its right.

The I Corps advanced as ordered, 2nd Division on the right, 1st Division on the left, and gained some ground, but, meeting strong forces of the enemy in front while, at the same time, the withdrawal of the French to the line of the canal exposed their left flank, they had to dig in on a line, 2nd Division Zonnebeke, to a point half-way between

Poelcapelle and Langemarck, 1st Division thence to Koekuit, and back to Steenstraat on the canal. The 6th Infantry Brigade was in reserve at St. Jean, the 2nd Brigade in Corps Reserve at Pilckem and Boesinghe. The 1st Battalion left Ypres at 5 a.m., and after spending the day in reserve, went into billets at St. Jean in the evening. The 2nd Battalion remained all day in Ypres, and in the evening went into billets in Boesinghe.

Seven and one-third British divisions and five Allied cavalry divisions, all below strength, were now holding a front of thirty-five to thirty-six miles against eleven German divisions (eight of them fresh) and eight cavalry divisions. Joffre, however, was despatching the French IX Corps to Ypres, and the leading division of Indian troops was arriving west of Hazebrouck.

On October 22, except for a slight withdrawal by the II Corps to a selected position, the front of the II, III, and Cavalry Corps remained the same, and there they repelled all attacks for the next few days.

The Germans renewed their attacks all along the line from La Bassée to the sea. The attack with which we are specially interested is that from the north and east against Langemarck: three German divisions against our 1st Division.

Our defences, at this time, chiefly consisted of short, disconnected lengths of trench, with very little wire, and a general shortage of engineer stores. Such was the skill with which our men held them, by their use of the ground, and even more by their overpowering superiority over the enemy in the use of the rifle, that the enemy were deceived into thinking they were up against a strongly prepared position.

An attack on the Zandvourde–Becelaere salient was easily repulsed by the 7th Division. The 6th Brigade, less two battalions, but including our 1st Battalion, were moved from St. Jean to Klein Zillebeke in reserve to this part of the line.

A strong attack on the 21st Brigade was repelled with very heavy loss.

Attacks on the 1st Division failed, except for a slight loss of ground about Kosteke Cabaret. Haig ordered Bulfin to retake this ground at dawn on the 23rd. Preparatory to this operation, the 2nd Battalion moved to Pilckem in the evening, and thence to near Het Sas at 1.30 a.m., 23rd.

Between the British Expeditionary Force and the sea there had been some hard fighting during the day, slightly in favour of the Germans, but the French 42nd Division had reached Nieuport, the French IX Corps was arriving west of Ypres, and the Lahore Division was arriving behind the right of our line.

On October 23 the 2nd Battalion advanced to the attack of the lost trenches at 6 a.m. The two leading companies pushed on till they reached the old support trenches, where they were held up, having pretty heavy casualties in the advance and from shelling after they had been held up. The Germans shelling their own front-line trenches, a good many of the occupants bolted and offered a good target to the riflemen, who got some 30 of them as they ran. About 2 p.m. General Bulfin ordered the Northants to attack the German left flank, but the attempt was unsuccessful. The North Lancashire were then sent in and, working farther round to the flank, were completely successful, driving out of the trenches the Germans, who, bolting across the open, gave a splendid opportunity to our leading platoons and machine guns. They left some 300 or 400 killed and wounded on the ground. D Company 2nd K.R.R.C. and part of C Company pressed on with the North Lancashire and occupied the lost trenches. D Company alone took 130 prisoners. The losses of the Battalion in the fight were 36 killed and about 60 wounded, including Major L. F. Philips and 2nd Lieutenant H. M. Heyland, wounded.

It was found after the trenches had been regained that the position taken up the evening before was a better one tactically, and the troops were therefore withdrawn to it after dark, so there was nothing gained except the moral advantage and a heavy debit balance against the Germans on the day's casualties.

German attacks on the I Corps line during the day were not very determined and were easily repelled. During the night the French 17th Division relieved our 2nd Division, which came into reserve.

The French IX Corps made an attack which had been planned for the previous day, but for various reasons could not be carried out. It proved to be an encounter battle, as it met a German attack launched at the same time. This German attack was repulsed, and nightfall found the French with 500 to 1,000 yards of ground gained from Zonnebeke to Langemarck.

Except for heavy shelling, things were quiet on the 1st Division front. During the night of the 24th/25th the 1st Division was relieved by French Territorial troops, and came into reserve about Ypres–Hooge–Zillebeke.

Early in the morning the Germans launched a heavy attack on the front of the 7th Division, and met with some success, almost annihilating the 2nd Wiltshire Regiment; but successive counter-attacks, first by the Divisional Reserve and then by the 5th Brigade (2nd Division) drove them back and cleared Polygon Wood, which they had occupied.

Shortly after this the 6th Brigade was sent in on the

right of the French attack and gained a line joining on the right with the 5th Brigade, who were holding the front of Polygon Wood, and on the left with the French IX Corps, in front of Zonnebeke. The 1st Battalion were in reserve.

In the afternoon the enemy made a violent attack on the right of the 7th Division, and General Capper had to call on the 22nd Brigade, which had suffered heavily in the morning fight and been relieved by the 6th Brigade, to counter-attack. The attack had, however, been repulsed by the troops in the line, and they were not required.

Heavy attacks had been made on the French and Belgian forces between Bixschoote and the sea, but had been beaten off fairly successfully.

Altogether, by the evening of the 24th the situation had improved. Attacks in superior force had been beaten back all along the line and some ground had been gained. The Allies had the 1st Division, a brigade of the 2nd Division, and nearly a whole French division in hand, whereas the Germans had put in their last reserve.

The fly in the ointment for the British Expeditionary Force was the shortage of gun ammunition.

A renewed attack was ordered for the 25th by the Cavalry, IV, I, and French IX Corps, to be carried out in succession from the left. In the outcome it took the French, whose advance was at once met by strong German counter-attacks, all morning to come up level with the left of our 1st Division. The French attack, therefore, did not begin till 3 p.m., and there was only a trifling gain of ground. At 8 p.m. the Germans launched an attack on the salient in the IV Corps' line, and captured the village of Kruiseecke, but were at once ejected by a counter-attack.

This left the situation practically unchanged from that of the previous night.

The orders for the 26th were that the operation of the 25th should be continued. The result was not unlike that of the day before, but there was harder fighting. The progress of the French IX Corps was very slight. The 2nd Division attacked, but gained no ground, the advance of the 6th Brigade being brought to a standstill by a heavy counter-attack. The Officer Commanding 1st K.R.R.C. had orders to fill a gap between the right of the King's Regiment and the Irish Guards, which gap would occur as these two regiments advanced. As D, the leading company, got clear of Polygon Wood, they came under heavy enfilade fire from rifles and machine guns from the left, and could get no farther. Part of the company got cover in some old trenches, and the remainder dug in where they lay, in a turnip field. The next company, C, came up later on the right of D to fill the gap between it and the Irish Guards. These two companies maintained their position all day. The other two companies, in the afternoon, were moved into Brigade Reserve. The Battalion lost 13 killed, and 34 wounded, nearly all in D Company, including 2nd Lieutenant G. Cronk, 3rd Buffs (attached), killed, Lieutenant E. G. W. Bourke and 2nd Lieutenant K. H. Ward, wounded. At 5 a.m., 27th, the two companies were relieved, and moved down to a farm in the valley south of Zonnebeke, where the other two companies had already arrived.

The salient in the line of the 7th Division was furiously attacked, and for a time things looked very serious, the salient being temporarily inverted into a re-entrant. Ultimately most of the lost ground was reoccupied during the night, though the village of Kruiseecke, at the point of the salient, remained in the enemy's possession. The 1st Brigade relieved the 21st north of the Menin road during the night.

The situation remained much the same as it had been for the last forty-eight hours, except that a fresh German division had been located a few miles east of the British lines. The French had been reinforced by their 31st Division.

The Allied attack was renewed on the 27th, but made little progress against an enemy of, at least, equal strength, with more and heavier artillery, and well dug in.

The orders for the 2nd Division were, for the 4th Brigade to stand fast, the 6th Brigade to advance in conjunction with the French 36th Brigade on its left, the 5th Brigade to support the 6th. The French were soon checked. The South Staffords and 1st K.R.R.C. continued to advance, and gained about 1,000 yards, which took them into the dip between the main Passchendaele Ridge and the Keiberg spur. Here they dug in.

The battalion lost 6 officers and 167 other ranks killed and wounded, including Lieutenant Prince Maurice of Battenberg and Captain W. Wells, 3rd Buffs (attached), killed; and Captain A. L. Y. Willis, 5th K.R.R.C., Captain W. W. Llewellyn, 3rd Somerset (attached), 2nd Lieutenant T. N. Hone, 2nd Lieutenant H. Sweeting, 5th K.R.R.C., wounded.

During the day Sir John French decided to break up the IV Corps, the 7th Division going to the I Corps, and the 3rd Cavalry Division to the Cavalry Corps.

The French attacked again on the 28th, but without much effect. Our 1st Battalion spent the day improving the trenches they had dug on the ground gained the day before. They were heavily shelled, and lost 2nd Lieutenant E. R. Waring, killed.

GHELUVELT

The Germans had been arranging to bring up another six divisions. These were to make a great attack on the part of the Allied front, Messines–Hollebeke–Zandvoorde. To cover the concentration of these troops an attack by three divisions and a Cavalry Division was ordered against Gheluvelt for the 29th.

This attack was launched at 5.30 a.m., and fell on the point of junction of the 7th and 1st Divisions, a mile west-south-west of Gheluvelt. Space will not allow that the fighting should be followed in detail, but the immediate result was a gap in the line and several battalions almost annihilated. A counter-attack was delivered under Major-General Landon, 3rd Infantry Brigade, with three of his battalions, and the 1st Loyal North Lancashire and 2nd K.R.R.C. were sent from Corps Reserve to take part in it; the two battalions being placed under the command of Lieutenant-Colonel Pearce-Serocold. The gap was filled with little ground actually lost, but casualties had been very heavy, and Haig was left with only five battalions out of the front line, instead of twelve.

On the night of the 29th/30th the relief of the II Corps by the Indian Corps was begun.

The Allied commanders were, as yet, unaware of the arrival of German reinforcements, whereas, during the night of the 29th/30th, one division and two cavalry divisions had been relieved by five fresh divisions opposite our 7th Division and Cavalry Corps; the situation being that, though north of Langemarck strength was about equally balanced, from the Menin Road to Langemarck the Germans had a superiority of about three to two and south of that road of more than three to one. Against our weak 7th Division and Cavalry Corps, augmented by two Indian battalions, the enemy had a superiority of about six to one.

The orders for the French IX Corps for the 30th were

to resume the offensive, those for our I Corps were to dig in and await orders for further advance till the situation should become clearer.

The Germans began the day by attacking the point of junction of our line and the French, where our 1st Battalion had been since the 27th. They met with no success, lost heavily and attracted no reserves—the probable object of the attack. Our 1st Battalion easily beat off the attack on them, but had a very heavy shelling, being lucky to get off with a total of 5 killed, 11 wounded, including 2nd Lieutenant J. Casey, killed, and 2nd Lieutenant R. H. Slater, wounded.

An attack on the 1st Division had the same result. The main attack fell on the Cavalry Corps and 7th Division, with the result that, after desperate fighting, although Hollebeke and Zandvoorde were lost and the line considerably pushed back, it still remained connected. Nearly all the reserves had to be employed, and the commander of the French IX Corps lent his Corps Reserve, which came into reserve at Zillebeke.

On October 31 the Germans resumed their attack on the Cavalry Corps, who put up a wonderful defence, though outnumbered six to one. The enemy penetrated into Messines, the opposing lines facing each other at the end of the day in the middle of the village. An attack on Wytschaete was beaten off. At nightfall our line was still unbroken, but losses had been appalling. The 2nd Cavalry Division had, in four days' fighting, lost 30 per cent. of troops engaged.

Equally fierce fighting and more vital in its consequences were the attack on, capture, and recapture of Gheluvelt.

This place was defended by the 3rd Brigade, supported by our 2nd Battalion and the 1st Loyal North Lancashire

Regiment, under Colonel Serocold. Two of our companies were in the front line with companies of the 1st Queen's on each side of them; two companies, with two of the Loyal North Lancashire, were in reserve. At daylight the Germans attacked. They captured an orchard, held by two platoons 2nd K.R.R.C. and two platoons 1st Queen's, whose trenches, which were in front of the line, they enfiladed with a machine gun; but elsewhere were beaten off. Attempts to retake the orchard failed, and from it the enemy could enfilade a part of the front line. Half of the Welch Regiment, in front of Gheluvelt, just north of the Menin Road, were simply blown out of their trenches. This left a gap in the line, the Queen's and detachment 2nd K.R.R.C., south of the gap, continuing to hold on. Thirteen battalions, six of which were fresh, were hurled against what was left of the K.R.R.C., Queen's, South Wales Borderers, and Scots Guards—barely a thousand men in all.

For an hour they were held off. At last the line was broken. Our two companies fell back on the reserve, which had already been almost wiped out by shell fire, and the whole then fell back again to a prearranged line south of Veldhoek.

> 'During the retirement Lieutenant Dimmer, with his machine-gun section, did excellent work on the main road. Although the Germans constantly got within a few yards of his guns he held them at bay, and inflicted very heavy losses on them, and eventually got back without losing either gun.'
>
> ('2nd Battalion War Diary.')

Our 2nd Battalion had lost 408 of all ranks, only 150 being left, whilst the Queen's were practically annihilated. Gheluvelt was taken.

An immediate counter-attack by the 1st Gloucestershire Regiment, reserve to the 3rd Brigade, with what was left of the 2nd K.R.R.C. and 1st Loyal North Lancashire, could make no progress, and the troops were withdrawn whence they started.

The Germans did not follow up, but started to widen the gap by wiping out the remaining two companies Loyal North Lancashire, still in the line, and the 2nd Royal Scots Fusiliers, the left-hand battalion of the 7th Division line. They also tried to widen the Gheluvelt gap by taking the château and its grounds, which they did, but were temporarily ejected by a counter-attack of the 1st South Wales Borderers.

Soon after 1 p.m. a counter-attack was delivered by the 2nd Worcestershire Regiment, lent by the 2nd Division, which relieved what remained of the South Wales Borderers and Scots Guards, who were surrounded in the grounds of Gheluvelt Château, and then cleared the village of Germans. This was, perhaps, the most critical moment of the whole war. If the counter-attack had been unsuccessful, an attempt would have had to be made to establish a new line in front of Ypres, and it is doubtful if any such attempt would have succeeded.

Colonel Pearce-Serocold was severely wounded by a shell during the course of the day, and the command of the Battalion devolved upon Major L. F. Philips. Other casualties among officers were: killed, Captain J. Spottiswoode, 2nd Lieutenant Hon. P. St. Aubyn; wounded, Lieutenant Hon. E. E. M. J. Upton, 2nd Lieutenant G. A. Fisher; missing (prisoner of war), 2nd Lieutenant J. F. E. Goad.

Farther to the right, the fighting had been as hard and as critical. Ground lost in the morning was recovered by a magnificent counter-attack, under General Bulfin, a reinforcement of 80 men of the 2nd Gordon Highlanders being joined by the remnants of the battalions that had been holding the line all day.

The 2nd Division had a much easier day, any threatened attacks being nipped in the bud. Our 1st Battalion lost 11 of all ranks wounded, including Captain B. Seymour, and after dark were relieved in the line by dismounted French cavalry and cyclists.

The programme for the next day (November 1) was that the French should launch three counter-attacks with fresh troops, one from the front held by our Cavalry Corps, another to the left of our I Corps, the third from Dixmude; but the question was less, how much advance they would make, than, to what extent they would relieve pressure on the exhausted British Expeditionary Force, wasted as it was to a quarter of its strength, and with hardly any reserves.

At 10 a.m. the Germans launched an overwhelming attack on the Messines Ridge and Wytschaete, which village changed hands several times during the course of the day, but was finally retained by the Allies; the result of the day's fighting being that the cavalry had to evacuate Messines, and the line was withdrawn so as to run from Wytschaete, south-west along the Wulverghem spur.

Bulfin's force and the 7th Division were heavily attacked nearly all day, but their line remained intact. General Bulfin was wounded.[1]

The 1st Division was not seriously attacked, which was as well, as it was reduced to an outpost line.

After dark our 1st Battalion and the 1st Berkshire relieved the remnants of the 2nd and 3rd Brigades in the line, the Berkshire taking over from our 2nd Battalion.

[1] 'Bulfin's force.' Three battalions from the Reserve of the 2nd Division, under Lord Cavan—2nd Grenadier Guards, 1st Irish Guards, 2nd Oxford and Bucks L.I.—had been put under General Bulfin's command in addition to his own brigade.

Altogether, it had been a good day for the Allies.

November 2 was much the same kind of day as November 1, in that the Germans and French both attacked, leaving the situation pretty well unchanged at the end of the day; but it is an eventful day in our annals, as our 1st Battalion had three companies surrounded and annihilated.

The following account of the disaster is taken from the 'Official History':

'Bernard's detachment of the IX Corps [French]—increased from eight battalions to ten, with four groups of artillery, and placed under General Vidal—was to attack south-eastward towards Becelaere, as on the previous day, but this village was strongly occupied, so, on Sir D. Haig's suggestion, the objective was changed. Pursuing the idea of a north to south counter-attack, Vidal arranged to pass through the left of the 1st Division between the Menin Road and Polygon Wood, and to attack south-eastwards against the curve in the German line near Gheluvelt. This was practically to follow the route of the Worcestershire on October 31. In co-operation with this movement of General Vidal, the British 1st Division was to attack eastwards, so that the enemy would be caught between two fires.

The infantry advance should have taken place at 10 a.m., and the artillery preparation began in good time; but, owing to various causes—the confusion due to the mixture of French and British troops, and the former being new to the ground—it was not till after 12 noon that Vidal's battalions began to approach the British line; but here, as near Wytschaete, the enemy took the initiative.

'To avoid interference with Vidal's advance, the artillery of the 1st Division had received instructions not to fire from 10.30 a.m. onwards on the ground near the Menin Road, which could not be overlooked by ground observers. This, unfortunately, gave the enemy a great opportunity. From 8.30 a.m. onwards his 30*th Division*, with the *XXVII Reserve Corps* north of it, had shown a disposition to push forward on either side of the Menin Road, where stood D Company of the 1st Royal Berkshire, three companies of the 1st K.R.R.C., and the

1st Coldstream, the last being under the establishment of a company in men and having only two officers. One company of the K.R.R.C. and two of the Berkshire were in support. These troops, it will be recalled, had only taken over from the 3rd Brigade after dark, less than twelve hours earlier, and had found but shallow disconnected lengths of trench, barely marking a front, without any wire or, of course, any dug-outs. Across the road [the Menin Road], where the 200 Coldstream stood, was a barricade. Behind this was a group of houses and a farm building which had not been prepared for defence; for, though the men in this sector worked hard during the night, they were too tired to effect much. When daylight came and they were thoroughly worn out, it was found that the field of fire, owing to a ridge on our side and a falling slope on the other, was limited to from 50 to 150 yards. This would have been sufficient if there had been a good obstacle in front of the trenches, and if the supporting artillery had had direct observation on the narrow field of fire. It was inadequate in the circumstances, particularly as hedges obstructed view along the line and interfered with mutual support. To make matters worse, less than 100 yards in front of the British line, bordering on the road, was a small house, to burn which all endeavours had been in vain.

'The barricade on the road was early blown away, and one machine gun of the K.R.R.C., which covered it, put out of action. Though held off elsewhere, the Germans managed to get up a machine gun into the small house about 9.30 a.m. Another party with another machine gun worked its way through a gap of over 60 yards between the Berkshire Company and the K.R.R.C. north of it, and now opened fire at a hundred yards range into the backs of the Rifles. This battalion had definite orders not to retire, and, with the Berkshire and the Coldstream, still kept off all attackers. Invaluable aid was rendered by the artillery, particularly by two guns of the 116th Battery, a couple of hundred yards behind the line.

About 11 a.m., soon after the British batteries had, according to orders, ceased to fire on the area near the Menin Road, the Germans of the 30*th Division,* under the covering fire of the machine gun in the small house, came on boldly down the road in parties of thirty and forty, followed on either side of it by others crawling in twos and threes. Getting up close to the British trenches they overpowered the Coldstream, taking prisoner Captain E. G. Christie-Miller, who was in command, and capturing or killing nearly one-half of their scanty number. They then turned against the three companies of the K.R.R.C., already attacked in front, machine-gunned from the rear, and bombed by parties working up the trench from their right. Then came a final rush. There was a mêlée between the Germans and the two left companies, but it lasted only a few minutes. The right company held out a little longer, but in the end 9 officers and 437 men of the Battalion were killed or captured.'

The officers missing, all of whom were prisoners of war, were: Captain W. P. Lynes, Captain H. E. Ward (3rd Buffs); Lieutenants A. M. Wakefield-Saunders, G. V. H. Gough; 2nd Lieutenants C. H. Reynard, C. F. Schoon, R. Richards, S. Lucas, and T. Wadner.

The troops on each side of the gap thus created managed to hold on and prevent the Germans widening it; the enemy poured through the gap, but were ejected by a counter-attack of the 3rd Brigade with its two attached battalions of the 2nd [our 2nd Battalion and the Loyal North Lancashire], with a French battalion on either side. This counter-attack was entirely successful, as it not only cleared out the Germans who had got through the line, but formed a fresh line only slightly behind the old one.

Though the line of the I Corps still held, it was woefully reduced. Of the 7th Division only a fifth remained of its original strength, of the 2nd Division about two-thirds, and of the 1st Division less than one-third.

On November 3 the French again attempted an advance, but without success. Otherwise things were fairly quiet on both sides.

Our 1st Battalion spent the day in close support of the 1st Royal Berkshire in the woods west of Gheluvelt. The 2nd Battalion, in the front line, were heavily shelled all day, the machine guns coming in for particular attention.

November 4 was a quiet day, except for heavy shelling. The Germans made a few ineffectual attacks. Major H. C. Warre, from the 2nd Battalion, took over command of the 1st Battalion. The British Expeditionary Force was feeling the shortage of field-gun ammunition, and one-third of the field artillery was taken out of the line.

On November 5 the French intended an attack on Messines, supported by two battalions of Allenby's command, but they were anticipated by the Germans, who took and held Spanbroekmolen (Hill 75). Our 1st Battalion moved to the north-west corner of Polygon Wood, where they came under the orders of the 5th Brigade, remaining in reserve to it.

The 3rd Brigade, with two attached battalions from the 2nd (including our 2nd Battalion), were relieved by the 6th Cavalry Brigade ; the 2nd Battalion going into reserve to the 4th (Guards) Brigade, a mile east of Zillebeke village.

On November 6 the Germans attacked astride the Menin Road, driving back some Zouaves, but the line was restored by a counter-attack of the 1st Royal Berkshire. They then attacked farther to the south with considerable success, taking Zwarteleen. In the evening, after dark, the 3rd Brigade—less one battalion, but plus the 2nd K.R.R.C.—counter-attacked, the 1st Gloucester and 2nd K.R.R.C. leading. They came under heavy machine-gun fire, got into considerable confusion, fell back and dug in, our 2nd Battalion relieving the Blues on Hill 60. The casualties of our 2nd Battalion were slight. On November 7 the Germans made numerous attacks on different parts of the line, but they gained no appreciable advantage.

The next three days were uneventful, except that on the 10th the Germans made a heavy attack on the French from Langemarck to Dixmude, and gained some ground.

November 11 was one of the most critical days of the

war, and one of the most glorious in the history of the "Old Contemptibles."[1]

The Germans attacked with twelve and a half divisions on the nine-mile front from Messines to Polygon Wood. In their attack on Cavan's detachment (Bulfin's force till that General was wounded), when the right flank of the London Scottish was surrounded, the situation was restored by a counter-attack by a few men of the 2nd K.R.R.C., which Battalion had a day or two previously taken over a part of the London Scottish line. Everywhere the attack was stopped with tremendous loss to the enemy, who gained no ground, except where the 1*st Guard Brigade* (fresh troops) took the first-line trenches of FitzClarence's 1st Brigade, which had been reduced to the numbers of less than one battalion. They penetrated some way, but the situation was saved by a counter-attack by the 2nd Oxfordshire L.I. The front-line trenches only remained in the enemy's possession.

FitzClarence was killed when reconnoitring for a counter-attack.

This was the turning-point of the First Battle of Ypres, as it was the Germans' last effort before detaching troops to their Eastern Front to meet the Russian danger. It was as well that it was so, as the original Expeditionary Force had almost ceased to exist.

Our 1st Battalion, this day, except for one company in the front line attached to the H.L.I., was in reserve, but even the Battalion Headquarters manned the windows of the house they occupied, and brought fire to bear on a wandering band of Germans who had broken through.

The 2nd Battalion, who were in the front line, with

[1] The Battle Honour 'Nonne Bosschen' was given for this day's fighting, though the name does not appear in the text. It was next door to Polygon Wood.

the 4th (Guards) Brigade, stopped the attack within 60 yards of their line. Next day, November 12, the French were shelled out of Zwarteleen; two platoons and a machine gun of the 2nd K.R.R.C. being lent to fill the gap. To quote from their 'War Diary':

> 'It was on this occasion that Lieutenant Dimmer behaved so splendidly and won his V.C. One gun was knocked out by shell fire early in the attack. Most of the men in his emplacement were killed or wounded, but he, although wounded in five places, continued to fire his own gun until the jacket was so riddled with bullets that the gun jammed from overheating. Dimmer then fell senseless into the bottom of the emplacement, but the Germans had already been stopped, and the few who were left alive fell back to their old trenches.'

Winter was now coming on. After cold rain on November 12, 13, and 14, there was a little snow on the 15th, with frost at night and hard frost on the 18th. There was a six hours' snowstorm on the 19th, the ground on the 20th being covered with snow. The physical condition of the men grew worse and worse, many men suffering from frost-bite (trench feet) from standing in cold water. The whole country became a sea of mud, and rifles constantly jammed in the trenches from getting clogged with mud. The 1st Division on November 12 was reduced to 68 officers, 2,776 other ranks. The 2nd Division was about double the strength of the 1st. The II Corps was equally reduced.

On November 13 there was a lot of shelling, and rather half-hearted attacks on both the French and British were beaten off with heavy loss.

On the 14th the *German Guard Division* again attacked, and were decisively beaten.

On the 15th the relief of the I Corps by the French began. A week of reshuffling followed, and by the 22nd the British front extended from the La Bassée Canal at Givenchy to opposite Wytschaete without a break, and with French on each side. The I Corps was in reserve behind Bailleul. On the 15th the 6th Brigade had been relieved by the French IX Corps. The 1st Battalion went into billets in Caestre on the 18th. The 2nd Battalion was relieved on the 16th, and after one or two moves, settled down in Hazebrouck on the 22nd. The Battalion had now rejoined its own Brigade, which was commanded by General Westmacott, vice Bulfin wounded.

The First Battle of Ypres was over, leaving the advantage to neither side. The opposing lines reached from the Alps to the North Sea, and both sides had tried and failed to break through or outflank the other.

The Germans, for the time being, definitely abandoned the idea of making progress in the West, and turned their attention to their Eastern Front.

The French G.Q.G. were still optimistic, and Sir John French was persuaded to take part in a renewed attack in the middle of December.

It was a half-hearted affair; none of the subordinate commanders seemed to believe in it; the British Expeditionary Force was quite incapable of taking part in a serious attack, owing to shortage of gun ammunition; everybody waited for everybody else, and no progress was made.

The enemy retaliated by attacking the Indian Corps on December 20. They met with some success, and two brigades of the 1st Division were sent to the support of the Indians. These had not been an unqualified success in the unsuitable conditions of trench warfare in the Flanders mud, and on the 22nd their relief by the I Corps began and was completed on the 27th.

Our 1st Battalion took over first-line trenches at

Cuinchy,[1] and remained there till the 29th, when they were withdrawn into billets.

On January 2, 1915, they relieved the 1st Hertfordshire Regiment and Irish Guards in the front line.

The 2nd Battalion moved on December 20, two companies going into the front line, the remainder of the Battalion being billeted in Le Touret.

[1] Map VIII.

CHAPTER IV

'GIVENCHY, 1915,' '**YPRES**, 1915,' 'GRAVENSTAFEL,' 'ST. JULIEN,' 'FREZENBERG,' 'BELLEWAARDE,' 'AUBERS,' 'FESTUBERT, 1915'

3RD AND 4TH BATTALIONS

So far, only the 1st and 2nd Battalions had taken part in the war. The 3rd and 4th Battalions, as related in Volume IV, were in India at the outbreak of the war, and sailed together from Bombay, in the s.s. *Ionian*, for England, about October 15, 1914; the 3rd Battalion under Lieut.-Colonel C. Gosling, the 4th under Major B. F. Widdrington, Lieut.-Colonel Hon. C. J. Sackville-West having gone to France previously on the Staff of Sir James Willcocks, the Indian Corps Commander.

They reached Plymouth, after a weary voyage under convoy, on November 18, and went into camp near Winchester. They were there brigaded, under Brigadier-General Hon. C. G. Fortescue (late Rifle Brigade), with the 4th Rifle Brigade, 2nd King's Shropshire Light Infantry and the Princess Patricia of Connaught's Light Infantry (Canadian) forming the 80th Brigade, 27th Division (Major-General T. D'O. Snow). They spent over a month there in continual rain, which reduced the camp to a bog. The men were never dry and never warm—a bad preparation for men just returned from a tropical climate to withstand the greater hardships of the trenches in a Flanders winter.

The Division went to France just before Christmas, and

after a fortnight in billets behind the line, during which officers and N.C.O.s visited the trench line to learn the work, which was entirely new to them—as siege warfare had long been looked upon in civilised armies as only of historical interest—they took over a line of trenches in the Ypres area, from French troops, on January 6, 1915.[1]

The trenches in Flanders during that first winter were neither safe nor luxurious in any part of the line, but the 27th Division seems to have struck them at their worst, and, with the whole country like a poultice—rain was incessant—and there being practically no fall in the ground to make drainage possible, it was difficult to improve them. The following extract from the 3rd Battalion 'War Records' gives a vivid description of what the troops, on both sides, endured :

'Our trenches at that time were very different from what most of the British line of trenches has since become. At that time our line consisted of a series of detached trenches at intervals of 30 to 50 yards between them, and either no communication trenches at all or, if any, they were nothing but water-logged ditches, in which water stood perhaps 2 feet deep, and which nobody ever thought of using. There was usually a line of support trenches behind, but it was of the same haphazard description as the line of fire trenches. All reliefs had to be carried out by night, and no one could approach or leave the trenches by daylight; even the wounded had to remain till it got dark. At night the reliefs or ration parties would flounder up through seas of mud, and would lose a good many casualties on the way. Individuals frequently got lost and even drowned.'

It took time before it was discovered to what a great extent 'trench feet' could be prevented by skilful treatment, and it is small wonder that the troops fresh from the tropics suffered more than others.

The 4th Battalion, after their first three days in the

[1] Map I.

trenches, came out, and somehow got back to billets in Dickebusch, three miles back, but next morning there were 6 officers and 500 men who could not walk.

Up to the middle of March there was no engagement of more than local importance on the British front, but there were several small attacks, in which the Germans were generally the aggressors, followed by counter-attacks to recover lost trenches. On February 14 the 82nd Brigade lost some trenches near St. Eloi, and our 3rd Battalion was lent to Brigadier-General Longley, commanding 82nd Brigade, to help him to recover them. The counter-attack took place during the night of the 14th/15th, and the Battalion took a successful and distinguished part in it. It sustained a great loss in the death of Captain A. D. Thursby, who, in addition to being a very promising officer, was one of the best gentlemen riders in the Army. He rode 121 winners in the first six years of his service and, at Quetta, in September 1912, he rode in six out of seven races and won them all. Lieutenant C. G. E. Clowes, the son of an old Rifleman, also was killed.

The 1st Battalion was in and out of the trenches, but without serious action, till March 10, when it took part in the subsidiary attack at Givenchy, intended to distract the enemy's attention from Neuve Chapelle. On March 2 Colonel E. Northey left to command the 15th Brigade, Major G. Shakerley succeeding him in command of the Battalion.

On December 31 a detachment of the 2nd Battalion, in a very exposed position in the La Bassée area, was driven out of its trenches by a concentration of *minenwerfer*, shrapnel, and machine-gun fire. An immediate attempt to retake the trenches failed. Next day one company of the Battalion took part in a more deliberately organised counter-attack, which was successful, but the position was untenable, and had to be abandoned. Second Lieutenants C. E. Parker and R. A. Persse (Rifle Brigade, attached) were killed, and Captain G. A. Tryon wounded.

On January 10 the Battalion made another most gallant attack to recover these trenches. This they accomplished, and maintained the position almost intact against German counter-attacks in superior numbers, in which the enemy lost heavily. In this operation were killed: Captain R. Tryon, Rifle Brigade, Lieutenants M. E. Lawrence and J. F. Amphlett-Morton; wounded, 2nd Lieutenants C. H. Dowden, D. Bullen, and W. P. Bristowe; 70 to 80 other ranks killed and wounded.

When the opposing forces first settled down to trench warfare the Germans very soon attained an ascendancy in sniping. The 2nd Battalion, during the winter of 1914–15, received a draft of Rhodesians. A section of snipers was made up from them under Lieutenant L. C. Rattray. In the words of the 2nd Battalion 'Records':

> 'Thanks to their enterprise and accurate shooting, we soon got the upper hand of the German snipers, and this ascendancy was maintained throughout the campaign and in every section of the line before the Battalion had been three days in the trenches.'

On March 1 the 4th Battalion was ordered to make an attack on a section of German trench line. It was a most gallant affair, but never had any chance of succeeding; out of about 300 of all ranks engaged, the casualties amounted to 113. The officers killed were Captain C. V. L. Poë, who had been Adjutant of the Battalion, and was one of the best officers in the Regiment; Captain R. O. Lagden, a Harrow Master who had joined for the war, and was one of those of whom it might be said that it seemed to be impossible to find anything which he could not do, and do well; and Lieutenant Hon. W. Eden; wounded, Major H. W. F. Bircham, Captain Sir G. A. H. Beaumont, Lieutenant E. H. Barker; other ranks, 108 killed, wounded, and missing out of about 300 in action.

GIVENCHY[1]

None of our battalions took part in the main attack at Neuve Chapelle, but the 2nd Division was ordered to make a diversion near Givenchy. The attack was delivered, on March 10, by the 6th Brigade. As happens too often with subsidiary attacks, the artillery support was insufficient, and the attack failed with heavy losses. Small parties of the 1st K.R.R.C., alone of the Brigade, entered the German position. In the words of the 'Official History':

> 'Here, too, machine-gun fire prevented the supports from getting forward and the captured sector had to be abandoned.'

Nothing could exceed the gallantry of the troops in the attack, but it may be doubted whether their object of pinning any of the enemy's reserves can have been attained. It is almost unbelievable how often in the Great War commanders failed to realise that to make a subsidiary attack or false attack or demonstration—horrible word—whatever you like to call it, of any effect it is not enough merely to 'go through the motions.' To prevent the enemy from sending his reserves elsewhere, the attack must have some measure of success—the more the better—so as to compel the enemy to counter-attack, at least with his local reserves or, better still, with reserves brought from a distance. It must be capable, should it meet with unexpected success, of being developed into a big affair. If it is easily beaten off, it not only fails in its object, but it 'gives the show away.' Demonstrations, in the way of

[1] Map VIII.

mock preparations, when they are well done and not made too obviously with the object of attracting attention, are useful before business begins; but, once the fighting has begun, it must be of the kind that does damage.

The 1st Battalion lost, of all ranks, 247 casualties in this affair, including, killed, Captains E. P. Shakerley, C. A. Grazebrook, Lieutenant P. J. Bevan, 2nd Lieutenants F. P. Crawhall, A. R. Herron, and Hon. R. Fellowes; wounded and prisoner of war, 2nd Lieutenant K. Ward; wounded, 2nd Lieutenant H. Else.

On March 24 the 27th Division had been relieved from the awful trench line of St. Eloi and had gone into reserve near Poperinghe.

They went back into the line, in the Polygon Wood area, about the middle of April, and the 3rd and 4th Battalions were alternately in the trenches or in billets west of Ypres till the outbreak of the Second Battle of Ypres, the story of which has now to be related. They seem to have found their new trenches comparatively luxurious after St. Eloi. After the outbreak of the battle and until the withdrawal of May 3/4, they had a fairly quiet time, being chiefly occupied in digging the new line.

The Second Battle of Ypres[1]

Gravenstafel Ridge—St. Julien—Frezenberg Ridge

Since the close of the First Battle of Ypres most of the salient had been held by the French. During the first weeks of April the British Expeditionary Force took over from the French from their former boundary to the Ypres–Poelcapelle Road. The sector taken over from the French was occupied by the V Corps (Lieutenant-General Sir Herbert Plumer) in the following order from right to

[1] Map. I.

left: 27th Division, 28th Division, Canadian Division. The line was practically the same as that held at the close of First Ypres.

On April 22, at 5 p.m., the enemy opened a furious bombardment, at the same time discharging a gas cloud which drifted down on to the French line, held by the 45th (Algerian) and 87th (Territorial) Divisions. This new and unexpected horror was too much for French and Algerian alike and, with the exception of a few scattered units, the garrison of the whole line from near Poelcapelle to Steenstraat became a stream of gasping, panic-stricken fugitives. The left of the Canadian Division was thus completely in the air.

The action of the Canadian reserves saved the situation, and they were shortly reinforced by all the reserves that could be spared from other parts of the V Corps line.

The enemy, who do not seem to have pressed on with any great vigour—probably because the complete success of this last breach of the rules of civilised warfare had rather taken them by surprise—were brought to a halt when they had penetrated as far as Kitchener's Wood. To quote from the 'Official History':

> 'Before daylight on the 23rd there were bodies of troops, amounting to some ten battalions, strung out to cover the gap from the original Canadian left to the canal * * * * with 3½ battalions of General Snow's Division [27th] as reserve.'

On April 23, after more or less impromptu efforts in the morning, a great counter-attack was launched in the afternoon, in which the Canadians, a mixed force under Colonel Geddes of the Buffs, the 13th Brigade, and some French troops took part, for the purpose of regaining the original line. It never had a chance of success, though nothing could have exceeded the gallantry with which it was delivered, and the casualties were heavy; but it at least prevented the enemy from penetrating any farther.

The next month was, for the British Expeditionary Force, as severe a trial as First Ypres.

In theory the French were going to restore the line they had lost, assisted by the British. In practice the British were left almost all the work to do of repelling an attack by the enemy, who, though not much superior numerically, were very greatly so in weight of artillery and available ammunition. The German tactics were to shell a trench line to fragments, and then to occupy it with their infantry and dig in anew.

On the 24th the enemy made a gas attack on the Canadians at the salient which had been formed by the retirement of the French. The Canadians made a magnificent defence and not much ground was lost, but by evening the situation was very precarious.

April 25 began with an attack by Brigadier-General C. P. A. Hull, with his own 10th Brigade and various other battalions attached to it for the operation, which was a repetition of that by the 13th Brigade, alike in its results, the gallantry of the troops, and the number of casualties. At the same time the Germans attacked the left of the 28th Division and the right of the Canadians, after a furious bombardment. The line held, though sections of trench were lost in places.

On the 26th the Lahore Division made an expensive attack which, if it did not gain much ground, at any rate considerably strengthened the position. The 149th (Northumberland) Brigade, which attacked somewhat later than and on the right of the Lahore Division, lost two-thirds of its strength.

By this time it had become more and more evident that the situation in the Ypres salient was an impossible one. The troops available could not restore the line; more could not be spared in view of the coming Allied attack in Artois; the only possible course was a withdrawal sufficient to flatten out the salient to an extent which would make it tenable.

Sir John French, incited by General Foch, would have none of it. Sir Horace Smith-Dorrien, who advocated the withdrawal, was ordered to hand over the greater part of his command to General Plumer, and returned home a few days later.

The very same day French, in a communication to Plumer, was admitting the possibility of withdrawal. Before he left for England, Smith-Dorrien was amply justified by the withdrawal taking place.

The Lahore Division had again attacked on the 27th, but without result, except for more casualties.

The next few days were uneventful, the British Commander-in-Chief now wishing to withdraw, but delaying the operation in deference to the wish of the French, who wanted to continue the attempts to retake the lost line.

The withdrawal began on the night of May 1/2. On May 1 the Germans made a gas attack on the 15th Brigade (Brigadier-General E. Northey) at Hill 60, which was beaten off, though the defence lost heavily from the effects of gas. On the afternoon of the 2nd the Germans attacked the 4th Division with gas, but were beaten off, and the withdrawal was resumed during the ensuing night.

During the 3rd the enemy twice attacked the part of the line held by the 85th and 11th Brigades, but was again beaten off, almost entirely by rifle fire, as most of the artillery had been withdrawn, and what was left was overpowered by superior weight of metal; during the night of the 3rd/4th the withdrawal was completed. This retirement from close touch with an enemy with whom they had been engaged for a fortnight, and who did not discover that they had gone till next morning, was a wonderful feat of arms on the part of the 4th, 27th, and 28th Divisions who carried it out. Our 3rd and 4th Battalions were in the front line of the 80th Brigade, and they retired through the new line, which had been taken up by the 4th Rifle Brigade and 2nd King's Shropshire Light Infantry, without a casualty. The process is described as follows in the 4th Battalion 'War Diary':

> 'It was arranged that the withdrawal should begin at the extreme end of the salient after dark, and that the remaining parts of the line should withdraw in rotation. First, half the garrison were withdrawn, then half the remainder, and then the whole of the remainder, with the exception of three or four men per trench under 2nd Lieutenant D. Morton, who remained firing rifles and Verév pistols until the last moment.
>
> 'The withdrawal was carried out with complete success, and the enemy were apparently in ignorance of the movement until after daylight.'

Second Lieutenant Morton was killed on the 10th.

In the new Ypres salient the 27th Division joined up with the 5th near Hill 60. The 80th Brigade, on the left of the 27th Division line, reached from the Menin Road to within half a mile of the Roulers railway.

On May 5 the enemy made a successful gas attack on Hill 60, which, in spite of several determined attempts to retake it, remained in his hands.

On May 8 the Germans continued their policy of attack by overwhelming bombardment and occupation of the battered trenches by infantry when the garrison had been driven out or wiped out. The attack on this day fell on the 28th Division and the 80th Brigade, on the left of the 27th Division.

The 83rd Brigade, whose trenches were in a very exposed position, after repelling several attacks, and after enormous losses during the bombardment, were almost annihilated, making a big gap in the line.

The 80th Brigade immediately to the right (4th K.R.R.C. and Princess Patricia of Connaught's Light Infantry in front line) were subjected to a like bombardment, and not only beat off all attacks during the day, but extended their front to the left and formed a flank towards the gap.

The 84th Brigade, next on the left to the 83rd, was gradually rolled up from its right and destroyed piecemeal.

Counter-attacks by the 85th Brigade, and by the 10th Brigade from the reserve of the 4th Division, filled the gap and restored the line, but the losses had been enormous, the 28th Division being almost destroyed. Of this day's fighting the official historian says:

> 'The stand of the 4th K.R.R.C., the Patricia's, the 1st King's Own Yorkshire Light Infantry, B Company 3rd Monmouthshire and 2nd Northumberland Fusiliers is indeed worthy to rank, with the counter-attack of the Rangers, among the historic episodes of the war.'

The 12th London (Rangers), in Brigade Reserve, 84th Brigade, had been sent forward to reinforce the front line, and were almost exterminated in the course of their advance, but the few who reached the front line held on gallantly for the rest of the day.

On May 9 the enemy subjected the 27th Division to another terrific bombardment. One small advanced trench of the 81st Brigade was taken, its garrison of one platoon 2nd Gloucestershire Regiment being all killed, and an expensive attempt to recover it failed. Several attacks on the 80th Brigade were beaten off by the fire of the 3rd and 4th K.R.R.C., 4th Rifle Brigade, and 2nd King's

Shropshire Light Infantry, with very heavy loss to the enemy.

On May 10 the enemy subjected the front line of the 81st and 80th Brigades, held by the 2nd Cameron Highlanders, 4th K.R.R.C., and 4th Rifle Brigade, to another intense bombardment from 10.30 a.m. to 1.30 p.m.

The front trenches of the K.R.R.C. and Rifle Brigade were destroyed, and the support trenches of those battalions became the line of defence.

The attack which followed was beaten off. The second line then became the first, as far east as Sanctuary Wood, which was still held by the 81st Brigade.

During the three days' fighting, 8th–10th, the 4th K.R.R.C. had lost 15 officers and 478 other ranks, leaving it with 3 officers and 100 men.

The losses of the 4th Rifle Brigade were almost as heavy. Our 4th Battalion was brought out of the line on the night of the 10th/11th.

On May 11 the Germans turned their attention entirely to the 81st Brigade, which was obliged to withdraw to its support line.

On the 11th the 4th Battalion moved back to Bosseboom, some miles west of Ypres, to reorganise, after twenty-six days in the trenches—a draft of 150 men had arrived the night before. On the 14th they were formed into a composite battalion with the Princess Patricia of Connaught's Light Infantry, but this arrangement does not seem to have lasted long, as the Princess Patricia of Connaught's Light Infantry was acting as a separate unit on the night of May 24/25. On the night of the 14th/15th the composite battalion relieved the 4th Rifle Brigade in the trenches, and were in turn relieved on the night of the 17th/18th by the 1st Cavalry Brigade and returned to Bosseboom.

On the night of the 12th/13th the 1st and 3rd Cavalry Divisions, under General de Lisle, relieved the 28th Division, which had had 15,000 casualties in the Second Battle of Ypres; the cavalry also taking over from the left-hand battalion of the 27th Division, the 2nd King's Shropshire Light Infantry.

On the 13th, after another intense bombardment—our 3rd Battalion 'War Diary' reports it as heavier than that of the 10th—the Germans attacked the 4th Division, Cavalry, and 80th Brigade. The 80th Brigade—4th Rifle Brigade and 3rd K.R.R.C. in front line, reinforced later by the 2nd Royal Irish Fusiliers (82nd Brigade)—maintained their position.

The cavalry lost some first-line trenches, obliterated by shell fire, but a counter-attack drove out the Germans, who had occupied the abandoned position. The line was, however, untenable, and another, 1,000 yards in rear, was taken up on a reverse slope.

Our 3rd Battalion was relieved, on the night of the 13th/14th, after twenty-five days in the trenches, during which time their casualties amounted to 17 officers and 525 other ranks. A comparatively quiet period followed the attack of the 13th.

Between the 17th and 19th the 27th Division was relieved by the 1st Cavalry Division. Laudatory orders and messages were poured on the 80th Brigade from everyone, from the Commander-in-Chief downwards. For a month they had been perpetually under shell fire, with long periods of intense bombardment, from an enemy strong in artillery and with apparently unlimited ammunition, while artillery support from their own side was negligible; what few guns there were being limited to an expenditure of ammunition which made their efforts positively pathetic.

On the 15th the French attacked and ejected the Germans from the west side of the canal, where they had secured a foothold on the day of the first gas attack.

Bellewaarde Ridge

In the early hours of May 24, the whole of the 27th Division being then in reserve some miles west of Ypres, the enemy made another attack, after a short but intense bombardment and under a gas cloud heavier than any they had before produced, along the whole V Corps front. Several gaps were made in the line, and the 80th and 84th Brigades were ordered up to counter-attack.

The 84th Brigade (Divisional Reserve, 28th Division), which had less distance to come, was ordered to counter-attack between Bellewaarde Lake and the railway, without waiting for the 80th Brigade, which was in Corps Reserve. The attack was launched at 5 p.m., and the attackers got some way and then dug in to await the 80th Brigade.

On the arrival of the 80th Brigade a night attack was arranged between the two Brigadiers, and the advance began at 11 p.m. The 80th Brigade advanced with two battalions in the front line, from right to left 4th Rifle Brigade, 3rd K.R.R.C.; the 4th K.R.R.C. and 2nd King's Shropshire Light Infantry in second line, with the Princess Patricia of Connaught's Light Infantry in reserve. The second-line battalions were detached, when the attack began, to support the 84th Brigade.

In spite of the bright moonlight, they got close to the German trenches without severe losses, but then came under such heavy rifle and machine-gun fire that they were forced to fall back to the line originally gained by the 84th Brigade. From the accounts in the 'War Diaries' of our 3rd and 4th Battalions, the attack seems to have been a haphazard affair, as a hastily prepared night attack is apt to be. No one appears to have known exactly where the enemy was, the 84th Brigade was evidently not in a condition to take part, and the attack just faded out when dawn began to appear and it became clear to the Commanding Officers on the spot that further advance would mean a useless sacrifice of life.

Our 3rd Battalion did not become very heavily engaged, and got off with a loss of 3 officers wounded and 65 other ranks killed and wounded. The 4th Battalion had 1 officer killed (2nd Lieutenant F. A. F. Baines) and 1 wounded out of 7 Company Officers present, and 159 other ranks killed, wounded, and missing out of 600 engaged.

The 3rd Battalion was relieved on the night of the 26th/27th, and went back into reserve at Bosseboom.

Various readjustments were then arranged all along the line, and the Second Battle of Ypres ended—the German Fourth Army having that day (May 25) issued orders to stop further operations.

During the Second Battle of Ypres the 3rd Battalion lost the following officers, killed or died of wounds: Captain J. F. B. Pearse, Lieutenant J. W. Maynard, and 2nd Lieutenant R. S. Timmis. The 4th Battalion lost, killed or died of wounds: Captain C. J. T. R. Wingfield; Lieutenants L. H. St. A. King, D. F. F. Shennan; 2nd Lieutenants N. M. K. Bertie, H. C. M. Farmer, D. Morton, G. T. Croft-Smith, and F. A. F. Baines. Captain Pearse was serving on the Staff.

Early in April a contingent from Fiji, 41 strong, had joined the 4th Battalion, and been posted as a platoon to B Company.

On April 29 the 4th Battalion lost a good officer in Captain C. J. T. R. Wingfield, who, a few days before, was wounded in a bomb accident and was again wounded, this time mortally, while being carried to the field ambulance.

In June the 27th Division was transferred from the V Corps, Second Army, to the III Corps, First Army, and moved down to Armentières, spending a comparatively quiet summer in the trenches in that area.

On July 23 Colonel C. Gosling went to command the 7th Infantry Brigade, and was succeeded by Major H. F. W. Bircham, D.S.O., till the return from England of Major W. J. Long.

On August 23 the 3rd Battalion suffered a great loss in the death of Captain Geoffrey Makins, M.V.O., who was picked off by a sniper.

Battle of Aubers Ridge [1]

The Allied plan for 1915 was to take advantage of the Germans' weakness in the West, owing to their great offensive against Russia, by making a big combined attack towards the plain of Douai and Aubers Ridge—the French on the right, the British on the left.

The British plan was to make two converging attacks about 6,000 yards apart. The I and Indian Corps were to attack south of Neuve Chapelle, the IV Corps north of it. The first phase for the right attack was to capture the line Rue du Marais–Lorgies–Ligny-le-Grand. The second phase was a good deal more ambitious, but, as the first objective was never reached, no more need be said about the second.

The British plan provided for only forty minutes' bombardment, the French for one lasting several days. Owing to the bad weather interfering with the French bombardment, the attack which was intended for May 7 had to be deferred till the 9th.

[1] Map VIII.

After the experience of Neuve Chapelle, in March, it was expected that, at least, the first line of German trenches would be captured without much loss. The German line here was, however, very much stronger than it had been in March. The forty minutes' bombardment had very little effect in damaging the enemy's parapets—owing to water near the surface, trenches could not be dug—destroying machine guns, or cutting wire. The attack was a costly failure all along the line.

The 2nd Infantry Brigade attacked with two battalions in first line, the 2nd K.R.R.C. being in support. [Since January our 2nd Battalion had had a fairly quiet time. On April 28, when in Brigade Reserve, they lost their transport officer, Lieutenant R. C. Fetherstonhaugh, son of Major-General R. S. Fetherstonhaugh, C.B., later the Colonel Commandant of the 3rd Battalion, a very promising young officer.] The first line advanced as soon as the bombardment became intense, but immediately came under machine-gun fire, and lost heavily. They lay down in some sort of a line in No Man's Land and as soon as the guns lifted, rose and dashed forward. Hardly a man reached the enemy's front-line trenches. The short bombardment had completely failed in its object. The wire was uncut, the trenches very little damaged and, when the guns lifted, the German machine-gunners were free to fire with nothing to disturb their aim.

On the whole 1st Division front only a few of the Northamptonshire and Munster Fusiliers reached the enemy's trenches, and these never came back. The 2nd K.R.R.C. advanced to the support of the Northamptonshire, but never got nearer than within 30 yards of the wire. The men were eager to advance, though it would have been useless sacrifice of life to do so. About 7.30 a.m. they received orders to withdraw to their original position.

It was with great difficulty that the remnant of the advanced companies was withdrawn, and many gallant acts were performed in bringing in the wounded under heavy fire. It was almost impossible to get a message of any sort up to the front line, and they, very properly, were taking no notice of mere shouts to retire. Corporal Bates, when he heard the order to retire shouted over the parapet, came back to his company commander for confirmation of the order before withdrawing his men—a very good testimonial to the training of the Battalion.

A fresh assault was launched by the 1st Brigade in the afternoon, with equally disastrous results. Two companies 2nd K.R.R.C. held the front-line breastwork during the attack. During the small hours of May 11 the Battalion moved back into billets in Corps Reserve. Their losses amounted to 11 officers and 240 other ranks killed and wounded.

Among the killed was the Adjutant, Captain the Hon. E. E. M. J. Upton, a very great loss to the Battalion. His father had served in the Regiment, and his grandfather, General Lord Templetown, had been one of our Colonels Commandant. 'Lipton,' as he was called, was devoted to the Regiment and his profession, and would have gone far. The other officers killed were: Lieutenants W. S. Bird, W. W. Melville, C. W. Morris; 2nd Lieutenants H. W. Hodges and J. I. Farmer. The wounded officers were: Captain the Hon. A. F. W. Harris, Lieutenant G. S. Walley, 2nd Lieutenants D. B. Morrieson, F. W. Crook, C. H. Dowden, D.S.O.

Although the IV Corps had some preliminary success, the attack on the whole British front ended in the same expensive failure. A renewal of the attack was ordered for May 10, but was deferred for some days owing to extreme shortage of gun ammunition. The big French attack farther to the south met with great success at the start, but, owing to the British failure, the Germans were able freely to reinforce their line, and the attack was brought to a standstill.

Festubert

Sir John French was in a difficult position. He had tried to support the French attack, but had failed even to contain the enemy. At the same time, he was anxious about the Ypres front, where the Second Battle was going none too well, and the French had done very little to implement their undertaking to regain the line they had lost on April 22. It was impossible to mount a fresh attack for some days, as this time it was to be preceded by a prolonged bombardment. As an immediate help he set free the left division of the French by relieving it with his shattered 1st Division and the 47th (London) Division.

The plan for the new attack was for the 2nd Division and the Indian Corps to make a night attack, and take the first two lines of the German trenches. At dawn the 7th Division were to attack immediately to the right of the 2nd Division, the whole to push on together when the 7th Division had gained their first objective.

At 11.30 p.m., May 15, the 6th and 5th Brigades attacked on a front of 1,300 yards. It was the first night attack made by British troops on the Western Front. The attack of the 6th Brigade was a complete success. The part taken in it by our 1st Battalion is thus described in their 'War Diary':

'The Battalion's first objective was the front line of German trenches which, in general, ran parallel to the British lines, but opposite our left, and immediately in front of the Ferme de Bois formed a re-entrant angle, and thence, to our left, ran out into a salient, on which several enemy machine guns were known to have been placed. (The salient was the objective of the Inniskilling Fusiliers, in the 5th Brigade.) The Germans were known to have one communication trench connecting their first and second lines in this piece of their defences, and their main communication trench running past the western side of the Ferme de Bois also led into this section. Their second line, apparently, came to a dead end almost opposite our left, but was known to continue again to the left in front of the 5th Brigade.

'The distance from our front line to the Germans' was roughly 350 yards, but on our left, opposite the salient, the distance was considerably less. The ground was flat, ploughed, with rough grass on it, and the furrows gave a good guide for direction. Parallel to our line, and 20 yards in front of it, ran a ditch 12 feet wide and full of water, and again on the far side of it was an old disused trench which, however, presented no serious obstacle. D Company (Lieutenant Alston) and B Company (Captain Bonham-Carter) were selected to form the first two lines. Each company, D on the right and B on the left, had two platoons in the first line and two in the second. C Company (Captain Bigge) was to form our third line, and A the fourth; the machine-gun section being kept in reserve to await orders.

'The two leading lines filed out quietly by two prepared openings in our parapets and lay down in front of the wide ditch ready to assault when ordered. The left party crossed the ditch by bridges which had been prepared; the right party's opening was in front of the ditch, being just to the right of where it entered our line. The Battalion left its billets at 9 p.m., and everything went smoothly. Ordinary sniping (into the air) was carried on from our trenches to disarm suspicion, and our artillery, which had been cutting the enemy's wire by deliberate fire for several days, fired an occasional shell throughout the evening. There was no moon, and the night was pretty dark. Three signallers accompanied D Company, taking with them a telephone instrument, two motor lamps, and paying out wire as they went. They were ordered to light one motor lamp if we captured the German first line, and two if we captured the second, and were also to signal back, if other means failed, with an electric torch, using the Morse code.

'For fully five minutes after 11.30 p.m., when the advance began, quiet reigned. The Germans fired no lights, and there was nothing more than the usual sniping. Then came a sudden burst of fire, mostly on our left, and the enemy began to send up lights in all directions. Our front line appeared to be quite close to the German trenches, advancing steadily, and as it gained them, the lights from that part ceased to go up. A very heavy machine-gun fire had been coming across our front from the salient on our left, and this fire did not seem to diminish much as time went on. Rifle fire also came from that salient.

'About midnight the letters K.R.B. were signalled back by electric torch, indicating, by previous arrangement, that we had secured the enemy's second line. The Commanding Officer, Major Shakerley, had started over with C Company, and A Company had followed. Messages were received that the Berks had got in, and also the 5th Brigade on our left. The Adjutant, Captain Knox-Gore, then went across with the Headquarters Staff, accompanied by the Machine-gun Section, which, thanks to the darkness, lost only one man from the heavy fire that swept the ground from the salient on our left.

'With vigorous bombing the third line of German trenches was taken before daybreak, when the Inniskilling Fusiliers, assisted by those who had already crossed, took the salient on our left with trifling loss. The new position was consolidated, and the making of communication trenches to our old lines, where the Staffords were now in support, was at once commenced.

'The trenches thus taken were retained.'

The statement of the writer of the 'War Diary' that the Inniskilling Fusiliers took the salient on the left 'with trifling loss' must have been written in complete ignorance of what had been going on in the 5th Brigade; the truth being that their attack, as also that of the Indian Corps on their left, had failed; only half of the Inniskilling Fusiliers, on the extreme right of the Brigade, reaching the enemy's front trench. The losses of the Inniskilling Fusiliers amounted to 19 officers and 630 other ranks.

It was this failure on our left and the consequent enfilade fire to which they were subjected that accounted for the heavy losses of our 1st Battalion in an attack which went off so smoothly, and does not seem to have met with much resistance from the troops who were its objective. These losses were: officers, killed 5, wounded 8; total casualties of all ranks, 307. The officers killed were: Lieut.-Colonel G. C. Shakerley, D.S.O., Captain the Hon. J. Bigge, Lieutenant W. H. Grenville-Grey, 2nd Lieutenants J. S. H. James and C. M. Cassidy; wounded: Captain and Adjutant W. S. Knox-Gore; Captain A. L. Bonham-Carter, E. A. Pauley; Lieutenants J. S. Alston, A. E. Messer, R. A. Banon; 2nd Lieutenants A. E. Dent and C. E. Hardy.

Geoffrey Shakerley was one of the best of his generation of Riflemen. He had distinguished himself in the South African War, and even more so as a commander of Mounted Infantry in Somaliland. He was an exceptionally good horseman, and won a lot of races in his younger days in Gibraltar, Malta, and South Africa.

The 1st Battalion held the captured German trenches till they were relieved on the afternoon of the 17th by the 2nd South Staffordshire, after which they took no further part in the battle, which dragged on till the 27th, when it died down, leaving the British gainers by a few square miles of country, but losers by some 15,000 casualties to the enemy's 5,000.

As in the battles round Ypres, the British were hopelessly handicapped by weakness in artillery and shortage of artillery ammunition.

On June 26, 1915, the 1st Battalion lost a fine old soldier in Captain and Quartermaster Arthur Harman, D.C.M., who had been wounded by a shell the day before. Born in 1865, he joined the regiment in 1883. After a few months in the 1st Battalion he went out to the 3rd, in time to take part in the Suakim expedition of 1884. He returned home with the Battalion as a sergeant in 1891, and went out with them as a Colour-Sergeant to the South African War in 1899. He served throughout the war, being honoured with the D.C.M. and two mentions in despatches. He became Sergeant-Major of the 4th Battalion in 1905, and Quartermaster of the 1st in 1909. Going out with the 1st Battalion in August 1914, he was promoted Captain for his services in the Great War, having been previously mentioned in despatches. He was one of the best that the ranks of our regiment has produced.

The 2nd Battalion took no active part in the battle of Festubert, though they were in the neighbourhood. They were, evidently, part of the time in the front-line trenches, as the following note from the 'Official History' shows:

> 'For crossing No Man's Land on the night of May 22, and bombing an enemy machine-gun emplacement which was hindering our working parties, Rifleman W. Mariner, 2nd K.R.R.C. (1st Division) was awarded the V.C. He was out alone for one and a half hours.'

We can now leave the four regular battalions, all of which were to have a fairly quiet time for the next few months, and turn to the New Army Battalions.

CHAPTER V

'Hooge, 1915,' 'Loos'

The New Army

Space will not admit of any detailed story of the raising and training of the New Army battalions, which began a few days after the mobilisation of the existing forces. All sources were tapped to find a nucleus of regular officers of the Regiment for the new battalions. The 1st and 2nd Battalions, before embarking for France, were ordered to detail several officers for service with the new battalions, much to the disgust of those selected, as few doubted but the war would be over long before the New Army could be fit for active service. A few officers at home on leave from abroad were snapped up, and of course a large number of Reserve officers were available. Most of the battalions were raised at Winchester, and these moved on to Aldershot or elsewhere, for training. For the purposes of this history their life must begin with their departure overseas.

The Regiment seems to have been particularly fortunate in its recruits, officer and man. The officers were for the most part of the best type which our universities and public schools produce. The men were of all sorts and from all parts of the world. The K.R.R.C. seems to have had a particular attraction for men from overseas.

The 7th Battalion, which started recruiting on August 9, and came officially into existence on the 19th, sailed for France on May 19, 1915, under the command of Lieut.-Colonel G. A. P. Rennie, D.S.O. Together with the 8th

Battalion K.R.R.C., and the 7th and 8th Battalions Rifle Brigade, they formed the 41st Brigade (Brigadier-General Oliver Nugent, D.S.O., A.D.C.) of the 14th (Light) Division (Major-General Victor Couper, late Rifle Brigade). Early in June the 14th Division moved up to near Ypres, and went through a course of digging in the line, being grouped with other troops that had been out longer. Later in the month it took over its own line of trenches in the Ypres salient, and went through the ordinary routine of trench life, till it took part in the action at Hooge, the story of which will be told later.

The 8th Battalion was formed towards the end of August 1914, and left for France, under Lieut.-Colonel H. C. R. Green, with the 14th Division.

The 9th Battalion went out under Lieut.-Colonel C. Chaplin, who had formerly commanded the 3rd Battalion. They, with the 9th Rifle Brigade, were in the 42nd Brigade (14th Division) under Brigadier-General C. J. Markham, who had commanded the 1st Battalion. The other battalions of the Brigade were the 5th Oxford and Bucks Light Infantry and the 5th King's Shropshire Light Infantry.

The 10th and 11th Battalions, under Lieut.-Colonels F. Douglas-Pennant (late K.R.R.C.) and W. H. L. Allgood (late K.R.R.C.), respectively, embarked for France on July 21, 1915.

Together with the 10th and 11th Rifle Brigade they formed the 59th Brigade (Brigadier-General C. D. Shute, late Rifle Brigade), 20th (Light) Division. They did nothing beyond the ordinary trench warfare during 1915.

The 12th Battalion was raised in September 1914, and went to France in July 1915, under Lieut.-Colonel A. I. Paine, D.S.O. (late K.R.R.C.).

Together with the 6th Oxford and Bucks Light Infantry, 6th Shropshire Light Infantry, and 12th Rifle Brigade, they formed the 60th Brigade, 20th Division.

The 13th Battalion was raised in October 1914, and went to France in July 1915, under the command of Lieut.-Colonel R. Chester-Master (late K.R.R.C.), forming part of the 111th Brigade, 37th Division. The other battalions in their Brigade were the 10th and 13th Royal Fusiliers and 13th Rifle Brigade.

The 14th Battalion was raised in the autumn of 1914 as a Service Battalion, but in 1915 became a Reserve Battalion, and continued to find drafts for the Service Battalions until in 1916 it was absorbed in the General Training Reserve, and ceased to form a part of the Regiment.

The 15th Battalion was raised in November 1914 under Lieut.-Colonel G. S. St. Aubyn (late K.R.R.C.). In the spring of 1915 it was converted into a Reserve Battalion and, until absorbed in the General Training Reserve on September 1, 1916, was employed in forming drafts for the battalions abroad.

At the instance of Field-Marshal Lord Grenfell, their Governor and Commandant, a Special Battalion was raised from past and present members of the Church Lads' Brigade. It was numbered as the 16th Battalion K.R.R.C. and recruiting was begun for it in September 1914. The full establishment was reached in November.

The Battalion left for France, under Lieut.-Colonel C. E. Wyld, late Coldstream Guards, in November 1915.

The 17th Battalion was raised by the British Empire League, and came into existence in April 1915. It left for France, under Lieut.-Colonel E. F. Ward (late K.R.R.C.), in March 1916.

The 18th Battalion (Arts and Crafts) was raised by Sir Herbert Raphael, M.P., who, on the outbreak of war, had enlisted as a private, at the age of fifty-six. In June 1915 he was given the rank of Captain, and commissioned to raise the Battalion, which left for France, under Lieut.-Colonel G. A. J. Soltau-Symons (late K.R.R.C.), in May 1916.

The 19th (Reserve) Battalion was formed by the amalgamation of the reserve companies of the 16th and 17th Battalions. Lieut.-Colonel E. Kelly Purnell, late Lancashire Fusiliers, was given command in October 1915. Till August 1916 it continued to supply drafts for the Service Battalions, when it lost its connection with the Regiment on becoming the 109th Training Reserve Battalion.

The 20th Battalion (British Empire League Pioneers) was raised in September 1915, and went to France in March 1916, under the command of Lieut.-Colonel E. Murray. It did good service there till the end of the war.

The 21st Battalion (the Yeoman Rifles) was raised by Lieut.-Colonel the Earl of Feversham in the autumn of 1915. Lord Feversham had gone to France in April 1915, in command of the Yorkshire Hussars. On the break-up of that regiment into Divisional Cavalry, he accepted the task of raising an infantry battalion from among the farming class in the north of England. He was the very man for the job, and the Battalion was full to establishment with men of the very best type by December. They went to France in May 1916.

The 22nd Battalion was another Reserve Battalion which had a brief existence before being absorbed in the General Training Reserve.

The 23rd (Reserve) Battalion was formed in December 1915, under Lieut.-Colonel J. A. Hope, M.P. (late K.R.R.C.). On September 1, 1916, it became the 111th Training Reserve Battalion, and was allotted to supply drafts for the K.R.R.C. and Rifle Brigade; officers and N.C.O.s retaining the uniform of the regiment.

The 24th (Reserve) Battalion was formed in April 1916, from the reserve companies of the 21st Battalion. In May Lieut.-Colonel H. P. Irby (late K.R.R.C.) took over command from Captain J. Lesley, of the 21st Battalion. They were disbanded in August 1916, on the formation of the Training Reserve Battalions.

The 25th (Pioneer) Battalion was formed in France in April 1918, and did much valuable work in France and Flanders during the rest of the war, under the command of Lieut.-Colonel J. G. Kirkwood, C.M.G., D.S.O.

With the exception of the 7th, 8th, and 9th Battalions, none of the new battalions took part in any operation beyond the uneventful round of trench warfare, with short periods out of the trenches for a little rest and a great deal of training, during 1915.

Hooge [1]

The 14th Division had been holding a part of the Ypres salient ever since the middle of June.

During most of that time there had been considerable bickering over the site of the village and château of Hooge. On July 17 a mine was successfully exploded under the enemy's front line, and the crater occupied by the 4th Middlesex (8th Brigade, 3rd Division).

Other attempts were made to capture a piece of the enemy's line on July 22, but without success. The area had become very 'unhealthy,' and was subjected to constant shelling.

To quote again from the 'Official History':

> 'Rumours of German retaliation, by an attack along the Menin Road, were current on the 26th, but it did not take place until the morning of the 30th, and then against the

[1] Map I.

Hooge sector, held by the 41st Brigade (Brigadier-General O. S. W. Nugent), of the 14th Division (Major-General V. Couper), which had taken over the sector a week before.

'The 8th Rifle Brigade (Lieut.-Colonel R. C. Maclachlan) held the front at the Hooge crater, with the 7th K.R.R.C. (Lieut.-Colonel G. A. P. Rennie) on its right. The crater itself was untenable, owing to constant trench-mortaring and "strafing," and the trenches, dry but dilapidated beyond measure, ran up to the lip on either side, with no definite connection round the crater. The sector had an evil reputation for being subject to incessant sniping and bombing, besides trench-mortaring and shell fire; but on the night of the 29th/30th, when the two battalions took over from the very tired and worn 7th Rifle Brigade and 8th K.R.R.C., there was ominous silence. No notice was taken by the enemy of the noise inseparable from a relief, and even a few bombs thrown by the new-comers into the German trenches—in places only 15 feet away—provoked no reply. Half an hour before dawn the trench garrison stood to arms, and there was still complete quiet. Then at 3.15 a.m., with dramatic suddenness, came the carefully planned German stroke. The site of the stables of the château was blown up, whilst a sudden hissing sound was heard by the two companies of the 8th Rifle Brigade on either side of the crater, and a bright crimson glare over the crater turned the whole scene red. Jets of flame, as if from a line of powerful hoses, spraying fire instead of water, shot across the front trenches of the Rifle Brigade, and a thick black cloud formed. It was the first attack on the British with liquid fire. At the same time fire of every other kind was opened: trench-mortar bombs and hand-grenades deluged the front trenches, machine-gun and shrapnel bullets swept the two communication trenches and the 300 yards of open ground between the front and support lines in Sanctuary and Zouave Woods; high-explosive shell rained on these Woods, whilst the ramparts of Ypres and all exits from the town were bombarded anew.

'The surprise was complete, and would probably have led to an entry even at the strongest part of the line. Most of the 8th Rifle Brigade in the front trenches were overwhelmed, the rest fell back gradually over the fire-swept open ground to the support line. The enemy did not follow: he at once set about consolidating the trenches he had secured, and trying to increase his gain by attacking the 7th K.R.R.C. in front, flank, and rear. There was desperate trench fighting, in which parties again brought up *Flammenwerfer*, but rapid fire was turned on to them at 20 yards range, and the attempt to use them broke down. In the end, however, after several counter-attacks, all but a small sector of the K.R.R.C. trenches were lost.

'The 42nd Brigade, on the left of the 41st, was not affected, and the 1/8th Sherwood Foresters (the left of the 46th Division) on the right, though attacked, managed to maintain its position. With the help of brigade reinforcements the new line on the edge of the woods was held, and at 11.30 a.m., by order from the VI Corps, Major-General V. Couper made arrangements for an assault at 2.45 p.m. to recover the lost ground. It was to be carried out by both 41st and 42nd Brigades (Brigadier-Generals O. S. W. Nugent and C. J. Markham) after three-quarters of an hour's bombardment by the divisional artillery and No. 2 Group Heavy Artillery Reserve—feeble indeed after the German tornado, but still, serving to encourage the assault —the 46th Division on the right and the 6th Division on the left co-operating by fire. The attack northwards of the 41st Brigade, with the 6th Duke of Cornwall's Light Infantry of the 43rd Brigade (Brigadier-General G. Cockburn) attached, failed, not a man getting within 150 yards of the Germans ; but the attack eastwards by the 9th K.R.R.C. of the 42nd Brigade succeeded in regaining part of the lost trenches.'

To the historian of the Great War the above is an account of a comparatively trivial incident of trench warfare, not affecting the general scheme ; a small section of trench line lost and partly regained, with no effect on the tactical situation ; at most another unhappy instance of useless loss of life owing to blind insistence by a higher commander, out of touch with the situation, on compliance with a hide-bound rule that every loss of ground must be met by an immediate counter-attack without any consideration of its chances of success ; the result being losses to ourselves out of all proportion to those inflicted on the enemy, an unfailing way to lose a war of attrition if followed with sufficient obstinacy.

To us it means much more. It means the first great trial of the New Army battalions—a trial in which they showed that in courage and devotion they were the equals of any of their predecessors in the Regiment.

No veteran troops could have shown greater tenacity than did the 7th Battalion when the line on their left had been penetrated and they were attacked on three sides at once. Nothing in First or Second Ypres was more resolute than the counter-attack made by battalions which had only just been relieved after a particularly arduous time in the trenches. The ground over which they attacked had not a vestige of cover, the three-quarters of an hour's preliminary bombardment had been devoid of effect, no one, from the Divisional Commander downwards, could have had any hope of success—General Nugent had, on the loss of the trenches, at once reported that it would want a Division to retake them—but the new battalions went forward as if they were determined to show that when called upon they could give their lives as freely as those whose blood had already soaked the ground for which they were fighting.

At 3.30 p.m. Nugent, seeing that persistence in the attack meant the loss of what remained of his brigade, ordered its suspension, and the attacking battalions were rallied on the edges of Sanctuary and Zouave Woods. The 41st Brigade was relieved after dark by the 43rd, but in the small hours of the 31st the Germans made a fresh attack with liquid fire, and the remnants of the 41st, which had just reached their bivouac, were recalled to the firing-line. The attack was repulsed, but the Brigade remained in the front line under constant shell fire, adding to their losses, till they were finally relieved on the afternoon of the 31st.

The casualties of the three battalions for July 30 and 31 were:

7th Battalion

Killed

Captain G. C. Dowling.
Lieutenant F. Seymour.
Lieutenant S. H. Snelgrove.
Lieutenant A. B. Findlay.
2nd Lieutenant R. B. Arnell.
2nd Lieutenant R. F. Robinson.
2nd Lieutenant R. Longbottom.

Died of Wounds

Captain J. D. H. Radcliffe.
2nd Lieutenant G. F. Carter.

Wounded

Captain and Adjutant A. P. Evans.
Captain H. M. B. de Sales La Terriere.
Lieutenant G. H. Gibson.
2nd Lieutenant H. W. N. Lawrence.

Other Ranks

Total casualties, 289.

8th Battalion

Killed

Captain and Adjutant W. J. Davis.
Lieutenant R. W. Watson.
Lieutenant J. C. Hawkes (R.A.M.C.).

Wounded

Captain L. G. Moore.
Captain J. P. Blane.
Lieutenant H. E. Tyndale.
Lieutenant T. L. Bourdillon.
2nd Lieutenant W. B. Todd-Naylor.
2nd Lieutenant H. E. Molsom.
2nd Lieutenant P. M. Pope.

Other Ranks

Total casualties, 190.

9th Battalion

Killed

Lieut.-Colonel C. S. Chaplin.
Captain A. A. T. Tanqueray.
Captain R. S. Durnford.
Lieutenant H. N. L. Renton.
2nd Lieutenant C. V. Faber.
2nd Lieutenant W. P. Geen.
2nd Lieutenant J. F. Lambert.

Died of Wounds

Captain N. J. Exell.

Wounded

Captain E. W. Benson.
Captain D. Young.
Lieutenant G. MacD. Warner.
Lieutenant H. S. Richmond.
2nd Lieutenant W. H. Bevan.

Other Ranks

Total casualties, 333.

The losses of the 8th Rifle Brigade were heaviest of all, being 19 officers, 462 other ranks.

Lieut.-Colonel C. S. Chaplin was killed leading his battalion, the 9th, in the counter-attack. He served with the 1st Battalion in the Chitral Expedition of 1895, and commanded a battalion of Mounted Infantry in the South African War. He had retired from the service on completing his time in command of the 3rd Battalion in 1912, and had commanded the 9th Battalion since its formation.

Loos [1]

The plan of the Allies for 1915 had originally been to accept the fact that they would not be strong enough till 1916 for a supreme effort; meanwhile, to stand fast on the Western Front, and relieve the pressure on Russia by an attack on the Dardanelles.

As the year went on, as things went from bad to worse on the Russian front, with no compensating advantage at the Dardanelles, the Allied statesmen came round to Joffre's view that the opportunity should be taken of the German weakness in France to launch a big attack which, even if it did not, as it was hoped it would, drive the enemy out of the country, would at least afford the much-needed relief to Russia.

Joffre's plan was an ambitious one. It was to make a big attack on a front of some fifty miles in Champagne, northwards, and a second one with his Tenth Army in Artois, eastwards. These attacks, if they succeeded as he hoped, would clear the enemy out of the whole of the big salient between them, and drive him back to the frontier. The British share was: firstly, to take over more of the French line, thus releasing more of their troops for the attack; secondly, to take part in the attack of the French Tenth Army, either on its right or its left.

[1] Map VIII and Sketch Map II opposite p. 114.

The scheme looked well enough on paper by counting noses on the opposing sides, but the truth was that the superiority of the Allies was more apparent than real. They had the men, but they had not the guns, still less the ammunition. Even the French were short of heavy guns; the British very much more so; while their ammunition supply with a big offensive in prospect was ludicrous. The Germans were also very much better off in quality and quantity in all the odds and ends of trench warfare.

Sir John French, fully realising all this, was strongly opposed to taking part in any big offensive before the spring of 1916.

Apart from the unpreparedness of his force, he disliked attacking on the left of the French Tenth Army, as Haig, commanding the First Army, had reported that the ground there was thoroughly unsuitable. He objected to coming in on the right of the French Tenth Army, astride the Somme, where the ground was more suitable, as he felt that he was thereby uncovering the Channel ports too much. He was ready to make a separate attack farther north, leaving a gap between him and the French, though the futility of small attacks on such narrow fronts that they could be enfiladed from end to end had already been proved.

Finally, matters between the Allied commanders had about come to a deadlock when Lord Kitchener stepped in and told French that the general situation demanded that 'we must act with all energy and do our utmost to help France in her offensive, even though by so doing we may suffer very heavy losses.'

French's position was not enviable. As the official historian puts it:

'Under pressure from Lord Kitchener at home, due to the general position of the Allies, and from Generals Joffre and

Foch in France, due to the local situation in France, the British Commander-in-Chief was therefore compelled to undertake operations before he was ready, over ground that was most unfavourable, against the better judgment of himself and General Haig, and, as we shall see, with no more than a quarter of the troops—9 divisions instead of 36—that he considered necessary for a successful attack.'

In fact, he was very much in the situation of any general who is ordered to make a subsidiary attack. He is, in the language of the Turf, 'on a hiding to nothing.' If he spares his troops and fails to attract the enemy's reserves, he probably loses his job, if he goes 'all out' and attains his object, he is faced with a disproportionate casualty list, and sees his operation referred to in despatches as a Demonstration.

Joffre fixed the date for the attack on September 8, but the preparations for the big attack in Champagne took longer than was expected, and it was deferred, firstly, to September 15, and again till September 25.

Joffre's final plan was that thirty-four divisions and eight cavalry divisions were to attack northwards, in Champagne, under General de Castelnau, on a frontage of some twenty miles. The Artois offensive also was to have a frontage of about twenty miles. It was to be delivered eastwards, between Arras and the La Bassée Canal, under the supervision of General Foch.

On the right the French Tenth Army—seventeen divisions—was to attack on a front of twelve miles, supported by 420 heavy guns. Next on the left came a French Territorial division, filling a gap of 4,000 yards with difficult ground in front of it, and with orders not to advance till the advance of the attacks on the north and south had forced the Germans in front of them to vacate their position. Next came the British First Army, which was to attack with six divisions on a six-mile frontage, supported by 114 heavy guns. Three more divisions were in General Reserve, and the Cavalry Corps and Indian Cavalry Corps were to be ready to pass through the gap when the infantry should break through.

Subsidiary attacks were to be made at other parts of the front to keep the enemy from reinforcing the threatened points.

There was to be a preliminary bombardment of ninety-six hours, the last four of which were to be intense. Joffre's hopes of success may be measured by the fact that the cavalry were given the line of the Belgian frontier as their final objective.

The main assault on the British front was to be made by the six divisions of the IV and I Corps, while the Indian and III Corps were to make subsidiary attacks north of La Bassée Canal.

The XI Corps in General Reserve was formed of the 21st and 24th, newly arrived, New Army Divisions, and the Guards Division.

In this attack gas was to be used for the first time by the British Expeditionary Force, and on its success or failure depended that of the whole operation.

The French were not using gas, and as their attack was to take place on the 25th, and we were pledged to attack at the same time as they did, it was not possible to defer the operation in case of the weather being unfavourable to our gas discharge.

If the wind should be blowing the wrong way the attack would have to be made without it. Haig had an alternative plan of attack to be made without gas, should the weather preclude its use, but he thoroughly realised that the weakness of our artillery support would make its failure almost certain. In fact, the success of the gas discharge was his only chance. The weather conditions gave some hope up to the last moment, and the gas discharge ordered for 5.50 a.m. on September 25—the assault was to be forty minutes later—was not counter-ordered. In the event, the wind was neither definitely favourable nor definitely unfavourable. On parts of the front it worked well, blew over the German trenches, and was a complete success; on other parts it hung about, dividing its attentions between both sides; on others it blew back on to our men, causing many casualties, and broke up the attack before it had started.

There seems to have been some misunderstanding between Haig and French as to the use of the General Reserve. Haig expected to have the 21st and 24th Divisions at his disposal as an Army Reserve, and consequently planned to attack with all six divisions of the IV and I Corps in one line. In the event, these two divisions were kept too far back, were not at hand when they were wanted, and their late arrival spoilt any chance Haig had of exploiting such initial success as he had.

The IV Corps were to attack on the right, the I Corps on the left. To deal first with the attack of the IV Corps: the 47th Division, which was next the French, and would therefore have a gap of 4,000 yards between it and the French Tenth Army's attack, was, after penetrating the enemy's front line, to form a defensive flank south-east of the village of Loos, facing south-east. The advance of this Division went pretty well. The gas drifted the right way and was a complete success, and after much hard fighting the Division was by 10 a.m. in occupation of the required defensive flank, but not in touch with the 15th Division on its left.

The 15th Division, on whose front also the gas discharge was successful, went forward with great dash, though losing heavily from machine-gun fire crossing No Man's Land, speedily overran the German first line, and one Brigade pushed on into the village of Loos, which, after hard fighting, was completely in their possession soon after 8 a.m. Other units passing north of Loos reached the Lens Road by 9.15 a.m.

After this, from heavy losses, intermingling of units and loss of direction, the impetus of the attack died out and, in the words of the 'Official History'—

'Nightfall found both the 47th and 15th Divisions on a line between the German first and second defensive positions ; from the Double Crassier to Chalk Pit Wood, along the western slope of the Cité spur, which bounds the Loos valley on the south.'

The plan for the attack of the 1st Division was a rather complicated one. Firstly, there was a gap of 600 yards between the left of the 15th Division's attack and the right of that of the 1st Division ; just as there was one of 4,000 yards between the left of the French Tenth Army and the right of the British Expeditionary Force, and for the same reason. Just as the gap between French and British was left because it was too strong to be attacked in front, and it was considered preferable to manœuvre the garrison out by penetrating on each side of them, so it was considered advisable to treat in the same way two trenches which had been run out from the German front line, known as Southern and Northern Sap, and believed to conceal machine guns. This system of turning a strong part of the enemy's line sounds plausible enough, but it has its dangers. Each gap so left means two more flanks in the attacking line to be enfiladed and, unless the garrisons of these strong points can be so treated by heavy artillery as to render them innocuous, the attack may lose more on the 'swings' than it gains on the 'roundabouts.'

Secondly, the 2nd Brigade, on the right of the Division, was to attack in a south-easterly direction, while the 1st Brigade, next on the left, was to attack due east. To fill this gap a separate force of two battalions, one from each of the leading brigades—these brigades had five battalions each—was detailed, under the command of Lieut.-Colonel E. W. B. Green, 2nd Royal Sussex, to advance behind the inner flanks of the two brigades, and to fill the gap between them when they reached the Lens–La Bassée Road.

The part of the line held by the 1st Division formed the right face of a slight salient, and therefore faced considerably south of east. At the time when the gas was discharged (5.50 a.m.) the wind veered to the south, and their own gas cloud, with that of the 15th Division, drifted right on to the jumping-off trenches, in which the 2nd K.R.R.C. and 1st Loyal North Lancashire were awaiting the word to advance. The gas was soon turned off, but not before the two battalions had each had about 200 men put out of action. Consequently, when the advance began, the second-line companies had to pass through those in the first line. This was not till a few minutes after the appointed hour, as, although the wind changed and the gas was turned on again, time had to be given to let it reach the German line. As the line advanced it was badly enfiladed by machine guns dug-in in front of the German line, which had not been dealt with by the bombardment. Then, when they reached the enemy's wire, it was found to be intact and, although heroic attempts were made to cut it, the attacking battalions had in the end to fall back to the jumping-off trenches.

The attack of the 1st Brigade was successful, in that it overran the German front line, an intermediate line, known as Gun Trench, and got as far as the Lens–La Bassée Road, but there found itself with its right in the air, and faced with a strong and intact belt of wire which covered the German second line.

Another attempt was made by fresh battalions of the 2nd Brigade and the remnants of the 1st Loyal North Lancashire, while the 2nd K.R.R.C., who had suffered the most, were left to reorganise in the front-line trenches, but it succeeded no better than the first.

The next attempt, made by the G.O.C. 1st Division, to fill the gap which existed, owing to the failure of the 2nd Brigade's attack, between the left of the 15th Division and the right of the 1st Brigade, was with Green's Force, but this also was soon held up. Later in the afternoon the Germans who had successfully held up the 2nd Brigade and Green's Force found themselves surrounded by the advance of the 3rd Brigade, which, in reserve to the 1st Division, had been sent in the tracks of the 1st Brigade to close the gap between the Brigade and the 15th Division, and surrendered; but their stout resistance had not only almost destroyed the 2nd Brigade, but had considerably affected the prospects of success of the whole British attack.

The surrender of the Germans enabled the remains of the 2nd Brigade and Green's Force to advance about 3.30 p.m. They met with no further opposition, and by nightfall were digging in just beyond the Lens–La Bassée Road, from Bois Hugo to near the Chalk Pit. There was a big gap between them and the 1st Brigade, facing Hulluch. These, not knowing of the advance of the 2nd Brigade, and thinking that their right was in the air, threw it back to occupy a German communication trench, running north-east and south-west, marked on the map as Alley 4. The 1st Division had thus, more or less, gained its objective, but owing to the heavy casualties and many men having lost their units, their strength was only a quarter of what it had been at zero hour, and the expected gap between the 2nd and 1st Brigades was beyond the capacity of Green's Force to fill to the extent of 1,500 yards.

In the I Corps the attack of the 7th Division and the right brigade of the 9th Division met with great success at the start, and reached right up to the German second line, parts of which were occupied. Owing to the total failure of the attack of the left brigade of the 9th Division, caused partly by the gas going the wrong way and even more by coming up against untouched wire, the left of the advanced line had to be thrown back to form a defensive flank, so that at nightfall the new line ran from a point in Gun Trench, facing Hulluch, where it was in touch with the left of the IV Corps, round the east side of the Quarries to Fosse Alley, where the 7th and 9th Divisions joined, round the front of the Corons, and thence back through the part of the German first line known as Little Willie to the original British front line. The left brigade of the 9th Division, which had been twice beaten back in a frontal attack, had been almost wiped out, and the other brigades of the 7th and 9th Divisions had suffered so severely that only a fresh division thrown in from the General Reserve could have exploited their success.

The plan for the 2nd Division was for the 19th and 6th Brigades to advance south of the La Bassée Canal, the 5th Brigade north of it; the whole were then to form a defensive flank, facing north-east, along the German communication trenches Canal Alley—Canteleux Trench, till they joined up with the Indian Corps.

The attack failed utterly, and does not appear, from the 'Official History,' to have been given much of a chance. The gas was turned on in spite of the protests of the officer in charge of it, and two mines, exploded under the German front line fifty minutes before the infantry were due to go over, only served to put the enemy on the alert. The attacking battalions, after losing heavily crossing No Man's Land, found themselves confronted by uncut wire, and when the remnants of them had, where possible, got back to their own front-line trenches, the Brigade, what with losses from the enemy's fire and their own gas, was not fit to renew the attack.

Only two battalions of the 6th Brigade took part in the attack, and our 1st Battalion was not one of them.

Subsidiary attacks were made at various points in the British line during the 25th.

In each case the result was about the same. The attackers met with some success at first, capturing trenches and prisoners, but were then bombed out by counter-attacks, finishing the day where they had started.

In an attack on Bellewaarde, by the V Corps, our 9th Battalion, near the scene of their losses on July 30, went to the support of the 9th Rifle Brigade, who had obtained a footing in the German second-line trenches. They had a hard fight, chiefly bombing on both sides, and lost 2nd Lieutenants C. W. Murray, P. H. Habershon, J. Howell, L. Pemberton, and E. P. M. Panes killed; and Captain M. Mallalue, Lieutenants F. S. Dansey and G. M. Warren wounded. Other ranks, 33 killed, 188 wounded, 29 missing.

In all these subsidiary attacks the losses were very severe; they were repulsed entirely by the local garrisons, and so did not attract to themselves any reserves, and it is very doubtful if they prevented any reserves from being drawn to the scene of the main attack. They deceived no one as to the locality of the main attack and, in fact, seem to have been a useless sacrifice of life; as, indeed, must be any, so-called, holding attack which is not strong enough to constitute a real threat to the enemy.

On the whole it may be said that the day had been very nearly a great success. Wherever the gas discharge went the right way, the enemy's resistance had crumpled up. Where it went the wrong way the attack failed.

It may fairly be said that, given a favourable wind, it would have succeeded all along the line.

But there was something more wanted to make success complete, and that was a reserve strong enough and ready to make use of the opportunity.

This is just what Haig had not got. The Commander-in-Chief had not only retained the XI Corps under his own orders, but he had kept them so far back that by the time they were ready to attack, the German line had shaken together, reinforcements were arriving, and the opportunity had passed.

To consider whether, if they had been near enough at once to follow up the blow of the IV and I Corps, they would have made a gap that would have let the cavalry through; whether, if the cavalry had got through, they would have done all that was expected of them; whether such a success by the British Expeditionary Force would have reacted on the opponents of the French Tenth Army sufficiently to turn failure into success; how much a big Allied success in Artois would have compromised the whole of the big German salient, is taking us too far into the realms of speculation.

It would fill too much space to follow the course of this long-drawn-out battle to the end, and unnecessary in this work, as our regiment took little further part in it.

The attack of the 21st and 24th Divisions which, to be effective, should have immediately followed the successes of the 25th, was not launched till the 26th. It failed, but it may be doubted whether two divisions of veteran troops would have succeeded. Except in the case of a very few of the senior officers, it was their first experience of war. They had not gone through the ordinary routine training in the trenches; their night march before the attack had been prolonged, possibly to some extent by their own inexperience, certainly in great part owing to the hopeless congestion in the traffic behind the lines, which was none of their fault. Whatever their military shortcomings may have been, lack of the will to be at the enemy was not one of them, and the losses in each division during the day exceeded 4,000 of all ranks.

A locality known as the Quarries, half-way between the two German lines, had been taken by the 7th Division on the 25th, and formed a part of the British front line on the night of the 25th/26th. It was retaken by a German counter-attack in the small hours of the 26th.

The possession by the enemy of this strong point would threaten with enfilade any renewed attack by the I Corps on their front.

The 2nd Division, which was not attacking on the 26th, was ordered to supply a composite Brigade to be attached to the 7th Division. This Brigade, under Lieut.-Colonel B. C. M. Carter, 1st King's, made up of 1st K.R.R.C., 1st Royal Berkshire, and 2nd Worcestershire, was ordered to retake the Quarries.

The attack was made by the 2nd Worcestershire, supported by two companies and the machine guns of the 1st K.R.R.C. They suffered heavily in the advance, and had reached an old communication trench 200 yards short of the Quarries when they got an order from the 7th Division to go no farther. They therefore dug themselves in. The rest of Carter's Brigade joined them after dark. They retained their position for the next three days, beating off heavy German bombing attacks on the 28th and 29th, and were relieved on the night of the 29th/30th. The

1st Battalion rejoined the 6th Brigade in Béthune on the 30th.

They were back in the same trenches by the night of October 1/2, where they beat off a heavy bombing attack on the 3rd, inflicting severe loss on the enemy.

Second Lieutenant F. D. E. Cayley was killed on September 29, and 2nd Lieutenants E. H. Bentall and K. J. B. Addy on October 3.

The 2nd Brigade, including our 2nd Battalion, had, on the afternoon of the 25th, reached the Lens–La Bassée Road with their right on Bois Hugo. In the early morning of the 26th they were relieved by the 21st Brigade, and went into reserve. In the evening of the 28th the Brigade went into the front line again, attached to the 47th Division, and the 2nd Battalion occupied cellars and trenches in front of Loos, where they endured a few days of heavy shelling. On the night of October 1/2 they were relieved by the French.

They were back in the trenches again once or twice before the end of the battle, but were not engaged in anything of importance.

The losses of the 2nd Battalion on the 25th were over 500 of all ranks. Among the killed were: Lieutenant C. H. Eyre; 2nd Lieutenants J. Scudamore, J. H. Simpson, J. C. Grahame Stewart, and G. G. Fowler (died of wounds). Lieut.-Colonel G. K. Priaulx, commanding the Battalion, was among the wounded, as also were Major J. E. N. Heseltine, Captains G. R. Dubs, J. B. Brady (gassed); Lieutenants W. P. Bristowe, L. C. Nash; 2nd Lieutenants W. H. Palmer, and H. K. Dinn.

Lieutenant Eyre was a Harrow Master, had been Head of the School at Harrow, and at Cambridge was distinguished both as a scholar and in the cricket field, having been captain of the Cambridge XI.

Rifleman G. Peachment, who was mortally wounded in attending to his wounded company commander, was awarded the V.C.

The battle dragged on till the middle of October. British attacks were made and failed, German counter-attacks were beaten off.

The last British attack, the only one on a large scale after the first three days, gained nothing, and incurred very heavy losses.

The French Tenth Army had met with little success; their main contribution, so far as assistance to the British attack is concerned, was that after the first few days they took over the line held by a division and a brigade on the British right, to enable Sir John French to create a reserve, all his reserves except the cavalry having been drawn into the fight; even a cavalry division having been sent in to fight on foot at a critical time.

The French attack in Champagne had some success at first, which came to nothing in the end. Finally, the weather came to the rescue of the hardly tried troops by making further operations impossible.

The British losses at Loos had amounted to over 50,000 of all ranks. The Germans opposed to them lost about 20,000.

The campaign of 1915 had gone badly for the Allies. Germany had turned her attention to her Eastern Front, and had seemingly put Russia 'down for the count.' The efforts of the Allies to take advantage of her temporary weakness in France had failed, and failed at the cost of far greater losses than they had inflicted.

France had about reached her maximum in man-power. The attempt to come to the rescue of Russia by opening the Dardanelles had been another costly failure.

The only glimmer of light in the outlook for the coming

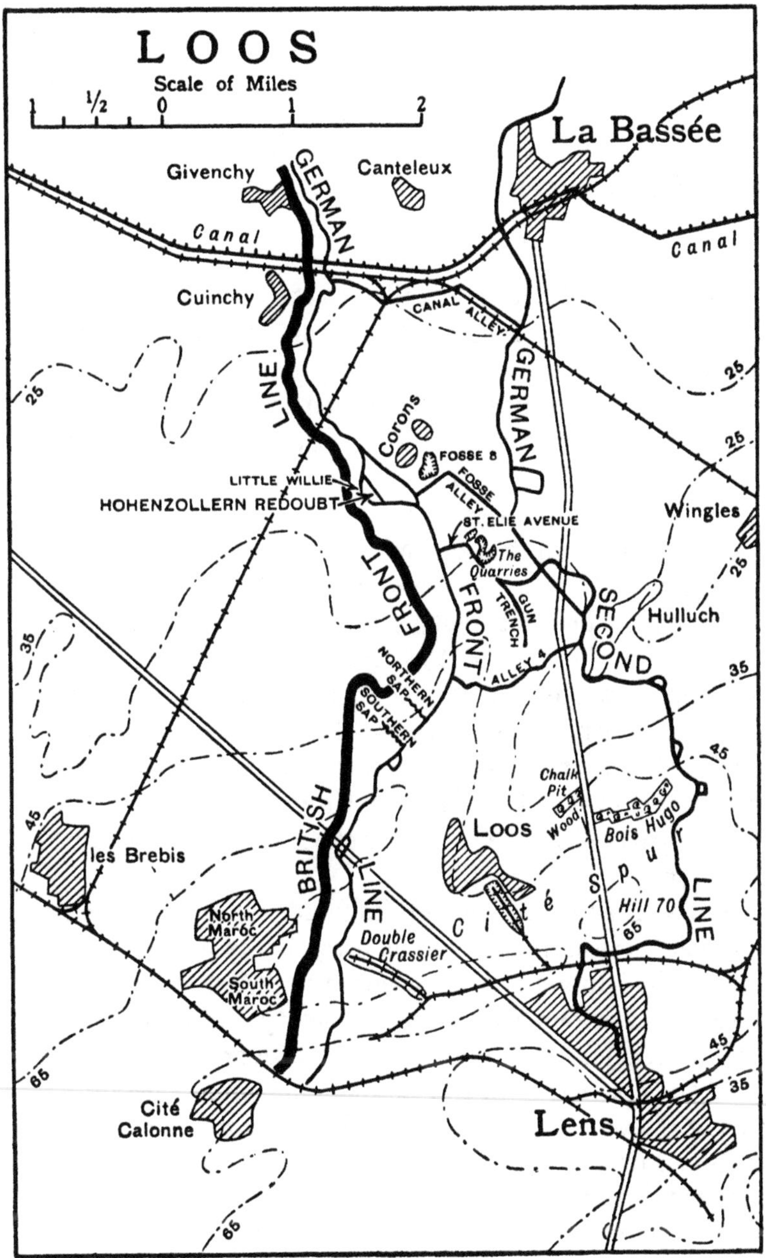

Emery Walker Ltd. sc.

year was that a large reserve of British man-power was still untapped, and there was a prospect for the future of an ample supply of all the munitions of war, the deficiency in which may decidedly be said to have been the one great cause of failure in 1915.

Salonika

The autumn of 1915 had added to the responsibilities of the Allies by the opening of a fresh campaign in the Balkans.

The French had for some time been considering the idea of another campaign in the Near East: to land on the coast of Asia Minor and work up the coast so as to clear the Turks off the Asiatic shore of the Dardanelles; to land at Alexandretta and cut the Turkish line of communication to Mesopotamia and Syria; or, lastly, to land at Salonika, this last being another attempt to bring in Greece on the side of the Allies. Circumstances, i.e. the enemy, made up the minds of the Allied Governments for them. Serbia had hitherto held her own against Austria. There were signs of a big attack against her being prepared by Austria with German assistance, and when Bulgaria started mobilising she was threatened with extinction.

Serbia called upon Greece to fulfil her treaty agreement, by which she was bound to come to the help of Serbia if attacked by Bulgaria. Venizelos, the Prime Minister of Greece, was anxious to stand by the treaty, but both he and Serbia asked for French and British support. The Allies agreed to go to the rescue of Serbia and, King Constantine refusing Greek help, were left to do the work themselves. The first move was to send one French and one British division to Salonika from the Dardanelles.

They arrived at Salonika on October 5, too late to

save the Serbian Army, and, on the same day, an Allied conference at Calais decided that the French would send two more divisions and two cavalry divisions, while the British would send three more divisions.

The British 22nd and 26th (New Army) Divisions, which had landed in France in September, were sent on to Salonika, where they arrived in November. The 27th and 28th Divisions, which had done such hard fighting in the Second Battle of Ypres, were also sent, as transport was available.

Our 4th Battalion embarked at Marseilles on November 18, disembarked at Salonika on the 25th, and went into camp on Lembet plain, outside the town, just in time to come in for the same blizzard that wrought such havoc in the Dardanelles.

The 3rd Battalion also embarked on the 18th, but, going by Alexandria, did not reach Salonika till December 5.

At the time of the arrival of our two battalions it was expected that the Bulgars would shortly attack, and the Allies set to work digging a defensive position covering Salonika. The Bulgars did nothing, and the winter passed off in peace and, after the trenches in France, comparative comfort.

CHAPTER VI

'SOMME, 1916,' 'ALBERT, 1916,' 'BAZENTIN,' 'DELVILLE WOOD,' 'POZIÈRES,' 'GUILLEMONT,' 'FLERS-COURCELETTE,' 'MORVAL,' 'LE TRANSLOY,' 'ANCRE HEIGHTS,' 'ANCRE, 1916'

1916

IN December 1915 Sir John French had been succeeded in command of the British Expeditionary Force by Sir Douglas Haig. The British public blamed French for the failure at Loos—little knowing that the battle had been fought against his wishes—and the British Government, doubtless realising that he had spoilt what chance he had of success there by the tardy use of his reserves, and probably, being honestly of the opinion that he was worn out by the strain of the last year, and that it was time that he gave place to a younger man, was not averse to letting him be the scape-goat.

Just before the change in command had taken place, the plans for 1916 had been sketched out at the meeting of the Allied War Council at Chantilly to this extent: that the coming year was to see the Allies take the offensive on a much greater scale on all fronts, and that, in the West, the British forces were to take something approaching to an equal share in the operations to that of the French.

The first question to be decided was: When was the great attack to begin?

The answer to the question appeared to be: whenever the British and Russians could be ready.

The French man-power had about reached its peak, and their gun-power and munition supply were in proportion to their numbers.

British man-power had still a great deal in reserve—conscription had not even been introduced so far—but gun-power and munition supply of all kinds, though rapidly growing, were still a long way behind requirements.

The Russian Army, after its defeats of 1915, required complete reorganisation.

Briefly, the decision finally arrived at was this: that the grand attack should begin in July, as the Russians could not be ready before that month; but if the Germans should attack the Russians in spring or early summer, the British and French should make preliminary attacks in the West, in order to hold the German forces in France, and prevent reinforcements from being sent to the Eastern Front.

The first step preparatory to the year's operations was the relief in the line by the British of the French Tenth Army, which, as will be remembered, was at the time of the battle of Loos sandwiched between the British First and Third Armies.

The next question for decision was: Where should the blow be delivered? Whatever illusions the Allied nations and statesmen may have had upon the subject, the Allied commanders seem to have realised that the time for great strategic combinations which were going to pinch out and surround huge sections of the German line, or for a break through and threat to communications which would compel the evacuation of all the occupied territory at a blow, was not yet; that the way to these ultimate objects must be prepared by first sufficiently breaking down the enemy's resistance; in fact, that the problem was one of tactics and not of strategy, and that the theatre of the attack should be that in which topographical and other considerations most favoured the attack—or, shall we say? least favoured the defence.

Before the plans for the combined attack were complete, they had all to be recast owing to the German attack on Verdun which, launched towards the end of February, engaged the chief attention of the French nation for the rest of the year.

This is not the place to tell the story of the battle of Verdun, which raged with greater or less fury for the next nine months. It was the longest, the most fiercely contested, and the bloodiest contest fought round any one spot in the whole course of the war. Looked on as an attempt to win the war before the British had fully developed their resources it was a German defeat; measured by ground lost and gained, and by the casualties on both sides it might be called a drawn battle. As to its effect on the war of attrition it is not so easy to decide. At the time, and for a year to come, it seemed that the Germans had been better able to stand their losses than the French, who had lost the flower of their Army; and Verdun was probably an indirect cause of the loss of morale which followed the Nivelle tragedy of the following year. By the middle of 1918, when the advantage in man-power had swung definitely over to the side of the Allies, the Germans were missing the men lost at Verdun more than did the French. Whether or not Verdun influenced the result of the war, it certainly brought the end nearer.

The immediate result, so far as concerns the British Expeditionary Force, was to make them the chief actors in the forthcoming Allied offensive. The objects of this offensive had been: 'To prevent the transfer of German troops from the Western to the Russian Front,' and 'To wear down the strength of the forces opposed to us.'

[Haig's despatches.] To these were now added a third: 'To lighten the pressure on the French at Verdun.'

The original plan for 1916 had been that the great attack should be preceded by a series of preparatory attacks, with limited objectives, and chiefly made by the British, in order to draw the German reserves. That done, the great blow was to be struck chiefly by the French. All that was now changed. Verdun was occupying the attention of the German reserves, as also of the greater part of the French striking force. The Germans had done the preparatory part themselves, in that they had found employment for what would have been their reserves if they had remained on the defensive. They had, however, at the same time, found employment for what would have been the Allies' chief striking force; so the battle of the Somme, with the British Expeditionary Force in the star part, great conflict as it was, was a very much smaller affair than it would have been if carried out according to the original plan.

Before coming to the battle of the Somme it would be well to give some idea of what our battalions were doing during the months of 1916 preceding the battle. It might have been thought that with such a stupendous struggle in progress round Verdun it would have been 'all quiet on the Western Front' at other parts of the line. There may have been parts of the line in the east of France where nothing ever happened, but certainly on the British front there never seemed to be much peace for the occupants of the trenches. Battalions would spend on the average a third of their time in the front-line trenches, a third in Brigade or Divisional Reserve, where they were never quite free from shell fire, and the remaining third in rest billets.

Minor operations of varying extent were constantly

being undertaken by both sides, who were equally anxious that the enemy should not be allowed to thin their line so as to send reinforcements to Verdun, were equally covetous of the possession of any point held by the enemy that gave some tactical advantage, and both sides made frequent trench raids, whether to secure identifications or merely done to annoy. The scale of comfort in the trenches had improved a good deal since the first winter, but still could not be described as anything better than beastly.

An extract from the War Records of the 2nd Battalion for April and May 1916, taken from the 'Regimental Chronicle' of that year, is given as a specimen of the everyday life of a battalion, in and out of the trenches:

April 1.—'Our billeting area in Les Brebis was shelled, but there were no casualties, and the next day we moved up into support line, relieving the 1st Gloucesters. A mine blown up in the Hulluch sector brought on some firing, which caught the transport coming down the Loos Road, and caused some casualties.'

April 5.—'On the 5th we moved up into the front line, and the next day the Germans sent up a small mine about 40 yards from our new trench, touching Seaforth Alley. It did us no damage. To keep us from being dull they shelled our communication trenches on the 8th during the day, and we had 2 killed and 5 wounded. The 1st Northamptons relieved us, and we went back into reserve.'

April 9.—'The next day the brigade on our right had an affair with much smoke and noise, and it appeared to be most successful. We had not forgotten the new crater, but for good reasons it was not advisable to meddle with it at present.

'On the 11th we relieved our friends, the Northamptons, and there was some liveliness with aerial torpedoes near the new crater, and there were signs that the enemy in front of us had been relieved. Our support line was shelled on the 13th, and our "heavies" retaliated. We returned to Les Brebis on the 14th. The next three days we spent in training, the Battalion being exercised through a smoke barrage.'

April 20.—'We were again up in the trenches at Double

Crassier with Battalion Headquarters in North Maroc. The weather being wet, the trenches were in bad condition, and the parapet falling down in many places, which kept us busy.

'Our routine was uneventful until the 29th, when at 4 a.m. gas gongs and bugle sounded "gas." The cloud came over from the direction of Hulluch. Thanks to the coolness of the men and their good gas training, there were no casualties, and the gas was not severe, but precautions had to be taken for some hours afterwards. The gas attack was between Hulluch and Chalk Pit Salient on the 16th Division front, the enemy penetrating our trenches at some points, but the line was immediately restored.

'An aerial torpedo dropped on the Southern Crassier into A Company's trenches. Captain [R. E.] Bullen was mortally wounded, 6 men killed, and 8 wounded, mostly belonging to a tunnelling company.'

April 30.—'We were relieved by the Sussex Regiment on the 30th, and returned to cellars in South Maroc.'

May 2.—'We left South Maroc and moved into rest billets at Petit Sans. Here we had a much-appreciated rest, and on May 8 we relieved the 6th Welch Regiment (3rd Brigade) in the Loos Sector. Headquarters were in the Loos cellars, and our front line extended from Carfax Road to Scrub Lane, our bombers holding Harrison's Crater.'

May 11.—'There was intermittent shelling of our front line and support trenches. A 6-inch gun from the direction of Wingles systematically and accurately searched our trenches for four hours, doing considerable damage. Eight men of D Company were buried in a dug-out, and their bodies could not be recovered, and our communication trenches were blocked. After a short spell in billets at North Maroc we returned to the front trenches on May 14.'

May 17.—'Our establishment of officers was now substantially increased. Second Lieutenants Edwardes, Sherlock, Cockerell, and Purdon joined the Battalion. On the 17th the 16th Division took over the Loos Sector as far as "Haymarket," the latter place now being the left of the 1st Division.

'We were relieved by the 1st Gloucesters, and after spending one night in South Maroc we marched to Les Brebis on the 18th, and became Divisional Reserve. The platoon of the Battalion which had been attached to the 1st Battalion S.W. Borderers returned, and the officer commanding that unit

(Lieut.-Colonel Collier) expressed gratitude for their help and appreciation of their gallant conduct in their attack on the craters in February.'

May 20.—'Captain L. G. Moore took over the duties of Adjutant. On the 21st the Battalion marched to the Bois Froissart for "a day in the country." On the way back to Les Brebis heavy shelling was observed to the right of Calonne and all along the ridge. On reaching Les Brebis the town was found to be under heavy shell fire. Our Headquarters got their full share, but there were no casualties, but some narrow escapes.'

May 23.—'We were informed by the G.O.C. 2nd Infantry Brigade that the Battalion would be selected for operations against "The Triangle," expected to take place about the 29th. The following days were spent practising this attack under the eyes of Major-General Holland, D.S.O., commanding the 1st Division, and Lieut.-General Kavanagh, commanding the 1st Corps.'

May 29.—'The villages round were actively shelled, and a deserter from the German IX Corps on our right front stated that the enemy contemplated a big gas attack, with Loos as the objective, at an early date. Our aeroplanes reported large movements of infantry columns about Douvrin, but it was not known what these movements indicated.'

May 30.—'The Battalion was addressed by the G.O.C. 1st Division, and he announced that the proposed attack was cancelled by G.H.Q.

'This caused the most lively disappointment amongst all ranks, who, after careful training and preparations, had been looking forward to getting to grips with the Germans.

'The next day we marched to North Maroc and took over the trenches from the Northamptonshire Regiment, being the left battalion of the left brigade.'

The attack on 'The Triangle,' which was postponed at the end of May, came off on June 30. It was one of several subsidiary attacks delivered just previous to the commencement of the battle of the Somme, presumably with the intention of misleading the enemy as to the locality of the coming onset, but the Germans knew a good deal about the forthcoming offensive, the preparations for which had been on too big a scale and too prolonged to escape notice, and it is doubtful if even a successful local attack elsewhere would have much affected their arrangements. Delivered as it was with too little artillery preparation and against uncut wire, it was only another useless sacrifice of life. The attacking troops were our 2nd Battalion and part of the 2nd Royal Sussex Regiment. The following is the account of the action given in the 2nd Battalion War Records (' Chronicle,' 1916) :

> 'On the last day of June, at 7.30 p.m., the companies selected for the attack moved to the starting-places allotted to them, and by 8.30 p.m. all was ready. At 9 p.m. the bridges were put up ; either the Germans saw them, or else observed the troops assembling in the trenches, as they opened a heavy fire, causing many casualties in the crowded trenches. At 9.15 three mines were sprung, and a few minutes later the storming parties went over the parapet. The two parties on the right failed to penetrate the heavy wire in front of the hostile trenches ; consequently, what remained of them turned south up the side of the north end of the Double Crassier, in an attempt to help the Royal Sussex Regiment, who had a company thereon. These efforts to carry the German sap north of Crassier did not succeed, due to wire and machine-gun fire.
>
> 'The centre column reached and entered the enemy's trench, but found its right in the air and exposed to bombing attacks, nor did it succeed in joining up with the left column. Under these circumstances Major Barber, the senior officer on the spot, ordered a withdrawal. This was carried out in good order. The left column reached the trench appointed for them, and remained in action there till 2 a.m., when they also withdrew.'

The Battalion lost 5 officers killed or died of wounds : Lieutenant C. S. Egerton-Green ; Temp. Lieutenant A. G. N. Dickenson ; 2nd Lieutenant O. Edwardes, F. A. Freeman, R. B. Holmes ; wounded : Temp. Captain C. R.

Fryre; Lieutenant F. Wadner; 2nd Lieutenants E. A. Warner, F. B. Walker, B. C. Munro, M.C., R. G. Bennett. Other ranks, 36 killed, 24 missing, and 167 wounded.

At the end of 1915 there had been some reshuffling in the British Expeditionary Force, a certain amount of exchanging of regular battalions for New Army battalions having been done with a view to strengthening the New Army brigades. Our 1st Battalion had gone from the 6th to the 99th Brigade. This Brigade had, however, been brought into the 2nd Division from the 33rd. Our 1st Battalion, therefore, although in a new brigade, whose three other regiments were the 1st Royal Berkshire, and the 22nd and 23rd Royal Fusiliers, still belonged to its old division.

The Somme[1]

Albert

On July 1 the British Expeditionary Force attacked on a front of about fifteen miles, with nineteen divisions either in the front line or in reserve close up—fifteen divisions were actually employed on the first day.

The French, on the right, under General Foch, attacked astride of the Somme on an eight-mile front with five divisions in front line.

The British Corps taking part in the attack were, from right to left: XIII (Congreve), XV (Horne), III (Pulteney), X (Morland), VIII (Hunter Weston), VII (Snow). Of these all but the VII, which was in Allenby's Third Army, formed the Fourth Army, under Rawlinson.

The results of the first day's fighting were disappointing. By evening the troops of the X, VIII, and VII Corps were, after in most cases considerable initial success, back on their starting-line, having sustained enormous losses. The III Corps had gained some ground, the XV more,

[1] Map II.

while the XIII Corps and the whole of the French had made a considerable advance. Though the penetration of the enemy's front line by the French and British right opened the prospect of further successes, the resistance met by the British centre and left was much greater than had been expected. The attack of the three left corps was as gallant and determined as that of the more successful ones, and the reasons for the repulse seem to have been as follows: firstly, that the enemy, though fully expecting the coming onslaught, had misjudged its exact locality, putting it rather too far north; the consequence being, that the part of their line attacked by the three left corps was much stronger than it was farther south—indeed, they had not expected a real attack from the French, thinking that all their energies were employed in the defence of Verdun. Secondly, the British were still comparatively weak in heavy guns, and their ammunition supply was still inadequate. 'On July 1 there were but 730 heavy guns on the whole British front from Ypres to the Somme. In support of his attack on an effective front of six miles, Foch was able to employ no less than 900 heavy pieces' ('Sir Douglas Haig's Command,' Dewar). There followed the inevitable consequence that the enemy's artillery was not kept under. Thirdly, the important lesson of the necessity for 'mopping up' had not yet been learnt. The British front line swept over the enemy's trenches, leaving behind them deep dug-outs full of men, the occupants of which came out as soon as the tide had passed. The enemy's artillery then put down a barrage which prevented the reserves from getting through, and the front line, their first impetus exhausted, found themselves held up in front and attacked in rear. Fourthly, that perfect co-operation of infantry and artillery, by which the infantry keep close up to the barrage, had not yet been attained, as, according to the German accounts, in some parts of their line, the attacking infantry was so far away when the artillery lifted that the defenders had plenty of time to come out of their dug-outs and man the shattered trenches and shell holes.

A fortnight was to elapse before any of our battalions took part in the battle, but it is necessary to give some brief account of what happened during that time, so as to give a right impression of the situation as it was when the first of them did arrive on the scene.

On July 1 the XIII Corps attacked with the 30th Division on the right, the 18th on the left, and the 9th in Corps Reserve. The heavy artillery had thoroughly done its work, and there was little response from the German artillery. The British losses were almost all from machine-gun fire. By the end of the day the Corps had gained the whole of its first objective on the Montauban Ridge. Its losses were over 5,000 of all ranks.

The XV Corps had attacked with the 7th Division on the right, the 21st on the left, and the 17th in Corps Reserve. As with the XIII Corps, the German artillery had been reduced to silence. By the end of the day the Corps had made a considerable advance on both flanks, but had failed in the centre. On the right they had gained 2,500 yards and taken the village of Mametz. The left had advanced almost as far, and occupied a line running across the top of the Fricourt spur. The Germans still held Fricourt. The Corps had taken prisoner 29 officers and 1,596 other ranks, but had losses amounting to over 9,000.

The III Corps attacked with the 34th Division on the right, the 8th on the left, and the 19th in Corps Reserve. The results for the day were some slight gains of ground by the 34th Division, while the losses of the Corps amounted to nearly 12,000.

The X Corps, 32nd Division on the right, 36th on the left, 49th in Corps Reserve, gained practically no ground, and had losses of over 10,000.

The VIII Corps, with the 29th Division on the right, the 4th in the centre, the 31st on the left and the 48th in Corps Reserve, also gained no ground, and had losses of over 10,000.

After the fighting of July 1 the X and VIII Corps were detached from Rawlinson's command, and came under that of Sir Hubert Gough in the newly formed Reserve Army, afterwards the Fifth.

Fresh divisions were ordered up to take the places of those which had suffered most, and throughout the five months' battle the composition of all the corps was constantly changing; the exhausted divisions going out of the line, not to rest and refit, but to undergo complete reconstruction.

At 10 p.m. on July 1 orders were issued by the Fourth Army to continue the attack next day: the XIII Corps was to consolidate gains and prepare for an attack on Mametz Wood, in conjunction with the XV Corps, which was first to capture Fricourt; the III Corps was to renew the attack on La Boiselle and Ovillers.

Gough reported that the X and VIII Corps would not be ready to renew the attack till July 3.

On July 2 a German counter-attack by twelve battalions, between 3 a.m. and 4 a.m., was beaten off by the XIII Corps, with heavy loss to the enemy. Consolidation went on uninterruptedly, and guns were moved forward.

Fricourt was occupied by the XV Corps soon after noon, and the advance went on to include Fricourt Wood.

On the III Corps front, La Boiselle was taken by the 19th Division in the afternoon. The remainder of the Corps did not move.

The French, north of the Somme, repelled a German attack on the night of the 1st/2nd, but made no advance on the 2nd. South of the river they continued their attack and captured portions of the German second position.

On the whole the Allies' situation had slightly improved during the day, but the artillery ammunition supply in the British Expeditionary Force gave cause for anxiety. Not only was the quantity still insufficient to allow of a really lavish expenditure, but the quality was poor, there being far too many 'duds.'

The plan of the Fourth Army for July 3 was unambitious, and only aimed at an improvement of the position of the three centre corps, with a view to the next advance. The results were not altogether satisfactory. The XIII and XV Corps each completed its programme, but in the centre there was a failure. The III Corps was to renew the attack on Ovillers, the X Corps co-operating on their left. The X Corps was unable to start their attack in time; consequently, though the partial capture of La Boiselle was completed, that on Ovillers failed; and the 12th Division, on the exposed left flank, lost 2,374 of all ranks. By the evening of July 3 the British losses for the three days totalled nearly 2,000 officers and over 60,000 of other ranks.

The French, south of the Somme, had a great day, reaching Assevillers, Herbecourt, and Flaucourt.[1]

At this stage of the battle Haig and Joffre differed as to what should be the next move. Haig wished to exploit the success of the XIII and XV Corps by attacking north, with the French securing his right flank. Joffre wanted Haig to renew his attacks where they had failed, on the fronts of the X and VIII Corps.

Judging after the event, there can be no possible doubt who was right, but Joffre—very naturally, considering the

[1] Map V.

drain of Verdun—preferred a plan in which the British Expeditionary Force would have it all to themselves to one which might increasingly involve French assistance. The success of his own troops and the comparative failure of the British in the first few days would no doubt intensify his fears that the calls on him would grow. In the end they amicably agreed to differ, and Haig was left to carry out his plan without any great expectation of active French co-operation.

The next big attack was not to come off till July 14, but there was much hard fighting to be done to pave the way to it.

On July 4 the Fourth Army handed over to the Reserve Army the 12th Division, which, from being the left-hand division of the III Corps, became the right-hand one of the X Corps. La Boiselle thus came into the Reserve Army front. On the 5th some small advance was made on the front of the XV and III Corps. July 6 was a quiet day except for a small but successful attack by one battalion on the III Corps front to fill a gap in their line which was found to be in occupation by the enemy. July 7, which was to have been a big day, proved disappointing. The XIII Corps, which was to have attacked Trônes Wood, had to stand fast, as the French, on their right, could not be ready to co-operate till next day. The day started badly, with the failure of a preliminary attack by the 17th Division (XV Corps), launched at 2 a.m., and after that nothing went right. The 19th Division, on the left of the III Corps, made a successful attack, but otherwise the Fourth Army had nothing to show for a day of heavy losses. On the Reserve Army front the 12th Division just obtained a footing in Ovillers.

On July 8 the 30th Division (XIII Corps) got a footing in Trônes Wood, and the French on their right made an equivalent advance; elsewhere there was not much done, and certainly no ground gained. On the 9th the 30th Division completed the capture of Trônes Wood in the morning, but was driven out in the afternoon. It was recaptured on the 10th, but only the southern edge retained. Fierce fighting for possession of the wood went on all day on the 11th. During the 12th a trench was dug and wired across the middle of the wood. On the night of the 12th/13th the 30th Division was relieved by the 18th, who, on the evening of the 13th, attacked and failed. In the early morning of the 14th an attack was made by a fresh brigade, and by 9.30 a.m. the wood was cleared of Germans. Thus at last the safety of the right of the big attack on the German second position, which had been timed for the 14th, was secured.

Meanwhile, there had been very severe fighting with the object of securing the other flank of the big attack.

On July 10, after continuous fighting all day, Mametz Wood was taken, all but the northern fringe, by the 38th Division. Next day a further attempt to get the rest of the wood failed. The 38th Division was relieved during the night of the 11th/12th by the 62nd Brigade of the 21st Division, which cleared the wood without difficulty next morning, the Germans having had enough.

On the III Corps front Contalmaison had been taken by the 69th Brigade, 23rd Division, on the 10th.

Bazentin

At dawn on July 14 was delivered the great attack on the German second position, for which all the heavy fighting of the last few days for Trônes Wood, Mametz Wood, and Contalmaison had only been a preparation. It was a great triumph for the training and staff-work of the New Army. Of thirteen battalions from the 9th, 3rd,

7th, and 21st Divisions that attacked in the first line, only one was a regular battalion. The 9th and 3rd Divisions had to make a night advance of over 1,000 yards across No Man's Land. All went like clockwork, and when the day was still young the German second position had been captured on a front of 6,000 yards. This day brings the first mention of the K.R.R.C. in the battle of the Somme, one company of the 20th (Pioneer) Battalion being attached to the 8th Brigade, 3rd Division.

During the morning the XIII Corps captured the southern portion of Longueval and Bazentin-le-Grand, while the XV Corps took Bazentin-le-Petit. By 2 p.m. the South African Brigade had cleared the northern portion of Longueval village.

During the afternoon a counter-attack drove our men out of Bazentin-le-Petit, but it was immediately retaken by the 7th Division. At 6.15 p.m. the 7th Division attacked High Wood, and by 8 p.m. had taken all but the northern tip of it. During the evening the 100th Brigade of the 33rd Division, which was in Corps Reserve, advanced and occupied the road line between the western corner of High Wood and Bazentin-le-Petit. Our 16th Battalion was in second line in this attack.

Everything seemed to be going well, nearly 10,000 prisoners had been taken during the day, an attempt had even been made to push the cavalry through, but the Germans rallied, and there was to be two months' hard fighting before any further big advance was to be made.

On July 15 Delville Wood was taken by the South African Brigade, XIII Corps, by midday, and counter-attacks were repulsed in the afternoon.

On the XV Corps front the 7th Division was fighting all day in High Wood, without getting the whole of it. The 33rd Division attacked the German switch line between

High Wood and the Martinpuich–Bazentin railway.[1] This attack should never have been made, as any possibility of success presupposed the secure occupation of High Wood by the 7th Division and Bazentin-le-Petit Wood by the 21st Division. Both these divisions were far too deeply engaged with their own affairs to be of any assistance to the 33rd. The attack was delivered by the 100th and 98th Brigades. The 100th Brigade attacked with the 9th Highland Light Infantry on the right and 1st Queen's on the left, in front line, the 16th K.R.R.C. being in support. The Highland Light Infantry were held up from the start by enfilade fire from High Wood. The Queen's reached the enemy's wire, and found it uncut. Our 16th Battalion was then put in to fill the gap between the two regiments. They advanced 1,000 yards over the open, under enfilading machine-gun fire, and lost heavily. Colonel Wyld was wounded and Captain E. Wenham succeeded to the command. The Battalion behaved most gallantly in this, its first big fight, and eleven Military Medals were awarded to N.C.O.s and riflemen for their conduct in the attack. Eventually the Brigade was withdrawn to its starting-line, and was relieved by the 19th Brigade. The Battalion lost on this day:

Killed: Major A. D. Cooban; Captain H. P. Deedes; Lieutenant J. B. Hichens; 2nd Lieutenants K. G. Denniss, R. D. Atkinson.

Died of Wounds: Lieutenant R. R. Lewer; 2nd Lieutenant E. H. Grant.

Wounded: Lieut.-Colonel C. E. Wyld; Captains C. C. F. Harrison, J. M. Donaldson; Lieutenants C. C. Watts, L. E. Francis, D. H. Derry (R.A.M.C.); 2nd Lieutenants A. R. Howell, C. E. Howard, L. Spero.

The attack of the 98th Brigade had been equally unsuccessful. The 7th Division was ordered to evacuate

[1] A light railway, not shown in Map II.

High Wood by dawn of the 16th, to allow of a fresh bombardment. This withdrawal was successfully carried out.

On July 16 the Reserve Army got practically the whole of Ovillers. During the ensuing night the 3rd Brigade, 1st Division, now in the III Corps, took a line of trenches running north-west from Bazentin-le-Petit Wood, inflicting heavy losses. On the same night the 33rd Division was withdrawn to near Bazentin-le-Petit, the 100th Brigade going into Divisional Reserve.

The next ten days produced little change in the situation, though there was constant fighting at different parts of the line. On July 17 the enemy were still firmly established in the northern portion of Longueval and the north-western corner of Delville Wood. A preliminary attack on the southern outskirts of Pozières failed. On the night of the 17th/18th the 76th Brigade, 3rd Division, cleared the northern part of Longueval. In the afternoon of the 18th the enemy counter-attacked, and retook the northern parts of Longueval and Delville Wood, inflicting heavy losses on the South African Brigade. Enemy attacks on Waterlot Farm were repulsed. The introduction of the I Anzac Corps into the Reserve Army necessitated a slight side-step by all Corps of the Fourth Army, the Anzacs taking over the operations against Pozières.

On July 19 there was fighting all day for Delville Wood, with no change in the situation. The XV Corps took over from the XIII up to Longueval (exclusive), and handed over Bazentin-le-Petit to the 19th Division, III Corps. The 34th Division handed over their sector to the 1st Australian Division.

On July 20 the XIII Corps attacked Delville Wood and Longueval in the early morning, but failed. Some trenches east of Maltz Horn Farm were taken, but found untenable, owing to being on a forward slope.

The XV Corps at the same time attacked High Wood and the roads Longueval–High Wood and High Wood–Bazentin-le-Petit.

All objectives were gained except the northern portion of High Wood. At one time the wood was clear of the enemy, but a counter-attack recaptured the northern half. The 33rd Division took part in this attack, but our 16th Battalion was not engaged. The 2nd Division, and with it our 1st Battalion, came this day into the XIII Corps area.

Nothing but the usual trench fighting took place on the 21st and 22nd, but even the quiet days meant an average of about 1,000 casualties a day. On the 22nd the casualties in the Fourth Army since the beginning of the battle reached 100,000.

Pozières

On July 23 the Fourth Army attacked all along the front, from Trônes Wood to Pozières, but failed everywhere.

Our 2nd Battalion was the right attacking battalion of the 2nd Brigade. They had the 1st Brigade on their right, and the 2nd Royal Sussex on their left. They took the trench that was their first objective (about equidistant from Bazentin-le-Petit, Martinpuich, and Pozières) on a front of 300 yards, but finding themselves isolated, owing to the failure of the units on their right and left, and being subjected to a severe bombing attack from both flanks, the remains of the Battalion were forced to withdraw. Their losses were: officers—killed 1; wounded 2; missing 5; other ranks—killed 11, wounded 48, missing 137. The Battalion had lost their Commanding Officer, Lieut.-Colonel H. F. W. Bircham, D.S.O., who had commanded ever since Loos, and whom they could ill spare. The officers missing, all of whom were killed except the last named, were: Captains E. M. Webb, R. F. Sherlock;

2nd Lieutenants F. B. Walker, G. H. Purdon, and F. S. Hancocks. On the 19th the Battalion had lost 2nd Lieutenant R. A. F. Eminson, who was killed when trying to bring in a wounded sergeant under a heavy fire. The failure of this attack seems to have been caused everywhere by well-placed machine guns, dotted about in shell holes and well hidden. The only success of the day was on the Reserve Army front, where the 1st Australian Division took most of the village of Pozières. The 2nd Battalion were withdrawn in the evening, and marched back next day to billets in Albert.

Nothing of importance occurred on the 24th, but it could not be called a quiet day, as there was very heavy shelling by both sides. The enemy counter-attacked at High Wood after dark, but were repulsed. During the afternoon the Germans massed large numbers of troops in trenches near Delville Wood, Ginchy, and Morval, where they were heavily shelled. Later they were reported to have moved most of them into Delville Wood, where they were again shelled.

Delville Wood

On July 25 the 2nd Division relieved the 3rd Division in the line, our 1st Battalion going into the front line in Delville Wood on the nights of 25th/26th and 26th/27th.

On July 27 a joint attack was delivered by the 2nd Division, XIII Corps, and the 5th Division, XV Corps, to clear Delville Wood and the north edge of Longueval village. The attack on Delville Wood was completely successful, and a line was established 150 yards inside the eastern, north-eastern, and northern edges of the wood. The left joined up with the 5th Division, which, however, had not been so successful. Extensive patrolling by the 1st K.R.R.C., the night before, had done much to locate the enemy's trenches in the wood. The bombardment began at 6.10 a.m. It lifted and the infantry advanced at 7.10 a.m. The 99th Brigade attacked, with the 1st K.R.R.C. (Lieut.-Colonel E. B. Denison) on the right; the 23rd Royal Fusiliers, commanded by Lieut.-Colonel H. A. Vernon, K.R.R.C., on the left; the 1st Royal Berkshire were in support, and the 22nd Royal Fusiliers had two companies in Brigade Reserve and two on carrying duties. The following account is taken, almost verbatim, from that of the Brigadier, 99th Brigade.

The 1st K.R.R.C. reached its first objective by 7.15 a.m. with small loss. The trench was full of dead and wounded Germans, and also contained three machine guns, destroyed by artillery fire. At 8.8. a.m. the second wave passed through the first wave, advanced to the next objective, and consolidated there. The advance was continued at 8.38 a.m., the final objective reached at 8.50, and a line dug, 150 yards from the edge of the wood, facing north and north-east. Two companies of the supporting regiment which came up on the right dug in too far inside the wood and left the right of the K.R.R.C. in the air. From 9 a.m. onwards the enemy shelled the wood heavily. About 9.30 a.m. the enemy were seen in large numbers north of the wood, massing for a counter-attack, while parties of them began to creep up to the eastern edge of the wood, and at 10 a.m. made a heavy bombing attack, effecting a lodgment 70 yards inside the wood.

The 1st K.R.R.C. at once attacked this party and drove them back about 40 yards, but suffered very severely in doing so; Sergeant Woodward, 1st K.R.R.C., here particularly distinguished himself at the head of his bombers, and his Commanding Officer reported that it was in great measure due to his efforts that the enemy were driven back with very heavy loss to them. The Commanding

Officer's report also mentions Captain Howell, who was wounded about this time, 'but continued to carry on his duties with great gallantry.'

About 11 a.m. the two companies 1st K.R.R.C., holding the northern and north-eastern edges of the wood, were heavily attacked from north and north-east, and fighting took place at 15 yards' range with bombs and rifle fire—both company commanders were wounded. This fighting then resolved itself into sniping from shell holes and crawling forward to bomb each other, which went on for some hours, till the enemy were finally driven off.

From 1 to 2.30 p.m. the right-flank companies along the eastern face of the wood were heavily attacked. They were reinforced by bombers from the 23rd Royal Fusiliers and 1st Royal Berkshire, of whom Lance-Corporal Bell, 23rd Royal Fusiliers, behaved with great gallantry, and the attack was repulsed.

Heavy bombardment of the old front line made reinforcement very difficult. There was a heavy mist all day, all communications were cut by the barrage, there could be no visual signalling or messages by aircraft, so all messages had to be sent by runners, who had to cross the barrage.

Reinforcements did, however, dribble up in the course of the evening. The 1st K.R.R.C. were partly relieved on the night of the 27th/28th, and were all withdrawn on the morning of the 29th. They had lost 14 officers and 308 other ranks killed and wounded. Captain and Adjutant A. H. Brocklehurst died of his wounds ; the other officers killed being: Captains E. L. Howell, R. H. Slater ; Lieutenant C. Collins ; 2nd Lieutenants A. Y. Bailey, C. R. S. Turner, 3rd Dorsets (attached), and J. W. E. Paul ; wounded : Lieutenant Hon. F. S. Trench ; 2nd Lieutenants H. E. Gill, 3rd Dorsets (attached), W. J.

Taylor, J. E. M. Skinner, C. Witt, T. I. Stevenson, N. H. Noble.

The Brigadier-General commanding 99th Brigade specially mentions in his first report of the fight Lieut.-Colonel E. B. Denison, Lieut.-Colonel H. A. Vernon, and Captain E. M. Allfrey, 1st K.R.R.C., Staff-Captain, 99th Brigade.

On July 28 the XV Corps completed the capture of Longueval, and next day gained some ground north of that village.

On July 30 the XIII Corps attacked Guillemont, the 30th Division, on the right, being sent against the village and trenches south of it; the 2nd Division, on the left, against the railway station and trenches north-west of it. Both attacks failed. Our 1st Battalion, which had only got back into a comparatively safe place in front of Montauban village at 8 a.m., started at 3 p.m. to go up into reserve in some old German trenches, where, except for two or three dug-outs, there was little protection from shell fire. During the day they received congratulatory messages on their taking of Delville Wood from the Commander-in-Chief, General Officers Commanding Fourth Army, XIII Corps, and 2nd Division, and their own Brigadier.

From July 31 to August 7 there were no operations of importance. The weather had begun to improve for the last few days, and there was noticeably less hostile shelling, owing to improved visibility enabling our aircraft to help in the counter-battery work. That does not mean that there was not still pretty constant shelling. On August 1 our 1st Battalion 'War Diary' reports that an 8-inch scored a direct hit on the Battalion Headquarters dug-out, and adds, 'as this hardly shook the dug-out, it speaks well for German workmanship.'

To enable the XIII Corps to concentrate on the capture of Guillemont, a slight rearrangement of corps' area took place from August 3, the III Corps taking over from the XV up to, but excluding, High Wood, while the XV took over from the XIII up to, and including, Delville Wood.

On August 3 instructions came from G.H.Q. describing the present phase as 'a wearing-out battle'; the object of the Allies being to have the 'last reserves' at the crisis of the battle, which was not expected to come before the latter half of September. The position of the British Expeditionary Force was to be gradually improved as far as could be done with due economy of men. The Commander-in-Chief hoped to get the Morval–Thiepval Ridge as a basis for further operations, the first necessity being to help the French forward by the capture of Guillemont and Ginchy.

On August 8 the XIII Corps again attacked Guillemont. The 55th Division, on the right, had for its objectives the whole of Guillemont village and trenches to the south. The 2nd Division was to capture the railway station, and join up with the XV Corps at the edge of Delville Wood. The attack failed everywhere. Troops that got into Guillemont were cut off by the enemy appearing behind them from deep dug-outs, reinforcement being stopped by the German barrage. On August 9 the attack was renewed and failed again. The 99th Brigade was not engaged this time, and on the night of the 9th/10th the 24th Division relieved the 2nd Division.

August 10 and 11 were uneventful, but on the 12th Lieut.-General Lord Cavan relieved General Congreve, who was ill, in command of the XIII Corps.

On August 12 an attack was made by the French Sixth Army from the Somme to Maurepas; the task of our XIII Corps being to conform to the French attack by pushing forward its right. The French attack was successful, except on their extreme left—next to our right—where their troops were unable to leave their trenches owing to the weight of the German barrage. On the XIII Corps front two battalions of the 165th Brigade (55th Division) attacked. The right battalion reached its objective, and began to dig in, but, as the battalion on its left failed to get on, it was left with both flanks in the air, and had to fall back to its original line during the night. On this day the Staff of the XIV Corps, from which Lord Cavan came, began relieving that of the XIII Corps.

On August 13, 14, and 15 there were no operations of importance.

On the 16th a combined attack was made by the French and our XIII Corps, to obtain a better jumping-off place for the next big offensive. The French XX Corps were to take Angle Wood[1] with their left. This they failed to do, though they gained their objectives farther to the right. Our troops were to connect Angle Wood with our front line west of Guillemont. The 3rd Division gained a little ground, and connected up with the French left, but generally speaking the attack was a failure. At midnight 16th/17th, the transfer between the XIII and XIV Corps was completed, the XIII joining the Reserve Army.

The 2nd Brigade, 1st Division, took a bit of trench just west of High Wood, and beat off counter-attacks, but our 2nd Battalion was not engaged.

On August 18 a general attack along the whole front of the Fourth Army took place in conjunction with the French on the right and the Reserve Army on the left. It was launched at 2.45 a.m., and was only a partial success. On the XIV Corps front the 3rd Division lost heavily and gained little ground. The 24th Division gained a little on

[1] Not marked. Is N.W. of Maurepas.

their left, but failed on the right; the enemy, preparing counter-attacks in front of them, were stopped by our field artillery and lost heavily.

On the XV Corps front the 14th Division, which had come into the corps area on August 11, gained nearly all its objectives. The 41st Brigade attacked Orchard Trench, just north-west of Delville Wood, and a trench beyond it, the 7th K.R.R.C. being on the right, the 7th Rifle Brigade on the left. Our 7th Battalion reached their second, and final, objective, and started digging in. They then came under heavy machine-gun and rifle fire from a strong point in the adjacent corner of Delville Wood, which caused many casualties. This fire was kept down by the bombers, under Lieutenant C. G. E. Farmer, bombing officer, who was soon killed. The attack by the brigade next on the left failed, and the 7th Rifle Brigade were left with their flank in the air, and lost heavily. The losses of our 7th Battalion were: killed, Lieutenants C. G. E. Farmer, Hon. B. D. Butler; died of wounds, 2nd Lieutenant S. T. Bird; wounded, Lieutenant J. N. Martin; 2nd Lieutenant A. C. Mackenzie, C. Whitley, C. H. Davidson; other ranks —killed 42, wounded 174, missing 4.

Next morning the Battalion suffered from accurate sniping from Delville Wood. At 8 p.m. the enemy put down a heavy bombardment on the captured trenches and a barrage behind. There followed a feeble counter-attack, which was easily beaten off. After things had quieted down the Battalion was relieved by the 2nd Worcester. Their casualties on the 19th were: other ranks—killed 9, wounded 28, missing 1.

On the 18th the III Corps made no progress, but the Reserve Army met with some success.

On August 19 the attack was not continued, as had been intended, owing to the exhaustion of the troops.

On August 20 there was heavy fighting all day on part of the III Corps front, in which our 2nd Battalion was involved. Their 'War Diary' gives the following account of it:

'Soon after daybreak our observers reported that the enemy was massing in rear of the crest of the high ground, upon the near slope of which our line lay. The Officer Commanding A Company called for an artillery barrage. This was not forthcoming, the attention of the guns being directed to that part of the line held by the 1st Northamptonshire. The threatened attack developed in great force. The enemy advanced, in spite of severe losses, drove in our outpost line and the Northamptonshire Regiment. A counter-attack was at once organised, and was carried out by C Company and by part of A and B. This attack was successful, and the original outpost line was again taken up. Captain J. S. Wilson was very severely wounded, and the immediate direction of operations devolved upon Captain F. J. L. Johnstone. Meanwhile, the Northamptonshire Regiment became very heavily engaged with the enemy, and hand-to-hand fighting ensued. At the same time Germans issuing from High Wood made a violent attack on our right flank. The brunt of this attack fell on the advanced post held by two platoons of A Company, under 2nd Lieutenant R. J. Stokes. This attack was repulsed. Later on the enemy made two further attempts to rush this post, besides keeping up a continuous and violent shell and machine-gun fire on it. All these attempts on the part of the Germans were crushed by the steady fire from the post. Second Lieutenant Stokes set a fine example of coolness and disregard of danger. He walked up and down under the heavy fire encouraging the men and controlling the situation. Our line remained in this position until dark, when the 3rd Brigade relieved the exhausted and shattered battalions of the 2nd Brigade. The 1st Battalion Gloucester Regiment relieved us. Two platoons of that regiment took over the advanced post from 2nd Lieutenant Stokes, but no officer was sent to relieve him. After sending away all the riflemen of the garrison with the exception of 1 corporal and 4 men, he remained in command of these two platoons. The enemy attacked again. While repelling this attack this gallant officer was killed by a shell.'

The Battalion also lost Captain F. J. L. Johnstone, who received the Military Cross for his gallant conduct that day, and Lieutenant G. S. Walley, both of whom died of their wounds, and Major G. M. Atkinson, D.S.O., Commanding, Captains J. S. Wilson, H. K. Ward (R.A.M.C.), 2nd Lieutenant L. A. Barnes, M.C., wounded; other ranks: killed 19; died of wounds 2; wounded and otherwise injured 110.

On August 21 troops of the XIV Corps made an unsuccessful attempt to increase their hold on Guillemont, of which they had only the western edge. At 4.30 p.m. the 14th Division did their best to carry out an order to capture a strong point in the enemy's line in Delville Wood. Our 8th Battalion were the victims, and the operation is thus described in their 'War Diary':

> 'Zero hour was at 4.30 p.m. A barrage was put up along the line. For some cause or other the barrage began *behind* our line, and lifted from here *over* our objective. In addition, the Stokes mortars managed to drop 15 shells into our lines, killing 2 and wounding 6. The platoon which was "establishing a post" was picked off by enemy rifle fire as each man emerged from a sap when the attack was to take place. Out of the first 8 men who emerged, 1 was killed and 5 wounded. The futile attempt was then abandoned.'

Artillery support for an attack in a wood, with trenches a few yards apart, cannot be an easy matter to arrange. No wonder the tone of the 'War Diary' is peevish.

The Anzac Corps and II Corps, Reserve Army, attacked at 6 p.m. and gained some ground.

On the night of August 22/23 the 24th Division was relieved by the 20th. At 8.45 p.m., 23rd, the enemy opened an intense bombardment on part of the 20th Division line, followed by a determined attack, which reached our parapet, but was everywhere repulsed. Our 10th Battalion, which was in the front line, lost a good officer in 2nd Lieutenant J. W. A. Maude, who was killed by a sniper while repairing a parapet.

A big attack had been arranged for August 24 by the XIV and XV Corps, but the bombardment of the night before upset our arrangements, and the attack was confined to the XV Corps.

The task of the 14th Division was to clear the remainder of Delville Wood, and secure a line of German trench running north-west and south-east, some 300 yards from and parallel to the north-eastern edge of the wood.

The 41st Brigade attacked on the right, the 42nd Brigade on the left. The attack of the 41st Brigade, of which the 8th K.R.R.C. was the left battalion, failed, and the following extract from that battalion's 'War Diary' explains the reason :

> 'At 4.50 p.m., after two hours' intensive bombardment, A and D Companies of the 8th K.R.R.C., with the 42nd Brigade on our left, attacked the enemy in and on the flanks of Delville Wood. . . .
>
> 'The preliminary bombardment has failed to cut the wire in front of A, and has not touched the enemy trench. The Stokes guns detailed to obliterate the enemy trench on the left fail to do so, and has some very good shooting at our trench instead. The field-gun barrage has been directed, unfortunately, behind the enemy trench all the time. Consequently, the enemy man their trench very strongly, and A Company's attack cannot develop, the first wave falling back dead on the second. Second Lieutenant Todd-Naylor is killed. On the right D Company has been held up nearly as badly, only about 6 riflemen and 2 sergeants reaching the enemy's line alive. This party made a post, and took 2 prisoners. They maintained themselves in the enemy trench till withdrawn after dark. Our extreme right bombing party progressed some way up an old trench, and established a block. This also had to be withdrawn after dark.'

The casualties among officers were, besides the above: killed, 2nd Lieutenant G. W. Huntington; wounded, 2nd Lieutenants F. G. Scott, T. A. Wood.

The Battalion was relieved by the 7th K.R.R.C. during the night.

The 9th K.R.R.C., on the right of the 42nd Brigade, were next on the left to the 8th K.R.R.C. Their objectives were: (1) Inner Trench, which ran parallel to the north-eastern side of Delville Wood and a short way inside it, but, in front of the left of the Battalion, slanted forward, so that it reached the edge of the wood opposite the centre of the Battalion's front; (2) Edge Trench, running along the north-eastern edge of the wood; (3) Beer Trench, 300 yards farther on. It will be observed that the attack of the 9th Battalion was at right angles to that of the 1st Battalion delivered on July 27.

The author so often has to regret the extreme brevity of the accounts of operations in battalion 'War Diaries' that, when he finds one like the following of the 9th Battalion, he is tempted to quote it in full.

'At 5.45 p.m. C and D Companies, who were assembled in Devil's Trench [some 300 yards inside the wood, running north-west and south-east], advanced to the attack in two waves with an interval of 100 yards between the waves. The battalion bombers accompanied the second wave in two parties, right and left, and at the same time A Company moved from the support trench, Devil's Help, and re-formed in Devil's Trench ready to advance as third wave. The distance from Devil's Trench to the first objective varied from 250 to 300 yards, the ground being pitted with innumerable shell holes, and obstructed with the debris of fallen trees, necessitating a slow advance. Immediately the barrage lifted and the assaulting troops climbed over the parapet, the enemy artillery fire became intense on Delville Wood, and machine-gun and rifle fire was opened from Edge Trench and the north-east corner of Delville Wood, causing many casualties. All the officers of both C and D Companies were either killed or wounded ; Captain H. S. Richmond, Commanding D Company, being killed, and 2nd Lieutenants G. G. Edgar and J. B. Heaton of D Company wounded, almost at the commencement of the assault. The men were rallied, and were led on by the N.C.O.s of C Company ; 2nd Lieutenant Farran was killed at the commencement of the assault, and Captain M. Mallalue killed and 2nd Lieutenant H. Robins wounded on nearing the enemy trench.

'On the right of Edge Trench the enemy wire remained to form a considerable obstacle, and the remains of C Company were unable to gain an entrance into the trench. The Company Lewis guns, both of C and D Companies, however, were brought into action close to the German trench, which was strongly garrisoned, and for a time, until the teams were killed, fired with effect on the enemy, who were also bombed. Sergeant Hamp of D Company and Corporal Ord of C Company in charge of Lewis-gun teams were both conspicuous in their daring, fearlessly exposing themselves to heavy fire close to the enemy trench, while they brought their guns into action, and maintained an effective fire on the enemy. Both gave their lives, and in the loss of these two N.C.O.s the Battalion has lost men who have always shown a steadfast devotion to duty, and a fine example of cool bravery. No history of the Battalion would be complete which did not record the service which Lance-Sergeant Hamp and Corporal Ord have always rendered to the Battalion, and the manner in which they served their guns and met their deaths with unflinching courage.

'At 5.45 p.m. A Company advanced . . . forming the third wave of the assault, maintaining its formation and direction splendidly. . . .

'At 6 p.m. the 8th K.R.R.C. on our right reported by runner to an officer in Devil's Trench that the enemy were advancing to meet them, and that they had sent an S.O.S. The attack by the 8th K.R.R.C. from Hop Alley on Ale Alley [outside the eastern corner of Delville Wood] made no headway. One party of battalion bombers under Sergeant Martin advancing towards the junction of Ale Alley and Edge Trench [the point of junction of the objectives of the two battalions] found the post there in the trench leading to the junction held by two men of the 8th K.R.R.C., and they were ordered by an officer of the 8th K.R.R.C. to hold this point at all costs. At this point they established a barricade from which they bombed the enemy, and held on there until relieved on the morning of the 25th. Second Lieutenant H. Le Mesurier, advancing with A Company together with two bombers, leapt over this barricade. Second Lieutenant Le Mesurier was immediately killed and the two bombers wounded. Lieutenant G. M. Warner, commanding A Company, was wounded, and 2nd Lieutenant P. W. Gould missing, and is believed to have been killed. Thus at an early stage of the battle every officer in the assaulting companies had become casualties, and at 7 p.m. Captain R. S. Daw, Commanding B Company, in reserve in Devil's Trench, was mortally wounded.

'On the right of Edge Trench the attack was entirely held up by wire and machine-gun and rifle fire, particularly from the enemy strong point at the junction of Edge Trench and Ale Alley. Edge Trench was afterwards found not to have been seriously damaged by shell fire. Towards the left of Edge Trench Sergeant Jordan of A Company and some men entered the enemy trench and drove the enemy towards Inner Trench, where they were made prisoners. Sergeant Jordan's party then left Edge Trench and entered Inner Trench, where they, together with other men who had entered Inner Trench, were organised by Lieutenant Clayton, of the Machine-gun Company, and bombed the dug-out there, and established a barricade at the junction of Inner Trench and Edge Trench. This trench and the dug-outs in it were found to contain a considerable number of German dead. When relieved on the following day 31 N.C.O.s and men of the Battalion returned from the right of Inner Trench and 7 wounded were evacuated.

'The attack having been held up on the right, and owing to the various losses suffered by the assaulting companies and the position of the 8th K.R.R.C., who reported being attacked and were asking for reinforcements, reinforcements were asked for at 7.45 p.m. to ensure the safety of Devil's Trench. The artillery were also asked to bring back the barrage on the battalion front on to Beer Trench and Ale Alley, east of Beer Trench [what was to have been the third objective]. One company of the 9th Rifle Brigade, under Captain Merewether, arrived at 8.15 p.m. to reinforce if necessary. However, Major H. C. M. Porter [Commanding 9th K.R.R.C.] having by this time assured himself by personal reconnaissance that the garrison of Devil's Trench was sufficient to defend it, in the event of attack, and that the reserve company holding it was in touch with troops on both flanks, this company of the 9th Rifle Brigade remained for the time being in Angle Trench [just outside the south side of Delville Wood.] Up to this time, 10 p.m., no news of events on the left had been received.

'At 10 p.m. a message was received from Brigade to get into touch with troops who had captured Inner Trench [i.e. farther to the left], and shortly afterwards Lieut.-Colonel Morris, 9th Rifle Brigade, arrived with news of the position on the left, and with orders to command the right and centre sectors of operations, and authority to draw reinforcements as required from his battalion. He at once detailed the company under Captain Merewether to dig, and connect Inner Trench with Devil's Trench, and this was carried out during the night.

'On the left of the Brigade front the 5th Oxford and Bucks had completely carried their objective, and were consolidating their position in Beer Trench. In the centre the 5th King's Shropshire Light Infantry carried and held their objective in Inner Trench, and gained their objective in Beer Trench, but later withdrew to Inner Trench.

'At 2 a.m. Lieut.-Colonel Morris organised a bombing attack from the right end of Inner Trench along Edge Trench. This was carried out about 5 a.m. on the morning of the 25th by his battalion bombers, under 2nd Lieutenant Day, and Edge Trench was then found to be evacuated by the enemy with the exception of the strong point at the junction of Edge Trench and Ale Alley. With this exception, Edge Trench was occupied and garrisoned by the 9th Rifle Brigade without opposition. This post, together with 50 prisoners, was captured on the 28th by the 43rd Brigade, with the loss of 6 casualties.

'As a result of the operations of the 24th/25th Delville Wood, with the exception of the post at the junction of the 8th and 9th Battalions' objectives, was entirely cleared of the enemy. One hundred and sixty-eight prisoners were captured by the Brigade, including 9 officers, and some machine guns. . . . The Battalion was relieved by the 9th Rifle Brigade midday on the 25th, and returned to the A 2 line in front of Bernafay Wood. . . . The losses of the Battalion during the course of the operations 21st–24th were severe: officers—5 killed, 1 missing, believed killed, and 6 wounded; other ranks —41 killed, 190 wounded, 46 missing.'

The casualties among officers were:

Killed: Captains H. S. Richmond, M. Mallalue; 2nd Lieutenants C. Farran, H. Le Mesurier, P. W. Gould.
Died of wounds: Captain R. S. Daw, Lieutenant G. G. Edgar.
Wounded: Lieutenant G. MacD. Warner; 2nd Lieutenants J. B. Heaton, H. Robins, E. Barlow.

We have not yet done with this day's operations, as our 16th Battalion took part in the attack of the 100th Brigade, 33rd Division, on a German trench known as Tea Trench, between the Longueval–Flers Road and High Wood. The day before, while Major C. A. Howard, Commanding the 16th Battalion, was going round his trenches, a shell had buried him and three other officers. One of them, Captain C. A. Thomas, was killed, and Major Howard was severely wounded, the command thus again devolving on Captain E. Wenham, who had commanded the Battalion in the fight in High Wood in July.

The Brigade attacked with three battalions: 2nd Worcester on the right, 16th K.R.R.C. in the centre, 1st Queen's on the left. All went well; the Brigade attained all its objectives, and kept them. The attack was over open ground, with good observation for artillery. There was no difficulty in the attacking troops keeping close up to the barrage, which lifted 25 yards a minute. The Battalion 'War Diary' says:

'The new front line was consolidated very rapidly, and a comparatively good trench established. The whole attack was carried out with surprisingly few casualties, partly owing to the troops moving out immediately behind our barrage (which, though it led to some casualties from our own shells, gave the troops the chance to get to the enemy's trenches very quickly), and partly because the reserve company was kept until needed in Carlton Trench [the jumping-off trench], and then sent up by half-companies when the barrage had partially stopped.'

The casualties of the Battalion in the attack were: officers—killed, 2nd Lieutenant A. C. Store; wounded, 2nd Lieutenants F. B. Whateley, A. F. J. Bevan; other ranks—killed 13, wounded 72, missing 39.

On this day the French attacked from the Somme to Angle Wood. On the right they failed, but on the left were most successful; 600 prisoners were taken, and the capture of Maurepas completed. The right of our XIV Corps pushed forward to get in touch with them.

There were no more operations of importance for some days, as the weather, which had been showery for some time, broke on the 27th, when it poured all day. On that day the post on the edge of Delville Wood, which had given such trouble on the 24th, was taken with slight loss and 50 prisoners with it. During the night of the 27th/28th both the III and XV Corps took over some line from the next Corps on their right, with a view to shortening the front of the XIV Corps for the forthcoming attack.

On August 29 there was some successful trench fighting just east of Delville Wood. About 6 p.m., during a thunderstorm, the enemy tried a raid on the 20th Division, now in the front line just west of Guillemont. They came up against our 12th Battalion, 60th Brigade, who drove them off with heavy loss, being helped by the 10th Battalion, 59th Brigade, with flanking fire.

On August 30 the garrison of a bit of German trench north of Bazentin-le-Petit, having been completely surrounded by troops of the 15th Division, surrendered. There were taken 2 officers and 124 other ranks.

On the 31st the enemy attacked the whole of the XV Corps front after 45 minutes' bombardment. They were, in most places, beaten off with heavy loss, but retained the extreme eastern point of Delville Wood and a trench in the 24th Division's line, between Delville and High Woods. The 7th and 24th Divisions, in the line, had heavy losses from the bombardment, especially the 24th. During the ensuing night the enemy, after a heavy bombardment, captured the eastern corner of Delville Wood from the 7th Division, our line being forced back to Inner Trench. At 6.45 p.m. on September 1 the 24th Division recovered the trench lost the day before. The weather was fine all day, and next morning the bombardment began, preliminary to an attack which was to take place on the 3rd, after having been several times postponed owing to bad weather. At 2 a.m. on September 2 the enemy attacked a trench held by our 2nd Battalion in High Wood, and were beaten off with heavy loss, our casualties being few. The Battalion was relieved the next night, and took no part in the fighting on the 3rd.

Guillemont

The programme for September 3 was the capture of Falfemont Farm, the south-west edge of Leuze Wood, Guillemont, Ginchy, Wood Lane, which ran south-east from High Wood, and the German front line in High Wood. The results were disappointing, as the capture of the edge of Leuze Wood was especially desired to prevent the enemy getting artillery observation from it.

The attack on Falfemont Farm failed. Guillemont and Ginchy were taken without difficulty, but in the afternoon heavy counter-attacks retook most of the last-named village. An attack on Tea Trench, north-west of Delville Wood, failed. The 1st Division took Wood Lane, and the front line in High Wood, but were immediately counter-attacked, and lost what they had gained. The only success of the day was the capture of Guillemont, in which our 10th and 11th Battalions took a distinguished part.

The 20th Division attacked Guillemont with the 59th Brigade on the right, and the 47th Brigade, attached from the 16th Division, on the left. Sickness, caused by the bad weather and gas shelling, had greatly reduced the strength of the 60th Brigade, and it had been relieved on August 31 by the 47th Brigade. On the night of the 2nd/3rd the 59th Brigade had relieved the 61st. All four brigades were greatly below strength. The 10th K.R.R.C. attacked in the front line on the left of the 59th Brigade. D Company, 11th K.R.R.C., was attached to the 10th Battalion, and acted as Battalion Reserve. Zero hour was 12 noon, and the intense barrage was only to come down on the German front line at that hour. For some unexplained reason—the company commander was killed—C Company, 10th K.R.R.C., went over the top just before zero hour, and suffered considerably from our barrage, as they had reached the enemy's front line when it came down. The 6th Connaught Rangers, on the right of the 47th Brigade, followed suit. At 12 noon the rest of the front line advanced very rapidly, and were into the enemy's front line with little opposition. The Connaught Rangers ran over their objective, the west edge of the village, without 'mopping up,' which exposed the left flank of the 10th K.R.R.C. to fire from the enemy who had been left behind. Lieut.-Colonel Blacklock, Commanding the 10th Battalion, very promptly rectified this by detaching A company and a platoon of D Company, 11th K.R.R.C., to clear up in rear of the Connaught Rangers, which they did very efficiently. The said platoon was led by the Forward Observation Officer of the supporting artillery, who, to the neglect of his own duties, had taken part in the attack, and had already been wounded. Neither his name, nor the remarks of his Commanding Officer when they next met, are on record. So close did the troops keep up to the barrage that the next objective, the eastern edge of the village, was reached before the advertised time, and by 1.30 p.m. a line was being consolidated just inside the eastern edge of the village. By half-past three the third objective, the road running due south from Ginchy, had been reached. As no further advance could be made owing to the failure of the 5th Division on the right and the 7th on the left, the 20th Division dug in on the line it had won, with flanks thrown back to connect with the divisions on its right and left.

In addition to the company attached to the 10th Battalion, all the companies of the 11th Battalion had taken their part in the battle. One company which had been in Brigade Reserve was employed consolidating in Guillemont and digging a communication trench; the other two had been carrying up bombs and Stokes-mortar ammunition all day. They all came in for a lot of shelling. The Battalion Headquarters of the 10th Battalion had to be changed five or six times during the day.

Our 12th Battalion, 60th Brigade, came up at 10 p.m., and relieved the Royal Irish, 47th Brigade.

On September 4 the 5th Division captured Falfemont Farm, upon which they and the 20th Division pushed out patrols to Leuze Wood, and the 20th Division occupied what was to have been their final objective on the 3rd, reaching from the west corner of Leuze Wood in a north-westerly direction to the railway. The Division was relieved by the 16th Division on the night of September 4/5, though the 10th Battalion was not relieved till 7 a.m., owing to the relieving battalion having lost its way.

The casualties of the 10th Battalion were: officers—

killed, Lieutenant R. de H. M. Bell; wounded and missing, later reported killed, 2nd Lieutenant S. L. Hocken; wounded, Lieut.-Colonel C. A. Blacklock, D.S.O.; 2nd Lieutenants R. S. G. Vigers, C. A. L. Rickett, S. J. Male, G. Richardson, G. N. Reles, D. G. Davies; other ranks—killed 39; wounded 202; missing 22.

The 11th Battalion lost 2nd Lieutenant A. L. Forrest, killed, and 2nd Lieutenant A. H. Horton, wounded.

Another of our battalions to be engaged on September 3 was the 17th, of the 117th Brigade, 39th Division, commanded by Lieut.-Colonel E. F. Ward. This Division of the Reserve Army attacked north of the Ancre, to cover the left flank of the 49th Division. The brigades in this division were all very weak. Of the two attacking brigades the 116th, with an extra battalion, 4/5th Royal Highlanders, attached, only amounted to 79 officers and 1,897 other ranks; the 117th Brigade, 89 officers, 2,714 other ranks. The 116th Brigade attacked on the right, the 117th on the left. Zero hour was 5.10 a.m. The German first line was entered with few casualties except in the 16th Rifle Brigade. The second-line companies then passed through to attack the support line. This attack was less successful and much more expensive, the failure of the attack of the 49th Division exposing the right of the 39th to enfilade fire. At 8 a.m. both brigades reinforced their front line, but the support line was only reached in a few places. At 9.33 a.m. the right battalion of the left brigade was reported to be back in its own front line. At 10.15 a.m. both attacking brigades of the 49th Division were driven back to their own line by strong counter-attacks. At 11.35 a.m. the enemy's first line was only held by the 39th Division in a few places. Owing to the failure of the 49th Division, the advance of the 39th became no longer necessary, and the Divisional Commander ordered a withdrawal to the original line. A few parties held out in the enemy's front line till after dark. The following account of the 17th Battalion's part in the action is taken from its 'War Diary':

'At 5.10 a.m., on September 3, 1916, the opening bombardment of the enemy's position commenced, and a barrage was placed on his front line. The two assaulting battalions of the brigade (the 16th Rifle Brigade on the right and the 17th Notts and Derby Regiment on the left) advanced to the attack. An intense barrage by guns of all calibre was placed by the enemy on No Man's Land, front line and communication trenches, through which B and C Companies again moved up and occupied our front line. [They had been relieved in the front line by the assaulting battalions the night before.]

'At 6.45 a.m. a message was received from the 17th Notts and Derby Regiment that the German first line had been gained, but that support was urgently needed. Orders were issued to officers commanding B and C Companies, and at 8 a.m. the two companies moved forward to support under a heavy barrage. During their advance across No Man's Land, all officers and a large proportion of the N.C.O.s became casualties, besides incurring heavy losses in the ranks. The German first line, however, was reached by several small parties, one at least pushing up a communication trench nearly to the second line. This party, originally consisting of two sergeants and about ten men, held their ground against repeated bombing attacks by the enemy for about five hours. The two sergeants were killed early in the fight, upon which C/4655 Rifleman T. V. Mills immediately took command. He kept the men together, and not until their supply of bombs had given out, and their depleted numbers made further fighting useless, did he withdraw into our lines, bringing his remaining men in safely.

'Communication between the advanced attacking troops and Battalion Headquarters was very limited, runners being unable to get through the barrage. Lieutenant K. T. Spinney, Signalling Officer, with an orderly, crossed over to the German line, but was unable to get in touch with either the 17th Notts and Derby Regiment or our own companies. He was forced to retire to our own lines, owing to the presence of small parties of the enemy, four of whom he shot. He returned safely to Battalion Headquarters, having, however, to leave his orderly, who was wounded, in No Man's Land. Shortly after his return Lieutenant Spinney was hit by a piece of shell at the entrance to Battalion Headquarters dug-out, and killed.

'By this time news was received that the attack on the right by the 16th Rifle Brigade had failed. They were ordered to attack again at 11.30 a.m., and A and D Companies of this battalion, who had moved up to the front trenches on B and C moving out, moved out to support them, assembling in No Man's Land. Shortly afterwards the attack was cancelled by Brigade orders, and at 1 p.m. orders from Brigade were received to withdraw all troops to our lines. Under great difficulty, and a heavy hostile fire, this was done, and at 7.55 p.m., under orders from Brigade, the Battalion, relieved by the 1st Cambridgeshire Regiment, withdrew from the trenches, and marched to Mailly Maillet Woods for the night.

'The casualties incurred throughout the operation were: officers—killed, Captains M. F. Hecht, H. J. Hulks; Lieutenant K. T. Spinney; 2nd Lieutenants A. J. B. Butcher, J. G. Goffey; died of wounds, 2nd Lieutenants A. B. Saunders, T. H. Lacey; wounded, Captains A. J. Powles-Curtis, T. W. Kirk; Lieutenant C. R. R. Gidney; 2nd Lieutenant G. Montgomery; missing, Lieutenant P. K. S. Ewen; 2nd Lieutenants A. J. Bailey and S. H. F. Woolmer. Subsequently, Captain Powles-Curtis died of wounds on September 11, and it was found that the three missing officers were all killed. In other ranks the casualties were: killed 36, wounded 149, missing 97, wounded and missing 9, died of wounds 1, wounded (shell shock) 7, and wounded (gassed) 5. The strength of the Battalion going into action was 21 officers (including the M.O.) and 635 other ranks.'

On September 4, as has been related, troops of the XIV Corps captured Falfemont Farm and reached Leuze Wood, but a renewed attack on Ginchy by the XV Corps failed. Next day most of the remainder of Leuze Wood was occupied, and on the morning of the 6th the whole wood was clear of the enemy. In the afternoon the 7th Division took Ginchy, but were driven out later by shell fire.

On September 9 there was an attack by the XIV and XV Corps on the whole front from Leuze Wood to High Wood (both inclusive).

On the XIV Corps front the 56th Division gained ground beyond Leuze Wood and the 16th Division captured Ginchy, but everywhere else on that corps front the attack failed. During the following night the Guards Division relieved the 16th.

On the XV Corps front the 1st Division attacked in High Wood and Wood Lane, a trench running south-east from the edge of the wood. The 2nd Brigade attacked this trench and a part of the wood. Our 2nd Battalion, in the command of which Major R. N. Abadie had succeeded Major Atkinson, attacked on the right, with the 2nd Royal Sussex on their left, and the 1st Northamptonshire beyond them in the wood. The attack was a brilliant success, and casualties were moderate as things went on the Somme. To quote the ‘ War Diary ’:

‘ At 4.45 p.m. our artillery opened an intense barrage on Wood Lane, and at the same time our men went over the parapet. The assault, which was delivered with much dash, was quite successful on the left. Here C Company carried their objective without any great effort or much loss. On the right D Company was held up by machine-gun fire, and the two platoons of B Company who were to support the attack on this flank were also stopped. Sergeant-Major Hyde was killed while endeavouring to lead forward the men of B Company. A fresh attack was organised on this flank. Stokes mortars and Lewis-gun fire subdued the enemy’s resistance, and on the threat of assault the remainder of the Germans surrendered. Their machine guns and the teams that had fought them had been put out of action by our Stokes mortars, and by 2nd Lieutenant Munro’s fire from a Lewis gun. The remains of D Company (every officer of whom had been hit), supported by B Company, then carried their objective. Connection was established with the 5th King’s Liverpool Regiment on the right, and with C Company on the left. C Company at the same time was in touch with the 2nd Royal Sussex, so that the whole line was firmly established in Wood Lane. The remainder of the day and the whole night were occupied in consolidating these positions.'

Next day the captured line having been turned, and being lightly held by posts and Lewis guns, the enemy began to shell it heavily, and parties of them were continually seen crossing the front into High Wood, in which, evidently, a counter-attack was being prepared. Our artillery put down a heavy barrage on the wood, and the attack never developed. On the night of the 10th/11th the Battalion was relieved by the New Zealanders.

The Battalion lost 2nd Lieutenants A. E. M. A. Hawke and A. H. B. Langton, both of whom died of wounds, and Captains F. G. Fison, L. A. Blackett, 2nd Lieutenants J. W. D. Sneddon, B. C. Munro, J. H. Lee, C. W. Beadel, wounded. The casualties among other ranks were 24 killed, 82 wounded, 36 missing. The Battalion took 59 prisoners and two machine guns.

On September 12 the bombardment opened for the big attack, now fixed for the 15th. The French this day attacked north of the Somme, captured Bouchavesnes[1] and L'Abbé Wood Farm, and took 1,500 prisoners. During the night of the 11th/12th the 14th Division commenced the relief of the 55th. On the 14th the weather, which the day before had been cloudy and showery and threatened another postponement, cleared, and it was fine all day.

Flers-Courcelette

On the 15th the great attack which had been so long awaited and so often postponed was launched, and brought the biggest advance made so far in the battle of the Somme, though it did not do all that was hoped for it. The fourth, and last, objective was to include the villages of Morval,

[1] Map V.

Lesbœufs, and Gueudecourt, and, if the best happened, the Cavalry Corps was to go through.

In the result the troops reached, roughly, the line of their third objective. In places they fell short of this (the two right Divisions of the XIV Corps failed to take even their first objective). The Guards Division took their second objective, but did not get near their third, being seriously handicapped by the failure on their right. The right of the III Corps did not get much beyond their first objective, which included clearing the enemy out of the northern part of High Wood, always a difficult nut to crack. Their left, however, even exceeded the day's programme by taking Martinpuich, as did the Reserve Army in the capture of Courcelette.

The chief interest of the day's operations was the appearance of the tanks for the first time on the field of battle.

The instructions for their use on their début are interesting. Their advance was to be timed to reach the first objective five minutes before the infantry, a gap 100 yards wide being left in the barrage as a route for each tank. Their pace was calculated to be 15 yards a minute over badly shelled ground and 33 yards on good ground, while downhill on good ground they might be expected to do 50 yards a minute. Advancing to the second objective they were to accompany the infantry behind a creeping barrage. For the third and subsequent objectives, when there was to be no creeping barrage, they were to take sufficient start to arrive ahead of the infantry. If delayed, infantry were on no account to wait for them.

Great things were expected of them, especially as regards their moral effect on the enemy, and by no one more than their own people. Much has been said of the misuse of tanks, in their early days, by generals who knew nothing about them, the suggestion being that they were asked to perform impossibilities. The writer's experience has been that the difficulty was to find anything that the tank-man would admit that a tank could not do. Their value was shown on this occasion by the way in which, where they were present, the infantry were never held up; on every occasion on which infantry was held up, the tank that should have been with it had broken down. The disappointment was in the number of breakdowns. Of forty tanks which were to go over the top with the Fourth Army only twenty-four crossed the front line, and of these seven more broke down in the early stages of the attack. By noon of September 18, out of forty-two tanks (two had been in support on the first day), thirteen were fit, fourteen to sixteen derelict, thirteen to fifteen repairable or under repair. Only three had been put out of action by shell fire when in motion.

As has been said, the attack of the right and centre of the XIV Corps was a failure. Of sixteen tanks allotted to the Corps, six broke down before reaching their point of assembly. The 6th Division was left with 1 tank for the attack of a strong point in the front line known as the Quadrilateral, which had already resisted several attempts to take it. This tank lost its periscope, and was blinded when close to the enemy's line, and this point held the Division up for the rest of the day. The Guards Division in their advance lost heavily from enfilade fire owing to the failure on their right.

The XV Corps made the biggest advance of the day, their final line forming a broad salient round the village of Flers. The Corps attacked with the 14th Division on the right, the 41st in the centre, and the New Zealand Division on the left.

The 14th Division had to make a preliminary attack,

before zero hour, to clear the eastern edge of Delville Wood and the trenches immediately to the east of it, an area of which they had had a bitter experience on August 24. The 41st Brigade were to take the preliminary, first, and second objectives, when the 42nd Brigade were to go through and take the third and fourth. The line of advance of their right led from half-way between Ginchy and Delville Wood to half-way between Les Bœufs and Gueudecourt.

The preliminary attack took place at 5.30 a.m., and was accompanied by a tank, but the trenches were found to be unoccupied.

At zero hour, 6.20 a.m., the 41st Brigade advanced; front line, 8th Rifle Brigade on right, 8th K.R.R.C. on left; second line, 7th Rifle Brigade right, 7th K.R.R.C. left. About 150 yards from the start our 8th Battalion met small outposts of the enemy in shell holes; these were easily driven in or disposed of, but 1 officer was wounded by a bomb. The first trench reached was carried by them with a rush, heavy casualties being inflicted on the enemy, but they lost a good many men from machine-gun fire, and from running into their own barrage. At 6.30 a.m. the enemy awoke to the fact of an attack, and put down a heavy barrage, but luckily most of it fell behind the attacking troops. The trench which formed the second objective had been almost obliterated by our bombardment, but the enemy, occupying the approximate line of it in shell holes, put up a stout resistance, and our first line suffered heavily before they had turned them out and started consolidating. The Officer Commanding 8th K.R.R.C., in his report, says that the tanks were a hindrance, owing to the barrage being timed so slow to keep back to their pace. (It must be remembered that he had come across no strongly held machine-gun nests or uncut wire. Other battalions are most grateful for the help the tanks gave them at critical moments.) He is full of praise of the heavy bombardment, and says he saw no bit of wire more than a foot long. The 8th Battalion held this line for the rest of the day, and were heavily shelled. They were relieved in the evening by the 21st Division. Their casualties for the day were: 11 officers wounded; 320 other ranks killed, wounded, and missing.

At the first objective the second line of the 41st Brigade passed through the first (7th Rifle Brigade on right, 7th K.R.R.C. on left), attacked and occupied the second objective, and started consolidating. The Officer Commanding 7th Battalion reports that they did not meet with much resistance, but lost heavily from shell fire in the advance; also that many men in their ardour went on with the next wave (42nd Brigade), and even some with the 41st Division, on the left, and that few of these returned. The 7th Battalion remained dug in on this line for the rest of the day, and were relieved at dusk by the 43rd Brigade. They then returned to trenches on the east side of Delville Wood, where they spent the next day, still under heavy shell fire. They were withdrawn to Fricourt in the evening. Their casualties for the two days were: officers—killed, Captain F. G. de Satgé; died of wounds, 2nd Lieutenants M. L. R. Romer, E. S. Blackbourn; wounded, Major R. Paget, Captain E. C. Bland, 2nd Lieutenants R. W. V. Midlane, W. W. Palmer, H. S. Brewster, J. E. C. Lamb, G. H. Edwards, G. L. Spreckley, Captain and Adjutant M. J. St. Aubyn, Captain W. Morrison, R.A.M.C.; other ranks—killed 21, wounded 189, missing 120.

The 42nd Brigade advanced at 7 a.m.; first line, 9th Rifle Brigade on right, 5th King's Shropshire Light Infantry on left; second line, 9th K.R.R.C. on right,

5th Oxford and Bucks Light Infantry on left. About 7.25 a.m. our 9th Battalion came under the fire of a machine gun about 100 yards from their right flank. This was in the area of the Guards Division, and it is not clear whether the Guards had not yet reached it, had missed it by going too much to the right, or had swept over it without mopping it up. Any one of these explanations is possible, as the Guards Division do not seem to have got on as far as the 14th Division, and it was not till the 42nd Brigade had been some time at the limit of their advance that their right could get any touch with the Guards. Anyhow, our 9th Battalion got the full benefit of this gun and, not only were there heavy casualties from it in the front line of the Battalion, but it wrought havoc in Battalion Headquarters, the Commanding Officer, Lieut.-Colonel E. W. Benson, being killed, the Adjutant, Captain C. D. Lacey, wounded, and all the battalion signallers knocked out. Lieut.-Colonel Benson was the only son of Sir Frank Benson, and had served for some years in the Cheshire Regiment. He had been gazetted Lieutenant to the 9th Rifle Brigade in September 1914, and had been transferred to our 9th Battalion, in which he became a Captain in June 1915. He reached the rank of temporary Lieut.-Colonel at the age of twenty-nine. He was severely wounded at Hooge in July 1915, being awarded the M.C., and was mentioned in despatches. His death was a great loss to the Regiment and the Army. The machine gun was silenced by two Lewis guns being turned on to it while it was rushed by a party of bombers of the Rifle Brigade. Six more officers were all hit about the same time. Between 8.30 and 9 a.m. the Battalion passed over the second objective, which was being consolidated by the 41st Brigade, following close on the heels of the 9th Rifle Brigade. Shortly after this Sergeant Elderfield, commanding the remains of a platoon in the front line, saw two German field guns firing towards Flers from the sunken road about 1,000 yards east of that village. He and his party immediately rushed the guns, chasing the gunners all down the sunken road, and killing seven of them. Soon afterwards, the barrage having either ceased or got ahead of the infantry, the 9th Rifle Brigade, pressing on to attack a trench in the third objective, which was strongly held, were brought to a standstill with very heavy losses. Major Porter, who had succeeded to the command on the death of Lieut.-Colonel Benson, decided to dig in where he was, being in touch with the 5th Oxford and Bucks Light Infantry on his left. His right was in the air, although about noon a party of Guardsmen from three different battalions, with a Lewis gun, joined his battalion, but none of them knew the whereabouts of their own units. During the afternoon the Irish Guards came up into the second objective, and sent forward a line of picquets to get in touch with the right of our 9th Battalion. The enemy seemed to be preparing counter-attacks all the afternoon, but only made one or two half-hearted attempts to carry them out. The night passed quietly, and at 4 a.m. the Battalion was relieved by a battalion of the 43rd Brigade. The casualties of the battalion were : killed, Lieut.-Colonel E. W. Benson and Captains H. K. Meek, H. Dowson, M.C. ; 2nd Lieutenant W. S. Glegg ; wounded, Captain C. D. Lacey ; Lieutenants A. Cook, C. R. Hollway, W. S. M. Brady ; 2nd Lieutenants R. Singlehurst, R. T. Ridley, R. B. Van Praagh ; other ranks—killed 22, wounded 144, missing 66.

Next to the left of the 14th Division came the 41st. It attacked with the 124th Brigade on the right with two battalions in the front line—10th Queen's on the right, 21st K.R.R.C. on the left ; the 122nd Brigade was on the left, with the 15th Hampshire on the right, the 18th K.R.R.C. on the left. The dividing line between the two brigades passed through the middle of the village of Flers. The 18th Battalion made an unfortunate start, which might well have affected the whole operation. Just as the attack was about to commence, the Commanding Officer (Lieut.-Colonel C. P. Marten, West Yorkshire Regiment), the Adjutant (Captain F. Walton),[1] the Signalling Officer (Lieutenant W. S. Mathews), and the Trench Mortar Officer (Lieutenant D. S. D. Clark) were all killed by one shell. It speaks volumes for the training and discipline of the Battalion that, after this catastrophe, the attack was carried to a successful conclusion. At 6.20 a.m. the infantry advanced behind the barrage, and the first objective was taken at about 6.45. The Germans did not stand except for the machine-gun detachments, which, as usual, stuck it out manfully, and inflicted heavy casualties on the attackers, especially among the officers. Seven out of ten tanks had crossed the front line, and reached the objective two minutes ahead of the infantry. Consolidation was begun at once, and at 7.20 a.m. the attack was continued behind the barrage, four tanks being still in action. The infantry got ahead of the tanks, but there was little opposition. The enemy's barrage, however, was very heavy. In one place the troops were stopped by uncut wire, but two tanks came up and made gaps in it. By 8 a.m. the second objective, a trench running through the extreme southern end of Flers, had been taken, and consolidation begun. At 8.10 a.m. 4 tanks entered Flers, followed by the infantry. The tanks did most effective work hunting out machine-gun nests. The village was cleared by 10 a.m., but there

[1] Captain Walton had served for sixteen years in the ranks of the Regiment. Going out as a Company-Sergeant-Major in the 2nd Battalion in August 1914, he was given a commission for gallantry in action. Before his death he had been twice wounded and mentioned in despatches.

was much disorganisation and mixing of units owing to the heavy casualties among the officers. The village was very heavily shelled, and at one time it looked as if the troops would be shelled out of it. At 10.20 a.m. a party of about 100 men and 2 machine guns, led by Captain R. Baskett, 18th K.R.R.C., reached the third objective, and established themselves in two works, called Box and Cox, just north of the village, in touch with the New Zealanders on their left. At this time the 124th Brigade had got out of touch to the east of the village, but in touch with the 14th Division. Lieut.-Colonel the Earl of Feversham, Commanding the 21st K.R.R.C., and Lieut.-Colonel Oakley, 10th Queen's, with as many men as they could collect, advanced against the third objective, the same trench which, farther along, had been the limit of the advance of the 9th Rifle Brigade, captured it and held it for some time against more than one counter-attack. During this time Lord Faversham was killed. This party was in the end obliged to fall back east of the village. However, by the end of the day a line was established by the Division running round the north side of the village and connecting up with the 14th Division on the right and the New Zealanders on the left. This was the greatest advance made by any division in the course of the day.

The casualties of our two battalions were: 18th Battalion: officers—killed, in addition to those already named, Major P. G. Sadd, Captain J. B. Lester, Lieutenant C. N. Curwen, 2nd Lieutenant J. J. Langford; wounded 7; other ranks—killed 57, wounded 227, died of wounds 3, missing 59. Total of all ranks, 360. 21st Battalion: officers—killed, Lieut.-Colonel the Earl of Feversham, 2nd Lieutenants T. P. A. Hervey, R. B. Nivison; wounded 10; other ranks—killed 54, wounded 256, missing 70. Total of all ranks, 394.

The 21st Battalion were relieved at 3 a.m. next day by the 11th Queen's; the 18th Battalion were not relieved till September 18.

As before mentioned, the III Corps had a lot of trouble with High Wood, and did not get far beyond it, but on their left the 15th Division reported the capture of Martinpuich at 5.15 p.m., and in the Reserve Army the I Canadian Corps had taken Courcelette by 6 p.m.

The attack was renewed next morning at 9.25 a.m., but little progress was made. The Guards Division slightly extended their gains of the previous day, and were relieved by the 20th Division during the night. The 14th Division gained a portion of the trench facing Gueudecourt which had stopped them the previous day, but were obliged to evacuate it later. The 41st Division made no progress. The New Zealand Division repulsed a counter-attack just before zero hour, and then gained their first objective, facing north-west. They beat off another counter-attack between 2 and 3 p.m. and, subsequently, several more were broken up by artillery fire. During the ensuing night the 14th Division were relieved by the 21st.

There were no important operations on the 17th on the British Expeditionary Force front, but, south of the Somme, the French captured three villages and took 1,000 prisoners. On the 20th Division front the 59th Brigade were ordered to capture a trench running almost at right angles to the one they occupied, as a jumping-off place for the next attack on Lesbœufs. The 11th Rifle Brigade were to attack on the right, the 10th Rifle Brigade in the centre, the 11th K.R.R.C. on the left. There was to be a heavy-artillery bombardment in the afternoon, followed by an intense field-gun barrage at zero hour, 6.30 p.m., September 17, when the infantry were to leave their trenches, make a complete right-form, and then attack.

The 11th Battalion 'War Diary' says: 'At zero hour the intense bombardment was imperceptible.' The attackers came under intense machine-gun fire as soon as they left their trenches. The 11th K.R.R.C. occupied a part of their objective, but were obliged to withdraw, as both battalions of the Rifle Brigade had been unable to get forward, and the battalion of the 21st Division, supposed to co-operate on the left, was not to be seen. The operation ended with the attackers back whence they started. Our 11th Battalion lost: killed 17, missing 6, wounded 84; officers—2nd Lieutenant A. J. Gilpin killed, and Captain E. S. A. Baynes, Lieutenant F. D. Steen, and 2nd Lieutenant K. D. Price wounded.

On this day the casualties of the Fourth Army in the battle of the Somme passed the 200,000 mark.

On September 18 a series of small attacks were made to secure jumping-off places for a renewal of the big attack which was due to take place on the 21st. The 6th Division at last captured the Quadrilateral, which had held up the whole XIV Corps for so long. On the 17th and 18th the enemy made heavy counter-attacks on the trenches held by our 12th Battalion, but was beaten off with severe losses. The Battalion's casualties included: Lieutenant S. R. Perry killed, and 2nd Lieutenants C. H. Bazeley and G. M. W. Bulkeley-Hughes wounded. The weather had broken again, and movement was very difficult. Several of the attacks failed, and there was not much gained anywhere. For the next few days the weather went from bad to worse, and the attack due for the 21st could not come off till the 25th.

Morval

On that day a general attack was launched, at 12.35 p.m., by the French and the Fourth Army, from the Somme to Martinpuich. The French gained some ground, but were not so successful as they had usually been in recent attacks. For the Fourth Army it was one of the best days they had had since the battle began. Most of the final objectives were gained, including the villages of Morval and Lesbœufs. The only failure was at Gueudecourt, which the 21st Division could not take, chiefly owing to uncut wire. Tanks were not used against Gueudecourt, as it was thought that in such very open country they would be sure to be knocked out. The Germans, on the whole, did not resist so stoutly as usual, and the casualties in the British Expeditionary Force were not so heavy as in most previous attacks. Some of the hardest fighting was on the 1st Division front, about half-way between Flers and Martinpuich.

The fight was renewed next morning. British and French together entered Combles, which the enemy had evacuated during the night. The 21st Division took Gueudecourt, and a strong counter-attack, approaching Gueudecourt and Lesbœufs, was broken up by our field artillery. There was hard fighting on the 1st Division front without any further gain of ground, but the Reserve Army made a successful attack with the Canadian and II Corps.

On the 27th the 55th and New Zealand Divisions made a considerable advance on a front of 2,500 yards, about a mile north of Flers. Further trench fighting on the front of the 1st Division was indecisive. Our 2nd Battalion had taken part in five bombing attacks in the last three days. The first was on the night of the 25th/26th, and was successful, 130 yards of trench being taken, chiefly—as the account in the 'Chronicle' says—'by the bravery and resolution of No. 8, Rhodesian, platoon.' At 2.30 p.m., on the 26th, another attack was made, this time unsuccessfully. Again at 11 p.m. they drove the Germans down 40 yards of trench, and two more attacks were made without result on the 27th. The Battalion was relieved on the night of the 27th/28th. During the three days they had lost Captain L. A. Ballance killed, Lieutenant W. P. Bristowe, 2nd Lieutenants A. W. Farman, N. F. E. Anson wounded; other ranks—21 killed, 80 wounded, and 8 missing, of whom 3 rejoined, the other 5 having been killed.

Le Transloy

During the night of the 27th/28th, the French took over from the Fourth Army up to half-way between Morval and Lesbœufs.

On the afternoon of October 1 the New Zealand Division (XV Corps) and all three Divisions of the III Corps attacked and gained a lot of ground east and west of Eaucourt L'Abbaye, the left of the attack getting right up to Le Sars. There was a failure in the middle which left a gap in the new line of some half-mile about Eaucourt L'Abbaye itself, but this pocket was occupied on the 3rd with little opposition.

After another spell of constant rain, the weather improved sufficiently to allow the attack to be renewed on October 7. It was launched along the whole front of the Fourth Army, and was generally unsuccessful. There were small gains by the 20th Division east of Gueudecourt, and greater ones by the 23rd Division at Le Sars. Our 12th Battalion had two companies engaged in the attack of the 20th Division and lost 90 of all ranks, including 3 officers wounded: Captain F. G. Read, 2nd Lieutenants D. G. Bennett, R. F. P. Howarth. The other half-battalion, in reserve, had 20 casualties from shell fire. The 18th Battalion was in support in the abortive attack of the

41st Division, but was not seriously engaged. The French, on the right, advanced 1,000 yards on a front of 3,500, but, owing to the failure of the neighbouring division of the British Expeditionary Force, they had to throw back their left to prevent having it in the air. The attack was renewed next day on various parts of the front, but generally failed.

The weather had by now completely broken down, the whole battlefield had become a pestilential slough and, so late in the year, a few consecutive fine days did little to improve it. For some time there were no serious operations, though there was constant trench fighting.

On the Reserve Army front a work called the Schwaben Redoubt was a particular bone of contention, each side holding a part of it. On October 14 troops of the 39th Division made a successful attack on the German half, and took 200 prisoners. Two companies of our 17th Battalion took part, under Lieutenants F. L. Brown and L. R. Rawson. They repulsed two counter-attacks next morning with heavy loss to the enemy. Our losses were: officers—wounded, Lieutenant F. L. Brown, 2nd Lieutenant D. Filtness; other ranks—killed 3, wounded 23.

At 3.40 a.m. on the 18th attacks were made by the French Sixth and British Fourth Armies to secure jumping-off places for the next attack. They were only very partially successful. The weather was very bad, and consequently the night was black dark, in spite of a good moon. There was nothing but rain, day after day, and the trenches were knee deep in water.

Ancre Heights

Our 17th Battalion, which had been relieved on the 16th, moved up again into the front line at the Schwaben Redoubt on the 20th. At 4.45 a.m. next day an intense barrage was put down on the front line by the enemy, who attacked at 5 a.m. By the use of *flammenwerfer*, they got a footing in the trenches occupied by C and A Companies (centre and left). They were ejected after fierce fighting, leaving 3 officers and 50 other ranks as prisoners. By 8 a.m. the line was firmly re-established, and 1 other officer and 30 other ranks had been taken, together with two *flammenwerfer* and a field telephone. The enemy's numbers were estimated at 400, and included picked storm-troops of the 28*th Reserve Division* and companies from four different regiments. The Battalion was flooded by a stream of congratulatory orders and messages. Their casualties were: officers—killed, Captain E. H. Kitchin, 2nd Lieutenant G. H. Le S. Honey; wounded, 2nd Lieutenant H. A. Attwood; other ranks—killed 14, died of wounds 1, wounded 66, missing 7.

On October 17 G.H.Q. had issued an appreciation of the situation, which showed that, owing to the delays caused by the bad weather and its probable continuance, and to the fact that, generally, progress had been less than had been hoped for, the Commander-in-Chief had abandoned the idea of winning a decisive victory in the autumn of 1916, and that his object was to gain a position on high ground which would both be a better line on which to spend the winter and a more suitable one from which to renew the attack in the spring. With this object the Reserve Army was to attack from the west on the right bank of the Ancre and from the south on its left bank. The ultimate line to be held would follow the ridge from Serre to the north of Miraumont, joining up with the Fourth Army, which was to gain the high ground west of Bapaume. With this object, attacks were to be launched about the 23rd, and it was hoped to gain the ultimate objective by the end of the month.

Meanwhile, the weather went from bad to worse. A few minor operations were attempted, but were generally unsuccessful. From October 30 the Reserve Army became known as the Fifth Army.

On November 2 a successful attack was made by one battalion on the XIV Corps front, doing a good deal of damage to the enemy with very little loss to themselves. This was repeated next day. It was reported that the state of the German trenches was as bad as or worse than our own, and that was about as bad as could be. Men were constantly being buried by the sides of trenches falling in, and the communication trenches were in such a state that there was the greatest difficulty in bringing up supplies except over the open.

On November 5, after a few days of comparatively fine weather, an attack was delivered along most of the front of the Fourth Army and by the French on the right. Nearly everywhere, either the attack failed from the outset or what was gained at first was lost later. The only success was gained by the 100th Brigade, 33rd Division, and our 16th Battalion took a distinguished part in it. It is thus described in the 'Chronicle' of 1916, the account being taken from the Battalion 'War Diary':

'The attack was made by C and D Companies. The objective for the Battalion was Hazy Trench [east of Lesbœufs]. The attack was very successful, and casualties were comparatively few. This was mainly due to the example of determination and heroism exhibited by Captain Hon. L. Lindsay, who reorganised and consolidated the line; and also to a new system of barrage adopted, which, instead of being the usual creeping one, was a rolling one. Platoons attacked in echelon, immediately the barrage rolled by, hence there was a constant attack on small sections of the enemy trench.'

Great credit was due to 2nd Lieutenant G. H. Cholmondeley, who was the leader of the right platoon, which went over in spite of the battalion immediately on our right failing to attack. The casualties were: officers—wounded, 2nd Lieutenants C. R. Lighton, H. G. Cholmondeley, C. M. Murray-Ainsley, G. A. Goody (died of wounds); other ranks—killed 39, wounded 113, missing 11. Hardly what one would call 'comparatively few,' considering that only half the Battalion went over. The Battalion was relieved on the night of the 6th/7th.

On the rest of the front the Anzac Corps, which had relieved the XV on October 30, and the III Corps, after considerable gains, were all driven back to their original line. The French Sixth Army, which had attacked at the same time, gained most of its objectives, but lost them all except immediately south of Saillisel.

On November 6 there was a conference at Fourth Army Headquarters, at which the Army Commander passed on to Corps Commanders the gist of the Commander-in-Chief's appreciation of October 17, saying that the chief object of operations was now not to break through, but to contain the enemy and prevent him detaching to the Eastern Front. Operations on this scale would be continued throughout the winter, when weather permitted.

Ancre

The bad weather continued, and no operations were possible until, on November 13, the Fifth Army (II, V, and XIII Corps), on whose front the ground was drier and had been less cut up by shell fire, attacked on a front of about 9,000 yards, from one mile north-east of Thiepval to one mile north-west of Serre. South of the Ancre all objectives were gained to a depth of 1,600 yards. This attack was carried out by the 19th and 39th Divisions. North of the Ancre the outskirts of Beaucourt were reached by the 63rd (Naval) Division. Beaumont Hamel was captured by the

51st Division. North of Beaumont Hamel the 2nd Division took trenches to a depth of 500 yards. The attack on Serre failed. On the whole front about 4,000 unwounded prisoners were taken.

The 63rd Division had made a very successful attack. The troops managed to keep close up to the barrage, which on some parts of the front was impossible owing to the state of the ground, though the barrage only advanced 100 yards in five minutes ; two tanks which accompanied the advance disposed of a strong-point which was holding out, and which disgorged 300 to 400 prisoners ; but, owing to the division next on the left not having got farther than the eastern outskirts of Beaumont Hamel, the left of the 63rd Division was in the air, their losses also had been heavy ; the 111th Brigade, 37th Division, were therefore sent up to reinforce them and to carry the attack farther next day. The 111th Brigade were placed under the orders of the G.O.C. 63rd Division (Major-General C. Shute, lately commanding the 59th Brigade, 20th Division). He sent them up to reinforce the 189th Brigade, then just west of Beaucourt. The trench occupied by this brigade's front line was held by Germans farther to the left. The 13th K.R.R.C. (Lieut.-Colonel R. Chester-Master) were ordered to prolong the line of the 189th Brigade to the left. To do this they had first to make room for themselves by bombing the enemy out, which was done by the Battalion Scouts under 2nd Lieutenant F. S. Pemberton and the bombers under 2nd Lieutenant R. G. Humphreys, taking 50 prisoners. The Battalion dug in, with C and D Companies, under Captains Proctor and Stocks, in front line ; A and B, under Lieutenant C. G. Johnstone and Captain R. S. T. Cochrane, in second line.

The orders for the 14th were that at 6 a.m. the 13th Royal Fusiliers and 13th Rifle Brigade should come up on the left of the 13th K.R.R.C. and take the prolongation of the trench held by that battalion. An hour later all were to go forward again, and take Beaucourt and the trenches to the left of it.

The attack launched at 6 a.m. was held up 200 yards short of its objective. At 7.30 a.m. the remains of the 189th Brigade and our 13th Battalion started their attack on the village and the 13th Royal Fusiliers and 13th Rifle Brigade moved forward at the same time. By 8 a.m. the 13th K.R.R.C. had taken the village. The two battalions on the left took the trench that had been their first objective, but could not get farther, as their left was in the air.

Just before the attack started a runner came from C Company bringing word that all three officers of the company, Captain J. Proctor, 2nd Lieutenant M. L. Jacks, and 2nd Lieutenant E. C. Holmes, were casualties; the last-named having been killed. Lieutenant G. W. Hawkins, Battalion Lewis-gun Officer, was sent up to take over the Company. As the Battalion advanced through the village, the enemy kept emerging from dug-outs, where they had taken shelter from the bombardment. These parties were engaged by the bombers and surrendered one by one. On reaching their objective, at the far edge of the village, the front line dug itself in under the direction of Captain Stocks, who was the only company commander left, and who had particularly distinguished himself in the attack. A great many prisoners were taken, 2 officers and 40 men being caught in one dug-out. The Battalion was relieved from the front line on the 15th, but was back in it again next day. On the 18th parties of Lewis gunners of the Battalion supplied covering fire for an attack going on across the river; 2nd Lieutenant Pemberton was wounded on this duty. The Battalion was finally relieved on the evening of the 20th, and passed out of the Ancre area. The casualties among officers at Beaucourt had been : killed—Lieutenant G. W. Hawkins ; 2nd Lieutenant E. C. Holmes ; wounded—Captains R. S. T. Cochrane, J. L. Stocks, J. Proctor ; Lieutenant C. G. Johnstone ; 2nd Lieutenants M. L. Jacks, F. Atkinson, H. Lines. A great many of the losses were due to the shrapnel barrage, put down for the 6 a.m. attack, and which overlapped on to the part of the trench held by our men.

On the 13th the 2nd Division had had a partial success against that part of the German line immediately south of Serre. The 5th Brigade and the right company of the right battalion of the 6th Brigade had gained their objectives, but the remainder of the 6th Brigade, and the 3rd Division on its left, were back in their original trenches. Our 1st Battalion had been in reserve.

The orders for the 14th were : for one battalion of the 6th Brigade to form a defensive flank, facing north ; two more battalions (1st K.R.R.C. on the right, 1st Royal Berkshire on the left) with the 23rd Royal Fusiliers in support, all three of the 99th Brigade, were to pass through the 5th Brigade and attack a trench known as Munich Trench. The barrage came down, and the advance began at 6 a.m. It was then quite dark, and there was such a thick mist that, even when daylight came, it was impossible to see more than a short distance. None of the officers or N.C.O.s had seen the ground before. Direction was soon lost. One party of 4 officers and 80 other ranks captured a communication trench running into Munich Trench from the front, and started consolidating under the impression that it was what they were looking for. On discovering their mistake they started a bombing attack on Munich Trench, but were stopped by their own barrage, which had not lifted. Being unable to get in touch with any other troops, and being enfiladed from Munich Trench, they withdrew, taking with them as prisoners 2 officers and 62 other ranks. The experience of another party was much the same. Finally, the Battalion dug in on the line of the sunken road north-east of Beaumont Hamel.

The casualties of the Battalion were: officers—killed, 2nd Lieutenants T. U. Royden and R. F. Lowndes; died of wounds, Lieutenants Hon. F. S. Trench and J. H. T. Liddell; wounded, 2nd Lieutenant G. M. Oakeshott; other ranks—killed 17, wounded 109, missing 12.

The Battalion was withdrawn to the old British front line on the night of the 15th/16th, and was relieved on that of the 16th/17th.

The prisoners taken by the Fifth Army for the two days were over 5,000.

This was practically the end of the battle of the Somme. Fighting went on spasmodically for some time, but there were no big operations. There were times when it had looked like being a big success. It is a very open question whether, if the weather had been, not continually fine, but something approaching to a normal season, the Germans would have been able to stand the succession of blows that would have been rained upon them. As it was, owing to constant postponements from bad weather, the programme simply could not be got through in the time; that is, before the date from which, in an ordinary season, operations might be expected to become impossible. Without going into the much-debated question of the comparison of the losses on both sides, one has only to read the accounts written by the German commanders to know that the enemy was pretty near the end of his tether.

CHAPTER VII

Operations of 5th Army, January to April 1917

On December 3, 1915, Joffre, who had hitherto been only Commander-in-Chief of the French forces in France, had become Commander-in-Chief of all the French Armies, including those in Macedonia.

During the year 1916 he had been losing the confidence of the French public. He was blamed for the defective state of the Verdun defences and for the losses at the Somme, and on December 13, 1916, was replaced by Nivelle.

Nivelle had a plan by which he was going to break the German front in from twenty-four to forty-eight hours. He had had more than any other commander the credit for the French successes at Verdun in the latter half of 1916, and had the full confidence of M. Briand, the Prime Minister.

Briefly, the plan was a series of minor attacks by British and French to pin the enemy down at various points from Arras to Rheims, while a big break through was to be made in Champagne by three armies (27 divisions).

Two armies were to make the break, the third to exploit the success. By the end of the first day the attack was to have penetrated eight or nine kilometres.

Nivelle had the gift, given to few soldiers, of being a persuasive speaker and, having talked over his own politicians, did the same by ours, with the result that, at a conference of the Allies held at Calais in February 1917, the British Prime Minister announced that the War Cabinet had decided to put Haig under the orders of Nivelle, for the period of preparation for and during the forthcoming operations. He had the brutality to make this announcement without having previously communicated it to Haig. Whether this was done through sheer want of tact or in the hopes of extracting his resignation from the victim, without taking the responsibility of asking for it, has not yet been made clear. Haig seems to have had doubts about the soundness of the plan, but was prepared to give it his loyal support.

In the French Army Nivelle does not seem to have inspired much confidence in anyone but his own Staff.

Joffre's desire had been to renew the battle of the Somme at the earliest date that the weather would permit—February if possible—so as to give the enemy no rest; or to deny him the chance of taking the initiative, should he contemplate another Verdun. Haig would have preferred to give his army more time to recover, and wait till the Russians and Italians were ready to join in. He had also, probably, had enough of Napoleon's 'fifth element,' and wanted to start his attack on dry ground. In the event, it turned out that the French themselves could not be ready till April. Joffre and Haig agreed on two main points: that the British Expeditionary Force should take a big part in the 1917 offensive, and that the battle should be a *bataille d'usure.*

If Joffre had survived, the course would probably have been for both allies to resume operations by preliminary attacks on both flanks of the Somme battlefield, to keep the enemy busy.

The coming of Nivelle changed all that. He had no use for the 'wearing out' idea. His plan was to win the war at a blow, which was to be delivered by the French Army. The British Expeditionary Force was to play a minor rôle, which was to consist, firstly, in taking over more line and relieving as many French troops as possible; secondly, in undertaking several preliminary operations, to engage the enemy's attention, and pin down his reserves.

On January 2 Haig informed his Army Commanders of the general plan of operations for the coming year. He tells them: 'The French will withdraw the maximum number of their troops into reserve with a view to the delivery of a decisive attack on a large scale. In order to give this attack the best chance of success, subsidiary attacks will be made north of the River Oise by French and British troops.

'The British attacks will be carried out in the Ancre Valley, opposite Arras, and against the Vimy Ridge by the Fifth, Third, and First Armies respectively.'

He goes on to say that he is going to relieve the French troops on the right of the British Army as far south as the Amiens–Villers-Bretonneux–St. Quentin Road. This relief was to be completed early in February. This was later extended to relieving to the Amiens–Roye Road by the end of February. It was at the same time laid down that the Fourth Army would not undertake offensive operations on a large scale, but was to be ready to carry out limited operations with the purpose of making the enemy think that the battle of the Somme was about to be resumed.

THE CAMPAIGN ON THE ANCRE

The Fifth Army was the first to get under way. Early in January Gough began a series of small, deliberate attacks with strictly limited objectives, by which he gnawed his way bit by bit into the enemy's line. The campaign began in the second week of January with a few small operations east of Beaumont Hamel, which resulted in the capture of some important trench lines and about 400 prisoners with slight casualties. The process continued for some weeks, the enemy not offering much resistance. Sometimes the bombardment was enough to make him retire, and the attacking troops found the trenches empty. The country was still a sea of mud, and life in the trenches was no better than in Flanders. We find in one attack the barrage advancing at the rate of 50 yards in five minutes, which was as fast as our men could move through the mud.

On February 17 our 1st Battalion took part in an attack on the high ground just south of Miraumont. Circumstances seem to have combined against them. Owing to a thaw on the top of a frost the going was even worse than usual and, consequently, some Stokes mortars, which were to have dealt with some strong points in the enemy's line, never arrived. The two leading companies of the Battalion gained the first objective with little loss. The two other companies which went through to attack the second objective came under very heavy machine-gun fire. One company was driven back by a counter-attack after losing heavily. The other got on a considerable way, but was left in the air from the attacks on both sides of it having failed. The Divisional Commander, describing how the attack next to them on the right failed, says:

'In the meantime one company of the 1st K.R.R.C. which had advanced so successfully . . . was entirely isolated, and the Officer Commanding Battalion reports that it was wiped out.'

There was for some time great confusion from troops of another division losing direction and getting mixed up with our men, but in the end consolidation was achieved on the line of the first objective. The casualties of the Battalion were 2nd Lieutenants C. V. Erwood, J. J. Craggs, W. A. D. Eley, and P. Mason killed; 2nd Lieutenant the Hon. G. C. Rowley wounded and missing, since reported killed in action; Lieutenant G. Allen, 2nd Lieutenants S. Barrand,

H. A. Jackson, D. McG. Wallis, wounded. Other ranks—killed 45, wounded 137.

The Battalion captured 180 prisoners, 1 machine gun, and 1 trench mortar.

During consolidation the enemy made several heavy bombing attacks, which the Officer Commanding says in his report 'were driven off mainly owing to 2nd Lieutenant P. Keevil, M.C.' The Battalion was relieved on the night of the 18th/19th.

Towards the end of February it became evident that the enemy was falling back on the line Bucquoy–Achiet-le-Petit–Le Transloy. He covered his retirement by small infantry detachments in a series of strongly wired posts with many machine guns. The object of the operations of the Fifth Army was to drive in or capture these detachments, and establish a line close up to the enemy's new position, previous to attacking it. This process went on gradually, but the state of the country made any movement very difficult. The Fifth Army Summary for the second week in March gives a good idea of it when it says:

> 'Roads in the shelled area have practically ceased to exist, and in many cases field guns and even 60-pounders had to be taken to pieces and pushed by hand over trench tramways, which were laid more quickly than the roads could be repaired. . . . Practically every round of field artillery ammunition has had to be carried up by pack horse, and as much as 80,000 rounds of 18-pounder and 20,000 rounds of 4·5-inch howitzer, representing a gross weight of 1,500 tons, was lately fired in 7 days.'

The conditions of life in the trenches can be imagined.

On March 10 the 2nd Division captured the Grévillers line, south-east of the village of Irles, which was taken at the same time by the 18th Division.

The part taken in this attack by our 1st Battalion is

thus described in the 'Chronicle' for 1917, in an almost verbatim extract from the report of the Commanding Officer, Lieut.-Colonel R. S. H. Stafford, D.S.O., M.C.

'On March 9 the Battalion was in dug-outs near Courcelette, and at midnight proceeded to their assembly positions along the dry ditch.

'There was little hostile shelling to annoy us during the march in, and only A Company suffered a few casualties.

'All the companies were in position by 3.30 a.m. on the 10th, and at zero, 5.15 a.m., it was fairly dark, with some mist.

'As soon as possible after zero we got up close to the barrage, and immediately it lifted we rushed and captured Grévillers trench.

'In two places the enemy tried to bomb us, but they were at once disposed of. A machine gun came into action on our right, but Sergeant Jacobs shot the gunner through the head and stopped the annoyance.

'We were lucky in finding the wire in front of the trench had been most thoroughly destroyed, and presented no obstacle at all. Grévillers trench was badly damaged, but the mist made the work of consolidation easy. On the capture of the trench, previously detailed parties with Lewis guns pushed forward and established posts. This part of the operations was admirably carried out, and its success was due to Captain E. M. Allfrey, M.C., who, though wounded immediately on leaving the assembly trench, was able to "carry on," and firmly established these posts.'

. . . . .

'The enemy's barrage following zero was feeble, and the impression was gained that the Germans were completely surprised. They soon recovered themselves, however, and at 8.30 a.m. on the 10th and the whole of the afternoon the shelling was very heavy.'

. . . . .

'On the night of the 11th/12th we were relieved by the 13th Essex Regiment. It will thus be seen that this operation was well carried out and entirely successful. The necessity of keeping well under our barrage was emphasised, even at the cost of a few casualties, and the gunners were splendid.

'Our casualties in this affair were slight: 1 officer killed

[2nd Lieutenant R. W. B. Levett], 3 wounded [2nd Lieutenant, Temp. Captain, E. M. Allfrey, 2nd Lieutenants J. Holdsworth, and H. L. Jewell], and 50 other ranks casualties. The strength of the Battalion prior to the attack was very weak, viz. 320; but they were all experienced fighters who knew their work and what was expected of them, and carried it out magnificently, earning the praise of G.H.Q., Corps and Divisional Commanders. We captured 3 machine guns [1 by a Company of 23rd Royal Fusiliers, attached], 3 trench mortars, and 120 prisoners.'

During the night of March 12/13 the enemy vacated the position to which he had fallen back towards the end of February.

He was immediately followed up, but his rearguards continued to put up a stout resistance, and not all of the attacks on them were successful. However, he never waited for a big attack, and by the end of the month he had pretty well completed his withdrawal to his prepared position across the base of the salient from Arras to near Soissons, known as the Hindenburg Line. Some of Gough's troops were required for the forthcoming operations of the Third and First Armies, and pressure on the Fifth Army front was gradually relaxed.

Though the Fifth Army had been doing most of the fighting, the Fourth Army had gradually advanced in touch with their right, and the 20th Division, to which belonged our 10th, 11th, and 12th Battalions, had been engaged in some minor operations.

On February 28 the 10th Battalion were in the front line near Lesbœufs. An attack was made by two platoons of the Battalion (total, 2 officers, 60 other ranks), under Captain H. C. H. Illingworth, against a post in a sunken road which ran at right angles into our line, the post being some 150 yards away. The attacking party came under very heavy artillery fire when forming up in the open. When it advanced it came under machine-gun and rifle-grenade fire, and then found the wire uncut. Captain Illingworth was reported as killed in the enemy's wire, and nothing more was heard of him till near the end of April, when news came that he was badly wounded and a prisoner in Germany.

The party then had to fall back with a loss of 42 of all ranks.

On April 4 a brilliant attack was made by the 59th Brigade, 20th Division, on the village of Metz-en-Couture.[1] Our 10th Battalion (Lieut.-Colonel E. M. Ley), on the right, and our 11th Battalion (Lieut.-Colonel G. K. Priaulx), on the left, led the attack. The night before was spent by the 10th Battalion in Dessart Wood, by the 11th Battalion in the village of Fins, from a mile to a mile and a half south of Metz. It had snowed all night, and was still snowing at zero hour, 2 p.m.

At that hour a barrage came down on the enemy's front line, just south of the village, and the two battalions advanced. For the first fifteen minutes the enemy's shelling and machine-gun fire was slight, but after that they came under increased rifle and machine-gun fire from the houses in the village. At 2.30 p.m. the two right companies of the 10th Battalion became heavily engaged with enemy posts on their right, lost heavily, and there was no sign of the troops which should have been next them on the right. At 2.35 p.m. the 11th Battalion and two companies of the 10th reached the outskirts of Metz, and paused while the barrage lifted. At 2.40 p.m. these troops entered Metz, and fought their way through the village against considerable fire from the houses and from the edge of Havrincourt Wood, to the north. The left flank of the 11th Battalion was for a time held up by wire and machine guns in a trench running towards the western

[1] Map IV.

corner of the village. The second line swung to the left, dashed up the hill, and captured the trench and its occupants, but came under intense machine-gun fire from the north-west corner of Metz. This was quickly silenced by a party under Captain O. B. Smyth.

On the right flank there was still no sign of the troops of the next-door division, and the enemy counter-attacked from the south-east. A company of the 10th Rifle Brigade from the Brigade Reserve was sent forward, but the counter-attack had been driven off before they arrived. This company then formed a defensive flank facing east, and eventually succeeded in gaining touch with their missing neighbours. By 3.25 p.m. the whole village was in the hands of our men, with the exception of a few houses in the north end. Cellars and dug-outs were cleared, and a number of prisoners taken. The 11th Rifle Brigade then went through against the second objective, and our battalions started digging in just north of the village. By 6.30 p.m. all the objectives had been gained.

The casualties in the Brigade amounted to 28 per cent. of the numbers actually engaged; those of the 10th Battalion were: killed, Captains J. Egerton Leigh, C. R. Blake, D. G. Davies, M.C.; 2nd Lieutenants A. Ashwell, A. L. C. Marlow; died of wounds, 2nd Lieutenant R. S. G. Vigers; wounded, Lieutenant J. B. Swan, 2nd Lieutenant E. D. Harvey; other ranks—killed 22, wounded 128, missing, 20. The 11th Battalion lost: killed, 2nd Lieutenants J. K. Pirret, H. C. Davis, and 27 other ranks; wounded, 4 officers, 96 other ranks.

CHAPTER VIII[1]

'**ARRAS,** 1917,' 'SCARPE, 1917,' 'ARLEUX'[2]

THE FIRST BATTLE OF ARRAS

THE retreat of the Germans to the Hindenburg Line, which flattened out the salient between Soissons and Arras, automatically did away with the idea of a converging attack on both flanks of the Somme battlefield. Nivelle's plan, to put all his eggs into one basket on the Aisne, left it to the British Expeditionary Force to carry out the only preliminary attack which was to open the campaign of 1917. This attack is what is known as the First Battle of Arras. During the progress of Nivelle's attack the battle of Arras would serve to pin down a part of the enemy's forces. In the event of Nivelle's attack being a success, it would become part of a great converging operation which would pinch out a large part of the centre of the enemy's line in France. Owing to the failure of that attack, it became an isolated operation without any great strategical object.

In 'Sir Douglas Haig's Command' there is an interesting comparison between the brilliant success of April 9, 1917, and the failure of July 1, 1916, and an analysis of the causes which produced such different results, which may well be reproduced in brief, as an introduction to an account of the fighting. The author points out that the front to be attacked at Arras was fully as strong as, if not stronger than, that to which the British Expeditionary Force were opposed on July 1. The southern part of the

[1] Map III. [2] Between Douai and Cambrai, Map VIII.

front formed a part of the new Hindenburg Line, the very latest thing in field defences. At the northern end was the Vimy Ridge, one of the strongest positions of the whole German line, which had repelled the best efforts of the French to take it. The centre was strengthened by a series of fortified villages and cut up by the marshes of the River Scarpe. The attack on July 1 was against a salient, and that on April 9 was against a straight line. He disposes of the idea that the difference was one of a moral weakening on the part of the enemy by pointing to the resistance the French met with on the Aisne. He concludes—it would appear rightly—that the change came from the improvement in the British forces. They had bought their experience on the Somme, and had profited by it both during that battle and in their period of training during the winter. The chief lessons had been the art of 'mopping up' and the perfection of co-operation between infantry and artillery. There were also the material advantages that the number of guns had greatly increased and shortage of ammunition supply was henceforth to be unknown to the end of the war. The quality of the ammunition had also improved proportionately to its increase in quantity.

On April 9 the Third Army (Allenby) attacked at 5.30 a.m. with the VII, VI, and XVII Corps, in the order named, from right to left, the XVIII Corps being in reserve, where it remained throughout the battle, supplying fresh divisions for worn-out ones, to which it acted as a repairing shop. The front of attack was about ten miles, from Croisilles to within a mile of Neuville St. Vaast. By 6.10 a.m. the whole of the first objective was captured without difficulty.

At 7.30 a.m. the advance was resumed on the second line. The enemy's resistance had hardened, and it was not till noon that this line, which by the time-table should have been taken by 8.15 a.m., was captured, and even then the enemy was still holding out in the Railway Triangle just south of the Scarpe. This was taken at 2 p.m., but, meanwhile, the check there had considerably delayed the advance of the troops farther south. By evening the third objective had been taken in several places, but only in one instance, where the 4th Division took Fampoux, was the farthest objective reached. On the whole, though results fell below expectations, it had been a very successful day. An advance had been made of from one to four miles, with, compared to the attacks on the Somme, a light casualty list.

The 14th Division, on the left of the VII Corps, was the only one containing battalions of our regiment which was engaged this day.

The Division attacked with the 43rd Brigade on the right, the 42nd on the left. They were to take the first two objectives, after which the 41st Brigade was to go through and take the third objective. The front of the Division was to decrease as it advanced, and after the capture of the third objective the Division would be squeezed out by those on its right and left, and would consolidate the positions won, and come into Corps Reserve.

The 42nd Brigade attacked with the 5th Oxford and Bucks Light Infantry on the right, the 9th K.R.R.C. on the left. This gave our 9th Battalion (Lieut.-Colonel H. C. M. Porter) the task of attacking a series of trenches known as the 'Harp,' so called from its appearance in plan. The frame of the 'Harp' was towards the east, and the trench forming its western string was the first one to be taken. Two hundred yards or so behind this trench was another, officially known as the 'String,' and this trench was the final objective of the Battalion. The 'Harp,' which was just south of Tilloy-lez-Mofflaines, had a frontage of about 1,000 yards and a depth of about 500, but it was only a portion of it which the 9th Battalion had to attack.

It should be explained that the enemy, having retired from their front-line trenches in front of the 14th Division some time previously, the 'Harp,' though the first objective for the 14th Division, was a part of the line which formed the second objective for most of the Third Army. Consequently, the 42nd Brigade, instead of advancing at zero hour, had to wait for their attack till the time for the advance of the rest of the army on their second objective. Fortunately, they were not 'spotted' in their assembly trenches, which were from 400 to 600 yards from the enemy's front line, and were only very lightly shelled during their two hours' wait.

The following account of the 9th Battalion's attack is taken from the 'Chronicle' of 1917:

'In conformity with 42nd Brigade Orders the 9th Battalion K.R.R.C. occupied their assembly trenches, and were in position there by midnight on the night of April 8/9, 1917.

'The objective allotted to the Battalion was the "String" of the "Harp," from the line marked Battalion boundary on our right, to line marked Divisional boundary on our left. Simultaneously with our attack the 5th Oxford and Bucks Light Infantry on our right, and the 4th Royal Fusiliers on our left, were to attack the "String" of the "Harp." Sixteen tanks also were to co-operate.

'Zero was fixed for 5.30 a.m. on April 9, 1917. At that hour, by the capture of Gateshead Trench, the 3rd Division on our left came up into line with the 14th (Light) Division, preparatory to the attack on the "Harp."

'Our advance on the "Harp" was covered by artillery barrage fire (half high explosive and half shrapnel).

'At 7.34 a.m., in accordance with Brigade orders, the Battalion moved out from its assembly trenches to commence the attack. Previous to this advance there had been very little hostile shelling of our assembly trenches, only 3 casualties being reported.

'The Battalion was distributed as follows :

'A Company, under the command of Lieutenant G. C. M. Leech, was the right leading company.

'B Company, under the command of Captain A. E. Dent, was the left leading company.

'These two companies advanced, each with a front of two platoons, the directing flank in each case being the left. . . .

'Immediately behind these two companies, D Company, under the command of Lieutenant T. A. Wood, advanced in one line as "moppers up" for the first trench of the "Harp." C Company, under the command of Lieutenant H. Stewart, advanced in one line as supports, being about 100 yards behind D Company.

'As soon as the advance from our assembly trenches started, the leading companies came under heavy hostile machine-gun fire from the direction of the "Harp." An enemy artillery barrage had been expected, too, but this was not in evidence at all. This machine-gun fire, however, caused many casualties among the two leading companies: Lieutenant G. C. M. Leech (died of wounds) and the 3 other officers of A Company—2nd Lieutenants A. J. D'Alton, F. Church, and J. G. Broadbent—were wounded, as well as 3 of the sergeants ; Captain A. E. Dent, commanding B Company, 2nd Lieutenant E. R. Clarke (4th London Regiment) of the same company, and 2nd Lieutenant R. B. Van Praagh of C Company were killed. The above were thus put out of action before the first line of enemy wire was reached. But the advance was not checked, and the first enemy trench was captured at 7.50 a.m. under our barrage. The wire in front of this trench, having been well cut by our artillery, proved no obstacle. Passing over the captured first-line trench, A and B Companies lay down under our barrage for the next advance on the "String." D Company came up into the captured trench and started "mopping up." C Company came up into the first-line trench.

'Battalion Headquarters moved forward towards our objective, reaching the first line about 8.30 a.m.

'The advance was continued on the "String," A, B, and C Companies all coming under the fire of two machine guns posted in the "String" opposite. Enemy snipers also were active hereabouts, from the direction of Noisy Work [in rear of the "Harp"]. The wire in front of the "String" had not been well cut by our artillery, and was a serious obstacle, making progress under machine-gun fire very difficult indeed. About this time the following casualties took place: Lieutenant H. Stewart, commanding C Company and 2nd Lieutenant R. Cook (7th Scottish Rifles), C Company, were killed, and Lieutenant V. Richardson, B Company, wounded for the second time.

'By this time the sixteen tanks told off to attack the "Harp" should have made their presence felt, and would have been invaluable in dealing with the machine-gun fire from the "String," but they had all stuck either in or before the first line.

'Owing to the machine guns and snipers, the only parties that succeeded in entering the "String," at 8.10 a.m., under our barrage, were two small parties which had worked up the communication trenches from the first-line trench, these communication trenches being fortunately at either end of our objective.

'The position about 8.20 a.m., when the Battalion Headquarters arrived on the scene, was that we had obtained a footing at either end of our objective, but the centre was held by two machine guns and snipers.

'A certain amount of hostile shelling was now taking place, particularly on the communication trenches leading from the first line to the "String."

'Two platoons of C Company were sent along F.1 communication trench to support a small party of B Company already in the "String" on the left. These together worked along the "String" to the right, dealing with the machine guns and snipers on the way, till touch was gained with the small party of A Company which had entered the "String" by the communication trench near the right of our objective. The dug-outs in the "String" were all picketed, and touch gained with the 4th Royal Fusiliers on our left and 5th Oxford and Bucks Light Infantry on our right, about 9.15 a.m.

'At 9.15 a.m. a message was sent to 42nd Infantry Brigade that the objective allotted to the Battalion had been gained. . . .

'Clearing up, consolidation, and reorganisation of captured trenches proceeded.

'Other units, proceeding with the capture of remaining

portions of the "Harp," had passed through our line previous to this.

'The Battalion remained in the captured trenches until 4 p.m., April 11, when it was relieved by the 9th Rifle Brigade. It returned to Wanquetin[1] that night.

'It is roughly estimated that rather more than 200 prisoners were captured by the Battalion, mostly of the *76th R.I.R.* (*Prussians*). Over 100 were extricated from the dug-outs in the first-line trench, over 60 from the dug-outs in the "String." About 40 or 50, including snipers and machine-gunners, were collected apart from the crew of the dug-outs.

'Besides prisoners and 2 machine guns, 1 medium trench mortar on wheels, and 2 *Granatenwerfer* were captured, together with a large quantity of ammunition and bombs.

'The casualties to the Battalion were as follows:

'Officers: killed 6, wounded 4; other ranks—killed 69, wounded 118, missing 17.

'All our wounded were evacuated by 5 p.m., which may be considered a good performance on the part of the medical personnel concerned.'

The 41st Brigade, with our 7th and 8th Battalions, was in reserve throughout the day.

It will be unnecessary to detail the events of the First Battle of Arras from day to day. The rate of progress after the first day slowed down, but it was more or less continuous.

The fighting went on almost without cessation for weeks, and it had its ups and downs. Its attacks were not always successful, but generally speaking the casualty list was kept low. The enemy's counter-attacks were numerous, were never more than temporarily successful, and were costing him very dear. As a part of the *guerre d'usure* the battle was favouring the Allies, and it was certainly doing its part in keeping the enemy's reserves employed during the French attack on the Aisne, the bad time that followed it, and the final preparations for Haig's next big offensive in Flanders.

[1] West of Arras.

It will be enough to give some account of the operations in which our battalions took a part in the order in which they came.

The attack was resumed on April 10, and the 41st Brigade went forward to relieve the 43rd, which was supposed to be holding a line from half a mile west of Wancourt towards Feuchy Chapel. The Brigade advanced with the 7th K.R.R.C. on the right, the 7th Rifle Brigade on the left. The 7th Rifle Brigade found some of the 43rd Brigade holding the line as expected, and relieved them. Our 7th Battalion found themselves opposite a gap, which the 43rd Brigade had somehow missed and was still strongly held by the enemy. Under cover of a snowstorm A and B Companies, under Captain G. H. Williamson, M.C., rushed the sunken road which formed the German front line, capturing some 20 prisoners, but lost heavily, as the wire was almost uncut, and they came under heavy machine-gun fire from a hill just south of Wancourt, on the front of the 56th Division. 2nd Lieutenant F. R. Williams, commanding D Company, Lieutenant F. J. St. Aubyn, and 2nd Lieutenant P. F. Walford were killed, and Lieutenants C. Pullinger, S. Wiggins, J. G. Johnson (Scottish Rifles), 2nd Lieutenants G. D. Ferard and K. H. Williamson were wounded (2nd Lieutenant Williamson died of his wounds). The 8th Rifle Brigade were sent forward to attack the hill from whence came the machine-gun fire which was causing the trouble, but came against uncut wire, lost heavily, and could not get on. However, by evening, the line they set out to occupy was held, the 8th Rifle Brigade prolonging the right, and connecting with the 56th Division. Next day a gallant but quite hopeless attempt was made to take Wancourt. It was arranged that the 56th Division should attack the hill mentioned above an hour before the attack of the 41st Brigade, in hopes of neutralising the machine-gun fire from it.

A creeping barrage was arranged for, and the attacking troops were withdrawn some 200 yards from the trench held by them to give it play. For some reason the barrage, in the words of the Brigadier, 'resolved itself into a little dispersed, intermittent fire which, beyond causing the infantry of the Brigade a considerable number of casualties, had no influence on the attack.' The attack by the 56th Division made no progress, and that of the 41st Brigade never had a chance. The losses, especially in our 7th Battalion, were very heavy. It snowed all day, and it was impossible to get the wounded in till after dark, so they must have suffered terribly.

That night our 8th Battalion relieved the 7th. Next morning Wancourt was occupied without a casualty, the position having been evacuated during the night.

The 14th Division was relieved on the night of the 12th/13th.

The casualties of the 7th Battalion during the 10th and 11th were, besides the officers already named: killed, Captain C. Whitley, M.C.; died of wounds, Captain G. H. Williamson, M.C.; wounded, Lieutenant C. C. Ommanney, 2nd Lieutenant W. O. Dring; other ranks—killed 20, died of wounds 15, wounded 140, missing 9.

Monchy-le-Preux

When the Third Army attacked on April 9, the 37th Division, in which our 13th Battalion (Lieut.-Colonel R. C. Chester-Master) formed a unit of the 111th Brigade, was in reserve to the VI Corps. It was intended that after the three leading divisions, 3rd, 12th, and 15th, had taken their third objective, the 37th should pass through and take the final objective, a line running north and south about 1,000 yards east of the village of Monchy-le-Preux.

The night of the 8th/9th was spent in bivouacs, from two to three miles west of Arras. The 111th Brigade marched at 4.30 a.m., and by 10.30 a.m. was in the old British front line at Blangy.

Two hours later it advanced to what had been the German first line, and about 5 p.m. was brought up to a point just west of the Feuchy Chapel–Feuchy Road.

It had been intended that the Brigade should go through and attack Monchy-le-Preux, but the 12th Division had failed to take their third objective, and further progress could not be made till this was done. During the night, a cold one with heavy snow, the 111th Brigade was moved to the left into support of the 63rd Brigade, of their own division. During the morning of the 10th, the 112th and 63rd Brigades made sufficient progress to allow of the 111th being launched against Monchy-le-Preux. The attack started at 2.30 p.m., with the 10th and 13th Royal Fusiliers in front, the 13th K.R.R.C. in support, and the 13th Rifle Brigade in reserve. The first objective was a group of enclosures about 800 yards north-west of the village. The first objective was taken after heavy loss from artillery and machine-gun fire, especially in the two Fusilier battalions. Our artillery support had been very weak, it having been impossible to get the guns which had been covering the previous advance forward in time. An effort was made to renew the advance at 7.30 p.m., but it had to be given up, and the troops dug in for the night. The attack was resumed at 5 a.m., April 11, but it seems to have been one of those affairs which are unduly hurried by higher authority without regard to the possibilities of the situation, as there was hardly any artillery support. The two Rifle battalions formed the first line—K.R.R.C. on the right,

Rifle Brigade on the left—the Fusilier battalions in 'second line.' Casualties were heavy and progress was slow; in fact, there is every likelihood that the attack would have failed but for the timely arrival of four tanks, which dealt with some machine guns in front of the village. This done, the trenches in front of the village were soon taken, and the riflemen cleared the whole village very quickly. Lewis guns, rapidly pushed out to the far side of the village, took a heavy toll of the enemy as he retreated across the open. About 150 prisoners were taken by the Brigade, of which 50 passed through 13th K.R.R.C. Headquarters. The village was cleared by 9 a.m., but the enemy had started a very heavy bombardment on it, which pointed to an impending counter-attack, and the Brigade was very glad of the assistance of the VI Corps Cavalry, 10th Hussars, 3rd Dragoon Guards, and Essex Yeomanry, who came up and assisted in preparing the defence of the position.

The Brigade had lost too heavily and the enemy were too strong for any further advance to be attempted, so consolidation went on under the worst of weather conditions. In the afternoon a storm passed over which left 3 inches of snow on the ground. In fact, the weather for the first few days of the battle of Arras seems to have been the worst the troops had suffered from since the early break-up of the previous summer. The Battalion was relieved during the night by a battalion of the Queen's from the 12th Division. Out of a battle strength of some 20 officers and 400 other ranks they had lost: officers—killed, Captain E. W. Webster, 2nd Lieutenant A. H. Dawe; wounded 11, of whom 2nd Lieutenant T. W. Penhale died of his wounds; other ranks—killed 26, wounded 162, missing 24.

Croisilles

On April 23 the 33rd Division attacked a section of the Hindenburg Line between Croisilles and Fontaine-lez-Croisille. The attack was made towards the north-east, astride the Sensée River, with the 100th Brigade on the right, the 98th on the left.

The following account of the attack is taken from the report of the G.O.C. 33rd Division :

'The attack of the 100th Infantry Brigade south of the Sensée River was carried out by the 1st Queen's Regiment, with the 16th K.R.R.C. in support.

'At this point our main line of defence was some 1,500 yards from the German line, and it was not possible to approach within assaulting distance during daylight. The approach to the enemy's position, therefore, resembled in all respects a night march, followed by an assault. Careful arrangements were made by the 100th Infantry Brigade to ensure the success of this movement. The 1st Queen's assembled . . . undetected by the enemy ; the 16th K.R.R.C. were kept in support in the quarry [some half-mile from the German line].

'At 4.45 a.m. the 1st Queen's advanced to the assault under cover of the barrage, and quickly took the front Hindenburg Line. The advance to the second line was continued almost immediately.

'Owing to (*a*) the wire in front of the second line not being properly cut, (*b*) and hence the barrage not dwelling sufficiently long on the second line, only elements of the 1st Queen's reached the second line, and a permanent footing in it was not gained.

'At 8.30 a.m. a message was received from 100th Infantry Brigade that a heavy enemy barrage on the Sensée Valley and Croisilles–Fontaine Road was preventing reinforcements being sent from the 16th K.R.R.C. (in the quarry) to assist the 1st Queen's. The counter-battery group were at once asked to deal with the situation, and enemy barrage ceased at 9 a.m., thus enabling the 16th K.R.R.C. to get forward. The first reinforcing waves of the 16th K.R.R.C. started before the barrage ceased, and they passed through it with great steadiness, as if on parade, although suffering considerable losses.

Before the 16th K.R.R.C. arrived, the 1st Queen's were driven out of the Hindenburg Support Line, and endeavours were made to block and hold the front line. Owing to the distance to be traversed, difficulty was experienced in getting supplies of bombs up. At 12 noon the Germans heavily counter-attacked the 1st Queen's and 16th K.R.R.C., and at 1.55 p.m. it was reported that they had been driven out of the front Hindenburg Line.

'Both battalions suffered very heavy losses in officers and other ranks.

'Two tanks had been allotted to the 100th Infantry Brigade for the operation, but owing to mechanical troubles, they never arrived at the starting-point, and took no part in the operations.'

The G.O.C. 33rd Division goes on to comment on the gallantry of the two battalions, and on the unreliability of tanks, which certainly in their infancy seemed to have suffered a most disconcerting number of casualties not due to the enemy's fire.

The losses of the Battalion were: wounded and missing—Captains E. M. Gonner, A. B. Bernard (both died of their wounds); killed, 2nd Lieutenants R. H. Garrard, G. L. Spreckley; 6 officers wounded; other ranks—killed and wounded, 260.

Arleux

On April 23 the Third Army renewed its attack on a big scale north of the Scarpe. The 37th Division was attacking westward to the south of Gavrelle, the 63rd Brigade on the right, the 111th on the left. The 13th K.R.R.C. was on the extreme left of the Brigade, and the 63rd (Royal Naval) Division, which was to take the village of Gavrelle, was on their left. The starting-point of the Battalion was about 1,000 yards south-west of the village. There were three lines to be taken. The nearest was within 250 yards; the farthest was the line of the road running south-east from Gavrelle to Plouvain, and about 2,000 yards from the starting-point. The barrage came down, and the advance began at 4.45 a.m., just as it was getting light. The 63rd Brigade were very soon in difficulties, coming under very heavy enfilade machine-gun fire, and making little progress—in places not even the first objective was taken. The 111th Brigade at first advanced without a check and with slight loss. This did not last long. When they reached Cuba Trench, about 1,000 yards from the start, the right and centre battalions also came under heavy enfilade machine-gun fire, and could make no further progress. The 13th K.R.R.C., though suffering from the same fire, went straight on, and at 8.25 a.m. were reported digging in on their final objective, on the Plouvain–Gavrelle Road, but out of touch with any other troops. They had lost heavily, but taken a number of prisoners. B Company, on the right of the second line, were for a time held up by a machine gun on their right. Captain L. D. Chidson, commanding the company, directed his bombers to bomb down a trench, which, after a stiff fight in which he and several men lost their lives, was cleared of the enemy, 1 officer and 40 other ranks of the enemy being taken prisoners. Hearing of the isolation of the 13th K.R.R.C. the Brigadier sent forward the 13th Rifle Brigade to get in touch with their right, but it was not till after dark that the gap was closed. The 13th K.R.R.C. had meanwhile thrown back one company on their right to form a defensive flank. They were not long out of touch on the left, as the 63rd Division had swept through the village without difficulty, and soon got up into line with them.

Besides Captain Chidson, the following officers of the Battalion were killed in this fight: 2nd Lieutenants F. E.

Mackenzie (Scottish Rifles, attached), F. W. Osborne, F. Atkinson.

Our 13th Battalion remained in their exposed situation for several days, where they were subject to frequent and heavy bombardments and several times counter-attacked. Some of the counter-attacks were stopped by our barrage, but others got near enough to come under our rifle and machine-gun fire.

Most of these counter-attacks were directed on the village of Gavrelle, and passing diagonally across the front of the 13th Battalion gave them some very pretty shooting, of which they took full advantage.

The Battalion was withdrawn into Brigade Reserve, in the old German front line, where they were still under shell fire; on the night of the 27th/28th and on the night of the 29th/30th they were relieved, and went into much-needed rest billets.

On April 26 the 14th Division came back into line again east of Wancourt, replacing the 50th Division in the VII Corps.

On May 3 the Third Army made a big attack along its whole front which was unsuccessful. Most of the troops gained their first objective, but vigorous counter-attacks drove them back, so that on the greater part of the front they ended the day where they began it.

The 41st Brigade attacked with the 8th Rifle Brigade on the right, the 8th K.R.R.C. (Lieut.-Colonel C. H. N. Seymour) on the left. The 8th Rifle Brigade had the 18th Division on their right, while our 8th Battalion had the 42nd Brigade on their left.

The first objective of our Battalion was a track running north-east from Chérisy, and was about 1,500 yards from their starting-line. The second objective was a line of trench about 500 yards farther on.

Zero hour was 3.45 a.m., at which hour it was still quite dark. Following close up to a very good barrage the leading companies reached their first objective at 4.35 a.m. with slight casualties and having accounted for a good many of the enemy on the way. Here they started to consolidate. Nothing could be found of the 42nd Brigade, who, as it turned out, had come under very heavy machine-gun fire, had had severe casualties, and never got farther than a couple of hundred yards from their trenches. The Battalion therefore had its left thrown back to form a defensive flank. They were in touch with the 8th Rifle Brigade, who also had taken their first objective without difficulty.

For half an hour all was well; then the trouble began. The enemy, in spite of incurring a good many casualties in the process, succeeded in establishing some machine guns in Triangle Wood, from which they swept our front line, which compelled them to leave off digging and lie flat. The supporting company, 200 yards behind, were better protected, and managed to go on digging. A visit from a German aeroplane which dropped lights over them was followed by a heavy bombardment of 5·9-inch shells.

The advance to the second objective was due to take place at 5.45 a.m., but Captain Leslie, in command of the front line, realised that to do this was quite impossible so long as his left was in the air. The 8th Rifle Brigade advanced and gained their second objective, with a battalion of the 18th Division on their right.

Meanwhile, farther on the right of the 18th Division the attack had failed. A reserve company of the 8th Rifle Brigade was sent up to fill the gap between their left and the right of the 8th K.R.R.C., which battalion sent up one of its reserve companies further to strengthen the defensive flank they had formed on their left. Meanwhile, the

Germans put down a heavy barrage which cut off Battalion Headquarters both from the front line and from Brigade Headquarters.

Later in the morning a retirement started on the right, and battalions of the 18th Division were seen falling back through Chérisy on to their old front line. The retirement extended to the left, as each battalion and company in turn found its right flank in the air. The retirement seems to have been a well-organised and orderly affair, and well covered by our machine guns, but the 41st Brigade lost very heavily from machine-gun fire in the process. By 10.30 a.m. the Battalion was back in the trenches it had started from.

The Germans threatened an attack, but lost so heavily from the fire from our trenches that they did not persevere with it.

The 7th K.R.R.C. relieved the 8th K.R.C.C. and 8th Rifle Brigade before midnight.

The total casualties of the Battalion were : officers, 10 ; other ranks, 270. The officer casualties were : killed, 2nd Lieutenant J. G. Lyndall ; died of wounds, 2nd Lieutenant J. Warham ; wounded and missing (prisoners of war), Captain J. W. Leslie, M.C. ; 2nd Lieutenants T. W. Lyle, C. E. Butcher, H. M. Cook, H. W. Liddle ; wounded, 2nd Lieutenants A. H. Mole, S. R. C. Sharpe, G. Lance.

The 7th, 8th, and 9th Battalions were in and out of the trenches in this area till the Division was relieved towards the end of the month. The 7th and 9th were lucky in the way of casualties ; those of the 7th for the month of May being : officers—wounded, 2nd Lieutenant G. A. Carr ; missing, Lieutenant A. H. Herbertson (later reported killed) ; other ranks—killed 16, wounded 63, missing 2. Those of the 9th Battalion were : officers—wounded, Lieut.-Colonel H. C. M. Porter ; 2nd Lieutenants L. Marks, J. P. Porteous,

T. S. Hodgson, P. H. Martin, C. N. Campbell; other ranks—killed 11, wounded 81, missing 2.

On May 20 our 16th Battalion, which had been out of the line since the affair of April 22, took part in another attack against almost the identical part of the Hindenburg Line where they had had such an unfortunate experience the month before. They behaved as gallantly, and had as bad luck as on the former occasion. The Brigade attacked with the 2nd Worcestershire on the right, the Glasgow Highlanders in the centre, and the 16th K.R.R.C. on the left; the 1st Queen's being in reserve.

The advance began in a thick mist, and there was no bombardment. The surprise was complete, and they took the first line almost without resistance, so presumably the wire had been well cut. The barrage then came down on the enemy's second line, and the advance was resumed under it. This line was strongly held, and the two leading companies were driven back on the other two, which were holding the German front line. The Battalion started consolidating this line with posts thrown out to the front, under heavy artillery fire all the time.

At 10 a.m. orders came to prepare to renew the attack. The Battalion started making preparations to comply, though it had already lost nearly half its numbers. In the afternoon the orders for the 100th Brigade to attack were cancelled, and they were informed that two battalions from another brigade would pass through. This attack failed too. Consolidation went on all next day, and the line was heavily shelled. On the night of the 22nd/23rd the Battalion was relieved.

Their casualties were: killed, Captain J. R. Smith, 2nd Lieutenants L. B. Forrest, E. F. Peacocke; died of wounds, Lieutenant H. B. Smith (London Regiment, attached); wounded, Captain G. J. Edwards, Lieutenant and Adjutant F. C. Giddens, 2nd Lieutenant W. Howat; other ranks—killed 23, wounded 133, missing 55.

The First Army had all this time been fighting in line with the Third to the north. Their operations had begun with the capture of the famous Vimy Ridge. Our 1st Battalion (Major R. S. H. Stafford) was the only one of our regiment which came under the First Army, the 2nd Division relieving the 51st on April 3 in the line west of Bailleul. They started with a good bit of patrol work, which is thus described in the 'Chronicle' of 1917:

'On the 13th it was decided that the Division would attack the railway line west of Bailleul the following morning, and orders were accordingly issued. Captain Anderson, however, rang up at 1.30 p.m. to say that he had occupied the railway as far as and including the station, and as far as he could see Bailleul village was clear of the enemy. This smart piece of patrol work was carried out by 2nd Lieutenant J. H. Lee, D.S.O., Sergeant Britton, Corporal Scott, and 6 men of A Company, who, in addition to collecting this valuable information, captured a field gun. The information was got through in time to prevent the bombardment of the railway and station at 2 p.m.

'Bailleul village was thus captured without serious opposition, although we were heavily shelled crossing the ridge near the railway cutting.

'We established our line [about 1,000 yards] east of the village on Hill 80. During the night 2nd Lieutenant J. C. Blyth was killed, and Captain F. Wadner and 2nd Lieutenant J. E. M. Skinner wounded. Our casualties in other ranks were very slight.

'We received a congratulatory message the next day from the Divisional Commander for our "bold and rapid advance."'

The Battalion was relieved on the 14th, and came back into the line on the 25th.

On the 28th the 2nd Division attacked the German line running north and south immediately west of Oppy, the

99th Brigade being in reserve. There followed two days' very hard fighting, the Germans putting up a very strong resistance, and counter-attacking furiously. Parts of the German front line were gained and lost more than once. The 99th Brigade took part in the attack on the 29th, but only one company of the 1st K.R.R.C. seems to have been involved in the fighting during the two days. This was B Company, which was sent up on the first day to form a defensive flank on the right of the divisional front, the attack of the division next on the right having failed entirely. When relieved the company, after a day and a half of heavy shelling, had lost 2nd Lieutenants T. M. Hext and A. C. Graham-Roe, killed, as well as many other ranks. Such had been the losses in the 2nd Division that on May 1 a composite brigade was made up under the 99th Brigade commander, one battalion from the 5th Brigade, one from the 6th, and two from the 99th, of which one, under Major Stafford, 1st K.R.R.C., was made up of three companies 1st K.R.R.C. and one 22nd Royal Fusiliers.

During the month of April, in addition to those already mentioned, the Battalion had two officers wounded, 2nd Lieutenants J. D. Sneddon and H. H. Pickett, and in other ranks had 8 killed, 64 wounded, 5 missing, and 17 wounded and missing.

On May 3, at 3.45 a.m., the Composite Brigade attacked the German trenches just north of Oppy, the 31st Division, on the right, attacking Oppy Wood and village. Two battalions attacked in front line with Major Stafford's Battalion in second line. The failure of the 31st Division made the task of the Composite Brigade very difficult. They took their first objective, but any of them who got into the main German line were driven out. They dug in on the line of the first objective with a defensive flank thrown back facing the village. This flank was formed by B Company, under Lieutenant G. Allen, M.C., who led his company forward on his own initiative at a critical time.

Attempts by the enemy from the village to bomb them out were stopped by a Stokes mortar. The new line was firmly established after dark, and the Battalion was relieved in the early hours of May 4.

The casualties of the Battalion on May 3 were : officers —wounded, 2nd Lieutenant L. J. Barnes ; other ranks—killed 13, wounded 37, missing 9.

The 1st Battalion was back in the line at Oppy on the 29th, but the First Battle of Arras was dead, and very soon every man that could be spared would be wanted for even bigger operations in Flanders.

CHAPTER IX

'**MESSINES,** 1917,' '**YPRES,** 1917,' 'PILCKEM,' 'MENIN ROAD,' 'POLYGON WOOD,' 'BROODSEINDE,' 'POELCAPELLE,' 'PASSCHENDAELE'

THIRD BATTLE OF YPRES, INCLUDING MESSINES AND NIEUPORT BAINS

NIVELLE's attack had been launched on April 16, and had failed to do anything approaching what was expected of it. It was at once evident that it was not going to win the war at a blow. It did, however, have enough initial success to make a promising beginning to a *guerre d'usure.* If it was to be continued on these lines, then it was worth while for the British to persevere with their offensive at Arras. If not, it were better for the British to switch off and open a new offensive in Flanders, which would have a great strategic object—the clearing of the Belgian coast, and a denial of its use to the enemy as a base for their submarine campaign.

The question was decided by the temporary loss of the will to win on the part of a large proportion of the French Army. How largely that disease had developed need not be discussed here. The fact remains that it was large enough to keep the French Army out of any aggressive operations for some months to come. The Russian Army, owing to the Revolution, was approaching final collapse, and it remained to the British Expeditionary Force to keep the enemy employed till the French Army should be back in fighting form again.

A conference was held at Paris on May 4 and 5, which was attended by most of the leaders, civil and military, of both Allies, and it was decided that Haig should go on with the operations in Flanders for which he had been preparing for some time. No one was more strongly in their favour than the British Prime Minister, though later, when 'Passchendaele' had become unpopular, he would have had it thought otherwise. That seems the only conclusion to be drawn from the fact that a reference to this approval was cut out of Haig's autumn despatch of December 17 after it reached home.

Preparations for an attack by the Second Army on Messines Ridge had been going on all winter, but it took a lot more to mount an attack there on a big scale. These preparations could not hope to escape the enemy's notice. If the operations in front of Arras had been at once suspended it would have made it obvious to the enemy where to expect our main attack. It was therefore necessary to carry on with the battle of Arras while the preparations at Messines were being completed, in order to keep the enemy guessing.

During the winter, in order to release French troops for Nivelle's big attack, the British Expeditionary Force had taken over from the French down to some miles south of what had been the French battle area of the Somme. It was now arranged that, in order to let the British Expeditionary Force continue their offensive on the Arras front while they mounted a fresh one in Flanders, the French should take over up to Havrincourt—due east of Bapaume. This relief was never fully carried out, the French taking over only six miles of front instead of twenty-one. The troubles in the French Army also prevented a show of activity on the Aisne, which might have kept the Germans in expectation of a renewal of the attack in that area.

Apart from the strategical reasons, which were overwhelming, for making Flanders the scene of the next attack, there was the tactical one that the capture of the high ground about Passchendaele would dispose of the abominable Ypres salient, which had been a running sore to the British Expeditionary Force ever since the autumn of 1914. Its situation was so bad, tactically, that nothing but the strongest reasons political and sentimental could excuse its retention. It had been a constant drain on British man-power for thirty months.

Messines [1]

The first step to an advance from the Ypres salient must be the capture of the Messines–Wytschaete position, from which the whole of the salient was overlooked.

On June 7 the attack of the Second Army on the Messines Ridge was launched to the sound of the biggest explosion in military history—19 mines, containing 470 tons of explosives, going off together at zero hour. The II Anzac, IX and X Corps attacked on a front of nearly ten miles, and met with the greatest success so far obtained by British troops in the war. This day's advance, followed by another on the 14th, not only went a long way to smooth out the Ypres salient, but deprived the enemy of the high ground from which he had overlooked it from behind our right flank ever since 1914.

Our 18th and 21st Battalions, both in the 122nd Brigade, 41st Division, X Corps, took part in the battle. On June 7 the 18th Battalion were in reserve to their brigade. Three companies were employed as carrying parties to the front line, while one company went up to support one of the front-line battalions. The Battalion came in for a good deal of shelling, and lost: killed, 1 officer, and 18 other ranks; wounded, 30 other ranks.

[1] Map I.

The 21st Battalion attacked in the first line. By 5 p.m. they had taken about 130 prisoners, including a machine gun with its team and, for an attack in the Great War, their casualties were very light, being: killed, 2nd Lieutenant G. Mason, and 6 other ranks; wounded, 2nd Lieutenant B. B. Beatie, and 63 other ranks.

On June 14 the 18th Battalion, in co-operation with the 11th Royal West Kent Regiment, captured a trench in the German front line called Olive Trench. The attack was launched at 7.30 p.m., and was entirely successful. Twenty prisoners, a dismantled battery of 5·9-inch howitzers, and 2 machine guns were taken. The enemy put up a stout resistance, and lost heavily. The casualties in the Battalion were: officers—killed, 2nd Lieutenants H. A. Salter (London Regiment, attached), V. L. Hamilton, and W. P. Calder; wounded, 2 officers; other ranks—59 killed and wounded.

By the middle of June the Second Army had secured all the ground that was wanted to protect the right flank of the Fifth Army when it should issue from the Ypres salient. Subsequent operations by the Second Army were only designed to keep the enemy in a state of uncertainty till the Fifth Army should be ready. For the same purpose fighting still went on along the fronts of the Third and First Armies, from near Bullecourt almost to Lens. Unfortunately, another six weeks were to elapse before the Fifth Army could be ready to attack.

The general scheme for the Flanders offensive was that the Fifth Army, after first attacking east and gaining the high ground which runs north and south across the Menin Road, should then push northwards along it. The French and Belgians were then to advance on the left of the Fifth Army, while the Fourth Army joined in on the extreme left, next the sea.

NIEUPORT BAINS[1]

For a great part of the distance between the Ypres salient and the sea the River Yser and its inundations were the boundary between the Germans and the Allies. From Lombartzyde to the sea the French had held a bridgehead on the right bank ever since 1914. With a view to the coming operations, British troops began the relief of the French in this area in the middle of June. The depth of the strip held on the right bank varied from 1,200 yards opposite Lombartzyde to 600 yards between that place and the sea. The left sector, a front of about 1,400 yards, from the small tributary, the Geleide, to the sea, consisted almost entirely of sand dunes. At the beginning of July this sector was held by the 1st Division with one brigade holding the line, another responsible for the coast defences, south of the estuary, and a third brigade in reserve. On July 4 the 2nd Brigade took over the front line, with two battalions beyond the river and two behind it. The battalions holding the front line were, on the right the 1st Northamptonshire Regiment, on the left our 2nd Battalion. The dispositions of our 2nd Battalion are shown in the sketch on page 221.

The capture of Messines Ridge must have been a broad hint to the Germans that there was something big in preparation in Flanders, if they did not know it already. The relief of the French troops by British in the bridgehead must have suggested an advance from that direction. They cannot have remained long in ignorance of the relief, as they raided our line on June 20 and obtained identifications. After that there was little attempt at concealment, as our troops replied with several raids, the last being made by the Rhodesians of the 2nd K.R.R.C. under 2nd Lieutenant T. P. McDowell, the very night before the

[1] Sketch Map III, opposite p. 220.

German attack. The scale of the German attack when it came showed that it must have been in preparation for some time, so it is evident that the enemy did not take long to make up his mind that if the British wanted to advance he would see to it that they should start from the left bank of the Yser. For some reason or other the troops beyond the Yser were supported by very few guns heavier than their own divisional artillery. What heavy artillery there was had only just arrived, and had not yet registered. Possibly the French had made difficulties about leaving theirs till relieved. Someone seems to have gambled on the chance that the Germans would keep quiet during the interval between the departure of the French heavies and the arrival of our own. It was just an instance of that happy-go-lucky trust in Providence which Providence so seldom forgives. The Germans did not wait.

It is impossible to do justice to the glorious defence of those two battalions in a volume which attempts to follow the fortunes of fifteen battalions through four years of war. Lieut.-Colonel Lewis Butler gave us, in the 'Chronicle' for 1917, the full story, of which the following is an abridged and inadequate edition :

On the night of July 9/10 the two battalions were holding the line as related above. The bridges shown in the sketch—the only means of approach to the left bank—were floating footbridges, easily destroyed by any sort of artillery ; the river was unfordable. The defences were, for the most part, not trenches, but breastworks. Now, trenches in sand dunes are just about the best to withstand bombardment. The heavy sand seems to smother the explosion, and nothing but the heaviest calibre has much effect on them, but their construction takes a desperate amount of labour. To get a trench of a certain depth it is necessary to make an excavation of about four times that width, build up the revetments—and every inch has to be revetted—and then fill up again. If sandbags are used, in order to prevent the sand from rapidly trickling out the bags must be doubled and only half filled, so that four times the number of bags are wanted that would be used if filled with earth. On the other hand, breastworks made of sandbags can be knocked out of shape by field artillery. It would have been quite impossible for the 2nd Battalion to dig themselves in properly in the few short summer nights before they were attacked. The last few lines are not borrowed from Colonel Butler, but are the writer's own, and he apologises for their insertion after he has so often complained of want of space; but military history is nothing if not instructive, so your historian must be forgiven if he is at times inclined to be didactic.

From the day on which the Battalion occupied the line the German artillery showed increasing activity. Up to the day of the attack the Battalion had suffered 70 casualties, of which 25 were inflicted on A Company, at that time on the left of the line, in one day. A was then relieved by C Company, and the line was held as follows: on the right B Company (Lieutenant B. C. Munro, M.C., 2nd Lieutenants A. C. Heberden and D. H. Taylor); in the centre D Company (Captain W. L. Clinton, Lieutenant A. Pinnock, 2nd Lieutenants H. Chevis, W. Sheepshanks, and A Simpson); on the left C Company (Lieutenant H. J. F. Mills, 2nd Lieutenants H. J. Lindsay and R. Madeley. A Company (2nd Lieutenants E. W. Barnes, A. G. Boucher, and N. F. E. Anson) was in Battalion Reserve, its company commander, Captain H. F. E. Smith, being at Battalion Headquarters as second-in-command. At Battalion Headquarters were also the Commanding Officer (Lieut.-Colonel R. N. Abadie), the Adjutant (Captain Humphrey Butler), the Battalion Intelligence Officer (Lieutenant

W. H. Gott), the Signalling Officer (2nd Lieutenant A. L. Gracie), and the Liaison Officer R.A. (2nd Lieutenant Henry).

At 6 a.m. on July 10 the enemy began a bombardment which, by 8.50 a.m., had become intense, and was of all calibres, including a few 15-inch shells. A Rifle officer taken prisoner was told by a German officer that their bombardment was the heaviest he had ever known. His own battery, consisting of ten *Minenwerfer*, fired 1,500 shells, each of about 250 lb.

At about noon Lieutenant Gott very gallantly volunteered to go and see how D Company were getting on. All telephone cables had early been cut, and the Commanding Officer had no means of communication, forwards or backwards, except for eight pigeons, of which one only reached Divisional Headquarters, at 5.15 p.m. Lieutenant Gott returned with a cheery message from Captain Clinton that so far all his officers were unhurt. Shortly afterwards 2nd Lieutenant Taylor reached Headquarters, wounded in the head and dazed, reporting that his Company Headquarters had been blown in, that Lieutenant Munro was presumably buried, and that 2nd Lieutenant Heberden had been killed earlier in the day.

There was a slight pause in the bombardment about 1 p.m., but it was soon as bad as ever again. At 2 p.m. Lieutenant Gott started to visit B Company, but was hit in the left arm and leg, and brought back to the dressing-station, which was close to Headquarters.

Between 2.30 and 3 p.m. a message came in from Lieutenant Mills that his officers were still unhit, and the company dug-out still intact.

Still the bombardment went on. The Divisional Artillery did their best, but without something heavier to help them they could do little except, perhaps, attract a little of the fire, and counter-battery work was practically 'nil.' German aeroplanes swarmed over our lines, coming down as low as 60 feet, and machine-gunning the trenches. Not one British aeroplane appeared during the day. At 3 p.m. it was found necessary to abandon the Headquarters dug-out, and move to the tunnel shown on the sketch. This tunnel was about 6 feet high, but only 3 feet wide. It was about 100 yards long, and had an air-hole every 30 yards, which let in a very small amount of light. It was found to be occupied by about 40 men of an Australian Tunnelling Company without an officer. These men, who were armed with rifles, but had only 20 or 30 rounds of ammunition apiece, Colonel Abadie put under the command of 2nd Lieutenant Gracie.

At 6 p.m. there was another short lull in the bombardment, and advantage was taken of it to get up rations and ammunition from the old Headquarters dug-out. The dressing-station was still intact, but Captain Ward, R.A.M.C., in charge of it, had been slightly wounded.

At 6.15 p.m. the bombardment broke out again as intense as ever, and at 7.15 p.m. the German infantry, a division of Marines, attacked. A part of them penetrated along the beach, and got in behind our line. The first the Battalion Headquarters knew of them was their appearance in the communication trench running parallel to the tunnel, whence they threw bombs down the air-shafts. They then appeared at the rear end of the tunnel, and threw in a species of liquid fire. This seems not to have had any very great effect. The Colonel then made for the front end of the tunnel and, apparently with the intention of making a last charge, went out into the open air, calling upon the party to follow him. In the narrow space, crowded with ammunition boxes, passage was difficult, and before the officers who were trying to get past to follow him could get through both entrances were blown in. Colonel Abadie was last seen by an Australian standing at bay outside the entrance firing his revolver, with which he killed five Germans before he himself fell. His dead body was afterwards identified on the spot where he fell.

Those left in the tunnel then went to work to clear the entrances. They had given up all hope of relief, and they made up their minds to break their way out and die fighting.

By the time the entrances had been cleared it was nearly dark. 2nd Lieutenant Henry, R.A., was the first to go out to reconnoitre. He returned to report that they were surrounded by the enemy. Rifleman Chaplin, Captain Butler's servant, then got as far as the old Headquarters dug-out, and reported that no wounded were left. Captains Smith and Butler then went out and got to within 10 yards of the German sentries. They came to the conclusion that, as the Germans were busy digging themselves in, there was a chance of getting through them and back to the river.

It was now about 10 p.m. The survivors in the tunnel were the four officers—Smith, Butler, Henry, and Gracie—15 riflemen, and about twenty Australians. Just as the party were about to emerge, it was seen that some Germans were approaching as if to enter the tunnel. Riflemen Smart and Allen were told off as a rearguard with orders to delay the enemy. This they did with great skill and coolness by blocking the passage at intervals with ammunition and biscuit boxes. The whole party then slipped out at the forward end of the tunnel. The enemy were only 20 yards away, but, fortunately, were busy digging. In spite of continuous shell fire and delays from having to lie flat whenever a Verèy light went up, they eventually reached the river-bank. Partly by swimming and partly

SKETCH MAP III

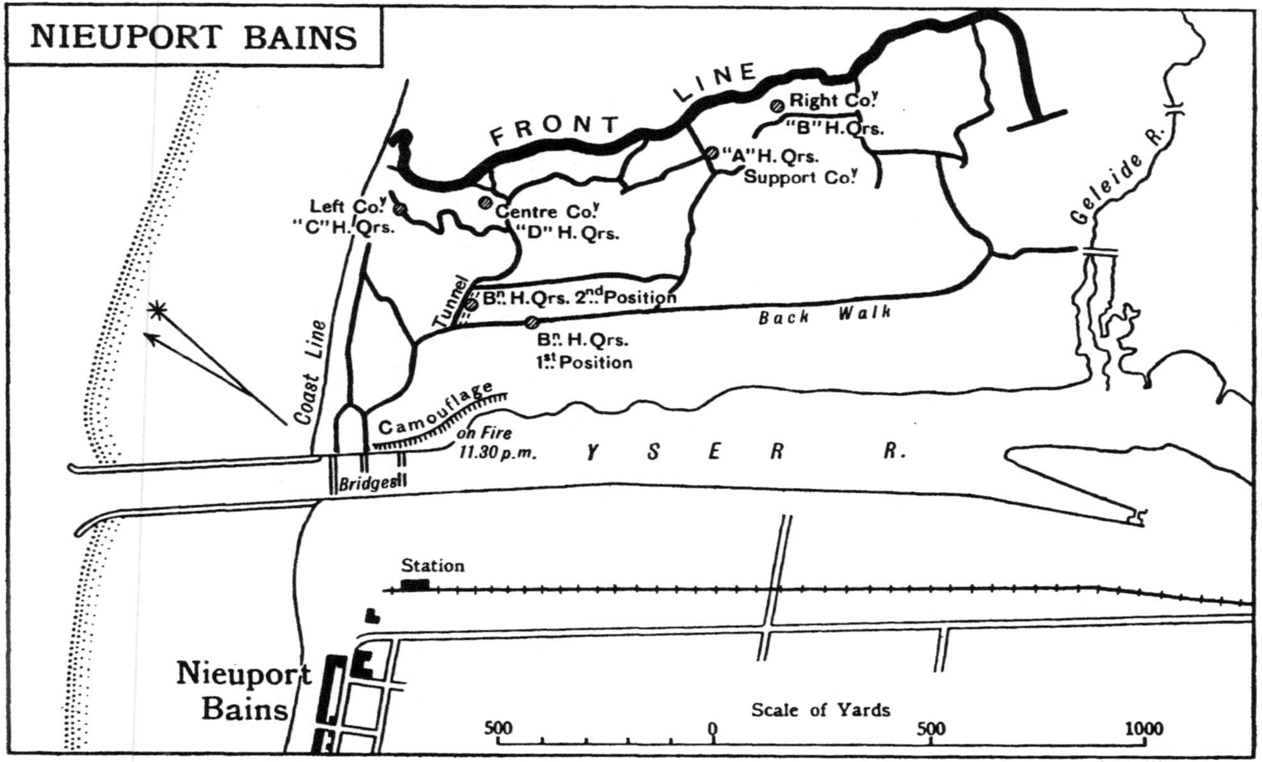

Emery Walker Ltd. sc.

by using what still remained of the bridges they at last got across. There were a few casualties by fire and drowning, but 4 officers and 32 other ranks reached the other side.

The companies in the front line had stuck it out to the end. When the German infantry arrived they found what was left of them half choked and blinded by sand, in spite of which they inflicted considerable loss on the attackers. The Germans took 404 prisoners, of whom about 100 were wounded, and of the remainder most were blinded by sand, shell-shocked, contused, or dug out of the sand.

Next day at 6 p.m. a party of 22 riflemen, under Lance-Sergeant J. H. Austin, having got clear of the dug-out in which they had been buried, walked back in broad daylight and crossed the Yser without a casualty, and without seeing a German.

The casualties of the Battalion were 17 officers out of 20 ; 481 other ranks out of 520. Seven officers were killed : Lieut.-Colonel R. N. Abadie, Lieutenant B. C. Munro, 2nd Lieutenants E. W. Barnes, A. G. Boucher, N. F. E. Anson, W. Sheepshanks, A. C. Heberden ; wounded and prisoners of war, Captain H. K. Ward (R.A.M.C.), Lieutenant W. H. E. Gott, 2nd Lieutenants R. Madeley, D. H. Taylor, and H. Chevis ; prisoners of war : Captain W. L. Clinton, Lieutenants A. Pinnock, H. J. F. Mills, 2nd Lieutenants H. J. Lindsay, A. Simpson.

For their conduct in the action Captain Smith received the D.S.O., Captain Butler a bar to his M.C., 2nd Lieutenants Gracie and Henry (R.A.) the M.C. ; Lance-Sergeant Austin the D.C.M. ; Riflemen Chaplin, Smart, and Allen, among others, the Military Medal. The conduct of one of the Australians named McGrady was, in particular, spoken of with the highest admiration, but he was killed during the course of the night.

The 2nd Battalion did not take long to recover. Before the end of July they had almost been brought up to strength, and on the 31st they joined the rest of the 1st Division in the 'mystery' camp at Le Clipon, south-west of Dunkerque. It was given out that the Division were in quarantine for some infectious pestilence, and they were shut off from the world. In reality they were in training for a landing on the Belgian coast, which was to take place when sufficient progress had been made by the Fifth Army for the Fourth to take a hand. In the end this stage was never reached. Under the command of Lieut.-Colonel F. G. Willan, who took over on July 21, and of Lieut.-Colonel G. C. Kelly, who succeeded him on September 6, when he was promoted to the command of a brigade, the Battalion made such progress that in the middle of September it was specially selected to give a demonstration of 'the Battalion in the attack' before a distinguished gathering, among which were several officers of the Higher Command of the American Army. Lieut.-Colonel Kelly took the opportunity to present the American General with a copy of the 'Brief History of the Regiment,' which was much appreciated by the recipient, who knew all about the origin of the Regiment.

THIRD BATTLE OF YPRES[1]

On July 31, at 3.50 a.m., after a twelve days' heavy bombardment, the Fifth Army attacked on the front Klein Zillebeke–Boesinghe, in conjunction with the Second Army on their right, and the First (French) Army on their left. The order of battle of the Fifth Army from right to left was, II Corps (24th, 30th, and 8th Divisions), XIX Corps (15th and 55th Divisions), XVIII Corps (39th and 51st Divisions), XIV (38th and Guards Divisions). The X

[1] Map I.

Corps, Second Army, attacked immediately to the right of the Fifth Army.

Unfortunately, after a long fine spell, the weather had broken a few days before the attack and already the going was bad. The day of the attack was dull and drizzling, bad for observation and aeroplane co-operation. A deluge set in on the night of July 31/August 1, and it was its continuation off and on throughout August and its renewal and persistence after one fine interval that ruined the prospect of any great success being achieved before the winter. The attack was fairly successful, but less so on the right than on the left. There was nothing like the results of the first day at Arras or Messines. The enemy everywhere made a stout resistance, and counter-attacked freely all along the line. Prisoners taken by the Fifth Army amounted to over 5,000, while the casualties amounted to over 20,000.

Pilckem Ridge

Over 1,000 of the prisoners were taken by the 39th Division, which attacked with the 116th Brigade on the right, the 117th on the left. The 17th K.R.R.C. (Lieut.-Colonel A. P. H. Le Prevost) were in the front line on the extreme left. The barrage opened at zero hour, and the advance began simultaneously. The enemy's barrage came down on our front-line trenches eight minutes later, but by that time our troops were well into No Man's Land.

By 4.20 a.m. the leading battalions had overrun the whole of the German front-line system without meeting very much resistance. They then started to consolidate, while the second-line battalions went through them. Our 17th Battalion lost 2nd Lieutenant P. C. Mann, killed; 2nd Lieutenant V. F. Turner, wounded; other ranks—killed 5, wounded 60, missing 8. They had captured 2 officers, 64 other ranks, and 1 machine gun. The second-line battalions and the 118th Brigade which went through to take the final objective found a much harder task, as they made their first acquaintance with the pill-box or concrete machine-gun emplacement. They dealt with them successfully by keeping their fire down with Lewis guns and rifle grenades, while they worked round them and bombed the garrisons. Though, owing to heavy losses, and having got out of touch with their neighbours on their right, the 118th Brigade had to give up some of the ground they had gained, the Division had made about the most successful advance of the day. Their losses, however, had been very heavy, amounting to 145 officers and 3,716 other ranks, killed, wounded, and missing.

The 122nd Brigade (41st Division) took part in the attack of the X Corps (Second Army). The Brigade attacked with the 18th K.R.R.C. (Lieut.-Colonel C. H. Kitching, D.S.O.) on the right and the 11th Royal West Kent on the left. The barrage came down, and the infantry advanced at 3.50 a.m. The enemy's barrage when it came down fell behind the attacking infantry, who took the first objective, the German front-line trenches, without difficulty. The second objective proved a much tougher proposition, consisting, as it did for the West Kent, of the village of Hollebeke, and for the 18th K.R.R.C., of Forret Farm, south-west of that village, both being strongly fortified and full of machine guns. The West Kent, after a very tough fight, had occupied the village by 11.30 a.m. Our 18th Battalion were less successful. The second wave of the Battalion, which went through after the capture of the first objective, seems to have lost direction, and got mixed up with the left battalion, leaving Forret Farm on their right. They thereby lost the barrage, and left Forret Farm unattacked. At 11.30 a.m. a Stokes mortar was sent up to bombard the farm, but was put out of action on its way up. Repeated orders were sent up for one of the first-line companies, engaged in consolidating the first objective, to go forward and rush the place, but the enemy's barrage was by this time very heavy, and all the runners were hit before they could get a message through. Captain Baskett, M.C., who had so distinguished himself at Flers the previous September, was sent up to find out the exact situation, and if necessary take command, but was wounded on his way up. The position was not taken, or touch gained with the division on the right, till August 2, by one of the reserve battalions of the Brigade. On July 31 Sergeant Diplock and a party of 8 men of the 18th K.R.R.C. did penetrate to the line of the second objective, between the farm and the village, and stuck it out there for twenty-four hours, taking part in a renewed attack by a company of the 12th East Surrey Regiment on the evening of August 1. Sergeant Diplock was rewarded with the D.C.M. The Battalion was withdrawn on the night of July 31/August 1, having lost: killed, Lieutenant G. A. G. Wilson (Royal Sussex Regiment, attached); 2nd Lieutenants J. H. Gibb, E. A. Claxton, C. Coburn; died of wounds, 2nd Lieutenant T. R. H. Webb; wounded, Captain R. Baskett, 2nd Lieutenant J. McL. Beatty; other ranks—killed 21, wounded 88, missing 37.

The Battalion remained in the trenches till August 14, when it went into the back areas for training, not returning into the front line till the middle of September.

The 124th Brigade, to which our 21st Battalion belonged, was in Divisional Reserve on July 31. At 7 p.m. two companies were sent forward to meet a counter-attack which the enemy was making on the 123rd Brigade. They repelled the attack with heavy loss to the enemy. Second Lieutenant W. B. Harmon was killed in the fight. Although they were not engaged in any big attack, and were out of the line for the last fortnight of August, this battalion lost during the month: killed, in addition to the officer already named, Major A. T. Watson and Captain C. O. Spencer-Smith (London Regiment, attached); other ranks—26; wounded, 10 officers, 253 other ranks; missing, 9 other ranks. They, too, did not return to the line till the middle of September.

The general result of the fighting of July 31 and the first two days of August was that the enemy's front system had been captured practically along the whole front of the attack, and, in spite of numerous and energetic counter-attacks, the British troops were firmly established on the ground they had gained. Incessant bad weather prevented any renewal of the advance on a big scale before the middle of August, but there was a good deal of local fighting in order to secure the best jumping-off places for the next advance. Especially was this necessary on the front of the XIV Corps, where a foothold had to be secured on the right bank of the Steenbeek, so that the first move of the big operation should not have to include the crossing of that stream.

On August 6 the 20th Division completed the relief of the 38th in the right sector of the XIV Corps front, and were thus confronted by the Steenbeek proposition. The situation on the front held by the Division was that the enemy were holding the opposite bank of the Steenbeek, while the British line was from 200 to 400 yards short of the stream. The 59th Brigade took over the line, the 60th and 61st being kept in reserve, the intention being that the 59th Brigade should gain a footing on the other side of the stream by a preliminary operation, where it would be relieved by the other two brigades the day before the big attack. The attack completed, the two brigades which had made it would, in turn, be relieved by the 59th, which would hold the position gained. Subsequent events prevented this scheme being carried out in its entirety.

The 10th K.R.R.C. was detailed to carry out the operation of crossing the Steenbeek. The attack was fixed for 4.15 a.m. on August 11. It was to be made by two companies of the Battalion, which were to form up in the open within 200 yards of the stream. Unfortunately, an enemy's patrol which had crossed the stream detected our troops in the act of forming up, and turned on a machine gun with very disastrous results, as the right company lost heavily, and was completely disorganised. The operation failed, only small parties ever getting over the stream, and they were never seen again. The casualties in this unfortunate affair were: killed, 8 other ranks; wounded, 1 officer and 32 other ranks; missing, 4 officers, of whom 2nd Lieutenant F. A. Haycroft was killed; Captain F. H. Tate died of wounds in German hands; Captain R. L. Jones and 2nd Lieutenant J. M. Lovatt (5th N. Staffs, attached) were prisoners of war, and 85 other ranks.

Three days later the operation was successfully carried out by the 10th and 11th Battalions Rifle Brigade, six companies being employed this time. Evidently no blame was attached to the 10th Battalion for their failure, as a few days later we find their Divisional Commander addressing a new draft, and congratulating them on coming to a battalion which 'always fought well.'

Langemarck

On August 16 the Fifth Army attacked again all along the line. The enemy had spent the time that the weather had given him in strongly reinforcing his line, and his resistance was more determined than ever.

The II and XIX Corps having captured their first

objectives failed to get any farther and, being everywhere vigorously counter-attacked, ended the day very much where they had begun it.

The XVIII Corps did very much better, taking the second of three objectives all along their front. They were obliged to fall back a bit on their right owing to the failure of their next-door neighbours, but on the extreme left they reached and held their final objective.

The XIV Corps had a great success. With the 20th Division on the right, and the 29th on the left, they gained their final objective all along their front. The 29th Division retained the whole of theirs, but in the centre of the 20th Division the front of one battalion was driven back a matter of 200 yards. The Corps had penetrated to a depth of 2,000 yards, including the village of Langemarck, and they were in touch with the XVIII Corps on their right and the French on their left.

The 20th Division attacked with the 60th Brigade on the right; the 61st, which had to take the village of Langemarck, on the left. The following account of the part taken by our 12th Battalion is from the 'Chronicle' of 1917:

'On the 15th we paraded in full battle order, and the companies marched independently to the point of assembly, where positions for each platoon had been marked out with tape by A./Captain Thornton-Smith, D.S.O. Positions were taken up without difficulty, although we were subjected to some fairly heavy shelling, and sustained a few casualties.

'During the night, preparations were made for the attack. Bridges of logs were thrown across the Steenbeek, as the depth of the mud made it practically impassable. Towards morning our shelling increased, and by the zero hour (4.45 a.m.) it had become terrific. It lifted five minutes later, and we advanced to our first objective, about 3,400 yards [*sic*] short of Langemarck [the first objective of the 61st Brigade was just short of the village, while that of the 60th Brigade was in the same line but to the right. The whole distance from the British front line to the village was about 500 yards. Presumably the printer's devil is responsible for an extra nought], with the 6th King's Shropshire Light Infantry on our right, and the 12th King's Liverpools on our left. On their left we saw the 6th Oxford and Bucks busily engaged in mopping up the Au Bon Gîte, a collection of pill-boxes on the bank of the Steenbeek.

'During this advance and a twenty minutes' halt to re-organise at our first objective, we were subjected to a very heavy machine-gun fire, and had many casualties, including A./Lieut.-Colonel Prioleau, M.C. (Rifle Brigade), who was wounded.

'The Adjutant, Captain T. Lycett, assumed command, and noticing a large pill-box on our left, which was holding up the advance of the battalion on our left, and also causing us heavy casualties by machine-gun fire, he ordered Sergeant Cooper (who was in command of a platoon, as his officer had been killed) to try and rush it.

'Accompanied by twelve men, Sergeant Cooper at once went forward, and with four of them succeeded in getting to a point about 100 yards from the pill-box, the remainder of his party having become casualties. From this point he tried to silence the fire from the pill-box by rifle fire, but failed, and the four men with him were killed. Sergeant Cooper then rushed forward alone, armed with a revolver which he had taken from his platoon officer after the latter had been killed. He succeeded in reaching the pill-box and began firing through the slit. Thinking that they were surrounded, an officer and 44 men came out and surrendered to him. There were seven machine guns in the pill-box, which were also captured. For this most gallant deed Sergeant Cooper was recommended for the V.C., which he was granted, and received later.

'By this time we had lost the following officers: A./Captain Thornton-Smith, D.S.O., and Lieutenant Carnegie (killed); 2nd Lieutenant Pollard (wounded, later died of wounds), and Captain Taylor (wounded); and had had about 100 casualties among the rank and file. At 5.45 a.m. the barrage began to creep forward, and we advanced in artillery formation to our second objective, just on the east side of Langemarck.

'At this point we deployed and obtained touch with the

6th King's Shropshire Light Infantry on our right, and the 12th King's Liverpools on our left.

'The barrage lifted, and we advanced to the attack of the final objective. To reach this, we had to cross about 4,500 [*sic*] yards [evidently a misprint for 450] of very boggy and shell-torn ground, during which we came under very heavy machine-gun fire, which caused many casualties, and encountered several pill-boxes which we accounted for, and from which we got some prisoners. Captain Lycett captured a German officer, and succeeded in eliciting some very valuable information from him.

'Notwithstanding the difficult nature of the ground over which we had to advance, and in spite of heavy opposition, especially on our left company front, we succeeded in reaching our final objective at 7.50 a.m.

'A few more prisoners were captured, but most of the enemy ran as soon as we reached their trench, which formed our final objective. We were able to account for a good many of them with rifle and Lewis-gun fire.

'At midday, messages were received from Captain Dove, M.C., who was in command of our left company, that he could see the enemy massing for a counter-attack. Fire was brought to bear on them with good effect, and the Brigadier was informed of the situation. We received orders that our positions were to be held at all costs. At 4.10 p.m. the enemy launched his counter-attack. The S.O.S. was at once sent in, and our guns responded immediately. They were, however, unable to stop the enemy, who advanced in large numbers. The weight of the attack seemed to be especially directed against the King's Liverpools, on our left, and after a gallant resistance they were pressed back. This let in the enemy on our left, but our left company, gallantly led by Captain Dove, put up a stout resistance, and fought until they were annihilated, only 1 sergeant and 4 men succeeding in rejoining the next company. Captain Dove was killed, and 2nd Lieutenant Munsey severely wounded.

'By this time conditions appeared desperate, as we had nearly exhausted our ammunition, and it was a matter of great difficulty to replenish it. A defensive flank was thrown back, and touch again established with the 12th King's Liverpools.

'This defensive flank was about 200 yards long, and was held by an officer and 15 men.

'Consolidation was begun that night, and continued for the two following days, during which time we were subjected to a lot of sniping, but not much shelling.

'On the night of August 18/19 the Battalion was relieved by the 10th Battalion Welch Regiment, and returned to Malakoff Farm, worn out, but cheery.

. . . . .

'The casualties during these operations amounted to: officers—5 killed, 1 died of wounds, 2 wounded and missing; other ranks—40 killed, 17 died of wounds, 47 missing, and 134 wounded.'

The missing officers were both killed. The corrected list is as follows: killed, Captains T. Dove, A. D. Thornton-Smith; 2nd Lieutenants E. D. Brown, T. A. Carnegie, W. F. Munsey, J. H. Molyneux; died of wounds, Captain G. L. F. Taylor (3rd London Regiment), 2nd Lieutenant E. M. Pollard.

Isolated attacks went on for the next few days with varying success on different parts of the Fifth Army front. On August 22 an attempt was made to retrieve the failure of the 16th by the XVIII, XIX, and the left and centre divisions of the II Corps. A lot of hard fighting did not produce any very satisfactory results, though some ground was gained, and most of the enemy's counter-attacks were beaten off.

On the night of the 17th/18th the 14th (Light) Division relieved the 56th Division and a brigade of the 18th in the centre of the II Corps front.

At 7 a.m. on the 22nd the Division attacked with the 43rd Brigade astride the Menin Road, the 42nd Brigade on their left. Neither K.R.R.C. nor Rifle Brigade was among the attacking battalions. The 41st Brigade was in Divisional Reserve. After very hard fighting most of the objective was gained along the whole front of the Division, but the enemy answered with very determined counter-attacks, and by 11 a.m. the right brigade, which had reached the far side of Inverness Copse, was pressed back almost to its western edge. About midday our 8th Battalion was ordered up to Sanctuary Wood, to be placed at the disposal of the 43rd Brigade, and got there about 2 p.m. At 10.30 p.m. they moved up into the old front line, just south of the Menin Road, from which the attack had started in the morning.

Next morning the enemy delivered a counter-attack between Inverness Copse and Glencorse Wood, which was beaten off. During the day the Division received orders to hold the 41st Brigade in readiness for a further operation. To carry this out the 42nd Brigade was ordered to relieve the 8th K.R.R.C. on the night of the 23rd/24th. The relief was interrupted by an enemy attack, and Headquarters, with 1½ companies of the Battalion, remained in the line, occupying a defensive flank facing south, running from Inverness Copse to Stirling Castle. Heavy counter-attacks went on all day, and at one time our troops were very nearly driven out of Inverness Copse. Things looked so critical that not only was the 41st Brigade ordered up to the front, but the 72nd Brigade (24th Division) was placed at the disposal of the 14th Division. By the end of the day the enemy had expended his efforts, and a line was firmly established about half-way between the starting-line and the objective of the 23rd.

During the night of the 24th/25th the 41st Brigade relieved the 43rd in the front line. The 8th Battalion went back the same night into Brigade Reserve. They had lost very heavily from shell fire, their casualties including Major T. L. Bourdillon, Captains R. L. Hardy (Adjutant), N. E. Lee, Lieutenant H. D. Simpson, 2nd Lieutenants A. E. Barrett, C. N. J. Spilling, killed; 3 officers wounded, and about a hundred other ranks killed and wounded.

For the next two days the 7th Battalion were in the front line repelling counter-attacks, losing 2nd Lieutenant A. J. Hooper (London Regiment, attached), killed, and Captain P. K. Howarth, wounded.

During the night of the 25th/26th the 23rd Division relieved the 14th, but the 41st Brigade remained in the line till the night of the 27th/28th.

The 41st Brigade were under orders to make a fresh attack on the morning of the 27th, but a renewal of the bad weather made movement impossible.

The bad weather persisted. During the last few days of August and first week in September various minor operations were undertaken on the Fifth Army front without success. A renewal on a large scale was put off till September 20, when it was arranged that the Second and Fifth Armies should attack together.

On September 3 the II Corps area was transferred to the Second Army and the II Anzac Corps relieved the II Corps.

On September 7 the V Corps took over from the XIX Corps.

There were several more unsuccessful local attacks made during the second week in September. There was a temporary improvement in the weather, but, of course, the big attack timed for the 20th was heralded by a downpour on the previous night.

At 5.40 a.m., on the 20th, the Fifth Army attacked with the V and XVIII Corps and the 20th Division of the XIV Corps.

Nearly all the objectives were taken, the only partial failure being in the 20th Division. The enemy made numerous counter-attacks, all of which were beaten off, except on the left of the XVIII Corps, where he made a considerable dip in the front of the 51st Division.

The 20th Division had taken over the right sector of the XIV Corps on September 11, and had on their right the 51st Division and on their left the Guards.

On the 20th the Division attacked, with the 60th Brigade on the right and the 59th on the left. Each brigade had two battalions in the front line, one in support—east of Langemarck—and one in reserve—just east of the Steenbeek.

Our 12th Battalion, the command of which had just been taken over by Lieut.-Colonel L. G. Moore, D.S.O., was in reserve to the 60th Brigade. The 59th Brigade attacked with the 11th K.R.R.C. on the right, the 10th K.R.R.C. on the left. The previous evening a shell landed on the Battalion Headquarters dug-out of the 10th Battalion and killed the Commanding Officer, Lieut.-Colonel T. M. Rixon, M.C., his Adjutant, Captain G. S. Wallington, and 8 other ranks, 8 other ranks also being wounded. The command was taken over by Major R. S. Cockburn, M.C.

The immediate result of the attack was that it was successful on the extreme left, partially so on the right, but in the centre was held up by a trench called Eagle Trench, some way short of the first objective. The left leading company of our 10th Battalion quickly reached their final objective, which in their case was coincident with the first objective. The right company were held up owing to enfilade fire from strong-points farther to the right. Our 11th Battalion came up against Eagle Trench, and a day of very hard and confused fighting ensued. The left of the Battalion seems to have got into Eagle Trench, and even beyond it, till they were brought up by further strong-points and, finding themselves in the air, were obliged to withdraw. The right of the Battalion was definitely held up. The 60th Brigade were successful on their right, but their left was also held up by Eagle Trench. Their situation was further complicated by the battalion of the 51st Division next on their right being driven back in the afternoon by a German counter-attack. By evening the situation was that, while on the left our troops were established in their final objective with a defensive flank thrown back towards Eagle Trench, on the rest of the Division's front the position was very obscure, parts of Eagle Trench being held by our men and parts by the enemy. This made it very difficult to assist a renewal of the attack by a bombardment. It was therefore decided to await the arrival of some tanks. The promised tanks had unfortunately got bogged, and it was therefore decided to attack on the morning of the 23rd without them.

The plan was for a hurricane bombardment by Stokes mortars to be begun at 7 a.m. on that part of Eagle Trench still held by the enemy. Following the bombardment a party of the 12th K.R.R.C. were to make a bombing attack from the south, while a party of the 10th Rifle Brigade attacked over the open from the west.

At 6.25 a.m. the enemy launched a counter-attack on the right front of the 60th Brigade, now held by our 12th Battalion, which had relieved the two battalions in the front line of the 60th Brigade during the night of the 21st/22nd. This attack was beaten off by machine-gun and rifle fire, 22 unwounded and 1 wounded prisoner being taken. The Stokes-mortar bombardment began at 7 a.m., and after three minutes of it the attacking troops—they only totalled 80 of all ranks—advanced to the attack under a barrage of rifle grenades. The party of our 12th Battalion—1 N.C.O. and 18 riflemen under Lieutenant J. McDonald, M.C. (Scottish Rifles, attached)—were the first to move. While the enemy was engaged with them, the party of the 10th Rifle Brigade advanced over the open and rushed the trench. A party consisting of an officer and 40 other ranks of the 6th King's Shropshire Light Infantry acted as moppers-up to McDonald's party. The attack was a complete success, and about 100 prisoners were taken with 10 machine guns.

Our casualties were slight, but Lieutenant McDonald was killed. While this was going on one company of our 10th Battalion took part with some of the 10th Rifle Brigade in a successful attack on a strong-point called Chinese House, some hundreds of yards behind the left of Eagle Trench.

By the evening of the 23rd the 59th and 60th Brigades were well established on the line which had been their first objective for the 20th. They had spent five days under incessant shell fire with little cover but shell holes, and had suffered severely, but had inflicted heavy loss on the enemy. The German troops that delivered the unsuccessful counter-attack on the morning of the 23rd and also those captured in Eagle Trench were special storm troops assembled for the purpose of a big counter-attack which our capture of Eagle Trench forestalled. The Division was inundated with congratulatory messages from the Army Commander (Gough), their own Corps Commander (Lord Cavan), and even from the G.O.C. Second Army (Plumer), under whom they had previously served.

On the night of the 23rd/24th the 61st Brigade relieved the 59th and 60th in the front line, and the Division was relieved by the 4th Division on the night of the 28th/29th, and went into Corps Reserve.

The losses of the 10th Battalion during the five days, 19th–23rd, were: killed—officers, Lieut.-Colonel T. M. Rixon, M.C., Captain and Adjutant G. S. Wallington, Lieutenant H. C. Lindop (5th South Staffordshire, attached), 2nd Lieutenants M. Hole, H. Lines; 35 other ranks;

wounded—officers, 2nd Lieutenants A. S. Bates, A. Wright, H. T. Fice; 90 other ranks; missing—20 other ranks.

The losses of the 11th Battalion, all incurred on the 20th—they were withdrawn into reserve on the night of the 20th/21st—were: killed—Captains H. J. Clifford, J. Bogle, M.C. (Scottish Rifles, attached), 2nd Lieutenants J. W. Pool (Scottish Rifles, attached), L. G. Edwards, R. G. Hobbs, E. Charleston; 36 other ranks; wounded—2nd Lieutenants E. P. Rider, W. J. Camplin, A. J. Sutters; 127 other ranks; missing—43 other ranks.

The losses of the 12th Battalion were: killed—Lieutenant J. McDonald, M.C.; 5 other ranks; wounded—69 other ranks.

Menin Road Ridge

The attack of the Second Army on September 20th was made on a front of nearly four miles, from the Ypres–Comines Canal on the right, to the junction with the Fifth Army, near the Ypres–Roulers Railway.[1] The Army attacked with one division of the IX Corps on the right; the 39th, 41st, and 23rd Divisions of the X Corps, in the centre, and two divisions of the I Anzac Corps on the left.

The Army had a most successful day. Starting at 5.40 a.m. the first objective was taken by 6.15 a.m., except on the front of the 124th Brigade, where machine-gun posts which had survived the bombardment held up the attack almost from the start. The advance was resumed at 7.15 a.m. by the IX Corps, which gained its second objective by 7.45 a.m. The other two corps, advancing at 7.40 a.m., except on the 124th Brigade front where the first objective had not yet been taken—met with much more resistance, but gained their second objectives by about 10 a.m. The 124th Brigade, after very hard fighting, had secured their second objective soon after

[1] Map I.

eleven o'clock, but were unable to get any farther during the day. Everywhere else on the Army front the final objective, which meant an advance of about a mile, was gained during the day. The enemy delivered three strong counter-attacks during the afternoon, all of which were beaten off, while several more concentrations were broken up by artillery fire before they could develop into counter-attacks.

Our 21st Battalion, attacking on the left of the 124th Brigade, almost as soon as they had started, came under very heavy machine-gun fire from Het Pappotje Farm, which was within 500 yards of their own front line. Owing to heavy casualties among the officers considerable disorganisation ensued, and it was by the personal efforts of the Commanding Officer, Lieut.-Colonel T. McL. Jarvis, D.S.O., who was wounded in the process, that the Battalion was pulled together, and parties detailed to deal with the machine-gun nests. By 9.25 a.m. it had been reported at Divisional Headquarters that Het Pappotje Farm had been 'mopped up,' and it must have been about this time that the first objective was captured. The attack on the second objective seems to have been a repetition of that on the first; that is, there were again heavy casualties from machine-gun fire, resulting in disorganisation and mixing of units. It is difficult to extract a very clear story from the meagre accounts of the fighting, but it seems clear that the right battalion of the Brigade had also been in difficulties. The battalions which were intended to go through and capture the final objective had become involved in the fighting for the second objective; consequently, when that was captured, between 11 a.m. and 12 noon, the Brigade was not equal to an attack on the final objective, and had to dig in considerably behind the line gained by the rest of the Army. The line on which the Brigade dug in was not taken till the evening. A German counter-attack was beaten off just before this advance, and another after it had been completed.

The 21st Battalion remained in the front line till the night of the 22nd/23rd, when they were relieved by the 1st Cambridgeshire Regiment, after beating off another counter-attack on the morning of the 21st.

The strength of the Battalion going into action was: officers 19, other ranks 487. Their casualties of all ranks totalled 282, being: killed—officers, 2 (2nd Lieutenants F. F. Norton, H. J. Kelly); other ranks, 45; wounded—officers 13 (Lieut.-Colonel T. McL. Jarvis, D.S.O.; Captains E. M. Worsley, H. C. Meysey-Thompson, G. J. L. Burton, H. C. Fein, N. A. Beechman; Captain and Adjutant W. Harrison; 2nd Lieutenants F. E. Hudson, G. R. Webb, H. Sandford, A. E. Thorn, E. Chart, D. C. Simpson); other ranks 192; missing—other ranks 44.

Our 18th Battalion (Lieut.-Colonel R. Pennell, D.S.O.) attacked on the right of the 122nd Brigade. Their task was to capture the first and second objectives and consolidate them, while another battalion went through to attack the third objective. This they carried out with comparatively little loss, and formed a defensive flank on the right, where the 21st Battalion had been unable to get on and did not get into touch till the evening.

Next day the Battalion came in for some heavy shelling, besides being machine-gunned and sniped from their right front. One company suffered from some 'shorts' from their own artillery, and lost 2 officers killed. Next day was more peaceful, as the situation on the right had improved. They were relieved on the 23rd.

Our 17th Battalion was, on September 20, attacking on the extreme left of the 39th Division, and were therefore next door to the unfortunate 124th Brigade. The 16th

Rifle Brigade were on the left in the attack on the first objective ; then the 17th K.R.R.C. were to go through and take the second objective, which done, they were to send one company on to take the final objective.

The first line was taken by 6 a.m. At 7.8 a.m. the battalions detailed for the capture of the next line went through, being at first much hampered by machine guns to their left front. These were successfully rushed and captured by the 17th K.R.R.C., and the second objective was attained. The battalion on the right succeeded in reaching the final objective, but owing to the failure of the 124th Brigade our 17th Battalion, instead of advancing to the final objective, were obliged to form a defensive flank to the left, to get in touch with the right of the 124th Brigade. The Battalion were relieved during the course of the ensuing night. Their losses were : killed—officers 2 (2nd Lieutenants A. H. Rice, O. A. Keeler, London Regiment, attached), other ranks 34 ; wounded—officers 5 (Lieutenant W. P. Sproul, 2nd Lieutenants R. E. Burgon, H. B. Marriott, M. G. Willmott, G. A. Parfitt) ; other ranks 132.

The 39th Division was again attacking on September 26, but the 117th Brigade was in Divisional Reserve, and our 17th Battalion was not engaged.

This attack was made by the Second Army on a front of 5,500 yards, astride the Menin Road, in connection with the Fifth Army on their left. The troops of the Second Army taking part were the X Corps (39th and 33rd Divisions) and the I Anzac Corps. Generally speaking, the attack was successful, but the 33rd Division had been subjected to a very vigorous German counter-attack the previous day and lost heavily, and were not in a condition to carry out the full programme. The plan of attack for them was therefore modified, but even this was beyond what they could completely perform, as the left brigade, 98th, was subjected to a very heavy barrage during the hour preceding zero, which prevented it from moving forward at that hour. The Division did, however, in the end, gain most of its objectives, and was specially praised by the Field-Marshal Commanding-in-Chief, who, in a letter to General Plumer, congratulating his Army, says:

> 'Please convey to all Corps and Divisions engaged my heartiest congratulations, and especially to the 33rd Division, whose successful attack, following a day of hard fighting, is deserving of all praise.'

Our 16th Battalion was in reserve, but was sent up by companies to reinforce other units, and had a lot of hard fighting during the three days September 25–27. C Company, under Captain L. Francis, acting in support of the 1st Queen's, particularly distinguished itself, capturing a machine gun, 6 officers, and 42 other ranks, prisoners.

The casualties of the Battalion during the three days were: officers—wounded, 2nd Lieutenants E. G. Fookes, W. A. Stratton, H. A. Manning, R. J. R. Day; other ranks: killed 33, wounded 152, missing 31.

The Division was relieved on September 28.

We may now say good-bye to the Third Battle of Ypres, as none of the battalions of our Regiment took further part in it.

The battle dragged on, as had that of the Somme, and met with the same fate—drowned out.

CHAPTER X

'Cambrai, 1917'[1]

Some time before the beginning of the Third Battle of Ypres, it had been pointed out to G.H.Q., that if the drainage system in the area of the forthcoming battle were destroyed by bombardment, the place would become a swamp, and tanks would be unable to operate.

That meant that either the operations in Flanders must be independent of tanks or the attack must be made elsewhere.

No doubt the great strategical advantages of the Flanders battle, which, it must be remembered, was to include the clearing of the Belgian coast, decided the Commander-in-Chief to stick to his original plan.

The question, however, soon came up for discussion whether use might not be found for the tanks elsewhere. It was finally decided that the Third Army (Sir Julian Byng) should make an attack in the direction of Cambrai, making use of tanks to an extent and in a manner which had not so far been attempted.

The theatre of operations was selected because the ground was suitable for tanks even in wet weather, there was plenty of cover under which the tanks might concentrate unobserved, and it was looked upon as a weak point in the enemy's line.

The scheme is best explained by an extract from Third Army Operation Orders :

'1. The object of the operation is to break the enemy's defensive system by a *coup de main*, with the assistance of tanks ; to pass the Cavalry Corps through the break thus

[1] Map IV.

made; to seize Cambrai, Bourlon Wood, and the passages over the Sensée River,[1] and to cut off the troops holding the German front line between Havrincourt and that river.

'2. The operation is designed to take advantage of the existing favourable local situation. Surprise and rapidity of action are therefore of the utmost importance.

'3. The intention of the Army Commander is, therefore: first, to gain possession of the quadrilateral formed by the Canal de l'Escaut–Sensée River [running east and west five or six miles north of Cambrai]–Canal du Nord; secondly, to clear up the area lying to the west of this quadrilateral.

'4. The operation resolves itself into three stages:

'(*a*) The infantry attack on the German organised lines, including the capture of the crossings over the Canal de l'Escaut at Masnières and Marcoing, and of the Masnières–Beaurevoir line east of those places.

'(*b*) The advance of the cavalry to isolate Cambrai, and to seize the crossings over the Sensée River; and of IV Corps to capture Bourlon Wood.

'(*c*) The clearing of Cambrai and of the quadrilateral Canal de l'Escaut–Sensée River–Canal du Nord, and the overthrow of the German divisions thus cut off.'

Of these, (*a*) and the latter half of (*b*) only were accomplished, so we need only concern ourselves with the operations of the Corps which carried them out, the III and IV.

The objectives of the two corps were, shortly, for the III Corps on the right to establish bridgeheads at Masnières and Marcoing, with a defensive flank occupying the high ground on the left bank of the Scheldt from opposite Crèvecœur to Gonnelieu. Advantage was to be taken of any weakening of the defence to occupy the crossings at Crèvecœur. The IV Corps was to capture Bourlon Wood, the importance of its being taken on the first day being particularly emphasised. When the river crossings were secured the Cavalry Corps was to push through.

The III Corps was to attack with the 12th Division on the right, the 20th in the centre, and the 6th on the left.

[1] Map VIII.

After the first objective, which was practically the main Hindenburg Line, had been taken, the 12th Division was to wheel to its right and form a defensive flank. When the second objective had been reached, the 29th Division, from reserve, was to go through and secure the crossings at Masnières and Marcoing, while the 20th Division was to form a defensive flank on the high ground west of the Scheldt connecting with the 12th Division on its right and the 29th on its left. To this division also fell the task of occupying the crossings at Crèvecœur, if the situation should permit.

At 6.20 a.m., on November 20, the attack was launched. It was led by three hundred and forty-two tanks in the first line, with thirty-nine in reserve, of which twenty-eight were used on the first day. There were nearly one hundred more tanks on various odd jobs, carrying supplies, etc. The day's fighting produced the greatest gains by the British for any one day since the war began, but there was a hitch here and there, which in the end made just the difference between success and failure.

The III Corps obtained nearly all its objectives, but the 20th Division, though it occupied the defensive flank laid down for it, had been unable to secure the crossings at Crèvecœur.

The 29th Division held the crossings at Masnières and Marcoing, but otherwise did not gain much ground beyond the Canal. The IV Corps had got on well on its right and left, but in the centre had failed to take Flesquières, much less Bourlon Wood. The enemy's line was dented, but not shattered, and the cavalry could not get through.

The 20th Division attacked with the 61st Brigade on the right, the 60th Brigade on the left. The 59th Brigade was to go through after the second objective had been carried, secure the crossings at Masnières and Marcoing, and hold them till the arrival of the 29th Division, at the same time forming a defensive flank, which would connect with the 12th Division on the right and the 29th on the left.

Our 12th Battalion (Lieut.-Colonel L. G. Moore, D.S.O.), on the left of the front line of the 60th Brigade, was to take the first objective, when another battalion would pass through to the attack of the second objective. Each battalion in the front line was accompanied by three groups of three tanks each. Each group of three tanks moved with one tank as advanced guard, the remaining two of each group were closely followed by the infantry, one platoon in file to each tank. Each company had three platoons and a small Headquarters platoon, instead of four platoons and Company Headquarters. The Battalion was distributed as follows: A and C Companies, under 2nd Lieutenants J. T. Keeping, M.C., and C. E. Austin respectively, were employed with the tanks. D Company (Captain G. B. Loyd) was in close support, and B Company (Captain A. Hoare) in Battalion Reserve. It must be remembered, in reading the following account from the 12th Battalion's 'War Diary,' published in the 'Chronicle' of 1917, that the first objective of the 20th Division was not one trench line, but the Hindenburg Line itself, a whole series of trenches.

'On November 19, at 3.10 p.m., the Battalion marched out of the camp (Heudicourt) and went up through Gouzeaucourt to Station Quarry at Villers-Plouich. Here the cookers, which had started later, met us, and at about 11 p.m. every man had a hot drink of tea. At 1 a.m. on the 20th hot tea was again served out. At 2.15 a.m. the Battalion moved off in file to the assembly position, at which the tanks had already arrived. Guides had been sent already to meet the tanks. As the Battalion moved up they led their respective platoons into their places without any confusion or trouble.

'The enemy did not interfere with the assembly in any

way. A few 4·2-inch shells fell near the tanks, but it was evident that no attack was suspected at that point. Officers and men lay down, or sat, in their places, waiting for zero, which had been fixed for 6.20 a.m. Precisely at 6.10 a.m. the tanks began to move forward. The long line of tanks, magnified to monstrous size in the dim light of early dawn, the columns of infantry with fixed bayonets which followed them, all advancing silently and in order, formed a spectacle which no one who saw it can ever forget. Not a shot was fired by the enemy until our leading tanks began to cross the British support-line trenches. Then at last the Germans opened with trench mortars and machine guns. Almost at the same moment our artillery, so long silent, burst into a roar. The barrage came down on the Hindenburg Line with a violence which must have shaken the stoutest of Prussians. Every gun of the many hundreds in action commenced by firing one round of smoke shells. These, as they burst, threw out volumes of fire and sparks. A proportion of the artillery put down a heavy smoke barrage beyond the Hindenburg Line. A few minutes afterwards the tanks smashed through the thick wire of Farm Trench [about 600 yards short of the main Hindenburg Line], and our men took it with scarcely any resistance on the part of its garrison. Up to this point remarkably few casualties had occurred, nearly all from machine-gun fire while crossing No Man's Land. D Company halted in Farm Trench, and set about its appointed task [to clear and consolidate this trench]. 2nd Lieutenant Gawthorp was wounded while leading his platoon down the trench, but no further casualties occurred. The remainder of the Battalion advanced on the Hindenburg Line. In the neighbourhood of Goodman Farm, a heap of ruins about 300 yards on the British side of the Hindenburg Line, C Company on the right came under considerable machine-gun fire. 2nd Lieutenants Austin and Finch were both wounded, and several others were hit also. The Company, however, continued to advance on its objective without checking in the least, and, following closely after the tanks, carried it. A Company also carried its objectives, but not without some resistance from the enemy. Six machine guns were taken by them, and 4 by C Company. What pleased the men still more was a German canteen full of beer, wine, cigarettes, and cigars, which fell to some resolute spirits of A Company, and provided, later, much-needed refreshment.

'B Company had not yet come into action. It had suffered but few casualties up to this time, including, however, 2nd Lieutenant Kay, who was severely wounded. Captain Hoare halted his company for a few minutes while he conferred with the Battalion Commander, who was with him at that time. It was decided to push on at once and capture the final objective. A Stokes mortar, which had been attached to the Battalion, came into action to support his advance. Captain Hoare led his company forward. The first enemy trench was crossed without opposition, but in the support line the platoon, under command of 2nd Lieutenant H. T. Paul, met with a party of the enemy. A hand-to-hand fight ensued, in which 2nd Lieutenant Paul was, unfortunately, killed, together with 3 of his men. Five Germans lay dead in front of him. The remainder of the enemy fled. Captain Hoare left the rest of this platoon to hold that part of the support line, and himself advanced with his two other platoons. Between the support line and the third line was a little mound, which, as appeared afterwards, contained a dug-out. On reaching this our men came under very severe fire from snipers and machine guns. The 6th Oxford and Bucks Light Infantry, on our right flank, had not yet pushed forward far enough to distract the enemy's attention; consequently, this fire was in direct enfilade from that direction.

'Round and upon the mound Captain Hoare and 14 other riflemen were killed, and many others wounded. The last remaining N.C.O., Sergeant Rowland, at once took command of the Company, and endeavoured to advance, when he, too, was wounded.

'Rifleman Shepherd, who was Captain Hoare's orderly, then took command. He ordered the others to keep up a steady fire, and by his gallant example encouraged them and inspired them with confidence. In spite of the severe and accurate fire, he then got up and walked back over some 70 yards of open ground to get assistance from a tank which he had noticed approaching. He succeeded in attracting the attention of the crew, and the tank moved forward to deal with the enemy. Rifleman Shepherd then returned, still under heavy fire, to the Company. Already that day he had rushed a machine gun single-handed, and had taken it after killing the gun team. Not many actions have been more gallant than those of this rifleman. Meanwhile, an officer who had been able to grasp the situation managed to get to a point in front of the mound near which B Company were, and signalled to them to advance. They did so ; and as the tank requisitioned by Rifleman Shepherd, together with the Oxford and Bucks Light Infantry on the right, had subdued the enemy's fire, they suffered no further losses. On calling the roll after the fight it was found that only 34 survived out of 3 officers and 94 N.C.O.s and riflemen of B Company who had gone into action. But the Company took its objective.

'Among the losses sustained by the Battalion on November 20 the name of Captain A. Hoare will always be remembered by those who knew him. His whole life had been devoted to the Regiment, to which he had given twenty-two years of spotless service, and in which he had risen from private rifleman to Captain. The example of coolness, courage, and skill he displayed in leading his company was such as might have been expected from a veteran of the old army. The devotion he inspired in his men was great. Himself conscientious, almost to a fault, in the exact performance of the smallest duty, he maintained among them a rigid discipline. But no man who did his best ever wanted help or encouragement from his Captain, and they all bitterly regretted his death.

'While these things were happening on the right, D Company on the left had pushed down the Couillet Valley and taken all its objectives with little or no opposition, so that the Battalion had now completed the task assigned to it. Our total losses were considerable.'

The Battalion started to consolidate, and the 12th Rifle Brigade passed through.

In spite of severe fighting in places, the day's programme of the 20th Division went off without a hitch. The first objective was taken about 9.30 a.m., and the second about noon. The 59th Brigade had advanced behind the two leading brigades with the two Rifle Brigade battalions in front, the 10th K.R.R.C. (Lieut.-Colonel A. C. Sheepshanks, D.S.O.) supporting them, and the 11th K.R.R.C. (Lieut.-Colonel G. K. Priaulx, D.S.O.) in Brigade Reserve. The 11th Rifle Brigade, as ordered, occupied the river crossings till relieved by the 29th Division, and, by evening, the two Rifle Brigade battalions were holding the high ground in the loop facing Crèvecœur, with the 10th K.R.R.C. in close support of them, and the 11th K.R.R.C. a mile or so to the west, in Brigade Reserve. During the morning's advance an enemy's strong-point was holding things up on the left, and was promptly taken by our 10th Battalion, yielding 200 prisoners.

The Third Army Orders for the 21st were for the III Corps to gain possession of the Masnières–Beaurevoir line east of Masnières, so as to admit of the cavalry being passed through, and also to take Crèvecœur ; the IV Corps to mop up Flesquières during the night, and in the morning to push on and capture Bourlon.

The rôle of the 20th Division in these operations was to seize the bridge at Crèvecœur and there effect a junction with the 29th Division. The 59th Brigade was detailed for this task. It was to have the assistance of twelve tanks.

At dawn on the 21st the 11th Rifle Brigade established connection with the 29th Division in Mon-Plaisir Farm between Masnières and Crèvecœur. At 6.30 a.m. the 10th Rifle Brigade attacked and occupied the bridge at Les-Rues-des-Vignes. They held it for an hour, but the Germans were still in the north end of the village in considerable numbers, and as these worked round behind them they were obliged to fight their way back to the high ground above the village, from which one company kept the bridge under Lewis-gun fire. The 11th Rifle Brigade had also been obliged to fall back a certain way, owing to enfilade fire from the other bank, and one company, 10th K.R.R.C., going up to support them, lost Captain W. Neilson (Scottish Rifles), killed by a shell.

Orders were then received for the 11th K.R.R.C.,

with one company 10th K.R.R.C. as reserve, to take Crèvecœur, assisted by tanks. There was to be a simultaneous attack by the 29th Division along the ridge on the north side of the canal. The attack is thus described in the Battalion's account in the 'Chronicle' of 1917:

'At 1.30 p.m. the Battalion moved off, disposed as follows: A Company on the left to cross the canal by the bridge a mile west of Crèvecœur and work along towards Crèvecœur. B Company in the centre, and D on the right, to advance on Revelon Château and seize the bridges, occupy the village, and hold the outskirts of it with the assistance of A and C Companies. C Company in support was to move on Revelon Château, help cover the advance, and assist in holding the village when captured.

'A Company of the 10th K.R.R.C. was in reserve. At the very outset of the advance it became obvious, from the very heavy machine-gun fire met with from the Masnières Ridge, that the 29th Division on our left had been unable to advance. This fire held up our advance and drew the remainder of the Battalion away to the left after A Company, who had in the meantime crossed the canal. This loss of direction was, however, rectified by Captain H. A. Denison, M.C., who reorganised B, C, and D Companies, and resumed the advance on Revelon Château.

'By this time four tanks had arrived, and proceeded towards the bridges, followed by the Battalion. They took up a position and opened fire on the bridges, but as it was then getting dark they decided that this fire was not likely to be very effective, and that they had better remain on this side of the canal. About 8 p.m. the tanks finally withdrew altogether, owing to shortage of petrol. We pushed on to the houses on our side of the canal, our rear wave being formed as a defensive flank to the right, and posts left in Revelon Château. After dark, Captain Denison withdrew to the high ground behind Revelon Château, whither the posts left in the Château were also forced to withdraw. A Company also recrossed the canal, and took up a position between the rest of the Battalion and the 11th Rifle Brigade. We were relieved that night, and went back into trenches near Masnières and Masnières Ravine.

'Our casualties were: officers—killed, 2nd Lieutenant

F. E. J. Richardson, F. Kearton, E. S. Hain ; wounded—2nd Lieutenants J. N. Marsh, G. T. Skinner, H. R. Beale ; other ranks : killed 15, wounded 99, missing 12.'

Farther to the right a company of the 10th K.R.R.C., about 4.45 p.m., rushed Rues-des-Vignes, but were subsequently withdrawn from it. The 59th Brigade was relieved in the line on the night of November 22/23.

During the day the 29th Division had not made much progress on their right, but had reached Noyelles on their left.

By this time the divisions of the III Corps were exhausted, and an order from Third Army to attack Romilly next day was cancelled, and they were told to hold on to what they had got.

The IV Corps took Flesquières at 8 a.m., and by evening had taken Fontaine and Anneux, but had failed to take Bourlon Wood or Moeuvres.

Nothing of much importance happened on the 22nd, but the enemy recaptured Fontaine.

On the 23rd there was no change on the III Corps front. The IV Corps failed to retake Fontaine, but took Bourlon Wood and part of Moeuvres. They also worked some way northwards along the Hindenburg Line.

There was little change in the situation for the next few days, though fighting went on almost incessantly for the possession of Fontaine and Bourlon Village.

On the night of November 26/27 the 2nd Division took over a portion of the line between Bourlon Wood and Moeuvres from the 36th Division, the 99th Brigade being on the right, the 6th on the left, and the 5th in reserve.

Our 1st Battalion took over the left of the front line of the 99th Brigade. Two nights later they were relieved by the 17th Royal Fusiliers, from the 5th Brigade, who had been lent to the 99th to take the place of the 22nd Royal

Fusiliers, sent to reinforce the 62nd Division, who were in trouble after the failure of an attack on Bourlon Village.

On November 29 one and a half companies of the 1st K.R.R.C. were ordered to capture and consolidate a new line of 500 yards in length, with a view to strengthening the Brigade's position. The attack was launched at 6.25 a.m., under an artillery and trench-mortar barrage. All went well till they topped the crest of a ridge, when they came under very heavy machine-gun fire, losing 75 per cent. of their strength and 3 officers. The remainder, unable to get farther, took cover in a partially dug enemy trench and shell holes, and proceeded to consolidate. They were soon afterwards reinforced there by two platoons. Though the line they had taken up was actually 150 yards short of their objective, they had achieved their purpose and, in the words of the 2nd Division's 'War Diary': 'Their action materially strengthened and straightened our line.'

Their casualties were: officers—killed, Lieutenant J. Goodwin; wounded, Lieutenant J. H. Lee, D.S.O., 2nd Lieutenant H. W. Richardson; other ranks—killed 18; wounded 53, missing 3.

By the evening of November 29, though their advance had been definitely stopped, and any chance of the cavalry getting through, or of a big roll up of the German line to the north, had long gone by, the Third Army had taken prisoner 185 officers and 10,323 other ranks, with 142 guns, 285 machine-guns, and 57 trench mortars.

The enemy, however, had no intention of leaving it at that, and had, with wonderful rapidity, made his arrangements for a big counter-attack.

On November 30 the storm broke. On the eastern flank of the salient which the Third Army's advance had formed in its line the enemy attacked on a seven-mile front from Vendhuile to Masnières. The general result of the day's fighting on this flank was that, after Gouzeaucourt had been lost and retaken by a counter-attack by the Guards Division, the line ran past the west side of Gauche Wood, by the western outskirts of Gonnelieu, east of La Vacquerie to Masnières, where the 29th Division had remained immovable, and we had lost more guns than we had taken in the last ten days.

Beginning a couple of hours later than on the eastern front, the enemy had been attacking all day on the northern front, but had met with no success, the line at the end of the day being practically unchanged.

On the 20th Division front the 59th Brigade had relieved the 60th Brigade in the right sector of the front line on the night of November 29/30. The 61st Brigade occupied the left sector. The 60th Brigade had gone into Divisional Reserve near Villers-Plouich. The main front line of the 20th Division ran from a point on the road 400 yards north-east of Lateau Wood, thence north-east for 1,500 yards, and thence to a point on the canal 800 yards south-east of the bridge at Masnières.

An outpost line ran from the right of the main line, round the spur overlooking Les-Rues-des-Vignes and Revelon Château, to the bridge on the canal half-way between Crèvecœur and Masnières. This bridge had been specially exempted from an order for the destruction of the bridges on the Division's front issued on November 23. However, none of those bridges can have been destroyed, as the troops of the Division never got within reach of them again after the 22nd.

The Divisional Order for the occupation of this line is dated the 23rd, but nothing much can have been done for the next few days, as another order, dated the 27th, shows how very much there was left to do. This latter order defines how the outpost line is to consist of a line of strong points, wired all round. The only thing it mentions as having been completed is a double-apron fence running along the whole front of the main line. With one night spent on reliefs, little can have been done by the morning of the 30th to carry out these instructions. The 11th Battalion 'War Diary' mentions that the main line was only partially dug, and there was only accommodation in it for two half-companies.

In the 59th Brigade sector, the 10th K.R.R.C. was on the right of the front line, the 11th K.R.R.C. on the left.

The German attack was made in echelon from the left, falling first on the 55th Division, then on the 12th Division and, half an hour later, on the 20th Division.

The following is the account of the fate of our 10th Battalion taken from the 'Chronicle' of 1917 :

'The night of November 29 was fairly quiet, but at 7.45 a.m., on November 30, the Germans made a strong attack on the 12th Division, which was on our right, and succeeded in piercing their line. They broke through Lateau Wood in great numbers, and thus got right behind our four companies, as we were in position north-east of the wood.

'At this time all was well with us in front, and Battalion Headquarters were in communication with our outpost company. Ten minutes later this line was cut. The events that followed were dramatic.

'Twice the Germans made desperate frontal attacks, but were splendidly repulsed by rifle and Lewis-gun fire, and many Germans bit the dust. Then we found ourselves attacked on three sides—in front, rear, and right flank.

'Fierce fighting followed, and the casualties on both sides were very heavy.

'Very few of the men, and none of the officers, succeeded in getting away.'

The Battalion Headquarters fell back, fighting all the way, till they joined the reserve battalion of the Brigade. The survivors totalled 4 officers and 16 other ranks.

The casualties among officers were:

Killed: Captain J. Davidson (R.A.M.C.), 2nd Lieutenants J. L. R. Bull, H. L. Hall.
Died of Wounds: Lieutenant W. A. Horner.
Wounded: Captain and Adjutant V. C. Holdcroft, 2nd Lieutenants A. E. Henderson, A. Mackenzie (prisoner of war).
Prisoners of War: Captain F. G. Fison, M.C., 2nd Lieutenants J. J. Lee, P. B. Diplock, J. T. King, W. E. Pristo, C. M. Penney, E. G. Prior, N. A. McLean, J. Hunter.

The fate of the 11th Battalion, which was in line on the left of the 10th, was much the same. The two companies in the front line found themselves attacked from three sides about 8.15 a.m. One company was completely surrounded, and was never seen again. The other company fell back on the two in the main line, but the enemy was on the top of them, and the remaining two companies were soon overrun. The Battalion Headquarters fell back fighting on to Brigade Headquarters. The combined Headquarters then fell back on to the reserve battalion of the Brigade, where a stand was made, and the enemy's advance was checked.

The losses of the Battalion were:

Killed: Major J. M. de Paravicini, Lieutenant G. D. Lugton (8th Scottish Rifles, attached), 2nd Lieutenant H. B. Broster; 7 other ranks.
Wounded: Captain O. B. Smyth, M.C., 2nd Lieutenant J. Bunnis; 67 other ranks.
Prisoners of War: Captains J. A. Watt (6th Scottish Rifles), C. N. Barlow, G. A. McArthur (R.A.M.C.), Lieutenant C. P. de Paravicini, 2nd Lieutenants G. H. Willis, A. Tayler, J. S. Porteous, R. Reader, W. P. Morris, G. P. Lowe; 296 other ranks.

The 'War Diary' of the 59th Brigade relates how the Headquarters of these two battalions fell back together and, collecting as many men as could be gathered, attempted or make a stand in several places, but the pressure was too heavy, and the retirement had to be continued until the positions taken up by the Reserve Battalion, about 3,000 yards to the rear, were reached.

So complete had been the break-through on the 12th Division's front, and so rapid had been the enemy's advance, that the Support Battalion of the Brigade (10th Rifle Brigade), which had orders to counter-attack at once if the enemy should secure a foothold anywhere in the front line, without waiting for orders from the Brigade, when it got the order to 'Stand to' about eight o'clock, found the enemy already in its right rear. This battalion was almost as completely destroyed as the two front-line battalions.

At the commencement of the attack the Reserve Battalion stood to and moved forward to their allotted position. They found some of the enemy there before them and, as both flanks of the position were in the air, they had to withdraw to a position in rear, where they covered a front of about 1,500 yards, facing east-north-east, with their right about 1,200 yards north-east of La Vacquerie, the 61st Brigade prolonging the line to the north. Here they were joined by the remnants of the other battalions of the Brigade, and held on there till the morning of December 2.

On that day, owing to heavy attacks on their right and persistent pressure from the front, they had to fall back another 500 yards on their right, the left remaining where it was.

On the night of December 2/3 the Brigade was withdrawn into Divisional Reserve in the old British front line.

On the night of the 3/4 the Division was relieved by the 61st Division.

At the time of the German attack the 60th Brigade was in reserve about Villers-Plouich, having been relieved the previous night, after a fortnight of incessant work and exposure. Just returned to comparative comfort they were looking forward to a few days' rest.

As soon as it was known that the 12th Division front had broken, the Brigade was ordered to send one battalion to La Vacquerie and three battalions to reinforce the Quentin Ridge–Gonnelieu line ; but, when it was reported that the 20th Division front had been driven in, these orders were changed to : one battalion to La Vacquerie, two to the Hindenburg Line—presumably with a view to a counter-attack—and one battalion to Gonnelieu. The two battalions for the Hindenburg Line had, however, already become involved in the fighting round Gonnelieu and Quentin Ridge, and could not be extricated. It was therefore impossible for the Divisional Reserve to counter-attack.

The 12th K.R.R.C. was the battalion detailed for La Vacquerie. They got their orders at 9 a.m., and marched off at 9.30. They managed to get up by a well-covered route, and had no casualties, except that 2nd Lieutenant W. Denton-Cardew and his acting Platoon-Sergeant, Lance-Corporal Cooper, were both killed by a shell. Arrived at La Vacquerie, they occupied a line of trenches round the east side of the village. In the afternoon they got an order to take up a line from La Vacquerie (exclusive) to the point where the old British front line crossed the Cambrai–Gouzeaucourt Road, where they would get touch with the 12th Rifle Brigade. They were to be relieved at La Vacquerie by the 59th Brigade. That Brigade, as has been seen, had only one battalion left, and the relief never took place. Lieut.-Colonel Moore, realising the importance of La Vacquerie, and judging that the valley to the south would be very well covered if the heights on both sides were held, left three companies to hold La Vacquerie and the ground to the south of it overlooking the valley, and, with D Company (Captain G. B. Loyd) and Battalion Headquarters, crossed the valley. He placed the company holding a line of shell holes and part of the old front line to the point of junction with the 12th Rifle Brigade. The gap across the valley was partly held by some stragglers, who had been gathered up during the morning. He was thus holding a front of about a mile with a very weak battalion. Battalion Headquarters were in an old communication trench called Foster Lane, close behind his extreme right.

Before we turn to the events of the 30th on the northern flank it will be as well to finish off with the 20th Division up to the time when they were relieved.

The story of how the 12th Battalion held their line is too good not to be given in full. The following is the account in their 'War Diary' from the time when they took up their position :

'No attack by the enemy took place, but La Vacquerie was shelled, though not particularly heavily. Battalion Headquarters moved over to the right flank into Foster Lane Trench, north of Gonnelieu, so as to keep in touch with the situation on the right, and with the 12th Rifle Brigade. In the evening news arrived that the enemy had been driven out of Gouzeaucourt. This proved to be correct subsequently, but it was, at the time, a mere rumour. Important as La Vacquerie was, Gonnelieu was no less so. About midnight Foster Lane was occupied by one company of the Essex Regiment, which had been in action that morning, and had had losses.

'Four Germans were captured near La Vacquerie during the night. On being questioned they stated that it was the intention of the enemy to attack next day, and, as they thought, about dawn. They expected that La Vacquerie would be one of the objectives. The prisoners seemed much elated by the success of the Germans during the day. At 8.30 a.m. on December 1 a heavy barrage from ·77 guns and 4·2-inch howitzers was put down on Foster Lane, and on the old British front line near the Cambrai Road. It lasted for about ten minutes. As the barrage lifted, a strong force of German infantry advanced from Gonnelieu and pressed forward down Fusilier Ridge, north-west of the village, while others came straight against Foster Lane. The whole of Battalion Headquarters at once lined this trench, and stopped the enemy, by rifle fire, from approaching it. The German advance down Fusilier Ridge was not appreciably checked, and it seemed likely that the enemy might outflank us badly. Battalion Headquarters therefore doubled across the Gonnelieu–Villers-Plouich Road, and took up a position next to the Grenadier Guards, who held a trench along the bank there. The company of the Essex Regiment, who occupied Foster Lane, would, it was thought, be sufficient to hold up the enemy in their immediate front. That Company had, however, lost a good many men from the barrage. Some 25 of them followed Battalion Headquarters, while the remainder do not appear to have been able to hold Foster Lane. The enemy, finding that no fire came from there, began to advance again.

'D Company was then ordered to bring up its left so as to place the whole company on the right flank of the enemy. This was done under a heavy machine-gun fire. A fierce and prolonged fire fight ensued. The Germans suffered severe losses from our rifle and Lewis-gun fire, but by means of trickling forward small parties they managed to occupy Foster Lane. All their attempts to advance any farther failed. Captain G. B. Loyd, while directing the fire of his men at the most critical moment, was mortally wounded; but his gallant example was not without its effect. Throughout the morning, and during the early afternoon, his company held its ground. While these events were taking place about Gonnelieu the enemy attacked La Vacquerie. Under cover of a violent bombardment, mostly with heavy guns, and of machine-gun fire from the Gonnelieu Ridge, they advanced down Barrier Trench [running due south from La Vacquerie], and in small parties over the open. These latter were brought to a standstill by our rifle and Lewis-gun fire. Their bombers, well organised, and accompanied by machine guns, had more success. They drove back the men of B Company some 70 yards.

A counter-attack restored the situation. A second attack, heralded by a most extreme artillery fire, then took place. After a preliminary success, the Germans were driven back in hand-to-hand fighting. Sergeant Chatt of C Company, Sergeant Steele and Rifleman Sergeant of B Company were most conspicuous in leading the counter-attack. They jumped out of the trench and threw bombs on the heads of the enemy below them. Their brave action and example inspired our exhausted men and, after a fierce struggle, the enemy were driven back to the Cambrai Road. The Germans who attacked La Vacquerie were brave and determined men. Their bombers were very well organised, and their attack was remarkably well supported by artillery, machine guns, and the ubiquitous sniper. Some of our men afterwards acknowledged that they scarcely expected to be able to beat back the second attack. Nevertheless they managed to do so, rather by resolute counter-attacks than by passive defence. This attitude may have deceived the enemy as to the strength of the force opposing him. No further attack took place, but the enemy's artillery fire was still maintained. Only towards evening did it lessen, and even then bursts of fire throughout the night contributed to make things very unpleasant. At dusk our positions remained intact. But the position did not present a happy picture. The men, many of whom had started very tired on the morning of the previous day, were now quite exhausted. Our losses had not been light. The Battalion was holding a front far wider than that allotted to it : not a man remained in support. It was only too evident that an attack by the enemy next day all along the line might force a breach in the weak defence. It was, therefore, with feelings of relief that orders were received to withdraw to the neighbourhood of Farm Ravine as soon as two fresh battalions of the 183rd Brigade, 61st Division, which had been brought up in buses, arrived. After this exchange had been effected, the Battalion moved to its fresh positions, occupying the old British front and support lines. After remaining here during December 2 the Battalion marched that night to Sorel by a circuitous route, about five miles.'

The casualties of the 12th Battalion during the twelve days were :

Officers—killed or died of wounds, Captain A. Hoare, wounded November 20, died November 27 ; 2nd Lieutenant W. de M. Denton-Cardew, killed November 30 ; Captain G. B. Loyd, M.C., died of wounds received on the same day on December 1 ; wounded, 7 ; other ranks—killed 31, wounded 109.

During the night of December 1/2, while our 12th Battalion was being relieved by troops of the 61st Division, the rest of the 60th Brigade were relieved by the Guards Division. On the night of the 2nd/3rd the 59th Brigade was relieved by a battalion of the 61st Division, and the 20th Division passed out of the battle of Cambrai.

We left our 1st Battalion in the front line between Bourlon Wood and Moeuvres after their brilliant little action of the morning of the 29th. The story of the defeat of the German attack on this front was issued as a special memorandum by the General Staff, and is such a tale of heroism, as instructive as it is thrilling, that I make no apologies for reproducing it in full.

THE STORY OF A GREAT FIGHT

(*Being an account of the operations of the* 47*th*, 2*nd*, *and* 56*th Divisions in the neighbourhood of Bourlon and Moeuvres on November* 30, 1917.)

Issued by the General Staff

On the morning of November 30, 1917, the 47th (London) Territorial Division, the 2nd Division, and the right brigade of the 56th (London) Territorial Division, were holding a front of about five miles extending from the eastern edge of Bourlon Wood to Tadpole Copse, in the Hindenburg Line, west of Moeuvres. From Tadpole Copse, the left brigade of the 56th Division formed a defensive flank across No Man's Land to our old front line.

The 56th Division had been in line prior to the British attack of November 20, in which its right brigade had taken part, and since that date had captured and held about a mile of the Hindenburg Line west of Moeuvres, including Tadpole Copse. Almost constant fighting had taken place in this area since our attack, and the Division, which at one time had been holding a front of 11,000 yards, had already been subjected to a very severe strain.

The Value of Work

On the night of November 26/27, the 2nd Division had taken over from the troops engaged in the original advance the position of our front lying between Bourlon Wood and Moeuvres. **The Division had recently completed a short period of progressive training, the great value of which at once became apparent.**

Work had been begun **immediately** to restore order to the line gained in our attack. Our positions had been straightened out at certain points and consolidated. Communications had been re-established and improved, strong-posts constructed and wired, and supplies of ammunition and stores of all kinds brought forward. **Had it not been for the promptness and energy displayed by all ranks in these tasks, it is doubtful whether the Division could have weathered the storm which broke out on its front on the morning of November 30,** when the concentrated attacks of three German divisions were beaten off with most severe losses to the enemy.

The 47th Division, which had previously been holding

another part of the line, on the night of November 28/29 had taken over our positions in Bourlon Wood and immediately to the west of it. Though the time at its disposal proved limited, on November 29 much had been done to strengthen and reorganise the defence, and, in particular, batteries of machine guns had been arranged in depth to cover the approaches to the Wood.

A PROUD DAY FOR ENGLISHMEN

The story of the subsequent fighting on the Bourlon–Moeuvres front is one so brimful of heroism that it deserves to take its place in English history for all time. The most determined attacks of four German divisions, with three other German divisions in support, were utterly crushed by the unconquerable resistance of the three British divisions in line. November 30, 1917, will be a proud day in the lives of all those splendid British soldiers who, by their single-hearted devotion to duty, prevented what would have become a serious situation had they given way.

THE ATTACK BEGUN

After considerable shelling during the night on Bourlon Wood, the enemy's artillery barrage opened at about 8.45 a.m., being directed on our front-line posts, and also with great intensity on the line of the Bapaume–Cambrai Road, severing all connection with the two right battalions of the 2nd Division [1st K.R.R.C. and 17th Royal Fusiliers].

Soon after 9 a.m. large numbers of the enemy were seen coming over the ridge west of Bourlon Wood, against the junction of the 2nd and 47th Divisions. Our artillery barrage, which at that time was intense, caught this advance ; but, in spite of their losses, the German infantry pressed on. The left of the London Territorials was being forced back. Four posts on the right of the 2nd Division were wiped out. The situation was critical.

As the enemy's infantry appeared over the crest of the hill, however, they were engaged with direct fire by our field artillery. Machine guns in position in a sunken road south-west of Bourlon Wood and in the Sugar Factory on the Bapaume–Cambrai Road swept their advancing lines. The survivors of the 2nd Division's posts succeeded in getting to shell holes farther back and held on. While the artillery of both British divisions maintained a constant and accurate fire, **rifle, Lewis-gun, and machine-gun fire** inflicted enormous losses on the enemy, held up his advance, and eventually drove him back after three hours' hard fighting.

A Rearguard's Sacrifice

Farther west, the enemy's advance broke upon the 17th Battalion Royal Fusiliers, 2nd Division, which was in the act of withdrawing from an advanced sap and trench, judged to be too exposed to be maintained in the face of so powerful an attack.

Owing to the enemy being concealed in some dead ground, the attack developed with unexpected speed, and the company holding the advanced position was ordered to leave a rearguard to cover the withdrawal of the remainder. Captain W. N. Stone, who was in command of the company, sent back three platoons, and himself elected to remain with the rearguard together with Lieutenant Benzecry.

This rearguard, assisted by our machine guns, **held off the whole of the German attack until the main position of the 17th Battalion Royal Fusiliers was fully organised, and they died to a man with their faces to the enemy.**

It is impossible to make comparisons in an action such as was fought on this day, in which so many glorious deeds were performed, but the report of the Officer Commanding the 17th Battalion Royal Fusiliers concerning this incident adds distinction to the history of the Regiment, and will be remembered as a devoted example of the greatest of all sacrifices. It runs:

'Of the heroism of the rearguard it is difficult to speak. Captain Stone and Lieutenant Benzecry, although ordered to withdraw to the main line, elected to remain with the rear-guard. The rearguard was seen fighting with bayonet, bullet, and bomb to the last. There was no survivor. Captain Stone, by his invaluable information as to the movements of the enemy prior to the attack, and his subsequent sacrifice with the rearguard, saved the situation at cost of his life. Lieutenant Benzecry was seen to be wounded in the head. He continued to fight until he was killed.'

The Importance of Straight Shooting

The 1st Battalion King's Royal Rifle Corps, on the left of the 17th Battalion Royal Fusiliers, were in action throughout this period, and masses of the enemy moved against them; but **by their well-directed and intense volume of fire delivered from rifles, Lewis guns, and machine guns, the enemy were literally mown down in heaps,** after topping the rise some 200–300 yards from our front line. Throughout the day formed bodies of Germans never got nearer than this to our position; though many individuals endeavoured to creep forward, until disposed of by our snipers and Lewis-gun detachments.

Before midday the enemy again attacked on the whole front of the right brigade of the 2nd Division, but was once more hurled back with great slaughter, offering very favourable targets at from 50 to 200 yards' range to machine guns, Lewis guns, and rifles.

Prompt Action by Local Commanders

Early in the afternoon, large masses of the enemy attacked on a front of nearly a mile west of Bourlon Wood. On the left of the front attacked he was once more driven off with heavy loss by the accuracy and volume of our fire; but three posts on the extreme right of the 2nd Division were captured, and on the left of the 47th Division a gap was formed between the 1/6th Battalion and 1/15th Battalion London Regiment. This gap was closed by the prompt action of the officers commanding these battalions, who, with a reserve company and the staffs of their respective headquarters, including runners, signallers, orderlies, and cooks, led immediate and successful counter-attacks.

Good Work by Small Posts

The garrisons of the three posts on the front of the 2nd Division fell fighting to the last, and when the line at this point was restored, such a heap of Germans dead lay in and around the posts that it was impossible to find the bodies of our men.

In this locality, five other posts held by a company of the 1st Battalion Royal Berkshire Regiment repulsed all the enemy's attacks, and maintained themselves until our reinforcements had restored the situation. This company showed the utmost valour and steadfastness in a most critical period, extending over some six hours. The enemy made attack after attack, always in vastly superior numbers, and time after time came right up to our posts, only to be mown down by our fire and driven back in disorder. The casualties of the Company were 46 of all ranks. They claim to have killed over 500 of the enemy.

The story of the gallant fight against odds put up by the garrisons of these posts, both those who survived and those who died valiantly, constitutes one out of the many examples furnished by the fighting of this day of the supreme importance of the resistance that can be offered by small parties of determined men who know how to use their weapons and are resolved to use them to the last.

Inflicting Heavy Losses on the Enemy

As the result of their efforts on this occasion, the 17th Battalion Royal Fusiliers reported at 1 p.m. that their line was intact, that they were in close touch with the units on either flank, and that the men were really enjoying the novel experience of killing Germans in large numbers at point-blank range.

During the afternoon, a strong hostile attack was made upon the 141st Brigade on the right of the 47th Division. For some days the German artillery had been steadily pouring gas shell into Bourlon Wood, until the thick undergrowth was full of gas. Many casualties were caused to our troops; and gas masks had to be worn continuously for many hours. None the less, when the enemy attacked, he was again hurled back with heavy loss. A distinctive feature of the defence was the gallantry of the Lewis gunmen who, when the attack was seen to be beginning, ran out with their guns in front of our line and from positions of advantage in the open mowed down the advancing German infantry.

Later in the afternoon, the enemy made two other

attacks against the right brigade of the 2nd Division [99th]. In each case he was beaten off with great slaughter, his losses being materially increased by the fire of an 18-pounder battery which got right on to his infantry in crowded trenches.

The Attack at Moeuvres

Similar events were happening meanwhile on the left of the 2nd Division and on the right of the 56th Division. At 9.20 a.m. the enemy had been seen advancing from the north towards the Canal du Nord, and subsequently attack after attack was delivered by him on both sides of the canal against the 6th and 169th Infantry Brigades.

South of Moeuvres the enemy succeeded in effecting an entry, but was driven back by a bombing attack after heavy fighting. In the fighting in this area Captain A. M. C. McReady-Diarmid, of the 17th Battalion Middlesex Regiment, greatly distinguished himself. When the enemy had penetrated some distance into the position, and the situation was extremely critical, he led his company forward through a very heavy barrage, and engaged the enemy with such success that the Germans were driven back at least 500 yards with the loss of many casualties and a number of prisoners.

On the following day this officer again led a bombing attack against a party of Germans who had broken into our positions and drove them back 300 yards, himself killing 80 of the enemy.[1] Throughout this attack he led the way himself, and it was absolutely and entirely due to his marvellous throwing that the ground was regained.

[1] The exact number hit was 88. This officer threw all the bombs himself; 67 dead and 21 wounded were actually counted after the recapture of the trench.

Captain McReady-Diarmid was eventually killed by a bomb, when the Germans had been driven back to the place from which they had started.

At this time, from Moeuvres westward to Tadpole Copse, a desperate struggle was taking place for the possession of the Hindenburg Line, in the course of which the enemy at one time reached the Battalion Headquarters of the 8th Battalion Middlesex Regiment, attached to the 168th Brigade, 56th Division. Here the German infantry were stopped by the gallant defence of the officer commanding the Battalion, who, with the assistance of his headquarters staff, held off the enemy with bombs until further help was organised and the trench regained.

Though much reduced in strength by the fighting of the preceding days, and hard pressed by superior forces, the troops of the 168th and 169th Brigades beat off all attacks. Queen's Westminsters, London Scottish, and men of the 1/2nd Battalion London Regiment and 1/8th Battalion Middlesex Regiment vied with one another in the valour of their resistance.

Another Most Gallant Exploit

Later in the evening, another attack in force was made south-east of Moeuvres, and the enemy once more effected an entry. In doing so, he isolated a company of the 13th Battalion Essex Regiment, 2nd Division, which was holding a trench along the west side of the Canal du Nord. Repeated efforts made by the enemy to gain further ground failed through the determined efforts of the 13th Battalion Essex Regiment and the 2nd Battalion South Staffordshire Regiment.

Their successful defence was undoubtedly greatly

assisted by the heroic resistance of the isolated company of the 13th Battalion Essex Regiment. It would appear that at 4 p.m. this most gallant company, realising the improbability of being extricated, held a council of war, at which the two surviving company officers, Lieutenant J. D. Robinson and 2nd Lieutenant E. L. Corps, the Company Sergeant-Major A. H. Edwards and Platoon-Sergeants C. Phillips, F. C. Parsons, W. Fairbrass, R. Lodge, and L. S. Legg were present. It was unanimously decided to fight to the last and have no surrender. Two runners, who succeeded in getting through, were sent back to notify Battalion Headquarters of their decision.

Throughout the night of November 30 many efforts were made to effect the relief of these brave men, but all attempts failed against the overwhelming strength of the enemy. The last that is known of this gallant company is that it was heard fighting it out, and maintaining to the last a bulwark against the tide of attacking Germans. It is impossible to estimate the value of this magnificent fight to the death, which relieved the pressure on the main line of defence.

Our Line maintained

At the end of this day of high courage and glorious achievement, except for a few advanced positions, some of which were afterwards regained, our line had been maintained intact. The men who had come triumphantly through this mighty contest felt, and rightly felt, that they had won a great victory, in which the enemy had come against them in his full strength and had been defeated with losses at which even the victors stood aghast.

Lessons of the Fight

Certain lessons stand out among the many incidents of the fighting, which will repay close study and attention :

(1) *Training.*—The first is the supreme importance of training, and the need for all ranks to make the best use of every opportunity for training that is given them.

(2) *The Rifle.*—Accurate rifle shooting played a very large part in the repulse of the enemy's attacks. Hundreds of men actually killed Germans, and there are instances of one man cleaning and loading a rifle for a comrade who was picking off Germans. When an attack had been beaten off men cleaned their rifles and collected small-arm ammunition to be ready for the next attack.

(3) *Trained Riflemen.*—In this connection trained riflemen proved most useful and accounted for many of the enemy. The enemy was prevented from working his way into our positions in small parties, and hostile attacks were disorganised by the picking off of their leaders.

(4) *The Bayonet.*—The bayonet was used on many occasions, and had a discouraging effect on a very determined enemy.

(5) *Lewis Guns.*—Lewis guns were in action the whole time, and proved their destructive powers. The true rôle of the Lewis gun, i.e. mobility with fire power, was utilised. Instances were many where Lewis gunners on their own initiative moved from point to point of the line being attacked and picked up targets of immediate urgency. They claim hundreds of the enemy, and by pushing forward in places which were not being attacked were able to bring cross fire to bear on massed German infantry advancing on the flanks.

(6) *Rifle Bombs.*—Rifle bombs were found to be very effective in assisting parties to work their way up trenches.

(7) *Machine Guns.*—Machine guns employed in batteries did magnificent work. They must have done enormous execution, as they frequently got long lines of men in enfilade, who fell where they were when our fire struck them, and did not rise again. One battery of 8 machine guns dealt with ten successive waves of Germans and fired 70,000 rounds into them. All the enemy attacks on the right of the 2nd

Division, near Bourlon Wood, were engaged by our machine guns with direct fire in enfilade, and their fire was a powerful factor in determining the issue of the fight on this flank.

(8) *Stokes Mortars.*—Stokes mortars were invaluable in driving back bombing attacks and ejecting forward parties of the enemy. The difficulty of rapid movement and traversing was overcome by the firer steadying the gun between his legs, without any platform.

(9) *Artillery.*—The great execution done by our artillery upon the massed bodies of the enemy was testified to afterwards by prisoners.

On the 2nd Division front, defence zones had been detailed in such a way that about two-thirds of the batteries covered the whole front on S.O.S. lines, the remaining third being superimposed upon them. This allowed the superimposed batteries to engage the masses of the enemy as they appeared over the crest line, without leaving any gaps in the screen of fire on the S.O.S. lines.

One or two sections were brought up on to the crest and fired direct, doing great execution until they were spotted by the enemy. They were then shelled so heavily that the detachments had to be withdrawn, but the results obtained on this occasion would seem to have been well worth the risk.

(10) Maintaining ground and counter-attack. Perhaps the most striking lesson of the day, and one to which reference has already been made, is the far-reaching nature of the results which can be achieved by the determined resistance of small bodies of men.

For attacking troops it is less costly in most cases to hold on to good positions than to evacuate them. A party of Germans who had established themselves in a sunken road in our line made no attempt to hold on but retired, and in doing so were caught by our fire and practically wiped out. In defence, the maintenance of advanced posts and isolated strong-points or positions of trench may involve the safety of the whole line.

In the course of the fighting, the value of immediate counter-attack by the unit on the spot was exemplified again and again. These counter-attacks were undertaken on the initiative of platoon and subordinate commanders, and were the result of recent training and the good discipline of all ranks.

Fighting still went on for the next few days on the Bourlon–Moeuvres front, but the Germans had had enough of it on the 30th, and their attacks were on a small scale, and were all beaten off. Our 1st Battalion were relieved in the front line on the night of November 30/December 1, but were back again in twenty-four hours. They were relieved again on the night of the 2nd/3rd, and went into the support line. On the night of the 4th/5th the Bourlon salient was evacuated, the line being drawn back to the Hindenburg Line. The 1st Battalion went back to the old British front line, one mile north-east of Hermies.

The fighting on the eastern flank of the salient was much more severe during the first three days of December than in the north, as the Germans tried to follow up their successes of November 30, while the British tried to regain some of the ground lost. There was no solid advantage to either side.

On the 1st the Guards Division and Cavalry Corps, with tanks, failed to regain Gonnelieu and Villers Guislain. The 29th Division repulsed nine heavy attacks during the day in the neighbourhood of Masnières and Rues-Vertes, but evacuated those two places, by order, during the night. On the 2nd there was heavy fighting without gain on either side. On the 3rd the enemy took La Vacquerie and Marcoing Copse.

On the night of the 4th/5th the salient was flattened out by our withdrawal to the Hindenburg Line and the battle of Cambrai came to an end.

CHAPTER XI

1918

THE FIFTH ARMY [1]

'ST. QUENTIN,' 'ROSIÈRES,' 'AVRE,' 'BAPAUME, 1918'

NINETEEN-SEVENTEEN had been a bad year for the Allies. It had opened full of hope of a big success with, it was considered, a good chance of seeing the end of the war; but nothing had gone right. The big event of the year, the French attack in Champagne, had been a total failure, and had nearly ruined the French Army. The various British offensives had not done more than give the French time to recover, though they had done that very effectively, as was shown by the success of the French in their autumn campaign. The 'crash' on the Italian front, though it had not had the effect which the Central Powers presumably intended of putting Italy out of the war, had compelled the French and British to detach to that front reinforcements which they could ill spare. There had been successes in Mesopotamia and Palestine which had no very great effect on the strategy of the war as a whole; in fact, the capture of Jerusalem had been a positive danger, in that it had put into our Prime Minister's head wild ideas about winning the war in the East. Both sides, on the Western Front, may fairly be said to have been thoroughly war-worn. It is no doubt perfectly true that the Allied armies, as a whole, never lost heart, but that does not say that they did not feel despondent and 'fed-up.' It would

[1] Map V.

be fair to say that the view of the individual was that there could be no possible doubt but that the Allies would win in time, but that he personally was not likely to see the end of it.

To the Germans, in the winter of 1917–18, the situation was obvious. Great Britain and France must be beaten before America could bring over a big army. With Russia out of it now was the time to win the war in France. Nothing else mattered.

For this purpose Russia had to be disposed of as quickly as possible; the armistice of the autumn was denounced, and hostilities resumed on February 18, 1918, and the treaty of Brest-Litovsk forced on the Bolsheviks.

British and French military opinion favoured a defensive attitude while waiting for America.

G.H.Q. calculated that Germany could transfer a minimum of thirty divisions from East to West. By the end of March 1918, they had transferred forty-six.

It is not necessary here to discuss the questions of the General Reserve which was to be under the orders of a committee at Versailles, of the disbelief of the British politicians in the danger of the threatened German attack, of the wild-cat scheme for winning the war in the East, of our unnecessary numerical weakness in France, or of the reserves of men in England and Palestine which might have been in France when the blow fell and had to be rushed there when it was almost too late; all that has been touched on in Chapter I.

It is enough to say that the result of all these futilities was that in March 1918 the British line was very much more weakly held than it might have been, and that in the weakest part, the right—that is, the part farthest away from the Channel Ports—Gough's Fifth Army was holding a front of some 30 miles with eleven divisions in the line and three more, with three Cavalry Divisions, in reserve; and, it must be remembered, British divisions had all been reduced by three battalions.

Both allies expected that the main attack would fall on themselves. The British Intelligence proved to be right. They were right as to the locality of the attack and the date, even to the very day.

An agreement was made by the two Commanders-in-Chief similar to that between Joab and Abishai in the war with Ammon. Each would be ready to give the other assistance should he require it. The assistance was to be given either by: (i) taking over more line, (ii) reinforcement by troops which would pass under the command of the ally they came to help, or (iii) intervention by troops whose commander would take command of any Allied troops that might be in the area in which he was to intervene.

The front the Germans selected to attack was that held by the British Fifth and Third Armies.

The Corps holding the line were in the following order from right to left—from Barisis, five or six miles south of La Fère, on the Oise, to and including Vimy Ridge: Fifth Army (Gough)—III, XVIII, XIX, and VII Corps; Third Army (Byng)—V, IV, VI, XVII, and XIII Corps.

The line was held in depth—that is, there was an outpost line in front of mutually supporting strong-points, and a battle zone in rear made up of similar posts. The system, which held for the first few years of the war, of one continuous front line, had been given up, the Germans, on the Ypres front in 1917, being the first to abandon it.

At 5.30 a.m. on March 21 the enemy put down a terrific bombardment, the like of which had not been seen before, and launched their attack some hours later. Their numerical superiority against the Fifth Army was at least three to one, and not far short of it against the Third.

A thick fog over the whole battlefield favoured the attackers, and enabled them to penetrate unseen between the strong-points.

The course of the battle can only be given very generally and very briefly. At first things seemed to be going fairly well on the Fifth Army front. The outpost zone was quickly overrun, but this was to be expected. Up to midday there were no reports of any penetration of the battle zone. Then bad news began to come in. The Germans were turning the extreme right. They had penetrated the line of the 18th, 14th, and 36th Divisions to the south of St. Quentin and that of the 16th Division about Ronssoy. Their advance was less marked in any one place, but greater generally on the Third Army front.

To make a long story short, the whole line was gradually forced back, fighting all the way. There were times of great anxiety when it looked as if the defence was going to collapse. At first it was the Third Army that looked like cracking, later it was the Fifth. Gaps appeared in the line, but were always filled in time to avert disaster. Reinforcements began to arrive. The French, by degrees, relieved the III Corps, on the right. Our troops, who had been fighting since the 21st, were worn out, but so were the Germans. By the end of the month the front was once again more or less stabilised, on a line running, roughly, from Barisis, south and west of Mondidier, to Hangard and Villers-Brettonneux—both within eight miles of Amiens—west of Albert, east of Arras, to Vimy Ridge.

On the Fifth Army front the enemy's thrust had, by the end of the month, more or less expended itself. It was exhausted by the pace of its own advance, and the series of rearguard actions it had fought. It could get no farther before the Allies had time to strengthen themselves on their new front. On the Third Army front the thrust, instead of gradually expending itself, was brought up with a jerk on March 28 in the Second Battle of Arras.

The Germans attacked on a twenty-mile front from Puisieux[1] to beyond Oppy.[2] This time there was no fog. The enemy was defeated with appalling losses, and did not gain a yard of ground. It must always be a matter of regret that none of our battalions were actively engaged in this battle, which was about the heaviest reverse the Germans ever met with when attacking throughout the war. So ended the first great German attack of 1918.

Let us now turn to the part our battalions played in the battle.

On the night of March 20/21 the 14th Division was in the front line of the III Corps, the right-hand corps of the Fifth Army, a few miles south-east of St. Quentin, with the 18th Division on its right and the 36th on its left.

The line was held as shown below :

	41st Brigade	*42nd Brigade*	*43rd Brigade*
Forward Zone .	8th K.R.R.C.	9th K.R.R.C.	6th Somerset L.I.
Battle Zone .	7th R.B.	5th Oxford and Bucks L.I.	7th K.R.R.C.[3]
Brigade Reserve	8th R.B.		9th Scottish Rifles (less two companies).

Divisional Reserve

9th Rifle Brigade ; 2 companies 9th Scottish Rifles ; Headquarters and one Company 11th King's (Pioneers).

Two companies 11th King's were attached to the 42nd Brigade.

The front of the Division was about 5,600 yards. The average strength of the infantry battalions was about 600 of all ranks.

The Forward Zone was on both sides of the main St. Quentin–Vendeuille Road ; the Battle Zone about the line Essigny–Benay.

On the 20th information was received from deserters

[1] Map IV. Seven miles W. of Bapaume. [2] Map III.

[3] The 7th K.R.R.C. had been transferred to the 43rd Brigade on the reduction of brigades to three battalions.

that the enemy intended to attack on the morning of the 21st. This confirmed the views of our Intelligence branch, but the troops in the line had heard the same story several times before, and were not very much impressed.

At 4.40 a.m. the Germans opened one of the most intense bombardments of the whole war. It went on for five hours, and then they launched their infantry attack. A dense fog had come on in the small hours of the morning, so that even when daylight came, no one could see more than a few yards. Long before the attack was launched all telephone cables had been cut by the bombardment, the fog rendered visual signalling and even pigeons useless, so that communication from company to battalion, battalion to brigade, brigade to division, and even, at times, from division to corps, was non-existent, except when an occasional runner got through. The artillery could do nothing but fire on their night-lines until, when after midday the fog cleared, they found themselves firing over the sights at short range at the enemy, who were by that time swarming round them. All the posts of the Forward Zone were quickly surrounded, the enemy being able to penetrate between them unseen. They fought it out with the utmost gallantry, but were finally overwhelmed. All three battalions were wiped out except for such details as were not up in the front line.

The fate of our 8th Battalion is described in the following letter, written some time after the event by Major Bowen, who was in temporary command on March 21 :

'I will tell you all I know about the show of March 21, but of course I know only what happened round about our Headquarters, and what I have picked up from other fellows. The fog was so appallingly thick that it was impossible to see even the wire surrounding the strong-points until about 3 p.m. The Germans started their bombardment about 4.45 a.m., and kept it going on us until 10 a.m. There was an awful number of gas shells, and we had to wear our gas helmets the whole time. At the same time they pelted Essigny with gas. All our communications, both back to the Brigade and forward, went in a very short time ; further, the fog was so thick that S.O.S. signals could not be seen at all ; in fact, we couldn't ourselves see whether they went off or not properly. As far as I ever could find out, the Germans attacked directly out of St. Quentin on to the 36th Division on our left about 9 a.m., and large columns came down the roads and valley. From there a great number turned southwards along the main road 44 [presumably that from St. Quentin to La Fère], and attacked our fellows in the front system from behind ; at the same time, about 10 a.m., they also attacked frontally from Itancourt. Some of the strong-posts with Lewis guns held out wonderfully well, and caused the Germans many casualties ; but they could not see anything much, and I believe at Madelon S.P.[1] they were overwhelmed before they even knew the Germans were there. Some fellows from here and some from the road seemed to have got back to Fluffy Work, which held out until 2.30 p.m. after very heavy fighting, during which Sergeant-Major Kidd of A Company was killed, leading a counter-attack on some Germans who had got into a portion of it. Finally, they were shelled out at point-blank range by field guns. Our first intimation at Headquarters was a runner from A Company, who arrived at 10.30 to say the Germans were overrunning the whole front. We tried to get runners back to Brigade Headquarters, and they found that the Germans had also got round behind us in the fog on the northern side through the 36th Division, and we couldn't get into touch with Brigade Headquarters at all. The fog was still very thick, and the Germans made no attempt to go for us at all. Later they drove the men out of a strong-point in Urvillers back on us, and tried to follow them, but we drove them off all right. Just after 1 p.m. we saw large numbers of prisoners being brought back from Essigny. Some of these we managed to release by shooting the guard and getting them back into Louvois [presumably the strong-point in which was Battalion Headquarters]. By them we were told that the 7th Rifle Brigade in Essigny and also Brigade Headquarters of both 41st and 42nd had already been captured by Germans coming

[1] Strong Point.

down from the north. Shortly after this the fog began to clear away a little, and the Germans made an attack on Calvairs and Louvois, which were both holding out, and in fair touch with one another through the communication trench. We drove them off successfully, and, in fact, Calvairs captured two German machine guns. They then lay down round us, and made no attempt to attack us ; it appeared at least as if a whole regiment were investing us. We sniped and picked off any we saw. Finally, about 4 p.m., they brought up two tanks—much larger and faster than ours—and took Calvairs. After a pause the tanks came on against Louvois and proceeded to trample down the wire and shoot into the trenches. We had nothing with which to beat off the tanks and, having picked up a lot of stragglers, our ammunition was getting scarce, and there were no Germans to shoot at, as they all lay low and let the tanks do the job. Under these circumstances we had no other course than to give in.'

The account of the 9th Battalion was written by the Commanding Officer (Lieut.-Colonel C. Howard Bury), and the following is a résumé of it:

'The night of March 20/21 found the 9th Battalion holding the Urvillers Wood sector of the front line, with the 8th K.R.R.C. on their left and the Somerset Light Infantry on their right. In support, at Montescourt, were the 5th Oxford and Bucks Light Infantry with the 9th Rifle Brigade in reserve at Jussy. [This is not strictly speaking correct. The 5th Oxford and Bucks Light Infantry was not in support of the front line, but formed part of the garrison of the so-called Battle Zone, which, however, seems not to have been any more strongly held than the Forward Zone.] The front of about 2,000 yards was held by posts, 300 or 400 yards apart, with no lateral communication. From the support line communication trenches ran out to each post. C and B Companies were holding the front line, each with two platoons in the front line and two in support. A Company was holding the three so-called strong-points, with one platoon on the St. Quentin Road. D Company was in reserve, over two miles behind, at Brigade Headquarters, so that the Battalion was very much scattered in small groups over a wide extent of country. At 4.30 a.m.

a heavy bombardment opened all along the line. By the time the bombardment had lasted two hours every telephone line from Battalion Headquarters had been broken. At 9.30 a.m. the hostile barrage gradually moved backwards, until it rested behind us. The fog was still as dense as ever, and it was impossible to see 5 yards in any direction.

'At 10 a.m. a runner came from C Company to say that the enemy had come over in the fog, and were already on the Pechine line (our main line of resistance in the outpost line). Immediately afterwards a runner from A Company came in to say that the Company Commander, Captain Singlehurst, had been killed, and that the Germans had reached the St. Quentin Road.

'Shortly afterwards Rifleman Blackwell dashed out into the fog and returned with a German officer, who, when he was asked what he was doing there, said that he was looking for his men, who had gone on ahead. On looking at his maps, I found that his objectives were places five and six miles behind us. The maps were at once sent off to Brigade Headquarters, but never reached their destination, as the Germans were already far behind us. The officer also told me that their Divisional front for the attack was two kilometres, and that they were attacking on this front with three divisions in depth, news which was not very cheerful for us. Several small parties of Germans stumbled into our trench in the fog, but were quickly driven away again. About midday the fog began to lift, and it was possible to gain some idea of what had happened. Most of our scattered posts had by this time been surrounded and mopped up one by one. Germans were to be seen everywhere: parties of them were to be seen hurrying along the St. Quentin Road, and to the south they were seen bringing up their artillery on to the ridge behind us. Our Lewis guns for a while had the time of their lives, and caused much confusion and delay to their artillery.

'At 1 p.m. we fired off rockets to show that we were still holding out, and had also sent a pigeon message saying that we were hard pressed, as the Boches had got into both ends of our trench, and were trying to bomb us out. In this they were not successful, as Lieutenant Mackie at one end and Lieutenant White at the other end, with a few men, managed to keep them at bay.

'The only effect of the rockets was to attract the attention of more Boches, who thereupon brought up all sorts of engines of war against us, *flammenwerfer*, trench mortars, and machine guns. The *flammenwerfer* were soon put out of action by rifle grenades, which were also very useful in searching out the dead ground, of which there was only too much around us, where the Germans were collecting preparatory to charging. The hostile machine guns proved much more troublesome, as they completely enfiladed our trench.

'By this time more than half the garrison were casualties, and the Lewis guns, which had done excellent work, refused to fire more than single shots. All this time the Germans had been collecting in large numbers, and just before 4 p.m. quite 500 rushed in on us suddenly from all sides, and it was all over.

'As a minor tactical operation, it was very well done, and they told me afterwards that they had had some months' training in this type of warfare.

'Their signalling and staff work appeared to be very good: their staff officers were well up in the front and when taken to their Brigade Headquarters we found it already established behind us on the way to our old Brigade Headquarters.

'The second division that was attacking on our battalion front were the ones that finally mopped us up, and our captors proved to be Bavarians. They could not believe that only one battalion was holding this front, and kept inquiring why we had already withdrawn our troops and guns.

'Of the Battalions in our Brigade that were in support and reserve we never saw a sign.' [1]

Here ends Colonel Howard Bury's narrative, and his last sentence gives food for much thought. What exactly was the intention of the higher commanders—Army and Corps—as to the way in which the enemy was to be opposed, taking the disposition of the 14th Division as a specimen of the front of the whole Fifth Army? Here we have a Battalion Commander, and one not in the least likely to misunderstand his orders, who evidently feels aggrieved

[1] The following officers of the 9th Battalion were killed on the 21st: Captain R. Singlehurst, 2nd Lieutenant H. D. Toogood.

that his battalion, in the Forward Zone, is allowed to be wiped out without any assistance from the other two battalions in the Brigade. Of these two battalions, one formed the garrison, and the sole garrison, of the Battle Zone—one would have expected to find the Battle Zone more strongly held than the Forward Zone—the other was in Divisional Reserve. The rôles of these Zones are given in a Divisional Order, evidently copied from a Corps Order, and presumably originating with the Fifth Army, as follows:

> 'Forward Zone: to break up and disorganise any enemy attack, and to compel him to expend large quantities of ammunition, and employ strong forces for its capture. The defence will be held by the units in depth, so as to admit of proper control and to simplify mutual support and immediate counter-attack.
>
> 'Battle Zone: is the zone selected in which to meet and repel any *serious* attacks on the part of the enemy. *It will be maintained at all costs.*
>
> 'Rear Zone: another Battle Zone in case of necessity. *Troops will not fall back from one zone to another.* All points will be defended whether the flanks are turned or not.' (The italics are mine.)

After reading the above, would not one expect to find the Battle Zone held in considerably greater strength than the Forward Zone? Now, the troops of a Forward Zone, or Outposts, or whatever one may choose to call those in front of the main line of defence, may accomplish their task in one of two ways. They may fall back fighting, in which case they are certain to mask the fire of the troops behind them, a very serious matter in these days of complicated artillery barrages; or, they may 'stick it out' to the last man. Now, no one will deny that there are occasions when one part of a force must be sacrificed to save the rest, when troops must be expected to 'stick it out' to the last man; but is it wise to make it a matter of routine? Would it pay in the end for all advanced troops to go forward, knowing that in the case of a serious attack they must, every man of them, be either killed or taken prisoner? One must give some consideration to human frailty, which is existent in the majority of us, even in the British Army. If a man knows that there is some remote chance of relief he will be inclined to see the matter out. If he knows that there is none, he will be under great temptation to put up his hands before all his ammunition is exhausted. But to return to Colonel Howard Bury: Is it not possible that the reason for his expectation of reinforcement was, that the scheme quoted above was looked upon by those who had to put it into practice as something very pretty on paper, but having no existence in fact? Could they altogether be blamed if they thought that the system of two, or three, weak zones, each 'complete in itself' (in the words of the Orders), and in which the troops of no one zone were to fall back on another, might resolve itself into a process of being 'scuppered' in detail; and may not this expectation, that when it came to the pinch, the garrisons of the rear zones would be sent up to reinforce them, have been an encouragement to them to make the heroic resistance they did? I offer no solution to any of these problems, but only put them forward as interesting and, I hope, useful subjects of discussion.

After overrunning the Forward Zone the Germans, leaving the posts that still held out to be dealt with by a fresh division, swept on to the attack of the Battle Zone. Our 7th Battalion (Lieut.-Colonel J. G. Birch) formed the garrison of that Zone in the 43rd Brigade Sector. Their fighting position was in front of Benay, but, until ordered to occupy it, which would only be when an attack was expected or had begun, they had Headquarters and one company at Montescourt, and the remaining three companies in the neighbourhood of Benay. It so happened that they had been ordered to have a practice occupation on the night of March 20/21. Consequently, the German attack found them already in position, with Headquarters a few hundred yards behind Benay (Brigade Headquarters being in the same spot), B, D, and C Companies holding a series of strong-points, from right to left, in front of Benay, with A Company in three more strong-points in close support. The following is the account of their share in the events of the 21st in the 7th Battalion 'War Diary':

'About 3.30 a.m. the Colonel and Major P. A. W. Laye returned to Headquarters, after having been round the Companies, and lay down for a few hours' sleep. Major M. J. St. Aubyn (Second-in-Command) had been left with the transport at Montescourt. At 4.45 a.m. everyone at Headquarters was awakened by the noise of a very heavy enemy barrage on the front line. All communication between Brigade and the front-line Battalion (6th Battalion Somerset Light Infantry) was cut before any message had come through, and dawn brought with it a dense fog, with a visibility of less than 50 yards. Runners from the companies brought news of enemy shelling on the strong-points; and although nothing definite was known it became sufficiently evident that an attack in force was about to take place. Two companies of the 9th Scottish Rifles at Remigny were sent for, and a party of fifty other ranks (transport details from the three battalions in the Brigade) from Montescourt, under 2nd Lieutenant T. G. Graham, of the Battalion. Before long the shelling of the Battle Zone became heavier and more accurate, and the combined Brigade and Battalion Headquarters were subjected to a considerable bombardment. The enemy barrage lasted approximately five hours, at the end of which he attacked. The Adjutant of the Somerset Light Infantry brought word to Brigade that the Boches were past his Battalion Headquarters, and by the time he reached Brigade Headquarters (about 11 a.m.) the companies in the Battle Zone were already engaged. The left (C) and support (A) Companies appear to have been attacked from the rear, and to have been practically surrounded, together with the centre Company (D). A few men from each of these companies eventually got back to Battalion Headquarters, and it was found that Captain H. Jackman (A Company) had been killed, Captain Hon. W. Borthwick (C Company) and Lieutenant W. L. Sanders (D Company) both severely wounded, and in the hands of the enemy. Captain C. H. D. King (C Company) succeeded in very skilfully withdrawing his company, and a line was taken up along a sunken road running east and west about 600 yards behind Benay, and on a level with Battalion Headquarters. This was reinforced by 2nd Lieutenant Graham's party, the two supporting companies of the Scottish Rifles, and a few of the Brigade Pioneer Company, under 2nd Lieutenant J. McDonald, of the Battalion.

'During the afternoon the fog lifted, and many enemy aeroplanes flew low over our lines, firing machine guns, and directing artillery fire. Brigade Headquarters had now moved back to their battle position near the Montescourt Railway Bridge. The line remained in this position until late afternoon, when it became apparent that the Boches were to our left rear, and a field gun was brought up to within 800 yards, firing with open sights on Battalion Headquarters, rendering the position untenable. The left was therefore brought back about 250 yards into a wired trench, where touch was established with the 42nd Brigade on our left. Headquarters moved into a dug-out in a sunken road 200 yards behind this line. During this period great execution was done by two of our field guns firing shrapnel at 300 yards' range from their position about 20 yards in front of our right (B Company). About 6 p.m. Captain King was unfortunately wounded, and shortly afterwards 2nd Lieutenant J. McDonald also. This position was maintained until midnight 21/22, when orders were received to withdraw without relief to Jussy, which was done. In addition to casualties already mentioned, during the day, 2nd Lieutenant D. O. Paget had been killed, Lieutenant Graham, 2nd Lieutenants Vincent, Rathbone, Day, and Allen were missing, 2nd Lieutenants Shaw and Jackson wounded and missing, and about 250 other ranks killed, wounded, and missing. Remaining with the Battalion were Lieut.-Colonel J. G. Birch, Major P. A. W. Laye, Captain P. Llewelyn Davies (Adjutant), 2nd Lieutenant V. A. Fair (A Company), 2nd Lieutenant T. G.

Graham, and 2nd Lieutenant F. V. Baker (Signal Officer), and about 130 other ranks.'

Of the above, 2nd Lieutenants J. W. Shaw, M.C., and F. C. Vincent, D.C.M., were killed.

The enemy do not seem to have had much difficulty with the Battle Zone anywhere on the 14th Division front, but, as in the case of the 43rd Brigade, a stout resistance was made a few hundred yards to the rear of it, which held him up for some hours. At 5.30 p.m. the Division reported their line to be running from left to right, from the railway cutting 1,000 yards west of Essigny—Hill 105, half a mile south of Essigny—sunken road 1,000 yards west of Benay to half a mile north-north-west of Hinacourt. They do not seem at that time to have been in touch with either the 18th Division on the right or the 36th on the left. In the evening the 5th Cavalry Brigade was allotted to the Division for the purpose of filling the gap between the 43rd Brigade and the 18th Division.

At 9.15 p.m. orders were issued for the Division to withdraw to the line of the Canal. The withdrawal took place without incident, and a line was taken up behind the Canal, with the 41st Brigade on the left, the 43rd in the centre, and the 54th, of the 18th Division, which appears to have been placed under the orders of the 14th Division at this time, on the right. The 42nd Brigade was in reserve at Petit Détroit. The 3rd Cavalry Brigade, which had been holding the line of the Canal on the 21st, also came under the 14th Division.

On the morning of March 22 the fog was as thick as ever, but at 10 a.m. it cleared. The enemy had brought up large numbers of machine guns and trench mortars to sweep the banks of the Canal, but the line was held all day. Orders came for the 14th Division front to be reduced, the

61st Brigade, 20th Division, taking over some of it on the left, and the 54th Brigade coming again under its own Division.

On this day our 7th Battalion were occupying a position 200 yards in front of the railway between Jussy and Flavy-le-Martel in support to a front line along the west bank of the Canal, held by the 9th Scottish Rifles and cavalry. They spent the day digging in.

At 2.20 a.m. on the 23rd the 14th Division received orders from III Corps that the 9th (French) Division would relieve them on the night of the 23rd/24th. At 3.30 a.m. the enemy got across the Canal at Jussy, but were driven back by a counter-attack delivered by a mixed body of details of the Division under the command of Major M. J. St. Aubyn, 7th K.R.R.C., who was killed in the operation. The enemy attacked all along the line of the Canal after daylight, and by 11.30 a.m. had crossed at several points. During the night Major Lacey, 9th K.R.R.C., had reported at 42nd Brigade Headquarters with a party of 400 details. At 12 noon on the 23rd he was ordered, by the Division, to form a reserve to the 41st Brigade south-east of Cugny. The 13th Entrenching Battalion, which was digging in east of Cugny, was placed under his orders.

During the afternoon the Division fell back to the high ground between La Neuville-en-Beine and Cugny. On this day Captain E. W. Tetley, 8th K.R.R.C., distinguished himself by holding the Canal crossing at Jussy with a party of details he had brought up from the rear, and then fighting a rearguard action back to Flavy, where the enemy was again held up. Major Lacey, 9th Battalion, before falling back to the position assigned to him with his details, took up a line with his right on Flavy station, and there offered a most determined resistance till obliged to fall back late in the afternoon. He was wounded the same evening. He mentioned the Regimental Sergeant-Major and his two runners, Riflemen Evans and Batton, as having particularly distinguished themselves in the action. By evening all the troops of the Division were thoroughly exhausted and units very much disorganised. The 41st Brigade was reduced to 9 officers and 160 other ranks.

Our 7th Battalion had been involved in heavy fighting during the day, which is thus described in the 'Chronicle' for 1918:

'On the 23rd dawn was for the third successive time accompanied by dense fog, and the situation became exceedingly obscure. The situation on the flanks was never satisfactorily ascertained, but on a report being received from the Division on our right that the enemy had effected a crossing in force, and that reinforcements must be sent to the right at all costs, 2nd Lieutenant T. G. Graham and about seventy other ranks were sent to occupy a trench about 600 yards to the right front of Battalion Headquarters. Later in the morning the enemy did undoubtedly force a crossing and advanced on to our left. In conjunction with the Scottish Rifles, the remainder of the Battalion lined the railway embankment to the left of Headquarters and astride the Jussy–Flavy Road, with the cavalry to the right of Headquarters. The enemy now began shelling the railway, and particularly the house in the cellar of which Headquarters were established. At the same time, under cover of the fog, the enemy succeeded in getting right up to the embankment to the left of Headquarters, and rendered the position exceedingly unpleasant by throwing bombs over it. We had run out of bombs, and the supply of S.A.A. was running low. Fortunately, the cavalry possessed a number of Hotchkiss guns which were turned on to fire through the fog and enfilade along the front of the embankment; this alone prevented the enemy from crossing the railway, and caused him a serious check. In response to urgent appeals for more S.A.A., a limberful came up the Faillovel Road at the gallop, and just reached Headquarters before both horses were killed by a shell.

'Headquarters moved about 11 a.m. a few yards to the right, with a bank running along the front of the railway, manned by the cavalry. By 11.30 a.m. the position was being apparently enfiladed by hostile machine-gun fire from the left rear, roughly from the direction of Flavy, and hostile machine guns were also heard firing from the right rear. The fog began to lift, and a party of the enemy, consisting of one officer and about thirty men, were seen advancing along the road towards the level crossing, but were wiped out by fire from two Hotchkiss guns at about 100 yards.

'The Colonel and the senior cavalry officer present (Captain Redmond, Scots Greys) decided that to remain longer in this position would mean being cut off, and it was determined to retire to a half-dug trench about 300 yards in rear. By the time this decision had been reached and orders issued, the fog had quite lifted, and the operation was effected at the expense of a considerable number of casualties from a very heavy and well-directed machine-gun barrage. The Colonel was seen to be hit in the face by a fragment of shell. It is presumed that he made his way to Flavy-le-Martel, and there fell into the hands of the enemy. Captain Redmond was killed, being shot through the head by a machine-gun bullet.

'The enemy advanced in force simultaneously with this withdrawal, and a gradual and orderly retirement, during which the enemy was constantly engaged with rifle fire, was effected by all units on to the Frières–Faillouel Ridge. Here a stand was made by the cavalry, in spite of low-flying aircraft directing artillery fire on to the position, where there were no trenches; and orders were received for all troops of the 14th Division to withdraw to a line between Ugny-le-Gay and Cugny. This was done, and the 43rd Brigade collected in front of the village of Riez-Cugny about 6.30 p.m. The Battalion now numbered about 70 all ranks, under Captain P. Llewelyn Davies, with 2nd Lieutenants Fair and Graham, Major F. A. W. Laye having taken command of a party of Corps reinforcements. The 9th French Division appeared along the line Ugny–Cugny, and the Battalion, in conjunction with the Scottish Rifles (under Lieut.-Colonel Lumsden), spent the night constructing an isolated strong-point 500 yards south of Riez-Cugny, behind the Bois de Genlis. 2nd Lieutenant F. V. Baker was not seen after the withdrawal from Jussy, and is presumed killed or wounded.' [He was killed.]

The French 9th Division had reported that they were ready to let the 14th Division retire through them, but, at 12.30 a.m. on the 24th, orders came from III Corps to say that the Division must remain in the line to fill any gaps. However, at 10.45 a.m., further orders came to retire through the French to Buchoire and Guiscard. Arriving at Buchoire at 5 p.m. the Division was ordered on to Crisolles, on reaching which place at 8.45 p.m. they were again ordered on to take up a position west of the Oise–Somme Canal, crossing at Beaurains and Haudival. The march was completed during the night. The Canal was found to be dry, forming no obstacle to the passage of infantry.

On the 25th the Division continued its retirement, and during the night concentrated at Thiescourt. On the 26th the Division reached L'Ecouvillon. On this day the strength of battalions, which on the 21st had averaged about 600 of all ranks, was as follows: 41st Brigade—8th K.R.R.C., 1 officer, 30 other ranks; 7th Rifle Brigade, 3 officers, 80 other ranks; 8th Rifle Brigade, 9 officers, 215 other ranks; 42nd Brigade—9th Rifle Brigade, 10 officers, 305 other ranks; 5th Oxford and Bucks Light Infantry, 15 officers, 232 other ranks; 9th K.R.R.C., 2 officers, 70 other ranks; 43rd Brigade—9th Scottish Rifles, 8 officers, 192 other ranks; 7th K.R.R.C., 5 officers, 140 other ranks; 6th Somerset Light Infantry, 2 officers, 9 other ranks; Pioneers—11th King's, 7 officers, 203 other ranks. These numbers do not include transport and other details brought up from the rear.

Corps reinforcements and two Entrenching Battalions which had joined the Division together brought about 1,000 men, so the infantry of the Division now totalled about 2,500.

On the 27th the Division moved to the neighbourhood of Estrèes St. Denis, and on the 28th to that of Pont-St.

Maxence.[1] Here they were to have gone into billets, but the arrangements broke down, as the place was found to be full of French troops, and it was not till 4 a.m. the next day that the troops were finally in billets in the neighbouring villages. At 9 a.m. on the 29th orders came to embus at Creil at 12 noon, but no buses turned up, and the troops finally embussed near Nogent at 9.30 p.m. They debussed at Hébécourt, some six miles south of Amiens, on the morning of the 30th, and went into billets; the 41st Brigade in Vers–Bacouel, the 42nd Brigade in Lœuilly–Tilloy and the 43rd Brigade in Plachy–Nampty, strung out along the right bank of the River Celle from four to ten miles south of Amiens. Next day the 13th and 14th Entrenching Battalions were absorbed by battalions of the Division as drafts.

On the night of April 1/2 the Division went up into the front line again, taking over from the 2nd Cavalry Division, with their left on the River Luce near Hangard. The following night the Division was relieved by the French 29th Division, and concentrated in the Bois de Blangy, west of Villiers-Bretonneux.

On the night of April 3/4 the Division relieved the 1st Cavalry Division about Hamel, the 6th Cavalry Brigade remaining in support.

The front taken over by the Division reached from Bouzencourt, on the Somme, on the left, to the main Amiens Road on the right. The 41st Brigade were on the right, the 42nd on the left, and the 43rd in reserve.

The enemy attacked next morning after a heavy bombardment. Reports of the fighting that followed are not very clear, and Divisional Headquarters seem, from their report of the action, to have had great difficulty in finding out exactly what was happening all day. The general

[1] Map VIII.

result was that the front-line resistance gradually collapsed, beginning on the right, and the end of the day found the remnants of the Division, interspersed with units of the 6th Cavalry Brigade, holding a position a few hundred yards in rear of their original front line. All attacks on this line were dispersed, chiefly by the action of the 16th Divisional Artillery, attached to the 14th Division, in running their guns up to the crest line and firing over the sights. Reading between the lines one gathers that the remnants of the 14th Division had about reached the breaking strain, and in this, their last fight as a Division, did not live up to their great reputation. Neither our 7th nor 8th Battalion appears to have been engaged this day. The share of the 9th Battalion in the day's fighting is described as follows in the 'Chronicle' for 1918:

'The next day, April 3, the Brigade moved into the line again. The Battalion marched into Hamelet, and the line ran in front of that village. The 41st and 42nd Brigades were to take over the line itself, whilst the 43rd Brigade remained in reserve. Of the 42nd Brigade, the Oxford and Bucks Light Infantry were to hold the line from Hamel east [*sic*] to Bois de Vaire, with the 41st Brigade on their right, the 9th Rifle Brigade on their left, and the 9th K.R.R.C. in support. Both the Oxford and Bucks Light Infantry and the Rifle Brigade were largely made up of drafts from the 13th Entrenching Battalion.

'After remaining in billets a few hours at Hamelet, the Battalion moved forward to Hamel. We were a sadly attenuated unit, only consisting of Captain Young, 2nd Lieutenants Gordon, Elwick-Harrison, and Whitehead, and 146 other ranks.

'We then took over three support positions from the 11th Hussars, the Battalion being formed into three parties, two just east of the village, and the third, under 2nd Lieutenant Whitehead, was to the north-west, communication with the latter being very difficult. The two former parties were in small shelters cut under two steep banks. No view of the front was possible, even from the top of the banks.

'At 5 a.m. on April 4, before the relief was complete, the German artillery became very active, which increased to a severe bombardment by 5.30 a.m.

'This continued and increased in violence until 9.30 a.m. Casualties were, fortunately, few, but it was impossible to move about, and communication with Whitehead's party was quite hopeless.

'During this period Sergeant Watkinson behaved particularly well, and in fact the example set by all officers and N.C.O.s was admirable, and the men were in good heart and quite ready for the attack which was obviously impending.

'At about 8.30 a.m. Major Labouchere, Commanding the 5th Oxford and Bucks Light Infantry, came to our Headquarters and informed us that, although he had received no news from the front line, a wounded man had stated that the casualties were not severe, and the wire was still in good condition.

'Half an hour later the 41st Brigade could be seen retiring in some confusion on the right flank near Bois de Vaire. Second Lieutenant Gordon did all he could to rally them, but could only check the men in his immediate neighbourhood.

'Major Labouchere then went up to the front line, and it was arranged that he should send back word if he required support for the Oxford and Bucks. No message ever came either from him or his Battalion. It was later ascertained that he was severely wounded before he reached his men.

'Meanwhile, the Battalion remained in its positions ready to move forward, and we saw the cavalry gallop forward to endeavour to restore the situation on the right.

'We were still in the dark as to what was going on forward, as no forward observation was possible from Battalion Headquarters, and the first indication we received that our line had gone in front was when the Oxford and Bucks dropped down the bank and made their way in some disorder through our positions. The reason for this retirement has never been satisfactorily cleared up. The right flank had admittedly gone, and the left flank went shortly afterwards, but the trenches and wire were practically intact; these troops had moreover gallantly withstood a severe bombardment without flinching; and no serious attack having developed, the movement was inexplicable. It must, however, be remembered that the men were very tired, and that orders to retire were most certainly given by someone.'

[The above account does less than justice to the 5th Oxford and Bucks Light Infantry, as the following extract from the Divisional account of the action shows: 'A message, timed 11.15 a.m., from 15th Australian Infantry Brigade stated "enemy reported coming over top about 400 yards right of the 11th Brigade drove out Oxford and Bucks (42nd Infantry Brigade), who retook trench but since driven out again. Bosch in great force." ']

'The Battalion fortunately was not involved in this retirement and held its ground. Our position was a difficult one; no observation, both flanks gone.

'The officers of the Oxford and Bucks Light Infantry stated they proposed to form a defensive line on the crest behind, some 300 yards in rear. When, therefore, the last of the front-line troops had passed through us, and we were coming under machine-gun fire from Hamel, and also from our right flank, orders were given to retire in artillery formation beyond the farther crest. No news had come in of Whitehead's party, and no message could be got to him.

'The men moved off in good order, but after passing the crest some confusion occurred, and by the time Battalion Headquarters arrived, only about thirty other ranks could be collected. Others had to be moved off by various officers who were endeavouring to rally the men, about twenty had become casualties, and there was no sign of the left party. Officers and N.C.O.s then assisted to rally the men of mixed units, and a line was eventually formed. The Germans then quickly occupied our old positions, but were there checked by our artillery fire, and the new line was not attacked.

'Orders then came from the Divisional Commander that the Battalion was to be collected, taken down to the transport, fed, and rested. Some fifty-seven men were marched to Blangy–Tronville, where the details of the Battalion were found.

'Ultimately our casualties proved to be 2nd Lieutenant Whitehead and 12 other ranks wounded, 20 other ranks missing (believed killed). The latter included Company Sergeant-Major Stamford and Company Sergeant-Major Ephgrave, who were probably buried in the original Battalion Headquarters. [Company Sergeant-Major Ephgrave was taken prisoner.]

'It was a bad day for the Division, but the Battalion to a man behaved extremely well, and it is only regretted that they did not have the chance of doing more.'

The 14th Division was relieved on the night of April 4/5, but the 43rd Brigade remained another twenty-four hours in the line, and on the 5th our 7th Battalion lost Captain G. F. Jessup, severely wounded, and of other ranks 6 killed, 23 wounded, and 6 missing.

This was the end of the 14th Division as a fighting formation. On April 14 a composite brigade was formed out of the remnants of the Division, our three battalions forming one battalion under Lieut.-Colonel B. J. Curling, but this arrangement did not last long. Towards the end of the month the Division became a skeleton formation—all superfluous officers and men being drafted to other units—and was used for the purpose of training the American Army. In June, what was left of it was finally broken up. The Cadre of the 7th Battalion went home, and there formed the basis of a new battalion, known as the 34th Battalion the London Regiment. The 8th Battalion was finally broken up on July 31, most of its remaining officers and men going to our 12th Battalion. The 9th Battalion lasted two days longer, its remains being absorbed by the 16th Battalion.

It was a sad ending to a grand Division, which had gloriously upheld the best traditions of the old Rifle and Light Infantry Regiments, and one wishes that it might have been allowed to see the end of the war, but the Adjutant-General's Branch is not governed by sentiment, and no doubt it was the most business-like method to select for extinction those formations which had suffered most.

It is reported that the G.O.C. 14th Division (Major-General Sir Victor Couper, who commanded it from start to finish) once got a letter from a friend at General Headquarters telling him that it was a subject of debate there whether the 14th Division or the Guards was the best in the British Expeditionary Force. His reply was that he was glad to hear that the Guards were so well spoken of.

11TH AND 12TH BATTALIONS

On the reduction of Infantry Brigades to three battalions our 10th Battalion had been disbanded, leaving only the 11th (59th Brigade) and 12th (60th Brigade) in the 20th Division.

After a winter in the Ypres salient that Division came down to the Fifth Army Area in February 1918. They were distributed in billets on both sides of the Somme in the neighbourhood of Ham, and were in General Headquarters Reserve, at twelve hours' notice, employed on the rear defences. Our 11th Battalion was at Chaulnes, the 12th at Offoy.

In the event of a big attack on the Fifth Army Front the Division was to come under the XVIII Corps as Corps Reserve, concentrated as follows: 59th Brigade, Villers St. Christophe-Douilly-Foreste-Ugny-L'Equipée-Vaux (incl.)-Omignon River, ready to man the Rear Zone; 60th Brigade, Fluquières-Douchy-Aubigny, to man from the River Somme to Vaux; 61st Brigade to man the Rear Zone forming the St. Simon Bridgehead.

The XVIII Corps was holding the line opposite St. Quentin, on the left of the III Corps, of which the 14th Division was the left Division.

On March 21, at 5.9 a.m., the Corps order for the front-line divisions (36th, 30th, and 61st) to 'man Battle Stations' was repeated to the 20th Division. Orders were at once sent out to the Division to be ready to move at one hour's notice. At 1 p.m. the order was given to move to concentration areas. Our 11th Battalion was moved by lorry to Foreste, the 12th marched to Douchy. At 8 p.m. the 59th and 60th Brigades were ordered to place covering troops in the Rear Zone; the 61st Brigade was attached to the 36th Division to cover their retirement over the Somme. At 11.50 p.m. the 59th Brigade was ordered to man the left of the Rear Zone of the Corps, Vaux to the Omignon River. The 11th Battalion moved to Vaux early on the 22nd. The enemy having been reported to have gained a footing at Happencourt, threatening the right of the 60th Brigade, the 59th Brigade was ordered, at 10.55 a.m., to withdraw from the Rear Zone, leaving a covering force, and assemble in the Germaine–Foreste area, ready to counter-attack south-east should the enemy press back the 60th Brigade.

Soon afterwards Fifth Army ordered a withdrawal south of the Somme.

The 20th Division was ordered to cover the retirement of the front divisions, and these fell back to the line Canizy (incl.)–Béthencourt (incl.).

At 5.50 p.m., the enemy having turned the left of the XVIII Corps, the 59th Brigade was ordered to fall back and occupy a previously sited rearguard position, Douilly–Lanchy. Meanwhile, the 60th Brigade had been heavily attacked. Our 12th Battalion was on the extreme left of the Brigade, with its right resting on Fluquières, its left just south of Vaux. Having both its flanks turned, the Battalion was ordered to fall back to Villers St. Christophe, which it did after losing almost the whole of one company, which was practically surrounded. The 20th Division, having covered the retirement of the rest of the Corps by holding the position Bray–Douilly–Lanchy, fell back behind the Somme during the night, not without severe fighting, in which Lieut.-Colonel A. F. C. Maclachlan, K.R.R.C., commanding 12th Rifle Brigade, was killed. By dawn of the 23rd the Division was holding its position south of the Somme. The 11th Battalion was behind the Somme at Voyennes, the 12th Battalion holding from Canizy (excl.) to the Bridgehead at Offoy (incl.).

At 8 a.m. it was reported that the enemy had crossed at Ham and was advancing on Esmery-Hallon. Troops of the 30th Division on the right, which were retiring to the line of the Libermont Canal, checked the enemy till a counter-attack could be prepared. This counter-attack, chiefly by the 182nd Brigade, attached to the 60th Brigade, was launched at 4 p.m., and restored the situation, the enemy being driven back nearly to the river opposite Ham. The 20th Division front along the river was held all day in spite of repeated attacks, especially against the 12th Rifle Brigade at Béthencourt and the 12th K.R.R.C. at Offoy.

On March 24, at 6 a.m., the enemy gained a footing on the west bank of the Canal on the 8th Division front, north of Béthencourt. A counter-attack by the 11th Rifle Brigade drove them back over the Canal and restored the situation. At 10.15 a.m. the enemy crossed at Pargny, and gained a footing on the high ground about Béthencourt. He was driven out by a counter-attack by the 183rd Brigade by 2.45 p.m.

About 8.30 a.m. the enemy attacking from the east drove the troops holding Canizy back to the railway embankment. An immediate counter-attack by the 12th K.R.R.C. drove them back into Canizy.

The position opposite Offoy and Voyennes was maintained all day, but our 11th Battalion suffered the loss of Lieut.-Colonel G. K. Priaulx by a shell which found the Battalion Headquarters, killing him and most of the Headquarters personnel.

At 12.20 p.m. anticipatory and confidential orders were issued for a retirement to the line of the Libermont Canal to Mesnil-St. Nicaise, as follows: 60th Brigade, line of Canal, Buverchy (excl.)–Quiquery (excl.); 59th Brigade, Quiquery (incl.)–Mesnil-St. Nicaise (excl.); 183rd Brigade, defensive flank, from Mesnil-St. Nicaise to the cross-roads, 1,000 yards south of Potte. Both flanks of the Division being in the air, the retirement on to this line took place during the afternoon, under heavy artillery and machine-gun fire. The 11th K.R.R.C. fell back to Languevoisin, the 12th to Breuil.

By evening the 8th Division on the left had withdrawn due west, and the enemy was reported at Morchain. The 59th Brigade was reinforced by the 20th Entrenching Battalion and the Divisional Reinforcement Battalion. The 183rd Brigade was ordered to occupy Potte. This was done, but no touch was obtained with the 8th Division. Heavy attacks forced our left back to a line facing north-east just in front of Mesnil-le-Petit. The line held till morning. Four companies of the 22nd (French) Division came up during the day, and were put under the 60th Brigade.

On the morning of the 25th heavy attacks from the north forced the left back to run from Quiquery to the high ground 1,000 yards west of Nesle. The 133rd (French) Division was reported to be digging in on the line Billancourt–Herly, and the 20th was placed under the orders of that division.

During the forenoon the left was further forced back to

the high ground north of Billancourt. Nesle was taken, and our 11th Battalion was very nearly cut off. At 2.30 p.m. information was received by the 20th Division from the XVIII Corps that the 61st Brigade, on its way back to the Division, would debus at Gruny,[1] with orders to send one battalion each to Gruny, Cremery, Liancourt, and man defences under construction facing east.

The Brigade, which was reduced to 450 of all ranks, arrived late in the evening and, although the enemy was already in the wood north-east of Liancourt, they held on long enough to enable the Division to withdraw west from Roye unmolested.

The 59th and 60th Brigades were ordered to withdraw to the line Cressy–Billancourt–Rethonvillers. This retirement was successfully carried out, but with considerable fighting. The trials of our 12th Battalion on this day are thus described in an officer's diary :

'The morning passed with only such casualties as were inflicted by our own artillery, who seemed incapable of finding the correct range [the Battalion had suffered many casualties from the same source the previous evening] ; but in the late afternoon the bridgeheads of Buverchy and Languevoisin gave, and the Brigade was again menaced on both flanks. Orders were received to withdraw in rear of the Rifle Brigade at 7 p.m., with the object of holding the Cressy–Ognolles line.

'At the last moment, even as the companies were moving out of their posts, the enemy forced his way over the bridge at Breuil, and the officer who was leading them, dressed in British uniform, called upon our men to halt. He was bayoneted at once. His men pushed on, and were seen surrounding Battalion Headquarters. It is believed that the whole personnel of Battalion Headquarters were captured. The retirement began in an orderly and organised way, but so disconcerting was the shell and machine-gun fire which caught us as we climbed the slopes of Oursey[1] that it ended in some disorder. We found the French in posts along the outskirts of Cressy,

[1] Not in Map.

and they asked us to form a defensive flank on their right until such time as another of their regiments should arrive. This we did, and remained with them till midnight, when a retirement to Roye, via Solente, was ordered.'

Soon after 3 p.m. the Division got orders to conform to the retirement of the French towards Roye, if necessary. From Roye the Division was to withdraw north-west to the area Hangest-en-Santerre–Le Quesnel. At 10 p.m. orders were issued for withdrawal at midnight. The retirement to Roye, where the Division was concentrated, was carried out without difficulty and, when there, orders were given for the march to the Le Quesnel area to begin at 7 a.m. on the 26th.

The diary of the officer of the 12th Battalion goes on:

'At 3 a.m. the Battalion, with the remainder of the 60th Brigade, arrived at Roye, where sentries had been posted to direct them to a grassy field south of the Carrepuis–Roye Road: here the details from the disbanded 20th Divisional Reserve Battalion awaited them. The whole Brigade sat down to rest in the field, while in a gutted building adjoining it, by the light of electric torches, the Brigadier held a conference of Battalion Commanders. The French, of whom weak detachments had taken over the front held by the 20th Division, were retiring, and the Division had to march at once to the neighbourhood of Le Quesnel, nine miles to the north-west of Roye.

'Of the officers and men who left Offoy with the Battalion on the 21st, 8 officers and about 160 men were now left. The officers were:

B Company—Captain Faddy, 2nd Lieutenants Bradford and Learnmouth.

C Company—2nd Lieutenants Dow and Everitt.

D Company—Captain Cranswick, 2nd Lieutenants Pearson and Rennie.

'Of the remainder, Captain Scott and 2nd Lieutenant Crooks had been killed; Captain Baxter, Captain Avent, 2nd Lieutenants Baddeley, Lamb, and Smith wounded; Colonel Moore, 2nd Lieutenants Taylor, Caldwell, Smitton,

Ward-Davis, and Scott were missing. Major Sampson took over command of the Battalion from the 26th.'

The 61st Brigade, not more than 400 rifles, which was to act as a flank guard, was, at 3 a.m., on the line Gruny–Cremery–Liancourt. Between 3 a.m. and 7 a.m. the Brigade slowly withdrew to the line Fresnoy-les-Roye–La Chavatte, from which line the villages of Parvillers, Damery, and Le Quesnoy were occupied in succession. Le Quesnoy was held till 6 p.m.; of which village the original garrison with only two officers, one being the Brigade-Major of the 61st Brigade, after holding up the enemy all day, withdrew, by order, to Beaufort during the night of the 26th/27th.

This flank guard enabled the Division to reach Le Quesnel unmolested. The march was only just completed in time. Touch with the 24th Division was regained between 11 a.m. and 12 noon towards Rouvroy-en-Santerre. The Division came under the orders of XVIII Corps at Le Quesnel, and the elements of the 61st Division were ordered to rejoin their division at Beaucourt-en-Santerre. At 2.30 p.m. detachments of the 30th Division reoccupied Bouchoir and Folies.

At 12.45 p.m. an air report came in saying that the enemy was advancing in large numbers along the Roye–Amiens Road, small parties being between Damery and Andechy.

At 1.10 p.m. the Division, which had reached Le Quesnel about noon, was ordered to take up the following positions:

The 61st Brigade to concentrate at Beaufort, block all roads, and hold on at all costs; the 60th and 59th Brigades to dig in just east of Le Quesnel.

This placed the Division in support of the 30th Division

holding Bouchoir–Folies–Rouvroy. Touch was obtained by the 61st Brigade at Beaufort with the 24th Division at Warvillers.

At 6.35 p.m. XVIII Corps ordered the 61st Division to take over the Le Quesnel defences; the 20th Division to move up in close support of the 30th; the 59th Brigade to Folies; the 60th Brigade to Arvillers (relieving the 36th Division); the 61st Brigade to remain at Beaufort, and the Divisional Reinforcement Battalion in Divisional Reserve at Le Quesnel.

On the morning of March 27 the Division was disposed as ordered, the 59th Brigade supporting the 30th Division, which was still holding the Folies defences.

At 10.5 a.m. parties of the 36th Division were reported falling back on Arvillers, saying their right was turned. The 60th Brigade was consequently ordered to form a defensive flank and hold Arvillers at all costs.

At 10.40 a.m. Erches was reported to be in the enemy's hands, and by 12.30 p.m. they had taken Bouchoir from the 30th Division. Folies and Arvillers held out all day. At 12 noon our 11th Battalion, which had been in reserve behind Folies, was sent up to relieve a battalion of the 30th Division in front of the village. There they beat off an attack, the first frontal attack they had experienced since the opening of the German offensive. At 8 p.m. the enemy unsuccessfully raided them, leaving behind a machine gun and some prisoners. Second Lieutenant H. A. Ramsden particularly distinguished himself on this occasion. At 9.30 p.m. orders came for the Division, leaving its artillery behind it, to be relieved by the 133rd (French) Division during the ensuing night and march to Domart.

The 59th and 61st Brigades were relieved before dawn of the 28th and, by 12 noon, were in bivouac south-east of

Domart. The 60th Brigade, which was not relieved till 11 a.m., owing to an attack on Arvillers, was in bivouac by 3 p.m. During its withdrawal from Arvillers, under heavy shell fire, the 12th Battalion lost 2nd Lieutenant J. Dow, who had taken over the duties of Adjutant only two days before, and the Medical Officer, Captain Wilson, both killed. The 20th Division here came under the XIX Corps, which had been heavily pressed all day. At 7.10 p.m. the Division was ordered to take up a position behind existing wire from Demuin (excl.) to Mezières (excl.): the 61st Brigade to hold the line, the 59th Brigade in support, the 60th Brigade to be in reserve ; the artillery of the 24th Division to cover the Division.

At 8.35 a.m. touch was obtained with the French, whose line on our right reached Moreuil. At 11.50 a.m. the French were reported to be falling back. The 50th Division, in support to the 20th Division, was asked to send a battalion to Villers Wood. The French were then reported to be heavily attacked at Moreuil. The 60th Brigade was then ordered to advance through Villers, and form a defensive flank on the right of the 59th Brigade and, if necessary, to counter-attack.

At 1.30 p.m. the enemy was reported to be advancing against the 61st Brigade, and assembling south-east of Beaucourt. At 1 p.m. the French holding Mezières withdrew, and the 59th Brigade, with both flanks turned, had to withdraw to a line running through Villers. At 2.15 p.m. the 60th Brigade was ordered to recapture Mezières in co-operation with part of the 59th Brigade and the 50th Division, formed as one brigade. The attack was launched at 4 p.m. and was partially successful, the outskirts of the village being regained and prisoners taken who reported that the enemy had suffered heavy losses in their capture of the village.

The following account of the share of our 12th Battalion in this attack is taken from the diary already quoted :

'At 2 p.m. orders were received from 60th Brigade that the Rifle Brigade and ourselves should counter-attack Mezières. As soon as the orders could be given [the attack was timed for 4 p.m. and took place at that hour] the three leading companies advanced in co-operation with the Battalion on our left, while the right was secured by the French on the high ground south of the village. At the cross-roads a number of prisoners with two heavy trench mortars, several machine guns, and two teams of horses with limbers were taken ; at the cross-roads 400 yards farther east we were held up, and after several attempts could not pass this point. D Company, which had been in reserve, now advanced round the southern edge of the village to a quarry, and began to work forward so as to take the eastern cross-road from the south.

'In the meantime, however, the enemy was continuing to advance north of us, and was beginning to occupy the western side of the woods north-west of Mezières, and the Brigade was forced to retire from the left. We withdrew again across the valley, and through Villers-aux-Erables under considerable machine-gun fire, leaving behind the mortars and machine guns which we had put out of action. We and the Rifle Brigade sent back 53 prisoners from Mezières.

'In these operations Lieutenant Allison, D.C.M., and 2nd Lieutenant Everitt were killed, and Captain Alpine wounded. Major Chadwick, of the 60th, in command of the 12th Rifle Brigade, was severely wounded when personally leading the attack of his battalion.'

By the evening the Division was holding a line just in front of the Moreuil–Demuin Road. On the 30th the whole Corps front was repeatedly attacked. At 4 p.m., the line having been pierced in several places, the whole Division fell back some distance. At 7 p.m. the 12th Rifle Brigade, 12th K.R.R.C., part of the 59th Brigade, and some French troops counter-attacked and regained the whole of the original line. This was a particularly fine recovery, as the troops had been fighting all day, and at times had about reached the limit of their endurance; in fact, the 60th Brigade 'War Diary' states that at 4 p.m. 'a general rot set in all along the line.' The 12th Rifle Brigade and 12th K.R.R.C. were organised into one battalion for the counter-attack, and they captured 49 prisoners and 9 machine guns. The 12th Battalion 'War Diary' says: 'This was the first time we had really good artillery assistance since Fluquières, and the bombardment, which lasted 20 minutes, was very effective. After the counter-attack we were subjected to an intense bombardment by field guns at close range, but we hung on to our positions.'

The night of the 30th/31st was quiet; but just after noon the enemy attacked the French at Moreuil, and the 8th Division, on the right of the 20th Division. The attack spread northwards, and the 20th Division was gradually forced back on to the River Luce.

On April 1 the Division was holding a series of bridge-head positions, with their left on Hangard, which was held by the French. A brilliant counter-attack by the 2nd Cavalry Brigade greatly improved the situation. The 59th Brigade assisted this attack by sending 100 men, of whom 1 officer and 50 other ranks belonged to the 11th K.R.R.C., to support the Canadian Cavalry Brigade.

No further attacks were made by the enemy on the position, and consolidation was continued.

At 11.20 a.m. orders arrived for the 14th Division to relieve the 2nd Cavalry Division on the night of the 1st/2nd; the 20th Division and remains of the 50th Division were to withdraw to the Quevauvillers Area. The withdrawal commenced at 8 p.m., and so the 20th Division passed out of the fighting area.

The casualties of our 11th Battalion during the twelve days were:

Killed: officers—Lieut.-Colonel G. K. Priaulx, D.S.O.; Captain D. C. O'Rorke, M.C.; 2nd Lieutenants E. McKie and A. M. Hopkins; other ranks—29.

Wounded: officers—Captain A. F. Nutting; Lieutenant G. H. Martin; 2nd Lieutenants N. H. Mason, J. P. Medwin, and C. W. Nicholas; other ranks—176.

Missing: officers—Captains L. E. James, M.C., and G. C. Webb; Lieutenant G. Rendall; 2nd Lieutenant B. Johnston; Captain P. Hughes and 2nd Lieutenant E. C. Griffiths (the last two officers were with the Divisional details); other ranks—220.

Of the above, Captain Hughes and 2nd Lieutenant Rendall were killed in action; the remainder were prisoners of war.

The losses of the 12th Battalion were:

Killed: officers—Lieutenant D. Allison; 2nd Lieutenants E. N. Crooks, J. R. Scott, J. D. Laird, and J. Dow; other ranks—37.

Wounded: officers—Acting Major M. T. Sampson, M.C.; Captains J. Alpine and C. F. Baxter; 2nd Lieutenants H. V. Smith, J. R. Lamb, C. R. Baddeley, A. W. Starling, J. W. Everitt, W. Wallace, J. Walker, and E. J. Simpson; other ranks—216.

Wounded, believed prisoners of war: officers—Lieut.-Colonel L. G. Moore, D.S.O.; Captain G. E. J. Scott; 2nd Lieutenants W. L. Ward-Davis, P. Smitton, and J. C. Caldwell; other ranks—6.

Missing, prisoners of war: officers—Captain A. N. Cranswick, M.C.; 2nd Lieutenant W. H. Taylor; other ranks—207.

Of the above, Captain G. E. J. Scott was killed in action on March 25; 2nd Lieutenant Everitt died of wounds as a prisoner of war on April 12.

These two battalions, though in and out of the trenches all the time till the Armistice, took no part in any more great operations.

17th Battalion

At the time of the German attack our 17th Battalion was with its Division (39th) in G.H.Q. Reserve, behind the extreme left of the VII Corps, the left corps of the Fifth Army. The Division was working on the rear defences, and the 17th Battalion was at Sorel, only three miles from the 1st at Equancourt, as will be seen later.

On March 21 the German bombardment began at 4.30 a.m., our 17th Battalion at Sorel getting some of the fire of the enemy's heavy artillery, from which A Company suffered 13 casualties before they moved. At 5.15 a.m. came orders from the VII Corps to 'Man Battle Stations,' which, in the case of the 39th Division, meant a move to assembly stations. Our 17th Battalion moved, soon after 6 a.m., to Sorel Wood, where they remained under shell fire for the rest of the day; their casualties for the day being 2 killed and 29 wounded. In the absence of Brigadier-General G. A. Armytage, D.S.O., Lieut.-Colonel A. P. H. Le Prevost, D.S.O., commanded the Brigade (117th), and Major E. Fairlie the Battalion. At 5.10 p.m. came the order for the 118th and 117th Brigades to dig, wire, and hold the Switch Line from Tincourt Wood to Saulcourt. The 17th K.R.R.C. had the 16th Sherwood Foresters on their right, the 16th Rifle Brigade on their left.

At 8.50 a.m., on March 22, the enemy was reported to be attacking St. Emilie, 2,000 yards south-east of Saulcourt. At noon the dispositions of the 117th Brigade were altered, the 16th Sherwood Foresters and 16th Rifle Brigade dividing the line, the 17th K.R.R.C. being withdrawn, and sending two companies to support each of the other two battalions. At 5 p.m. the enemy attacked heavily, causing the 16th Rifle Brigade to withdraw to a position north-west of Tincourt Wood, after suffering many casualties. The whole Brigade was then forced to withdraw. C and D Companies, 17th K.R.R.C., supporting the 16th Rifle Brigade, suffered severely, Captain A. W. Harvey (8th Scottish Rifles, attached), and Lieutenant F. C. Pepler being wounded, and the former left behind when the Battalion withdrew. Captain Harvey died in German hands on March 27.

A and B Companies covered the retirement of the rest of the Brigade from positions in Tincourt Wood. C and D joined them two hours later, and were placed in close support.

At dawn on March 23, which was as misty as had been the two previous mornings, the enemy attacked our 17th Battalion in great strength, but were beaten off after very fierce fighting. The Division then again withdrew, the 117th Brigade taking up a fresh position between Bussu and Aizecourt, with the 17th K.R.R.C. in support. During this withdrawal the Battalion lost 2nd Lieutenant P. V. Fifield, killed, 2nd Lieutenant P. Freer, wounded, and 2nd Lieutenant W. A. MacIntyre, wounded and a prisoner of war. Soon after 1 p.m. the Brigade fell back to a position east of Mont St. Quentin, which they only held long enough to allow the transport, with which the road was blocked, to get away. At 5 p.m. the Brigade, which was by this time very weak, and had the enemy round its left flank, retired again, and crossed the Somme at Cléry. They occupied a line south of the Canal, but at 10 p.m. were ordered back to Feuillères in Divisional Reserve. The line was held by the 118th Brigade on the right, the 116th on the left.

After getting some hot food and a night's rest, the 117th Brigade went back into line on the morning of the 24th, on the right of the 118th Brigade. The 17th K.R.R.C. was responsible for the Feuillères Bridgehead. The enemy did not attack, and the bridge was blown up at 10.30 p.m.

March 25 was uneventful on the 39th Division front, but at 7.30 p.m. orders came for a fresh retirement. At

2 a.m. on the 26th the 117th Brigade, which was by this time reduced to less than half its original numbers, withdrew to a line of trenches between Herbécourt and Frise, the 17th K.R.R.C. being on the right with the 118th Brigade next to them. The 116th Brigade was in Divisional reserve. At 4.30 a.m. the 39th Division came under the XIX Corps, the boundary between that Corps and the VII being the River Somme.

At 7 a.m. the enemy attacked heavily about Herbécourt, and turned the right of the 118th Brigade, forcing it back. The 117th Brigade conformed. The 116th Brigade was brought up to cover the retirement, and the Division fell back to a line between Framerville and Proyart, fighting all the way.

Our 17th Battalion reached a position astride the Cappy–Herbécourt Road, south of Eclusier, and at 11 a.m. were ordered to retire to Proyart. This movement was successfully carried out, covered by the 13th Gloucestershire Regiment (Pioneers), Lieutenant G. B. Barber and 2nd Lieutenant C. Wallace being wounded. At 5 p.m. the 117th Brigade, on the left of the 39th Division, established a strong line in front of Proyart with the 16th Sherwood Foresters on the right, the 17th K.R.R.C. in the centre, and the 16th Rifle Brigade on the left. Touch was gained by the Division with the 50th Division on the right and the 16th Division on the left. During the night the enemy was reported north of the Somme as far west as Chipilly.

At dawn on March 27 the enemy launched a faint-hearted attack along the whole front of the 39th Division, making no headway, but at 11 a.m. the 16th Division reported that the enemy had broken through between Proyart and the Somme. This compelled the 117th Brigade to form a defensive flank, while the 116th Brigade and 13th Gloucestershire (Pioneers) prolonged this line along the spur south-east of Morcourt. Lieut.-Colonel Le Prevost, who had returned to the Battalion on the 24th, was wounded at this time, and Major Fairlie again took command.

At 12.15 p.m. the 117th Brigade were again compelled to withdraw, but a counter-attack by the 118th Brigade temporarily restored the line on the right. About 2 p.m. the enemy succeeded in forcing a passage over the Somme at Cérisy, thus getting behind the left rear of the 39th Division; on the north bank he was as far west as Sailly-le-Sec. At 4 p.m. a counter-attack was launched by a battalion each of the Durham Light Infantry and Devons, which regained a certain amount of ground. In the evening the 17th K.R.R.C. and 16th Rifle Brigade were amalgamated into one battalion under Colonel Hon. E. Coke, D.S.O., 16th Rifle Brigade. At 7.30 p.m. the enemy was reported to be in Lamotte-en-Santerre.

At 4 a.m. on the 28th the 39th Division received orders to withdraw at once to the line Vrély–Guillaucourt–Marcelcave. The withdrawal commenced at 7 a.m., the 117th Brigade moving first, covered by the 118th. The enemy advanced rapidly into Harbonnières, and the Brigadier-General commanding the 118th Brigade with his Brigade Major was taken prisoner. By 1 p.m. the 117th Brigade had taken up a position along the Marcelcave–Cayeux Road, with the 16th Sherwood Foresters on the right, the Rifle Battalion in the centre, and the 13th Gloucestershire on the left. Several attacks against this line were broken up. The Rifles caught some guns unlimbering at 1,700 yards and brought rifle fire to bear on them with good results. During the night the Division again fell back, the new position being: the 117th Brigade along the Démuin–Marcelcave Road, the 118th Brigade continuing the line to the right to the River Luce. Carey's mixed force was on their left, holding Marcelcave, and thence northwards. During the night the enemy occupied Marcelcave. The night passed quietly, and endeavours were made to sort out units and get stragglers back to their battalions.

On March 29 Major-General E. Feetham, C.B., C.M.G., commanding the 39th Division, was killed by a shell. Otherwise, the day was uneventful.

During the early hours of March 30 the 39th Division was withdrawn into reserve, and assembled in a wood 2,000 yards north-west of Aubercourt. The enemy attacked the front-line troops heavily, driving them back. In the afternoon a counter-attack was delivered, in which Major E. Fairlie, 17th K.R.R.C., was killed, 2nd Lieutenant T. G. Eastman wounded and taken prisoner, Lieutenant A. H. Boney and 2nd Lieutenant F. Warren (3rd Dorsets, attached) wounded. It gained a temporary success, but at 5 p.m. the line was again forced back. The 3rd Australian Division then went through and counter-attacked, reoccupying the position. The 39th Division then received orders to withdraw to Longeau, just east of Amiens. Our 17th Battalion reached that place at 6 a.m. on the 31st.

There the Battalion was re-established as a separate unit under command of Captain and Adjutant W. R. Low, M.C. Their losses in the operation had been : officers—killed 2, wounded 7, wounded and missing 3, missing 1 ; other ranks—killed 17, wounded 181, missing 163.

The officer killed who is not mentioned above was 2nd Lieutenant E. A. Norris ; he was killed on the 22nd.

CHAPTER XII

'ARRAS, 1918'

THE THIRD ARMY IN MARCH 1918[1]

ALL indications during March pointed to an attack on the 21st. On the morning of that day, the Third Army was disposed as follows: on the right—from its junction with the VII Corps, Fifth Army, near Gonnelieu—the V Corps, with three Divisions (47th, 63rd, and 17th) in the line, and two (2nd and 19th) in support; on the right centre the IV Corps, with two Divisions (51st and 6th) in the line, and one (25th) in support; on the left centre the VI Corps with three Divisions (59th, 34th, and 3rd) in the line, and one (40th) in support; and on the left the XVII Corps—to where it joined with the XIII Corps, First Army, north-east of Arras—two Divisions (4th and 15th) in the line, and one (Guards) in support. The 41st Division, which had just returned from Italy, was in G.H.Q. Reserve, twenty-five miles behind the line.

The relief of the 2nd Division, which had been in the line since January 24, by the 47th, began on the night of the 19th/20th, and was only completed at 2 a.m. on the 21st. Command was due to pass between the two Divisions at 6 a.m. on the 21st.

While in the line during March the 2nd Division had been, for days at a time, very severely shelled with 'mustard gas,' and had suffered proportionately. Consequently, battalions were either below strength or full of young

[1] Map IV.

soldiers, and many of those who had not been evacuated were still suffering from the effects of the gas. The condition of our 1st Battalion is thus described by their Commanding Officer, Lieut.-Colonel R. H. S. Stafford :

'During the last tour in the front line, ending March 18, the Battalion had lost 320 men from gas. This completely accounted for two companies, B and D, and, what was still more serious, for all Battalion Headquarters personnel. A considerable number of men from the other two companies had also been lost. On the 20th two drafts, amounting to 150 men, joined the Battalion, but a considerable proportion of the men had not been out before. There was a very great shortage of senior N.C.O.s throughout the Battalion, and this proved a great handicap during the operations. In short, of the 320 men who went into action on the 22nd, not more than 70 had been with the Battalion more than a month.'

The German attack on March 21 opened at the same time as that on the Fifth Army, and, so far as the right of the Third Army is concerned, with much the same results ; that is, the whole army, pivoting on its left, was forced back, fighting all the way, until, at the end of six days' fighting, though the left, in front of Arras, was not much behind its original position, the right was in touch with the left of the Fifth Army near Albert.

The German attack found the 2nd Division, with the 99th Brigade at Manancourt and Equancourt and the 5th and 6th Brigades, just relieved from the line, on their way, the 5th to Ytres and Lechelle, the 6th to Rocquigny. The Division was not employed on March 21, but, on the 22nd, the 5th and 6th Brigades took up positions in the Rear Zone to cover the retirement of the front-line troops. The story of the 99th Brigade for the next few days is a very involved one, as they were constantly passing from one command to another, at one time being directly under the V Corps, at another under the 9th Division, Fifth Army, returning to their own Division on the 24th. It will be sufficient to give the account of the share of our 1st Battalion in the fighting, as told by Lieut.-Colonel Stafford, without trying to connect it with that of the rest of their Brigade, as they seem most of the time to have been acting almost independently and rarely getting any order from their Brigadier.

'Shortly before dawn there was a very heavy bombardment all along the front, and at 9.30 a.m. some gas and smoke shells fell into Equancourt. Nothing of interest occurred during the day, but the air was thick with rumours, but no news!

'The morning of March 22 passed as the previous day, constant orders came to move, but were at once cancelled.

'At 5 p.m. a report reached us that the enemy had broken through to the south, and were approaching Nurlu. A party was therefore sent to picquet the Green Line [Rear Zone] north of Nurlu, and send back frequent reports. At 5.45 p.m. a report from 2nd Lieutenant P. Hambro confirmed the seriousness of the situation, and half an hour later orders came to move and garrison Dessart Switch Line, north of the Equancourt–Fins Road, if any gap existed between the 9th and 47th Divisions. This Line was reconnoitred, and at 8 p.m. a badly wounded officer from the South African Brigade, 9th Division, came to Battalion Headquarters and reported that his whole Brigade had been cut to bits, and that the Germans were advancing towards Equancourt. Touch had previously been obtained with the 8th Black Watch (9th Division), who were to hold the Green Line, south of the Fins–Equancourt Road.

'At 8.5 p.m. companies were ordered up to occupy the Green Line, C Company on the right, in touch with the 9th Division, A Company on the left, in touch with the 23rd Royal Fusiliers; D Company was held in reserve.

'By 9 p.m. all companies were in position. The Germans by this time had approached close to Equancourt, and were firing machine guns into the village.

'The night passed quietly; our patrols reported enemy digging in west of Fins, and our front companies were doing the same on the Green Line, where the trenches were well wired but shallow.

'The position so far was satisfactory, but the 23rd Royal Fusiliers reported that no touch could be obtained with the 47th Division on our left. This was ominous.

'Up to 11 a.m., apart from a good deal of rifle and machine-gun fire in front of the 9th Division, all was quiet. A message then arrived, saying that the 9th Division were withdrawing, and that we and the 23rd Royal Fusiliers were to conform, holding the line up to the Canal, where the 1st Berks would be on our right. This necessitated withdrawing A and C Companies over 1,000 yards of open ground. The movement was carried out very well in broad daylight, under heavy fire from field guns, machine guns, and low-flying aeroplanes, and our new positions were occupied by 12.30 p.m. Our casualties were not heavy. This position on the top of a hill was subjected to intense machine-gun fire, and we suffered many losses while we were digging in. This was particularly the case on the right, where no touch could be obtained with the 1st Royal Berks Regiment. Wave upon wave of the enemy were seen advancing upon Etricourt. Fire was opened upon them with our Lewis guns, but no Vickers could be found, otherwise the enemy advance could have been checked.

'We were now in touch with the 23rd Royal Fusiliers on our left, and the commander of that unit informed me that the 47th Division had been forced back on his left, and he was swinging his left back to Mouette Trench. C Company, on seeing this movement, thought the whole unit was retiring, and so fell back to Vallulart Wood, thus leaving the right of the 23rd Royal Fusiliers in the air.

'Our withdrawal, however, would in any case have been necessary almost at once, as the Germans were working round our right flank in very large numbers, and were enfilading our line. At 3 p.m. we were holding the east edge of Vallulart Wood. Hearing that some Brigadiers of the 47th Division were in a Casualty Clearing Station close by, I went to see them, and as I had not been in touch with our own (99th) Brigade Headquarters since early in the morning, I did not know where they were, so put myself under the 140th Brigade. This did not help me much, as the Brigade suddenly vanished. I then put myself under the 142nd Brigade. This Brigade formed the line from the hangars, running north-east in front of Lechelle towards Little Wood, Ytres. We were to be on their left.' At 4.30 p.m. we accordingly withdrew and dug in. Our left was in the air, but troops could be seen coming back to Little Wood.

'From 5.30 p.m., for two hours, Lechelle and all the ground round was heavily shelled, and many enemy aeroplanes also circled over us about 100 feet up, and we were unable to fire at them owing to a shortage of ammunition. At 7 p.m. the situation was quieter, and the Commanding Officer of the 15th Londons came from the left and said there was no ammunition there. Large numbers of troops could still be seen withdrawing.

'It was then that my right company reported that the 142nd Brigade had disappeared, thus leaving our right completely in the air, a fact of which the Boches soon took advantage.

'It was obvious that if the enemy reached the hangars we could never withdraw at all. I therefore ordered the companies to retire from the right and go back to Bus.

'Fortunately, this was carried out with few casualties, though the shelling was still heavy and the machine-gun fire severe.

'The Battalion now (7.45 p.m.) reorganised west of Bus; there I found the Officer Commanding 24th Royal Fusiliers, 5th Brigade, and leaving Major J. B. Brady, D.S.O., in charge of the Battalion, went to Barastre to see the G.O.C. 5th Brigade, as it was obvious that part of the 2nd Division, then facing north, had no idea how serious the situation was to the south. This proved to be the case, as the V Corps could not believe that the enemy were in Lechelle. On returning to the Battalion at 8.30 p.m. I found Major Brady had gone to get touch with the 63rd Division on the left and the Adjutant to see the 47th Division on our right. D and C Companies then picqueted Bus. At 9 p.m. D Company's picquets were driven in, so a counter-attack was ordered and organised, but just as it was starting a large dump of big shells just west of Bus caught fire, so the operations ceased. Heavy enemy pressure on C Company caused them to fall back. As usual, both our flanks were in the air. A line was therefore formed about 200 yards west of Bus, with the 24th Royal Fusiliers on our left, and some men of the Hawke Battalion on the right. The Officer Commanding this Battalion wished to make a frontal attack, but I considered this quite impossible, so he sent a company to work through the village from the south end; this effort was held up at once.

The night passed with a great deal of rifle and machine-gun fire, and as daylight approached, shell and trench-mortar fire increased. It was very cold, the men had no rations or water, and there was a serious shortage of S.A.A.[1]

'About 6.30 a.m. it appears that orders were issued to evacuate the most dangerous Bertincourt–Ytres salient ; these orders never reached us ; in fact, we had almost given up hope of receiving any orders.

'Fortunately, 2nd Lieutenant H. D. West saw the Officer Commanding Hawke Battalion, who was about to retire on our right. I therefore ordered all Companies to withdraw north of Villers-au-Flos, where the Battalion would be re-organised, and also sent the adjutant to inform the 24th Royal Fusiliers. There was extremely heavy artillery fire on the left all the morning, as the Germans endeavoured to harass the withdrawal from the Bertincourt Salient.

'11 a.m. What was left of the companies reached the rendezvous. D Company had been completely wiped out, and the others had suffered severely. Had this withdrawal been carried out at night, many casualties might have been saved.

'Our guns were now, for some reason, shelling the line, Barastre–Rocquigny. We still had many troops east of this line! After vainly trying to get the gunners' F.O.O.s[2] to stop this, I obtained a horse, and galloped round all the batteries I could find.

'The Naval Division were forming a line with the 17th Division on their left, when, at 2.30 p.m., I suddenly heard that the Naval Division were going to retire to Bazentin. As usual, no orders came to us. I decided to go and look for the 2nd Division, whom I had heard were somewhere on our left. All the country was full of troops moving back. At 4.30 p.m., as no one was acting as rearguard, I occupied a line for a short period, and then fell back on Guedecourt. On the way I heard the 2nd Division was at Destremont Farm. We reached this place at 8.30 p.m., and found the Division. The men could now hardly stand for fatigue. We were then ordered to join the 99th Brigade the following morning. Rations arrived, and we passed a very cold night, some bombs falling close by. We now heard, to our great sorrow, of General Barker's[3] death,

[1] (Small Arms Ammunition.) [2] (Forward Observing Officers.)

[3] Brigadier-General R. B. Barker, D.S.O., Royal Welsh Fusiliers, Commanding 99th Infantry Brigade.

and also that Captain Bell (Staff-Captain) and Lieut.-Colonel Hunt, of the 1st Royal Berks, had been killed.

'5 a.m. The Officer Commanding 1st King's informed me that the 2nd Division was taking up the line Courcelette–Pys. Our previous orders had been to move to Albert. I had received no orders from our Brigade, and presumed they were also withdrawing from the Eaucourt–L'Abbaye Line. Two hours later, at 7 a.m., I sent the adjutant to obtain orders, and started to move back to Courcelette. Soon after starting I met the G.S.O. (2) of the 2nd Division, who told me that the whole Division were moving back to the Pys–Courcelette Line, and as he was going up to the 99th Brigade he would tell them where we were. At 9 a.m. orders came to come back to Eaucourt-L'Abbaye, as the Brigade was not going to withdraw. I then went on in advance, and at Destremont Farm found the 99th Brigade, who had just reached there. I was ordered to move into support at Blue Cut, just north of Eaucourt-L'Abbaye. I then proceeded to Eaucourt-L'Abbaye, and saw the Officer Commanding 10th Duke of Cornwall's Light Infantry, who was holding a line just north-east of the village, with the 23rd Royal Fusiliers and the 1st Royal Berks on his right, and some of the 51st Division on his left. He told me Blue Cut was untenable.

'The Germans could now be seen advancing from the north-east, and there was a great deal of rifle and machine-gun fire on both sides. As the Officer Commanding 10th Duke of Cornwall Light Infantry did not think he could hold on long, I placed the Battalion to cover his withdrawal. This was at 10.15 a.m., and the 10th Duke of Cornwall's Light Infantry and 1st Royal Berks commenced to withdraw; we covered them with rifle fire as much as possible. As these units came back they were reorganised and thickened the line we held, and extended it to the left, where the 51st Division were rapidly falling back.

'This position was held until about 11.15 a.m., and heavy rifle fire was brought to bear on masses of the enemy, who were advancing from the north-east.

'It then became evident that the troops on the right were withdrawing. The 23rd Royal Fusiliers were finally forced to withdraw, suffering very heavy casualties in so doing. The Germans were now working round our right flank, and the situation was most dangerous. After consulting with the Officer Commanding 10th Duke of Cornwall's Light Infantry, I decided to withdraw the Battalion, and reform on a line west of Le Sars. This withdrawal was carried out, as usual, under very heavy machine-gun fire, and casualties were many. Major J. B. Brady, who had done most invaluable work, was wounded.

'As I passed through Le Sars I detailed a rearguard, under 2nd Lieutenant D. G. Buxton and an officer of the 1st Royal Berks, with two parties to cover the retirement until the Battalion was in position on the line I proposed to hold.

'This line was successfully occupied at 12 noon, and we then had the 17th Division and some of the 63rd Division on our right, and some men of the 5th Division on our left. Those on the right did not appear very anxious to hold on, however, and soon withdrew, leaving our right once more in the air. We were therefore also forced to fall back, though the position ought to have been held for some time, as it was a strong one, with the 5th and 6th Brigades behind holding the Pys–Courcelette line.

'At 1.15 p.m., soon after passing through the 5th and 6th Brigades, they also withdrew. Large numbers of our troops could be seen retiring from Loupart Wood. I did not understand the reason of this withdrawal, but presumed that orders had been given to that effect. I had received no orders, and was again out of touch with Brigade Headquarters. The men were most exhausted, so I decided to rest them, and then moved to Grandcourt.

'I then heard that the Division was to move back to Auchonvillers, and was about to set off when I met Major Lane, M.C., who told me that the V Corps wished the Pys–Courcelette Line held for some time longer.

'4.30 p.m. I met the Officer Commanding 1st King's with the remnants of his battalion. I then went back myself towards Pys, and met the rearguard of the 63rd Division, who were falling back towards Thiepval. They reported there was no one between themselves and the enemy, and after satisfying myself that that was so, I returned, and moved off towards Beaucourt.

'The shelling had now become quite heavy. Together with the 1st King's, the Battalion moved to south-west of Beaucourt, where we halted to rest, as the men were quite worn out. I was about to move on again, when I met the Adjutant of the 52nd Light Infantry, who told me that the Division was to hold a line near Beaumont-Hamel for the night. I went back, therefore, and crossed the Ancre by Beaucourt, and met the Officers Commanding the 52nd Light Infantry and the 24th Royal Fusiliers, together with several mixed units of the 17th Division. No one knew exactly what was to be done, so it was decided to stay near Beaumont-Hamel. After some discussion, I decided to bring back the Battalion to the north of the Ancre. I then found the situation clearer, and located the 99th Brigade Headquarters up Stanton Road. From them I received orders to place the Battalion in support in Green Cut. The 5th Brigade were on the right guarding the crossings of the river Ancre, with the 99th Brigade in the centre and the 6th Brigade on the left.

'The night passed quietly. Cookers arrived about 5 a.m., and the men had some hot food for the first time since March 22. I then received instructions that the Division was moving back to the old British Line as held before the Somme offensive, the order from right to left being 6th Brigade, 99th Brigade, 5th Brigade. The 1st Battalion K.R.R.C. was to be on the right of the 99th Brigade.

'We moved off at 6 a.m., and were in position by 8 a.m., with the 1st King's on our right and the 10th Duke of Cornwall Light Infantry on our left. The position was a fairly good one, as the old trenches had stood the weather wonderfully well.

'9.30 a.m. Enemy patrols were observed in the Ancre Valley on our right, and half an hour later large numbers were seen coming over the ridge.

'10.30 a.m. Lorries full of troops were reported moving up the Ancre Valley from Miraumont. The artillery was informed, and opened fire; the range was too great for Lewis guns.

'Orders had previously been received that this line was to be held at all costs. This anyhow was satisfactory after all the withdrawals of the last few days. From now on the Germans could be seen pouring over the ridge on our front and on our left. A heavy fire was opened on them, and on many occasions they were turned back.

'At 12.15 p.m. the Battalion was heavily shelled, and this continued, with intervals, until dusk.

'A message was received at 2 p.m. from the right company that the enemy was massing on the right. In the meantime the situation on the left of the Division was obscure; apparently a gap existed there, which was closed by tanks and Australians. As the afternoon wore on a New Zealand Battalion came up, and expressed great surprise at seeing us there, as they were told they were to fill a gap. At 6 p.m. our battalion front was full of New Zealanders, who were also reported to have reoccupied Beaumont-Hamel, and three hours later we received orders that the Battalion was to move out to Mailly-Maillet.

'It was, indeed, essential that the Battalion should be relieved, as all the officers and men were utterly exhausted, and could not have been relied on to stop another heavy attack. In fact, it was only because they had many very excellent targets during the day, and undoubtedly had taken a heavy toll of the enemy throughout the retreat, that they were able to hold on at all.

'The Battalion moved back to Mailly Wood and bivouacked there. Cookers came up and gave the men a hot meal, but we obtained little sleep, as there were 10° of frost and no blankets.'

The casualties of the Battalion during the period March 21–27 were :

Officers : wounded, Major J. B. Brady, D.S.O. ; Captains G. Allen, E. C. F. Vyvyan, P. F. C. Jourdain ; 2nd Lieutenants A. J. Bray, H. V. Slingsby, D. M. Macgregor, Hon. J. C. C. Jervis, R. R. Wheatley : died of wounds, 2nd Lieutenant P. Hambro ; wounded and missing, 2nd Lieutenant H. M. Barnet ; missing, 2nd Lieutenants H. D. West, M. G. Bland. Of the above, 2nd Lieutenants Barnet and West died of wounds in German hands. Other ranks : killed 13, wounded 391, died of wounds 14, missing 57.

The Battalion was reorganised on the 28th as one company of a composite battalion formed from the remnants of the 99th Brigade, and went back into the line the same evening. After twenty-four hours they came out again into support and, on April 1, on receipt of a big draft, they became a battalion once more. There followed several months of alternate periods of training and trench-warfare.

18th Battalion

Our 18th and 20th Battalions had gone to Italy with the 41st Division in the autumn of 1917 after the Caporetto débâcle, and had there spent a quiet winter.

The Division was brought back to France in the first few days of March 1918.

On the 16th the 21st Battalion was disbanded, the officers and other ranks being distributed among various battalions of the Regiment.

On March 21 the Division came into Corps Reserve to the IV Corps, and entrained for their concentration area. The 122nd Brigade of which our 18th Battalion formed a part, arrived at Achiet-Le-Grand in the small hours of the 22nd. At 6 a.m. on that date the Division received orders to move into the Favreuil area, one Brigade to be ready to man and hold the Rear Zone between Beugnâtre and Vaulx. The 124th Brigade was detailed for this duty, and later in the day two battalions of the 123rd Brigade were attached to it. The 122nd Brigade, marching from Achiet-le-Grand, was concentrated just east of Sapignies by 12 noon. During the afternoon it appeared from reports received that the 6th Division was being forced back from Vaulx south-westwards on to the Rear Zone. About 3 p.m. orders were received for the 41st Division to relieve the 6th Division and 7th Infantry Brigade after dark. The 123rd and 124th Brigades were detailed to relieve the front line, the 122nd Brigade to be in reserve. At dusk the 122nd Brigade took up a position just clear of the western edge of Favreuil Wood, the 18th K.R.R.C. being on the right, the 12th East Surreys in the centre, and the 15th Hants on the left. During the night the 12th East

Surreys were sent away to the left to cover the left flank of the Corps in case of a break through on the front of the VI Corps, next on the left to the IV. At 7.35 a.m. on the 23rd the 15th Hants were ordered to reinforce the East Surreys, and the 18th K.R.R.C. were left to dig in astride the Favreuil–Beugnâtre Road. At this time everything pointed to the likelihood of a break through on the VI Corps front. Just before midnight, 23rd/24th, our 18th Battalion was ordered to move into the line west of Beugny, in relief of the South Staffords, 7th Infantry Brigade. The relief was completed just before dawn on the 24th, and the Battalion then came under the orders of the 123rd Brigade.

The situation on the 41st Division front at this time was as follows: the 123rd Brigade, with the 18th K.R.R.C. and 19th Middlesex (Pioneers) attached, held from a point half a mile north-west of Beugny—which village was in the hands of the enemy—where it was in touch with the left of the 19th Division. From thence the line ran north-west, with the 7th Infantry Brigade next to the 123rd, and the 124th beyond them. A mile short of Mory, which was held by the enemy, a defensive flank was thrown back due west, held by two battalions of the 122nd Brigade. The 123rd and 124th Brigades had both suffered heavily during the 23rd. Throughout the morning of the 24th reports kept coming in of a withdrawal by the V Corps, next on the right to the IV, and of the massing of heavy enemy forces in front of the IV Corps. The IV Corps therefore began a general withdrawal during the afternoon, which was carried out under heavy pressure from the enemy.

The 41st Division fell back to about the line of the Bapaume–Ervillers Road, but, in the process, the 123rd Brigade, and with it our 18th Battalion, were almost wiped out. At 10 a.m. on the 24th, the Commanding Officer, Lieut.-Colonel R. Pennell, D.S.O., had been wounded, and the command had passed to Major W. P. Bristowe. Neither the reports of the Division nor of the Brigade give very clear accounts of what happened, but the Brigade seems simply to have been overwhelmed by superior numbers. The following extract from the Battalion's own account, in the 'Chronicle' for 1918, tells as much as can be known of its dissolution.

'The morning passed fairly quietly. The Brigade Headquarters warned us that our right flank was the likely danger-spot. Early in the afternoon troops were seen to be withdrawing from their positions on the right, and C Company was therefore thrown out as a defensive flank. Very heavy rifle and machine-gun fire developed on the right, but the smoke from a burning dump obscured the enemy's movements in that direction. A little later troops on the left were seen to be falling back in good order.

'An attempt was made to extricate the Battalion to avoid being cut off, but all the companies were by that time heavily engaged, and the Germans were making rapid progress on both flanks, especially on the right.

'The situation was serious, as it was not possible for more than a small proportion of the garrison to be withdrawn. Casualties amongst those who did fall back were very heavy, as the Germans had pushed forward some machine guns on the railway line east of Frémicourt and enfiladed the embankment. At the same time a heavy artillery barrage was put down behind our front line, and under its protection the hostile infantry pressed forward. The remains of the Battalion were then collected, and occupied a continuation to the south of the line we had dug on the 21st/22nd, but they were soon forced to leave the position, as the troops on both flanks were withdrawn. What was left of the 123rd Brigade was collected on the night of the 24th/25th at Bihucourt.

'Two lines of trenches were dug and occupied in front of Biefvillers, to protect the road to Achiet-le-Grand, as the enemy was then in the outskirts of Bapaume.

'This position was, however, rendered untenable the next

morning by the Germans working up the valley between Biefvillers and Favreuil.

'During the day the line gradually fell back to a final position on the line Albert–Achiet-le-Grand Railway, and at 9 p.m. the remains of the Division were withdrawn on relief by the 62nd Division, and what was left of the Battalion went in search of the 122nd Infantry Brigade. As they could not be found the night was spent at Essarts, and at midday on the 26th we discovered them, and also picked up a party belonging chiefly to C Company. The Battalion, now consisting of only 60 other ranks, was formed into one company, and during the night of the 26th/27th we were withdrawn to Bienvillers, and spent the remainder of the hours of darkness in a field.

'We did our best to clean ourselves on the 27th, and the following day moved up to support behind Gommecourt.

'We were relieved on the night of the 29th/30th by the 42nd Division, and moved to support line behind Bucquoy.

'Thus ended an eventful month. Our fine Battalion of nearly 900 other ranks had been reduced to about 80. We had fought against heavy odds and suffered much, but the Germans did not break through. The officer casualties on March 24 were: killed in action, Captain W. A. J. Willans; wounded, Lieut.-Colonel R. Pennell, Captain J. N. Waldy, 2nd Lieutenants G. F. Lewis, J. Pennie, P. Hope-Johnstone; missing, Captain J. B. Gray, 2nd Lieutenants J. A. Harris, E. C. Bullivant, C. T. Uren, G. Richardson, P. W. Shepheard, P. T. Loft, G. Calder, H. J. Pickup, M.C.'

Of these, 2nd Lieutenants Bullivant and Loft had been killed in action.

CHAPTER XIII [1]

'YPRES, 1918,' 'MESSINES, 1918,' 'LYS,' 'BAILLEUL,' 'KEMMEL,' 'BÉTHUNE'

THE ATTACK IN THE NORTH

IT is unnecessary to discuss what the enemy's original intention was in his next move, after the breakdown of his attempt to separate the Allied armies. It may be that his attack in Flanders was merely to be a distraction, to keep the British occupied while he prepared for a renewal of his thrust towards Amiens, and that he was tempted, by his initial success, to make the Flanders offensive a bigger thing than he had intended. Ludendorff's 'Memoirs' do not support this theory, and it is enough for the purpose of this book that the next big thrust came in Flanders, and that that on Amiens was never renewed.

The Report on the Operations of the Second Army tells us:

'The situation of the Second Army at this time [April 9] was as follows: During the fighting on the Third and Fifth Army fronts, which commenced on March 21, it had been necessary to draw on the Second Army for fresh troops, and of the 14 Divisions in the Second Army on March 21, all had been transferred to the south, with the exception of the 29th and 49th, which were both under orders to go.

'These Divisions had been replaced by others from the south, which had all been heavily engaged, and had since been filled up with reinforcements, and officers and N.C.O.s who had only lately arrived in this country.

'There had, however, been no indications whatever of

[1] Map I.

attack on the Second Army front, and the whole front, including the Passchendaele salient was held intact.'

In the beginning of April two Portuguese divisions had been a long time in the line, in the Neuve Chapelle area, and were about to be relieved. As a preliminary, one division was taken out on April 7, and the remaining division took over the whole front of 10,000 yards. It was arranged that on the night of the 9th/10th the right brigade of this Division should be relieved by a brigade of the 55th Division, which was in the line on their left, and the remaining two brigades by the 50th Division, which had recently been through a bad time on the Somme.

Unfortunately, the Germans attacked on the 9th, again in a fog, starting the bombardment at 4 a.m. and launching the attack at 7 a.m. A Portuguese division consisted of four brigades, but to hold 10,000 yards of front against a concentrated German attack was too much for them, and they simply faded away. As their 10,000 yards of front were attacked by seven German divisions, who can blame them? The front attacked was much less than on March 21, but the numerical superiority of the enemy was fully as great. On April 9 the front attacked was only 11 miles, occupied by two British divisions and one Portuguese. Against them the enemy put in 14 divisions in the front line or close reserve. They poured through the gap. The 55th Division held their ground at Givenchy, and never lost their hold there during the whole battle, thus preventing the front of the First Army being rolled up to the south. The 40th Division on the left of the gap held their front for a time, but very quickly had the enemy all round and behind their right flank. Warned by the weight of the bombardment, and having no faith in the capacity of the Portuguese Division to hold the line, the commanders of the XI and XV Corps had, even before the attack was delivered, ordered the 51st and 50th Divisions to take steps to occupy the Second Line, a couple of miles back, and to secure the crossings of the rivers Lys and Lawe,[1] while at the same time the reserve brigades of the 55th and 40th Divisions were ordered to connect the inner flanks of their Divisions with the Second Line; but events moved too fast for them, and before the reserve brigade of the 40th could get into position, the flank of that Division was turned and the whole of it had to fall back.

By 11 a.m. the enemy had reached the Lys at Bac St. Maur,[1] and by 3 p.m. were across it.

On April 10 the Germans extended the front of their attack to the Comines–Ypres Canal, their greatest weight in the new sector being applied on each side of the river Douve. The fighting of the next few days was perhaps the severest test to which the British Expeditionary Force was put throughout the war, and certainly produced one of its most critical times. In the days which followed—as compared with those coming after March 21—reinforcements arrived sooner, resistance hardened more rapidly, and the crisis came sooner. On April 12 Haig issued his famous 'backs to the wall' order, and by the end of the next day the worst was over. A line was for a time stabilised running from Givenchy [2] back to the east end of the Forêt de Nieppe, by Bailleul to Wytschaete. To shorten the line the Ypres salient had returned to its old dimensions of before the Passchendaele offensive.

The enemy was not yet done with. On the 15th he attacked and took Bailleul, but was brought up by a previously prepared second position. On the 17th and 18th he had a try at Kemmel Hill, but failed both times, as he did in another attack near Givenchy. His efforts then died down for a week. Meanwhile, the French had been

[1] Not in Map. [2] Map VIII.

arriving, and between the 18th and 21st they took over the Kemmel sector. On April 25 the enemy attacked and took Kemmel Hill from the French, after which, though fighting went on well into May, he made no further serious effort on this front. Our 16th Battalion, 100th Brigade, 33rd Division, was the only Battalion of our regiment which had part in these operations.

On April 5 the 33rd Division had been relieved in the Passchendaele sector, and had, next day, been transferred to the Third Army, where they came under the XVII Corps, and were in G.H.Q. Reserve. On the evening of April 10th the Division entrained to go back to the Second Army, detraining next day at Caestre and Strazeele, coming under the IX Corps.

The 100th Brigade finished detraining at Caestre by 10 a.m., April 11, moved to the Ravelsberg area, and came under the 25th Division at 5.30 p.m. Immediately after dusk the Brigade took over a part of the line from Le Romarin to east of Neuve Église, with the 16th K.R.R.C. on the right, the 2nd Worcestershire on the left and the 9th Highland Light Infantry in reserve. Le Romarin was in the occupation of the enemy. Touch was obtained on the right with the 75th Brigade, on the left with the 148th Brigade.

On April 12, at 4 p.m., the troops next on the right of the 16th K.R.R.C. fell back, causing a gap, which was partially closed by troops from the reserves of all three regiments. The gap not being completely closed, and the 75th Brigade, apparently, having been wiped out, a company of the 9th Highland Light Infantry was sent to gain touch between the right of the 16th K.R.R.C. and the left of the 88th Brigade, 29th Division. The report of the 100th Brigade tells that at 8.25 a.m. the Worcesters were in touch on their left, but not on their right, and that there was no news of the 16th K.R.R.C. After relating how the enemy got into Neuve Église, behind the Worcesters, and were ejected by a counter-attack of the 9th Highland Light Infantry, it goes on to say that during the afternoon nothing could be heard of the 16th K.R.R.C., but that their line had been turned and taken in reverse in the morning, and that most of the Battalion were casualties or prisoners.

It will presently be shown that their line had indeed been turned, but that fragments of the Battalion continued to fight a soldier's battle for the next three days.

The 100th Brigade again had very hard fighting on the 14th, and in the afternoon they were relieved by the 49th Division, and were sent to dig a fresh position in rear. On the evening of the 15th a Composite Battalion was formed of 150 rifles each, of the 16th K.R.R.C. and 9th Highland Light Infantry.

The new position was attacked at 7.45 a.m. on the 16th, and by 8.30 a.m. the attack had been repulsed with the help of French field artillery. Another attack was beaten off in the afternoon.

On April 17 the enemy launched a fresh attack, under a very heavy bombardment, and secured a lodgment in the position from which counter-attacks failed to eject him, but he gained no more ground. The Brigade was relieved, on the night of the 17th/18th, and moved to Mont-des-Cats, where it rejoined the 33rd Division. On April 20 the Division was transferred to the VIII Corps, and moved to areas west and south-west of Cassel.

The 16th Battalion War Records, in the 'Chronicle' for 1918, give a very full account of the fortunes of that Battalion in these operations. After telling how the Battalion beat off a heavy attack on the 12th, doing great execution, it goes on :

'The morning of the 13th was very misty.

'Word was received that a Composite Battalion, which had taken up positions on the right, had fallen back, and accordingly two platoons of the very small remaining reserve had to be sent to endeavour to cope with the new situation, which was rapidly getting beyond the powers of one Battalion. At about 6 a.m. a very heavy barrage was put down along the whole line, and as soon as this lifted it was seen that the line on the right of the Battalion had given way in the face of a heavy attack. Almost immediately the Battalion Headquarters were attacked and cut up, Lieut.-Colonel A. V. Johnson, D.S.O., and his Adjutant being wounded in their endeavour to save the situation. Word was received by the right support Company (A Company) to endeavour to swing back and get into touch with troops at the rear, and so keep some portion of the line intact, but it was not possible to get a message of any sort to the remaining companies, who held on in their positions, fighting until all their ammunition was exhausted before they were overrun and killed or captured. A Company, already heavily engaged, endeavoured to break off the action to carry out the orders received, but Captain Scott and Lieutenant Cheetham were wounded almost immediately, and in the mist it was not possible for the remaining officers to fight the whole Company, which by this time was completely surrounded. A position was taken up by the remnant of A Company in the streets of Neuve Église, and a patrol was sent out to gain touch with the Glasgow Highlanders [9th Highland Light Infantry], who were known to be in a support position nearby. This patrol tried several directions, but encountered the enemy on all sides, and accordingly it was decided to fight a way through the lines, and take up a defensive position until the situation became known. The Company was enabled to take up a prepared position on the Dranoutre Road, being by this time 1 officer and 20 strong. Stragglers were collected, and set to work on the positions and, later in the day, an officer from the 75th Brigade handed over 200 other ranks to this party to assist in the defence of the position. A Company were lightly attacked, but were able to hold the position.

'At about 3 p.m. Lance-Corporal Dean, of D Company, reached this position with a verbal message from Lieutenant Hannay, of D Company, to say that they were entirely surrounded but holding on, killing many Germans, but that, owing to lack of ammunition, they could not hold much longer. Lieutenant Hannay was by this time some two kilometres behind the advanced elements of the enemy forces, and with the troops available it was not possible to give him any relief. Several stragglers from the Battalion were collected after this, and the position consolidated in depth, in spite of enfilade machine-gun fire, which caused casualties.

'Events moved very rapidly at about this stage of the fight, and owing to the fact that Battalion Headquarters were cut up almost immediately, the action of the Battalion developed into several isolated fights, in which the initiative and judgment of junior officers were taxed to the full. Two platoons of B Company (left front company) suddenly found that their flank had gone, and that the enemy were actually in occupation of the same trench as themselves. The events following are perhaps best told in the words of 2nd Lieutenant Wilder, who with 2nd Lieutenant Talbot was called upon to face this difficult situation. The former, in a letter to the Battalion, says that he went to discuss the situation with 2nd Lieutenant Talbot, and that they decided to construct a block and strong point at the right of their position, and to hold on pending instructions from Headquarters. 2nd Lieutenant Wilder then says:

> "Runners were sent out—but never returned. On learning this I went to the Company Commander on my left (2nd Worcestershire Regiment), and informed him that our C Company had given way, and asked him to send a message to Battalion Headquarters to this effect. On the morning of the 13th Captain Sargent came with a ration party and informed me that he had received my message regarding C Company. As dawn approached we saw several enemy stragglers behind us, and it gave us conclusive proof that the enemy were in the direction of Neuve Église, and as we had no support the question of holding about 300 yards of front became rather a serious one. We dared not jeopardise the right flank of the Battalion on our left, so we continued to hold the line, hoping for action by Battalion Headquarters. Unfortunately, however, our own artillery were firing short, and were shelling our line. I sent up word to the Battalion on our left to get a message sent through to the artillery, and this

was successful, but only for a short time. About two hours later we were subjected to shelling from both our own and the enemy artillery, consequently another message was sent through. This was of no avail, and the continuance of the shelling caused us to close upon the Battalion on our left. This was done about 2 p.m. and we had no sooner got into position than we discovered that the enemy was preparing to attack, he having assembled his troops under the cover of two farm-houses in front. This was about 3 p.m., and soon after the enemy was seen to leave the farm-houses and was coming in open order towards us. By this time some of the enemy were coming up the trench we had just vacated, and we were being fired upon from the rear, making our position a precarious one. Orders were given to fight to the last, and after a fight of about half an hour we succeeded in breaking up the enemy attack, killing or wounding about 100 of the enemy, and saving the right flank of the 2nd Worcestershire Regiment. Just before the attack started a large number of the enemy were seen to enter Neuve Église in close formation, so it was known that we were likely to be surrounded at any moment, and accordingly it was decided to move to a position near Neuve Église Church. When withdrawing, however, the road we had to traverse was held under fire by the enemy, and in the process of withdrawal several of our men were hit and the party broken up. I arrived at the rendezvous, collected what I could, and took up a position north of Neuve Église Church. The others, who did not get to the church, became attached to the Worcestershires, who had commenced to dig in a field about 300 yards south of the church. Owing to our party being broken up Lieutenant Talbot remained with the Worcestershires and collected those of his men who had become attached to that regiment. Later on in the evening, after consultation with Lieutenant Talbot, it was decided that both parties should remain where they were, and be held in readiness for the defence of the remaining portion of the village. In this I had the support of a motor machine-gun, and I remained near the church till the following morning, when I took up a position in a ditch on the Neuve Église–Kemmel Road. During the night the enemy had taken the village and had numerous machine guns posted in the houses, but as we had cover from view nothing untoward happened until about 11 p.m. [a.m. ?], when he shelled our part of the road. The shelling did not cease until about 2 p.m. Shortly afterwards heavy machine-gun fire was brought to bear from the school house, Neuve Église. This firing continued until about 5 p.m., when the Hallamshires thought fit to withdraw to two farms east of their Headquarters, with the object of making a stand around these farms. In taking up this new position, however, so many men were hit that it seemed to me that by attaching myself to this new Battalion my men were being unnecessarily exposed to machine-gun fire, as there was no cover at all, and the enemy was on the high ground. I therefore collected my men and got them under cover from view, and went to seek Lieutenant Talbot (the Worcestershires having withdrawn to an adjoining field), but could not find him. I returned to my men, and as the Hallamshires were moving back, led them to the high ground towards Mount Kemmel, where we had a good field of fire and not so exposed. Here I attached myself to a Battalion of the Notts and Derby Regiment, which had dug two lines of trenches earlier in the day, and prepared to stay the night before seeking the 16th Battalion Headquarters. At 8 p.m. on the 14th I sent a message to the Battalion to the effect that my men had had no food at all, and that they were completely worn out and could therefore hold on no longer. Receiving no reply, I went in search of Battalion or Brigade Headquarters, and ultimately was able to join my Battalion at Hill 70, south of Mount Kemmel, at about midday on the 15th of April."

'The action quietened a little on the 14th, but the situation was still obscure on the right. The 6th Division sent up a battalion to the position held by A Company and stragglers during the early morning, and a fighting patrol was sent towards Neuve Église to ascertain if any British troops were still holding out there. They got right to Neuve Église, but found no British there. They were fired on and got back with difficulty, having 1 killed and 5 wounded.

'On the early morning of the 15th the 6th Division took over A Company's position entirely, and later on in the morning the stragglers joined the minimum reserve at Keersebrom,[1] where they were ordered to stand to almost immediately. Major Wenham, M.C., took over command of the whole. The Battalion received orders to find 4 officers and 150 other ranks to form a Composite Battalion, with a similar number of the 9th Highland Light Infantry, under Major Lamberton, M.C. (Highland Light Infantry), and these were to clear up the situation at the Crucifix. Lieutenant Brough and 2nd Lieutenants Cram, Grey, and Jeffery were sent. Orders were to form up at Keersebrom Farm, and thence go on to the railway cutting. Lieutenant Grey was wounded on the way. Brigade Headquarters moved to Locre Château. At 8.15 p.m. our troops were seen retiring. Ravelsberg Farm from 5 p.m. onwards was subject to heavy shelling, and enemy machine guns swept our front. We got in touch with the Loyal North Lancashire on our left, and also patrolled during the night to Composite Battalion in front.

'The 16th was a dull wet morning. At 12.20 a.m. orders were received that no attack would take place on the Crucifix, and that the Brigade would hold the line dug by them the previous day, which would become front line from then onwards. The Composite Battalion, under Major Lamberton, would withdraw from railway and move back, taking over line held by the North Lancashire. This move was completed by 6.30 a.m., 16th K.R.R.C. occupying front line, with the 9th Highland Light Infantry in support. 2nd Lieutenant Mather remained in the two posts in front of Headquarters. Battalion Headquarters moved down to Hill Farm. There was heavy shelling throughout the day, during which time Lieutenant Brough and 2nd Lieutenant Cram were wounded, leaving three parties without officers. 2nd Lieutenant Bottoms was sent up to take their place.

'In the early hours of the morning of the 17th the enemy attacked the line held by the Composite Battalion, and forced in their advanced posts, and during the day two endeavours were made to regain these, both of which were unsuccessful. This made the situation of the party under 2nd Lieutenant Mather extremely uncomfortable, but in spite of heavy fighting throughout the afternoon the position remained intact until the Battalion was relieved the same evening.

'The following is the casualty list for the period of the operations April 12–17 :

[1] Not in Map.

Officers

Killed

Captain N. K. Balshaw.
2nd Lieutenant F. B. Holborow.

Died of Wounds

2nd Lieutenant H. A. Cram.
2nd Lieutenant B. Hodges.

Wounded

Lieut.-Colonel A. V. Johnson, D.S.O., Commanding Officer.
Captain S. S. Scott.
Lieutenant and Adjutant C. H. Wilkins.
Lieutenant G. Brough.
Lieutenant B. J. Crowe (at duty).
2nd Lieutenant L. W. Cheetham.
2nd Lieutenant W. A. Talbot.
2nd Lieutenant J. Grey.

Wounded and Missing

Lieutenant W. Staggers (U.S.A.), M.O.

Missing

Captain C. H. Cork, M.C.
Captain L. E. Francis, M.C.
Captain E. F. Sargent, M.C.
Lieutenant J. Hannay, M.C.
2nd Lieutenant L. J. Goldsack.
2nd Lieutenant H. W. Considine.
2nd Lieutenant R. W. Edwards.
2nd Lieutenant J. E. Riches.
2nd Lieutenant W. H. McLean.
2nd Lieutenant R. H. M. Lea.

Other Ranks

Killed	27
Wounded	125
Wounded and missing	55
Missing	337
Total	544

CHAPTER XIV[1]

'Drocourt-Quéant,' 'Hindenburg Line,' 'Havrincourt,' '**EPÉHY,**' '**CANAL DU NORD,**' 'St. Quentin Canal,' 'Courtrai,' '**SELLE,**' '**SAMBRE**'

From the German High-Water Mark to the Armistice

The next blow fell on the French. On May 27 the enemy attacked on a front which reached from Rheims to the river Oise. The result was a deeper and more rapid penetration than that following the March attack. By June 2 the new line formed a rough triangle: Rheims–Château-Thierry–Noyon. The Germans were nearer Paris than they had been since 1914. In the history of the British Expeditionary Force the advance is chiefly famous for the magnificent defence by the British IX Corps, consisting of four divisions, reinforced by a fifth, all of which had suffered very heavily in the attacks on the British front, and, having been relieved by French troops, had been sent to a supposedly quiet part of the front to refit. By the first week in June the German effort had exhausted itself, and the enemy was left holding a pronounced salient which, when the tide turned, was to be the first objective of Foch's counter-attack.

By the time the German offensive in Flanders was over there were ten French divisions in that part of the British front and two more in reserve behind our Third Army. The attack west of Rheims was followed by the gradual

[1] Map VIII.

withdrawal of these divisions, all of which had gone by the end of the first week in July.

Meanwhile, our losses of March and April were being made good by drafts from home, and by complete divisions and separate units from other fronts. By the beginning of August the strength of the British Expeditionary Force was not far short of what it had been on March 21. Also, except for the five unfortunate divisions that had been sent to Champagne for a rest, there had been three quiet months, during which the shattered divisions could regain their fighting efficiency. Throughout these three months a succession of minor operations had been carried out—all of them successful—so that when the time came to counter-attack on the big scale the troops had regained—if they had ever lost it—a distinct moral superiority over the enemy.

On July 15 the Germans made one last effort to keep the initiative by making an attack on both sides of the Rheims salient. This met with no success, and on the 18th Foch launched his first great counter-attack, as told in Chapter I.

On August 8 Haig delivered the first of that series of blows which only ceased with the Armistice.

The attack was made by the Fourth Army, south-eastward, from the point of the salient nearest to Amiens almost to Albert.

A French army attacked immediately on the right, and the front of the French attack was widened more and more on subsequent days. The success of the attack was great and immediate, and by the 10th the salient had been flattened out till the line ran through Roye–Rozière–Bray-sur-Somme.[1]

The enemy's resistance had now begun to harden, so a fresh attack was let loose on him by the Third Army on

[1] Map V.

August 21, from about the northern edge of the old Somme battlefield nearly to Arras. This attack was equally successful, and on the 23rd the advance was resumed on the Fourth Army front.

The orders from G.H.Q. to the Third Army were 'to press the enemy back energetically in the direction of Bapaume without delay, and to make every effort to prevent the enemy from destroying road and rail communications.'

Orders were issued by the Third Army for a preliminary operation, to take place on August 21, which was to include the capture of Bucquoy, Ablainzevelle, and the Ablainzevelle–Moyenneville Spur. Then, if this operation should prove successful, the IV and VI Corps were to exploit the success by pushing infantry and tanks to the line Irles–Bihucourt–Gomiecourt, thence northwards along the Achiet-le-Grand–Arras Railway.

At the same time, the IV Corps was to capture the remainder of the Serre–Miraumont Ridge including Beaurégard Dovecote.[2]

The V Corps were to be prepared to push across the river Ancre in a south-easterly direction towards Pozières, and to prolong the right of the IV Corps.

On the night of August 20/21 the Third Army was disposed as follows: on the right, from the junction with the Fourth Army, north of Albert, the V Corps, with two divisions (38th and 21st) in the line, one division (17th) in support; in the centre, the IV Corps, with three divisions (42nd, New Zealanders, and 37th) in the line, and two divisions (5th and 63rd) in support; on the left, joining with the First Army east of Mercatel, the VI Corps, with three divisions (2nd, Guards, and 59th) in the line and two divisions (3rd and 62nd) in support.

[1] Map IV. [2] Not marked in Map.

The 37th Division, which included our 13th Battalion, was ordered by the IV Corps to attack and capture, with the assistance of a battalion of tanks, the high ground east of Bucquoy and Ablainzevelle.

The VI Corps ordered the 2nd and Guards Divisions, the first of which included the 1st Battalion, to capture the spur Ablainzevelle–Moyenneville.

The Third Army Diary says that the attack was to be carried out as a complete surprise, and that no alterations, prior to August 21, were to be made in artillery expenditure, aeroplanes, and anti-aircraft activity, road and railway repair and construction. The 37th Division Diary, however, tells us that the bombardment of the enemy trench systems and known machine-gun positions about Ablainzevelle and Bucquoy by heavy artillery was intensified.

During the night of August 20/21, the 37th Division moved into position of assembly in the forward trench system west of Bucquoy and Ablainzevelle. It was a still, foggy night, very favourable to the enemy for the employment of gas shell. The enemy, however, only put down a slight harassing fire with gas shell which did little damage. A captured order showed that a gas bombardment had been designed for the following night.

The 37th Division attacked as ordered, with the 63rd Brigade on the right, the 111th on the left. Zero hour was 4.55 a.m., and there was a heavy ground mist, which did not lift till 10 a.m. Each of the attacking brigades had a battalion of the 112th Brigade attached as a supporting battalion, that Brigade (less two battalions) being in Divisional Reserve.

By 6 a.m. all the objectives of the Division had been taken with slight loss, and consolidation begun. As soon as the objective was gained the leading troops of the 5th Division on the right and the 63rd Division on the left began passing through the 37th on their way to attack the next objective. As described in the 'Chronicle' of 1918 :

'In the 111th Brigade the 13th K.R.R.C. were on the right, the 10th Royal Fusiliers in the centre, and the 13th Rifle Brigade on the left.

'By 4.30 a.m. on the 21st all companies were reported to be in position.

'As the fateful hour approached each moment became more intense. The tanks, working into their positions, seemed to our straining ears to be making a hideous noise, and the covering noise of the machine-gun fire altogether inadequate ; every minute we expected the counter-preparation.

'The morning was thick and misty, louder sounded the roar of the tanks, but the other side was strangely silent.

'The minutes now passed quickly, and still not a shell from the Germans ; then at zero, minus two and a half minutes, the fight began.

'Whizz !—crash !—bang ! down came our shells, a magnificent barrage and beautifully timed ; surely nothing could live in such a rain of fire.

'At zero plus five minutes we began to move forward. Still no sign of the tanks. It was an anxious moment as wire, imperfectly cut, might hold up the attack. Three minutes later one tank was seen to follow ; what became of our supporting tanks is not known.

'Visibility was very bad, and increased by the smoke of the barrage, so no aeroplanes appeared.

'At 5.30 a.m. the first tangible proof of our success came to hand in the form of prisoners. They belonged to the 15*th Bavarians*. At 5.47 a rumour from A Company reported that the Company was in their objective, but not in touch with the flanks.

'Shortly before this the men of the 63rd Royal Naval Division passed through our position. All signal communications which had been established prior to the attack became disconnected. An officers' patrol was now sent forward to get into touch with the forward companies. At 6.10 a.m. more troops passed through us accompanied by eight tanks. A Company now reported they were in touch on their flanks. Prisoners continued to come back in considerable numbers, and it was reported that B Company was in touch with the 10th Royal Fusiliers on the left flank at 7 a.m.

'Our artillery ceased firing at 7.30 a.m. Generally speaking, the enemy's reply to our artillery was not very pronounced, and did not in the least interfere with our progress. The machine-gun fire was negligible on our front. D Company then reported liaison was established on our right with the 8th Somersets (63rd Infantry Brigade).

'Carrying parties were now sent up to the front companies with fresh supplies, and the Germans now shelled Bucquoy for about an hour.

'At 9.30 the 19th Hussars passed through our position, and were cheered by our men. It was an inspiring sight. They returned in the evening, and it is not thought that they came into action.

'After the cavalry came the R.F.A., who took up position in the valley in front. Visibility now improved, and in a moment the air was filled with our planes, but not a sign of a Hun. There was no doubt of our mastery of the air.

'From now on for the rest of the day there was a regular procession of guns passing forward. Indiscriminate bursts of enemy shell fire characterised the afternoon, and the remainder of daylight was spent consolidating and wiring our new positions.

'The night passed quietly.'

Meanwhile, the 2nd and Guards Divisions were attacking the Ablainzevelle–Moyenneville Spur. They, too, met with little opposition, and by 8.15 a.m. Third Army had received the report that the objective was taken. The Division consolidated its gains, and was relieved in the evening. Our 1st Battalion was in reserve, and suffered only a few casualties, including 2 killed by the enemy's barrage.

The divisions which were launched on the next attack, after the first objective had been taken, met with much more opposition, and heavy fighting went on for the rest of the day. However, though the cavalry failed in an attempt to get through, and were withdrawn in the evening, by dusk the line of the Third Army ran along the railway south and east of Beaucourt–west of Baillescourt Farm—east of Achiet-le-Petit—west of Achiet-le-Grand—just east of Moyenneville–west of Hamelincourt–thence north along the railway to the original line.

There was no further advance by the Third Army on August 22, but strong enemy counter-attacks were beaten off with heavy loss, and by dusk the line held was practically the same as that of the night before.

The attack was to be renewed on the 23rd, and in the course of the operations the 3rd Division was to attack Gomiecourt at 3 a.m.; the 2nd Division was to pass through at 11 a.m.; the 5th and 37th Divisions were to attack the position from Irles to Bihucourt at 11 a.m. Farther to the right the 42nd and New Zealand Divisions were to make a preliminary attack at 2.30 a.m., and then co-operate with the attack on their left.

The attacks took place as ordered, and by evening the line of the 2nd Division ran west of Behagnies and east of Ervillers; the 37th Division had taken Achiet-le-Grand and Bihucourt.

The attack of the 1st Battalion, which had been resting during the 22nd, is thus described in the 'Chronicle' of 1918:

'Early on the morning of the 23rd we began to move forward, and by 8 a.m. the Battalion had reached a point of assembly at a place between Ablainzevelle and Courcelles. The companies were in preliminary battle formation, as follows:

A Company . .	Captain L. P. Walsh, M.C.
C Company . .	Captain A. E. Austin, M.C.
D Company . .	Captain C. A. V. Porter.
B Company . .	Captain W. E. Thomas.

'The idea was that the 5th Infantry Brigade of our division was to attack Behagnies and Sapignies villages, whilst the duty of the 1st Battalion K.R.R.C. was to protect the right flank of the 5th Brigade. Meanwhile, the IV Army Corps on our right were to attack Achiet-le-Grand, and Bihucourt and vicinity. The 5th Brigade crossed the railway line east of Courcelles at 11 a.m., and our battalion conformed. The enemy put down a fairly heavy barrage. It is difficult to speak with restraint about the riflemanlike dash and tactical ability which was displayed on this day by the company commanders and platoon officers. They were soon engaged with the enemy. D Company turned south, leaving Gomiecourt to their left. They found heavy machine-gun fire coming from the south-west. They were helped by a tank, and had soon taken 30 prisoners and 20 machine guns.

'Having cleared this area, D and C Companies went on almost to Achiet-le-Grand. They then turned east towards Behagnies. Meanwhile, A Company had attained their objective, and B Company had done splendid work, capturing quantities of prisoners, and getting in touch with the 24th Royal Fusiliers (of 5th Brigade) on our left. At night we held a line facing east, and about a mile and a half west of Behagnies; we were in touch with the 5th Brigade on our left and with the 37th Division (IV Corps) on our right. Captain Austin captured a German officer with his orderly in a dug-out. There was a good deal of enemy gas shelling during the night, and some fairly heavy shelling early on the 24th, but we had good cover in a sunken road. During the 23rd 500 or 600 enemy prisoners had been taken, with 200 machine guns and 6 pieces of artillery. The Battalion casualties were 3 officers wounded, namely: 2nd Lieutenants D. W. Robertson, A. Boyle, and R. L. G. Burney, and of other ranks, 10 killed and 60 wounded.'

The 13th Battalion had spent the 22nd on the ground taken by them on the 21st. The following extract from the 'Chronicle' of 1918 describes their share of the fighting on the 23rd:

'At 10.30 p.m. 22nd the Brigadier informed us that the original plan had been altered, and that before our attack on Favreuil could take place, Gomiecourt had to be captured, and another attack made on our right flank.

'Zero hour would depend on how these operations succeeded.

'The Battalion commenced to move up to relieve one of the Naval Division battalions in the line. The march up was exceptionally quiet, and all went well until we were about half-way through Logeast Wood, of evil fame. Here we ran into a zone of gas shelling, one shell landing plumb in the middle of a platoon ; several men were laid out.

'The relief being completed, the companies commenced getting into their assembly positions. Movement in the open in the neighbourhood of the jumping-off places was impossible, owing to aerial and ground observation.

'4 a.m. The attack on Gomiecourt on the left flank now commenced, and the enemy was very prompt in putting down his barrage, and the machine-gun fire was particularly heavy ; nothing could have got through the region of its area of fire.

'This fire directly enfiladed the line of our advance, and we began to feel a bit anxious, as we had not been promised the aid of any tanks.

'Zero hour was fixed at 11 a.m., and an hour previously all companies were reported in position.

'Our barrage came down to the tick, the attack commenced, and progress was very rapid. Several hundred prisoners and many machine guns were captured, and the final objective was gained at 1.30 p.m. The fight, however, was not finished, as the positions were subjected to very heavy shelling, and there were numerous counter-attacks. Our Commanding Officer, Lieut.-Colonel A. N. Strode-Jackson, D.S.O., was wounded in the right arm, and Major W. S. Johns took over command of the Battalion. The night was quiet.'

The Third Army gave orders for the advance to be pushed vigorously on the 24th, all Corps being given objectives well to the front ; those of the IV Corps being Le Transloy–Fins–Boursies [1] ; of the VI Corps, Quéant and Vis-en-Artois.[2] Ground was gained on the 24th all along the Third Army front, and by evening the line of the IV and VI Corps ran east of Biefvillers–east of Bihucourt–west of Behagnies–west of Mory–west of Croisilles [2]–east

[1] Not marked in map. [2] Map III.

of Henin,[1] and then westward for a few thousand yards, to where it connected with the First Army.

During the morning our 1st Battalion was relieved from its place in the line, and sent off to take part in an attack on Mory, but soon after its arrival at the rendezvous it was reported that the attack had already succeeded.

Their brigade was relieved during the night, and marched back to rest near Ayette. During the three days, August 22, 23, and 24, the Battalion had captured one and a half times its own strength of German prisoners. Its total casualties had amounted to 66, which included three officers wounded.

Our 13th Battalion was not engaged on the 24th.

Orders were given for all corps to push on next day, the XVII Corps taking over part of the VI Corps front on the extreme left.

Another considerable advance was made during the day, but an attack by the 37th Division on Favreuil was help up, the village not being finally cleared of the enemy till the early morning of the 26th.

The 'War Diary' of the 13th Battalion gives the following account of their share in the action:

'Zero hour was fixed at 6.30 p.m. on August 25, and at 5 p.m. the Companies began to move forward into position.

'The Germans had obviously got wind of our intentions, as we were immediately subjected to heavy artillery and machine-gun fire. The barrage commenced at 6.30 p.m., and our men went over. They had 700 yards to cover in six minutes. Our 18-pounders were firing short, and unfortunately killed Company Sergeant-Major Raybould.

'A Company of the West Riding Regiment went over in our rear; this was obviously an error, and we endeavoured to turn them towards our left flank, where there was a gap.

'At 7 p.m. 2nd Lieutenant Haddow reported that C and D Companies were held up by machine-gun fire from the ridge on

[1] Map III.

our left, so the support company of the 10th Royal Fusiliers was diverted to try and deal with the situation.

'Prisoners now came through in considerable numbers, 349 being sent back by 8 p.m. At 7.25 Haddow reported that he had formed a defensive flank on the left, and had pushed out some guns to hold the position. Twenty minutes later Company Sergeant-Major Bertouche, of the 10th Royal Fusiliers, sent back a message that they had succeeded in breaking through the enemy's resistance, and that they were surrendering 400 yards from the village, but the village was strongly held by machine guns.

'Our casualties were now very heavy. and Haddow reported personally that he had very few men left. At 8.50 the position was obscure and undoubtedly disorganised on our left.

'At 9 p.m., in spite of the men's gallant effort, it was obvious we could not gain our objective owing to the intense machine-gun fire. Accordingly, a defensive flank was organised, and at 3 a.m. on the 26th we were relieved by the King's Own Scottish Borderers and moved to Logeast Wood.'

The casualties of the Battalion during the month were:

Officers—killed, Captains C. Landale, R. E. Stavert (4th London Regiment, attached), F. C. Taylor; wounded, Lieut.-Colonel A. N. Strode-Jackson, D.S.O.; Captain P. N. Russell, M.C.; Lieutenants S. T. Harvey, D. J. Hay, C. E. Carr, C. Pickering; 2nd Lieutenants J. C. Bolton, L. F. Carter, T. M. Barrie, P. H. Warwick, A. M. Yates, M.C.; other ranks—killed 39, wounded 279, missing 32.

The Battalion received the following complimentary message on the 22nd:

'The G.O.C. wishes me to convey to you his appreciation of the wonderful rapidity with which you organised the objective. The enthusiasm shown throughout by troops already tried by a long spell in the battle zone more than confirms the statement of the Commander of the First Army that, in the 13th Battalion K.R.R.C. he had a Battalion upon which he could entirely rely at all times.'

(*Signed*) A. N. Strode-Jackson, *Lieut.-Colonel.*

On August 26 the First Army joined in on the left of the Third, on a front of seven miles, widening the advance of the British Expeditionary Force to a front of forty miles.

Meanwhile, on the 17th, the French Tenth Army (Mangin) had joined in on the right of the French, extending their front almost to Soissons.

The enemy was gradually forced back all along the line. On the 28th the French First Army (Debeny) occupied Nesle, and next day the French Third Army (Humbert) took Noyon. By September 1 Bapaume and Péronne had fallen to our Third and Fourth Armies. On September 2 the Third Army broke through the Drocourt–Quéant line,[1] and the Germans fell back again, until by the 8th they were again on the line to which they had retired in the spring of 1917. The French advance west of Soissons had turned the German position on the Vêsle, where our allies had been held up for the last month, and the enemy fell back across the Aisne. He had already evacuated the Lys salient, so he had now lost practically all his gains of the first six months of the year.

The 1st Battalion 'War Diary' describes, as follows, their share in the fighting of the first few days of September:

'Orders were received at about 10 a.m. September 2 to prepare to move, and the Battalion moved off at 12 noon via Courcelles–Ervillers, and took up a position in the old "Army Lines," 2,000 yards west of Vraucourt.

'On arrival there the Commanding Officer received verbal orders from the Brigadier-General that the Battalion would attack at dawn on the 3rd, with the ridge between Lagnicourt and Morchies as its objective.

'The Battalion was moved off at about 8 p.m. to rendezvous at the Sugar Factory, the Commanding Officer, Lieut.-Colonel C. A. Howard, D.S.O., and company commanders having ridden forward to reconnoitre the ground forward of

[1] Map III.

Vraucourt. On their return the Companies moved forward to the assembly positions: A Company (Captain L. P. Walsh, M.C.), B Company (Captain J. Lee, D.S.O.), C Company (Captain A. E. Austin, M.C.), D Company (Captain C. A. V. Porter).

'C and B Companies led the attack, C being on the left, D supporting C and A supporting B.

'At 4.45 a.m. Battalion Headquarters moved forward to its battle position (zero was at 5.20 a.m.), and a fairly heavy barrage was put down. The barrage put down by the Guards Division on our immediate left unfortunately did not coincide with our advance, thereby causing some casualties to our leading companies. By 6 a.m. it was reported that our companies had reached their objectives, meeting with practically no opposition. Strong patrols immediately pushed forward. At 6.25 a.m. Lieutenant R. S. Eckersley reported not a sign of the enemy, and by 7.15 a.m. our patrols had taken Eye Copse (about 1,200 yards beyond our objective). At 8.10 a.m. the patrols reported no enemy north-west side of Bapaume–Cambrai Road. Beaumetz was found to be in flames. We continued to push forward, but did not succeed in getting in touch with the enemy. At 9.30 a.m. the Brigade was ordered to stand fast while the 6th Brigade advanced through us, accompanied by cavalry and "whippet" tanks. Orders were issued accordingly, and our advanced patrols withdrawn, the Battalion occupying a line 1,000 yards south-west of Morchies, with the right of the Brigade resting on Chaufours Wood. During the day's operations we captured 4 field guns, 1 trench mortar, and a considerable number of machine guns. Only 6 prisoners were captured and a few Boches killed.

'Our casualties for the day were: Lieutenant H. W. Ponter (attached from 4th Queen's Regiment) killed; 2nd Lieutenant D. W. Davies wounded; 4 other ranks killed; 20 other ranks wounded.

'The Battalion stood fast for the remainder of the day, and information was received in the evening that we should probably move forward next morning.'

Next morning the Battalion moved forward to near Beaumetz, and during the night of the 4th/5th relieved some of the 6th Brigade in the Hindenburg Line near

Demicourt (west of the Canal du Nord). The enemy had ceased to retire and was getting troublesome again.

He became more active during the day, attacking a post in the middle of the day, from which he was ejected by a counter-attack of a platoon under 2nd Lieutenant R. D. C. Trench. In the evening he forced back some posts on the left of the Battalion's line. The casualties for the day were about 20. Captain J. H. Lee had been wounded on the 4th, and Lieutenant R. S. Eckersley, M.C. (Intelligence Officer) was wounded on the 5th. Nothing happened on the 6th except a considerable amount of shelling, and the Battalion was relieved on the night of the 6th/7th. The total casualties for these two days in the line amounted to 29.

By this time the American Army had come into being as a separate force, and taken over their share of the line east of Verdun. Their first big operation was the flattening out of the St. Mihiel salient, in which they took 16,000 prisoners and 450 guns.

The stage was now set for the final advance which was to end the war.

The main line of communication for the whole of the German forces in northern France ran through Liège, Namur, and Mons. All the eastern half of their line was supplied by the railway running south from Mons to Aulnoye and thence south-east to Hirson, Mezières, Montmédy. If this line could be cut at Aulnoye the German Army would be cut in two, and the eastern half would have behind it the Ardennes, railless except for one branch-line from Namur to Mezières, and almost roadless. This object was to be attained by a general advance all along the Allied front from St. Mihiel to the sea. On the right the Americans, with some French troops, were to advance north-west in the direction of Mezières. Next on their left, almost to Soissons, came a French Army Group (Maistre) advancing north. Thence to about St. Quentin came another French Army Group (Fayolle) to advance north-east. Then came the British Expeditionary Force, making the main thrust against the vital point on the enemy's communications, while on the extreme left the Second Army and the Belgians were to clear the Belgian coast and western Belgium, and prevent the enemy detaching troops to reinforce the danger zone.

Opposite the British Fourth and Third Armies the enemy was now back on the Hindenburg Line, or holding positions immediately in front of it—it had even been forced in places—but there were some preliminary operations to be undertaken before the great advance should begin.

On the night of September 8/9, the French crossed the Crozat Canal. On the 10th an attack by the III Corps (Fourth Army) at Épéhy[1] failed. On the 12th the Third Army took Trescault, Havrincourt, and Moeuvres.

The capture of Trescault, mentioned above, is thus described in the records of our 13th Battalion :

'Next morning [September 10] news came. An operation on a fairly large scale was to be undertaken. The 37th Division with the New Zealanders on our right was to take the Trescault spur, while on our left the 62nd Division was to attack the village of Havrincourt and the Hindenburg front system from the south-west. On the 37th Division front the 111th Brigade were to attack—13th K.R.R.C. on the left, and the 13th Rifle Brigade on the right, with the 10th Royal Fusiliers in reserve. The day was spent in reconnoitring. The Trescault spur runs north from the high ground between Gouzeaucourt and Bois de Gouzeaucourt, and ends in Bilhem Farm [a quarter of a mile east of Trescault]. The farm stands high, commanding the country to the north and east, and was rightly suspected of being strongly held ; indeed, it was subsequently found that orders had been issued to hold it at all costs. From the

[1] Map V.

eastern side of the Bois d'Havrincourt, now in our hands, the ground slopes down to the edge of the village of Trescault, which stretches up the reverse slope and could be looked into from the edge of the wood.

'On the 11th, Major Johns, who was in command, went through his orders with the company commanders, and preparations for various eventualities were made. The plan was for A Company (Captain E. J. Putman), supported on the left front by the Lewis guns and rifles of B Company, to take the village. As soon as A Company was in the village, B Company (Lieutenant G. A. Carr) was to send two platoons to mop up, and the remaining two platoons were to form a defensive flank in Queer Street (north of the village) and connect up with A Company's left. Meanwhile, C Company (Acting-Captain A. L. Seagar) was to follow A Company to the cross-roads on the south-east of Trescault, form up in the sunken road leading to Charing Cross [a cross-roads three-quarters of a mile to the south-east], and from there attack Bilhem Farm and the ridge. Once the ridge was held the 62nd Division could establish themselves to the north, and as soon as the Officer Commanding A Company satisfied himself that they were consolidating, he was to send out a patrol to Bilhem Chapel Wood switch [to the north-east] and dribble his Company forward to link up the line. D Company (Acting-Captain C. W. Beadel) was to remain in reserve. A light trench mortar and two machine guns were attached to the Battalion. The former was kept in reserve, while the latter were attached to the reserve platoon of A Company, to act as guns of opportunity and to assist in the consolidation.

'The attack was carried out very much as planned. The Companies, which were in position forty-five minutes before zero hour, timed to coincide with dawn, were subjected to heavy shell fire with Blue Cross gas. Our barrage, when the time came, was magnificent, and the prompt launching of the attack took full advantage of it. Machine guns were active from the village, but the opposition was soon overcome, and Trescault was in our hands.

'In the meantime C Company had reached the sunken road and formed up to take the second objective. As soon, however, as Captain Seagar launched his attack, the Company came under very heavy fire from a strong-point about 300 yards in front, and further advance would probably have been impossible but for the timely help of our sister Battalion, the 13th Rifle Brigade, who had not met with so much resistance, and seized the moment to bring a cross-fire to bear on the strong-point.

'Our casualties were heavy, as there was no vestige of cover. 2nd Lieutenant Wilding shot a machine-gunner through the head from a distance of about 200 yards, and after a fierce struggle the strong-point was rushed and 40 prisoners, 2 machine guns, and a trench mortar were taken. Heavy fighting continued from here onwards, and the outstanding feature lay in the number of the enemy killed at their battle posts, and the manner in which encircling movements pinched out the defence.

'By 7.30 a.m. the final objective had been taken. A Company had pushed up, and B Company, which had followed the attack as supports (two platoons to each Company) now reinforced the front line; altogether 190 prisoners, 18 machine guns, 3 trench mortars, an anti-tank gun, and 2 field guns were taken. The latter continued firing at point-blank range until their crews were knocked out by our Lewis guns and rifle fire. Throughout the day the enemy shelled us heavily, and dosed Trescault and the ground back towards Havrincourt Wood with Blue and Yellow Cross gas. In official parlance, "the spirit of the troops was excellent." If we had suffered heavy casualties, the Boche killed and wounded outnumbered ours, and the contentment that arises from a good haul of prisoners and material of war is a refreshing thing by itself.

'Battalion Headquarters was moved to Butler's Corner [600 yards north-west of the village] as the attack progressed, and at 11.30 a.m. D Company moved to Trescault Trench, just in front of the new Battalion Headquarters, their old position ********* being shortly occupied by a Company of the 10th Royal Fusiliers. Soon after noon two platoons of D Company were sent up to reinforce on the right, and one platoon on the left, and Major Johnstone, Second-in-Command, visited the front line to see that the positions taken up were satisfactory for withstanding counter-attacks. A little later a carrying party of forty men of the 10th Royal Fusiliers brought a supply of ammunition to the front line. About 6 p.m. the counter-attack came. After heavy bombardment the enemy came up Queen's Lane and succeeded in forcing their way along Shaftesbury Avenue [about three-quarters of a mile east of the village]. Our liaison post with the Rifle Brigade, which was a little to the north of the junction of these trenches, was wiped out either by the attackers or by shell fire. 2nd Lieutenants Tregarthen and House counter-attacked promptly ; hand-to-hand fighting and bombing ensued, and the enemy were driven back on to the Rifle Brigade. It is believed that they entered Shaftesbury Avenue about fifty strong, with three light machine-guns. They left behind 20 dead and 6 prisoners. A strong liaison post with the Rifle Brigade was now established in Queen's Lane. Our casualties were considerable from the preliminary bombardment. Indiscriminate shelling continued through the night, but no further attacks were made.'

2nd Lieutenant H. J. Devitt was killed in this attack.

Another German attack was repelled next evening, during which 2nd Lieutenant H. H. Wilding was killed whilst lying out in front of the parapet firing a Lewis gun. The Battalion was withdrawn on the 16th, and their Brigade went into reserve. Here 2nd Lieutenants J. E. P. Nicholson (Loyal North Lancashires, attached), and A. B. Walton were killed by a direct hit on a dug-out. Next day the Battalion again withdrew to the Beugny area.

On September 18 the Fourth Army (III Corps) and Third Army (V and IV Corps) attacked on a front of seventeen miles, from Holnon[1] to Gouzeaucourt. The line was advanced to a depth of three miles, and, in the course of the next few days, our troops got within striking distance of the main defences of the Hindenburg Line, taking 12,000 prisoners and 100 guns.

The 1st Division was at this time in the Fourth Army, and attacked with the 6th Division on their right and the 4th Australians on their left. The Division attacked with the 1st Brigade on the right, the 2nd on the left. Each brigade had two battalions in front line, the 2nd K.R.R.C. being on the right of the 2nd Brigade with the Royal Sussex on their left. Zero hour was at 5.20 a.m., and by

[1] N.W. of St. Quentin.

7.30 a.m. both battalions had captured their first objective. The following is the account of the action taken from the 2nd Battalion's 'War Diary'[1]:

'On the 18th the Battalion was formed up for the attack by 4.30 a.m. The Battalion frontage was about 800 yards at the start, but gradually narrowed down to about 500 yards at the final objective. The front extended from the marsh ground of the River Omignon on the left to the road running north-east from Maissemy to Berthaucourt. The 2nd Royal Sussex Regiment was on our left, and the 1st Cameron Highlanders on our right. The first objective was an enemy trench system on the high ground half-way between Maissemy and Berthaucourt, and the second and final objective, Berthaucourt. There was a final objective for the exploiting of success, but this was not attempted on account of the battalions on our right being held up.

'We moved forward at zero hour, which was at 5.20 a.m., A Company, under Captain Barnes, M.C., being in front, supported by B Company, under 2nd Lieutenant Cunningham, M.M., and C Company, under Captain Cook, M.C., on the right and left respectively. D Company under 2nd Lieutenant Cotton, was in Battalion Reserve.

'The morning was very wet and unpleasant, but cleared up towards noon. Prisoners soon began to come in, but it was difficult to get any information as to how things were going owing to the heavy "Scotch" mist which hung thickly in the valleys and prevented any visual signalling or direct observation of the attack. The Colonel went forward and got into touch with the company commanders of B and C Companies, and learnt that the Battalion was held up by machine guns on the left and right flanks. C Company was ordered to work round the left flank, and B Company, together with a portion of the left company of the Camerons, was to work round the right, while A Company held the machine guns in front. This worked very well, and the position was turned, chiefly due to the splendid leadership of 2nd Lieutenant Cunningham. He took charge of the whole situation on our right, and himself dealt with the crew of one enemy gun.

'All this caused considerable delay, and as it was not till 9.45 a.m. that the position was turned, our barrage had gone

[1] Map V.

far ahead. However, without the aid of the barrage, the Battalion pushed forward quickly, C Company on the left, A Company (now commanded by 2nd Lieutenant Nugent-Head, Captain Barnes having been seriously wounded) in the centre, and B Company on the right. D Company was still in full strength, and was in reserve.

'The Battalion fought its way right through the village of Berthaucourt to the eastern outskirts, and finally consolidated there, throwing out sentry groups in front of the main line of resistance. Battalion Headquarters took up a position in a half-dug trench just short of the village, from which an extensive view of the country round could be obtained.

'During the operations the enemy shelling was practically negligible, and most of the opposition was from machine guns. We had been told to expect a counter-attack from Pontruet, a village 500 yards east of Berthaucourt, and sure enough much movement in the shape of small groups of men moving forward from that village was observed at about 4.45 p.m. We had a telephone line back to Brigade Headquarters, which was laid as we advanced, and our Artillery Liaison Officer was able to get back to his Brigade, so that within a few minutes an excellent barrage of shrapnel and high explosive was put down in the area where movement was seen, with the result that the counter-attack did not develop.

'Lieut.-Colonel E. G. St. Aubyn had unfortunately been hit in the foot earlier in the day, and was eventually evacuated, Major Butler taking command.

'Besides the Colonel, we had the following casualties:

Killed

2nd Lieutenant J. T. Eldridge.
2nd Lieutenant E. H. Best.
And 23 other ranks.

Wounded

Captain L. J. Barnes, M.C.
2nd Lieutenant A. Winter.
2nd Lieutenant M. D. B. Lister.
And 95 other ranks.

Missing

6 other ranks.

'On the 19th, about 3 p.m., the enemy attempted to bomb down an old communication trench on our right, but was stopped by counter-bombing. Unfortunately, in this minor operation Lieutenant W. F. A. Chambers and 2nd Lieutenant A. P. Cunningham, M.M., were wounded; the latter afterwards died from his wounds.

'A small fighting patrol, under 2nd Lieutenant O. L. Marlow, was sent out that night along the main road to Pontruet, but they bumped into some strongly held enemy posts, suffering casualties, and having to withdraw, 2nd Lieutenant Marlow being missing, 2 other ranks killed, and 13 other ranks wounded.

[2nd Lieutenant Marlow was a prisoner of war.]

'On the night of the 20th/21st the Battalion was relieved.'

On the 23rd the 33rd Division, on the right of the Third Army, attacked in co-operation with the left division of the Fourth Army. Our 16th Battalion came in for some hard fighting, in which great gallantry and determination were shown on both sides. It is thus described in the Battalion's 'War Diary'[1]:

'The Battalion moved into the line on September 22, taking over trenches of Villers Guislain from the Cameronians and from the 5th Scottish Rifles, who had encountered serious resistance at about this point and suffered heavy losses. A number of minor operations were carried out here by the Battalion to clear up an obscure situation, but very determined resistance was encountered, which made it apparent that the enemy intended to make a strong stand. As a result of these operations, casualties to 5 officers and 82 other ranks were sustained.

'The largest of these operations deserves special mention, owing to the very determined resistance put up by the enemy, and also the gallant and sustained attack made by A and C Companies of the Battalion.

'These companies were commanded at the time by Captain G. MacD. Warner, M.C., and Captain G. B. de Courcy Ireland, M.V.O., M.C., respectively. The position taken over by the

[1] Map IV.

Battalion was as follows: on the right of the line was a strong-point, rectangular in shape, called Meath Post, and this was extended to the left (north) by a single, well-constructed trench to a sunken road about 800 yards north of the strong-point mentioned. About 200 yards of the northern extremity of this trench was occupied by the enemy, between whom and the Battalion a block had been established, and the intervening portion of the trench was freely sprinkled on both sides with barbed-wire "gooseberries." Accordingly it was decided that a minor operation should take place in conjunction with a Battalion on the left, who were to work down the trench to the south whilst we were working to the north. The portion occupied by the enemy was obviously regarded by him as of much importance, and he was assisted in his foothold by the sunken road, which formed a very useful covered approach.

'It was decided that two platoons of A Company and two platoons of C Company should work up either side of the trench, whilst a bombing party from A Company should operate in the trench itself. The night September 23/24 was chosen for the operation. This proved to be a particularly bright night, and this fact was undoubtedly largely responsible for the failure of the attack. In order to be sure of their direction, it was necessary for C Company (deploying on the east side of the trench) to move into position at right-angles to our front. This deployment was observed by the enemy, and a heavy machine-gun fire opened, which committed this company to their advance a few minutes before zero. At the outset, heavy losses were experienced, including 2 officers of C Company taking part in the operation, Captain Ireland and 2nd Lieutenant Pinnington. Notwithstanding this the advance was continued, and to some extent a diversion was created, which was taken advantage of by the bombing party of A Company and the two platoons operating on the west side of the trench. Led by 2nd Lieutenant Hogan the bombing party advanced with great dash, and cleared the trench to the point where the flanking battalion (1st Middlesex) were to be met. Unfortunately, that battalion was not in sight, but preparations were immediately made to hold the ground gained. Immediately, however, supporting parties of the enemy arrived *via* the sunken road, counter-attacked, and drove A company back some distance by a very determined bombing attack. Though already badly wounded, 2nd Lieutenant Hogan secured more bombs, and once again found himself at his objective. During this short hiatus it was subsequently found that the Middlesex Regiment had also gained [their objective], but had been driven back before the second arrival of 2nd Lieutenant Hogan's party. A second counter-attack was delivered by the enemy again with fresh supporting troops, once again driving 2nd Lieutenant Hogan's party back, and this time, owing to the approaching daylight, the engagement could not be renewed. In the second attack Hogan was again hit, and was left unconscious and apparently dead in the hands of the enemy. The personal exploits of this very gallant officer are worthy of fuller mention, and a copy of the recommendation submitted by the Commanding Officer, who was on the spot throughout the action, is appended.

' " For conspicuous gallantry and devotion to duty on the night September 23/24, 1918. During a minor operation, south of Villers Guislain, this officer was in charge of a platoon detailed for bombing along a trench. Immediately the attack started he was hit in the left arm severely, but in spite of this he carried on, encouraging his men to further efforts in spite of a very determined resistance. Later he was again hit dangerously in the head and slightly in the right arm, and with his men was driven back to his starting-point. Rallying his men again in spite of growing weakness and loss of blood, he led them once more to attack, but on reaching his objective his right foot was blown off by a bomb and he was rendered unconscious by the concussion. On regaining consciousness he ordered his men to move him to a place clear of the trench and to continue their efforts, as the enemy were counter-attacking. He lost consciousness again and his platoon was finally driven back, leaving him apparently dead and in the hands of the enemy." '

The officer casualties in this operation were :

Reported Killed

2nd Lieutenant G. S. Hogan [subsequently reported a prisoner, wounded].

Wounded

Captain G. McD. Warner, M.C.
Captain G. B. De Courcy Ireland, M.V.O., M.C.
2nd Lieutenant A. H. Pinnington.
2nd Lieutenant F. G. Budd [remaining at duty].

In this action the Battalion earned the following decorations: D.S.O., 1 (Hogan); bar to M.C., 1; M.C., 3; bar to M.M., 1; M.M., 13.

Our 2nd Battalion was again engaged on the 24th in the capture of Pontruet. The attack by the 2nd Brigade was made with the 2nd Royal Sussex on the right and the 1st Northamptonshire on the left. Our 2nd Battalion were 'mopping up.' The following is the account from their 'War Diary':

'On the evening of the 23rd the Battalion moved up to the line again to attack on the 24th. The enemy apparently suspected the attack, because they were shelling all the roads and valleys and likely forming-up positions very heavily with gas. The Royal Sussex were attacking on our left and the 3rd Infantry Brigade on our right. [The Northamptons appear to have been held up and the 2nd K.R.R.C. pushed up into the front line very early in the attack.] Their objectives were two hills about two miles from the assembly position, and the Battalion's task was to clear the valley running in between, and the final objective was known as Le Duc Trench, about 400 yards south of Pontruet.

'The attack progressed very well, and all objectives were gained except on our right, where a party of about 200 of the enemy held out in a trench redoubt till dusk, when we captured the positions. A further advance was made at dusk by A and C Companies, and a sunken road on an important ridge was captured. This attack had to be arranged and carried out at very short notice, and was most successful. About 2 p.m. the next day, the 25th, the enemy attempted to counter-attack, after heavy artillery preparations. They were heavily repulsed by our rifle and Lewis-gun fire and the excellent barrage from our guns. Enemy shelling remained very heavy all day, but no further counter-attack was attempted.

'The next morning Lieut.-Colonel E. G. St. Aubyn was wounded [he had rejoined on the 22nd] and Major H. W. Butler, M.C., came up and took command.

'The 26th the Battalion was relieved, and marched back to Vermand.'

Our casualties for this battle were :

Killed

2nd Lieutenant C. B. D. Wake.
And 21 other ranks.

Wounded

Lieut.-Colonel E. G. St. Aubyn.
Lieutenant P. D. Ravenscroft.
Lieutenant H. B. Dawson.
2nd Lieutenant S. T. Bolton.
2nd Lieutenant T. W. Cotton.
2nd Lieutenant E. V. Davies.
2nd Lieutenant P. J. Smith.
2nd Lieutenant A. C. Mee.
And 61 other ranks.

Missing

3 other ranks.

CANAL DU NORD

HINDENBURG LINE

The great advance was begun on the morning of September 26 by the attack of the Americans with nine Divisions, equal in strength to about thirty French or British, on a twenty-mile front west of the River Meuse. On their left the French Fourth Army attacked on a twenty-four mile front. In the course of the next day or two the whole of the French forces were in movement. We need not record further the advance of our allies on the right, but will deal solely with the operations of the British Expeditionary Force.

It must be remembered that on the front of the Fourth, Third, and First Armies the British Expeditionary Force had a much harder task than had the Allies elsewhere. On the extreme right and left the Allies had great numerical superiority which lessened as the centre of the line was approached, until, on the greater part of the British Expeditionary Force front, the numbers were on the side of the Germans. Against forty British divisions in the central attack the enemy had concentrated no less than fifty-seven.

On September 27 the left of the Third Army and the right of the First attacked on a front of thirteen miles, and by evening had penetrated four miles, from Beaucamp to Oisy-le-Verger. Ten thousand prisoners and 200 guns were taken on the first day. Next day bridgeheads across the Scheldt Canal were secured five miles from the starting-line.

The Fourth Army attacked on September 29, the Third and First Armies joining in on a total front of over thirty miles from St. Quentin to the River Sensée.

The chief thrust of the Fourth Army was on a front of nine miles from Gricourt[1] to Vendhuille.[2] In spite of a partial failure by the American II Corps, the Hindenburg Line was broken on a front of five miles.

On October 3 the Fourth Army breached the Fansomme–Beaurevoir Line, and the attack, started on October 8 by the Fourth and Third Armies, drove the enemy back on to a line running through Le Cateau.

On the 27th the 2nd Division was, with the 62nd, in the second line of the VI Corps, with the Guards and 3rd Division in front line. The events of the following days are described, as follows, in the 'War Diary' of our 1st Battalion:

'Zero Day. [September 27th.] Zero, 5.20 a.m. The Battalion was ordered to be ready by 6.20 a.m., and then to advance by bounds, to the east of the Canal du Nord.

'At 6.15 a.m. the Battalion moved to the 1st bound, which was complete by 8 a.m.

[1] Map V. [2] Map IV.

'Battalion was ordered to move to 2nd bound with instructions to halt west of the canal in Sunken Road, near the crossing, but not to cross until further orders. This bound was complete by 1.30 p.m. At 4 p.m. Battalion was ordered to take up position in Sunken Road, and be dispersed in depth; this was carried out by 6 p.m.

'Casualties during the day were 2 officers wounded, 2 other ranks killed, and 6 other ranks wounded.

'At 9 p.m. commanding officers were assembled at Brigade Headquarters, and orders were received to relieve the 3rd Guards Brigade in Beet Trench, and to attack the following morning at 4.45 a.m.

'As there was not much time for arrangements, the Commanding Officer issued verbal orders to company commanders at 11 p.m., these being followed later by written orders. The Battalion moved into position of assembly at 1.30, being met by guides from the Welsh Guards at Beetroot Factory, just east of Flesquières, at 2 a.m. The Welsh Guards gave every assistance in putting the Battalion into position.

'*Operations near Flesquières*

'Position of assembly: two leading companies B and C just west of the Guards outpost line, 200 yards east of Beet Trench, which is 500 yards west of Flesquières, two supporting companies in Beet Trench. Battalion Headquarters in Sunken Road, just west of Flesquières.

'At 4.45 a.m. a barrage was put down on Premy Trench, remaining there three minutes, until reaching the Graincourt Line, resting there ten minutes, and lifting then 100 yards every four minutes, running from Nine Wood to Marcoing.

'It was very dark at the start, but the two leading companies reached Premy Trench with slight opposition, and passed on to the Graincourt Line, capturing it and taking a few prisoners on the way. The two supporting companies passed through the leading companies, and advanced to the Sunken Road. This was reached with little opposition. The original idea was to hold the line firmly, and to send out strong patrols to gain the river and canal crossings. Such slight opposition being encountered, the leading companies pressed on towards Noyelles and the canal[1] crossings, being followed by the two

[1] This was the Canal de l'Escaut, not the Canal du Nord. The Canal du Nord was crossed the previous day.

other companies, which had now become the supporting ones. Up to this point excellent direction had been maintained, although the night was dark; but from this point the leading companies inclined rather to the left, as the 1st Battalion was moving somewhat to the north. During the advance from Premy forwards, the barrage of the 62nd Division came down, this attack not starting till 7 a.m.

'Unfortunately, the barrage came down between the supporting companies and Battalion Headquarters, completely cutting off communication from front to rear, and *vice versa*, for some time.

'During the advance to the Sunken Road, one platoon had been detached to work through the northern portion of Marcoing. This platoon, under Lieutenant R. J. Anderson, actually advanced through Marcoing in front of the barrage of the 62nd Division. This officer surprised two German guns limbering up; the first got away, but the second was captured, the team being shot down by this officer; the artillery officer, his orderly, and the drivers were taken prisoner.

'A number of other guns were captured in this area. This platoon advanced through the northern part of Marcoing, and left one Lewis-gun section to cover the bridge over the canal. This section remained there until the arrival of the advanced troops of the 62nd Division, when it rejoined its company. Meantime, the two leading companies advanced to Noyelles, taking prisoners on the way, and reached the village at 8.15 a.m.; the leading company going straight to the bridge over the canal at the factory. Several prisoners were taken in Noyelles in pyjamas, and a number taken out of various dug-outs in the village. The whole Battalion had now practically reached Noyelles, and while there, was joined by the Commanding Officer, who disposed the Battalion as follows:

'Two companies to seize the crossing over the canal south of the village, one company to hold the river crossing, and one company in reserve with Battalion Headquarters.

'It was found necessary to keep one company at the crossing over the canal in Noyelles near the factory, so only one company went forward to seize the canal crossing. Two platoons reached the bridge, but were unable to cross owing to heavy machine-gun fire. They, however, established themselves on the western bank, controlling the bridge, and driving off several attempts to blow it up. When crossing the river bridge the leading platoon of this company had captured seven Germans trying to destroy the bridge. The company at the factory effected a crossing, but were compelled to retire over the canal again. Posts, however, controlled the bridge and kept it intact; eventually we handed over this bridge to the 1st Royal Berks, the left battalion of the Brigade. The situation at the end of the day was as follows: two platoons holding the canal bridge, supported by the remaining platoon of the Company, and the other company holding the river bridge. One company in the neighbourhood of the canal bridge in Noyelles, and one company with Battalion Headquarters at the entrance to the village. These positions were maintained throughout the night of 28th/29th.

'Ninety-seven prisoners had been taken; all, with few exceptions, were artillery signallers. Our casualties were 1 officer and 12 other ranks wounded.

'At 6 p.m. on the evening of the 28th the Brigadier-General gave orders for the next day.

'These were to cross the canal, establish ourselves on the eastern side, and push forward to secure the general line from just north of Mont-sur-l'Œuvre, to Range Wood, east of Noyelles.

'Company commanders were assembled and orders given out as follows: zero, 5 a.m. Barrage to come down for ten minutes on Marcoing Switch and Marcoing Support and Flot Farm.

'C Company: Lieutenant A. Armstrong to have two platoons in position near canal bridge ready to slip across when barrage lifted. One platoon to support. This company to seize Flot Farm and work south to gain touch with 62nd Division.

'A Company: Captain L. P. Walsh, M.C., to follow C Company, and secure Marcoing Switch and Marcoing Support and work north to meet 1st Royal Berks, crossing the canal at Noyelles. In the event of the Brigade on the left (5th Brigade) getting forward quicker, the Battalion was to push forward to the general line already mentioned, and to get into touch with the Brigade on the left.

'B Company to be ready to cross canal and reoccupy Marcoing Support and Flot Farm, as leading companies went forward. D Company to remain in reserve at Noyelles.

'At 5.45 a.m. the leading company and four machine guns

were reported all over. Prisoners began to come in, and about 200 had been taken by 7.15 a.m. A Company, following close behind C Company, had established itself in Marcoing Support, connecting with C Company in Flot Farm. The 1st Royal Berks being unable to cross by Noyelles Bridge, it was decided that Captain L. P. Walsh, M.C., should extend his front in Marcoing Support to east of the Factory; this he did, taking 10 or 12 prisoners, and thereby established the Brigade front, and enabled the Berks to carry on. At midday the situation of the Battalion was as follows: two platoons to the south of Flot Farm. One company in and around Flot Farm, supported by two platoons of the 1st Royal Berks. One company and one platoon just north of Flot Farm and along Marcoing Support. Four Vickers in Marcoing Support, south of the farm, and three just north of it, in the Sunken Road. About 2 p.m. the enemy made a counter-attack against Flot Farm, but it was not pressed, and easily repulsed.

'At 2.30 p.m. a fresh attack started. Three Companies took part in this, B on the right, D on the left, and C in support. It was thought that the 62nd Division was trying to co-operate on our right, but they did not do so. The right company, which was ordered to move against Mont-sur-l'Œuvre, soon came under heavy machine-gun fire, and though supported by C Company, was forced to form a defensive flank facing east. These companies suffered some casualties, Lieutenant A. Armstrong, commanding C Company, being wounded. Meanwhile, D Company had gone on and reached the trench which was their objective, and passed some 200 yards in front of it. Both flanks being exposed, this company fell back, getting into touch with the 1st Royal Berks on the left, and also with the two companies forming a flank towards Mont-sur-l'Œuvre.

'A considerable number of the enemy were seen to concentrate farther north as if to counter-attack, but nothing developed. The Company during the advance captured 2 light field guns. At 7 a.m. A Company was ordered to attack Mont-sur-l'Œuvre under a barrage, in conjunction with the 62nd Division.

'The 62nd Division again failed to co-operate, so A Company's advance was stopped, and the position was as follows: two platoons, 23rd Royal Fusiliers, in Flot Farm, A Company in Marcoing Support, and about the Cross-roads, C and D Companies along the Sunken Road, D Company being in touch with the Royal Berks, on its left. The Vickers and light trench mortar, still in their original positions, north and south of Flot Farm. Orders were received to organise this position, and hand it over to the 23rd Royal Fusiliers that night.

'At 1 a.m. the Battalion was relieved by the 23rd Royal Fusiliers ; and returned to billets in Noyelles.

'The casualties during the fighting were :

	Killed.	*Wounded.*	*Missing.*
Officers .	Captain G. Fardell, M.C.	4	—
Other Ranks .	14	71	7

2nd Lieutenant J. Lever, M.C., died of wounds on October 1.'

To return to the 16th Battalion, which had been relieved in the front line on September 25, and had spent the next few days in support, still under artillery fire from which they continued to have a few casualties :

Their 'War Diary' relates that :

'On September 28 the Battalion made ready to relieve the 2nd Worcesters in the line, but no orders of any sort were received, and a curious silence was maintained by the Brigade. Accordingly Colonel Seymour and the Adjutant paid a visit to Brigade, and in response to inquiries found that there would be a conference at the Headquarters of the Worcestershires in the line that evening.

'At the conference it was explained that the operations farther south made it conceivable that the enemy would withdraw from the positions he held in front of the Brigade during the night, and accordingly an operation was planned to attack to a great depth. The jumping-off place for the attack was a trench running across the crest of a hill and commanding a very extensive view of the country over which the attack was to be made. The first objective to be reached was a sunken road with a powerful strong point constructed at its junction with another road. Intersecting these cross-roads was a communication trench which was a part of the very complicated system of trenches over which we were fighting, which system was possessed partly by ourselves and partly by the enemy. The communication trench in question led both to the British and German positions ; a complication of doubtful advantage to either side. After passing the line of this road, open country for about 1,000 yards would be encountered, and then Pigeon Trench, about 1,000 yards west of the canal, which, in view of the open ground to be traversed, was a formidable obstacle. The line of this trench was the objective of the Glasgow Highlanders (north) and the 2nd Worcestershire Regiment (south). After this trench the country fell fairly rapidly until the Scheldt Canal was reached. The village of Ossus, on the west bank of the canal, was assigned to this battalion as its objective. The approach to this village was by two converging sunken roads, and it was necessary to give special orders for the avoidance of these roads, owing to the almost unique opportunity they afforded for the successful use of machine guns in defence.

'By 5.20 a.m. [September 29] the Battalion was in position in a maze of trenches behind the Worcestershire Regiment, a moonlight night having assisted greatly in a rather difficult move across-country without landmarks. Zero hour was 5.30 a.m., and consequently the tedium and nerve-strain of waiting were largely avoided. In default of news from the leading battalion, B and D Companies (B Company left and D right) were ordered to dribble up to the jumping-off place vacated by the Worcesters.

'From reports received it appeared that the attack was going well. At about this time the enemy put down a very thick smoke and gas barrage, with startling and unfortunate results for the attacking troops. Landmarks were lost sight of immediately, and, worse still, the company and platoon commanders could not see their troops or ascertain the direction they were taking. Following B and D Companies, A Company in turn vanished into the blue, and only C Company was left. This Company was immediately put into the line to garrison the jumping-off trench, and Battalion Headquarters moved to the place occupied by the Worcestershire Headquarters to ascertain the situation and do what was possible. After some time two company commanders were found, each of whom had lost his company in the fog. Communication with the troops in front was impossible owing to the continuous and heavy machine-gun fire which was maintained from the strongpoint described above. Isolated platoons pressing on had most exciting experiences. The two leading platoons of B and D Companies pressed on resolutely, though completely hidden from their objective by the fog, and missed the advanced elements of the German defences, and were only stopped by machine-gun fire at close quarters from Pigeon Trench. All these platoons got to earth immediately and sent out patrols to gain touch with the flanks. The patrols returned to report that they were completely surrounded, and that in many cases the enemy were only about 50 yards distant. 2nd Lieutenants Levitt and Knight thereupon went out again with small parties to find or fight a way through. During all this time the only protection for these platoons was the fact that the smoke barrage had not lifted, and they were covered from view. Unfortunately both 2nd Lieutenants Levitt and Knight were killed in their very hazardous enterprise. 2nd Lieutenants Wilson and Budd then remaining, decided to steer their way back by compass, taking the whole force with them, and trusting to weight of numbers to force a way back to their comrades. They were successful in this, and were just back in our lines when the smoke cleared. In both their advance and retreat they had passed by on the south and vulnerable side of the strong-point, ignorant of the fact that the Worcestershires were held up on the north side, and that it only needed the pressure of their blow from the south to make the attack a success. The whole of the Battalion had been located by about noon; and in view of the heavy losses sustained by the Worcestershire Regiment it was found necessary to take over the major portion of their front and to organise for defence. Patrols were undertaken, and towards 7 a.m. returning patrols reported the evacuation of the enemy foremost positions. Accordingly two companies were pushed forward with orders to occupy the village of Ossus and to cross the Scheldt Canal if possible. These companies took up positions north and south of the village, but were unable to cross the canal owing to the fact that the bridges were destroyed and that the eastern bank was held in strength by the enemy with machine guns.

'The night of September 30 was spent in taking up and organising positions. Movement was impeded by the fact that the night was extremely dark, and that rain, which was falling continuously, made the going extremely heavy. Patrols, however, made reconnaissances of the west bank of the canal, and a daylight patrol by 2nd Lieutenant Wilson on October 1 brought extremely valuable information as to the state of the crossings on the Battalion front.

'Universal time started on October 1, i.e. the counting of hours from 01.00 to 24.00, instead of in two periods of twelve hours.

'There was considerable activity on the part of the enemy trench mortars and machine guns throughout the day, and information was received that an enemy patrol had crossed the canal at Honnecourt, and was moving south towards the Battalion's area. Nothing was seen, however. The British artillery was extremely active on the 3rd, but retaliation on the part of the enemy was extremely feeble.

'The Battalion was relieved by the 5th Scottish Rifles on October 3, two companies in the afternoon and two companies at night.

'The Battalion moved to the area south of Vaucelette Farm.'

The following casualties were sustained during the action of September 29 and the subsequent days :

Officers

Killed .	2nd Lieutenants S. N. Levitt, P. Knight.
Wounded .	2nd Lieutenant W. C. Whitmore.

Other Ranks

Killed	6
Wounded	40
Missing	9
Total .	55

Though the V Corps was held up at this point from September 29 till October 4, the successful crossings of the canal to the south and north caused the enemy to retire, and on the morning of the 5th the V Corps began to cross at Honnecourt.

Our 4th Battalion had left the Macedonian front towards the end of June, and reached France early in July.

They joined the 151st Brigade of the 50th Division, and were fortunate enough to get a long spell of training in which to make up their numbers and get rid of the effects of malaria. On September 24 Lieut.-Colonel J. B. Brady, D.S.O., from the 1st Battalion, took over command.

Towards the end of the month their division joined the III Corps, Fourth Army. On October 3 they joined in the attack by that army which had begun on September 29, and the following account of their share in the battle is taken from the Battalion War Records in the 'Chronicle' of 1918:

'The Battalion was allotted the task of clearing the villages of Le Catelet and Gouy, and of consolidating the high ground north of Le Catelet village; orders were accordingly issued, but very great difficulty was experienced in moving companies to positions of assembly, the ground being entirely unknown, and no guides were available. The night was dark, with frequent bursts of very heavy rain. The attacking Companies, B and D, were under the command of Captain Nutting, M.C., and Captain Hayhurst-France, M.C., respectively.

'The whole operation was successfully carried out, but our losses were heavy; at 9 p.m., on October 3, units had become scattered and disorganised owing to the severe nature of the fight, and the task of holding a line 2,000 yards long, north of the village, was therefore found impracticable. All troops appearing beyond the western front of Le Catelet came at once under heavy machine-gun fire from the road which had not been dealt with by the Brigade on our left; troops therefore dug in on the outskirts of the village north-west and north-east, covering the approach on the north as far as practicable.

'It was noticed about noon that the enemy were endeavouring to work their way to the outskirts of Gouy; owing to the heavy casualties we were too weak to hold that position. A company of the 3rd Northumberland Fusiliers were ordered to support us, and a second company of the same battalion were ordered to take up the position in readiness for a counter-attack should the enemy penetrate.

'At 1 p.m. our artillery swept the ground to the north and

north-east of Le Catelet, with the result that any chance of a successful movement of the enemy up the valley was frustrated.

'We were relieved in the evening, and withdrew to Bony in the Hindenburg Line. We had lost during the fight, 3 officers killed and 6 wounded; the losses in the other ranks were also heavy. We captured 1 officer and 252 other ranks, and 35 machine guns.

'Both villages had been organised with great skill and thoroughness; nests of machine guns covered every way of approach, with snipers in the upper stories of the houses; the task set the Battalion called for very resolute leading, and rapid handling of both the rifle and Lewis gun. Throughout a morning of bitter fighting all ranks of the Battalion did their duty.

'On October 4 we were placed at the disposal of the commander of the 150th Infantry Brigade, and this officer was not going to let us rest long.

'We first received orders to hold the line of the Escaut River, from Marquincourt Farm to Quincamp Mill, to protect the gap which was then believed to exist between the canal and Le Catelet village. Two companies were therefore sent forward to hold the line of this river.

'The Commanding Officer, with Lieutenant Bennett, the Battalion Intelligence Officer, reconnoitred the line of the river, and, on reporting to Brigade Headquarters, received orders to attack at dusk the enemy's system of fortified posts on the high ground across the river. This operation was entrusted to the 4th Battalion, under the command of Lieut.-Colonel Brady.

'The attacking companies were under the command of the following officers: C Company, Lieutenant H. R. Preece; B and A Companies, under Captain Nutting; D Company, Lieutenant Debnam.

'The attack was launched with such energy that the Boche soon decided that he had had enough of it. All positions were taken and held. We captured 2 officers, 51 other ranks, 25 machine guns, and 2 trench mortars. Our casualties were slight. For the second time in a week the Battalion had distinguished itself.

'The real difficulties of this operation were overcome by the rapidity and skill of the company commanders, who led their men to positions of assembly over rough and unknown country, across a formidable river obstacle, without any previous reconnaissance.

'The movement, as executed, could not have been carried out by other than highly disciplined and well-led troops. The enemy's opposition melted away owing to the rapidity and determination with which the actual assault was launched and carried through.'

The enemy was given no rest, and on October 8 the Fourth and Third Armies were attacking again.

The 99th Brigade, 2nd Division, attacked to the south of Cambrai, with the 23rd Royal Fusiliers on the right, the 1st K.R.R.C. on the left, and the 1st Royal Berks in reserve. The 3rd Division were attacking on their right and the 63rd Division on their left. The first objective was a trench running north-west and south-east to the west of Seranvillers and Niergnies, of which the Fusiliers were to take 750 yards and the K.R.R.C., with three companies only, were to take 550 yards. The second objective, the La Targette–Cambrai Road, was to be taken, including the village of Forenville, by the 1st Royal Berks, except for the left 400 yards, which was to be taken by the company of the K.R.R.C. not engaged on the first objective. Zero hour was 04.30.

The following is the account of the action from the 1st Battalion's 'War Diary':

'At 2.30 a.m. the Companies were in position, having suffered no casualties. B and C Companies, having recently been a good deal knocked about, had been combined, under Captain W. E. Thomas. A Company was under Captain L. P. Walsh, M.C., and D Company under Captain C. A. V. Porter, M.C. Battalion Headquarters were in a dug-out. Zero was 4.20 a.m., and at that hour our barrage came down, and the front-line companies moved up behind it. There was a certain amount of enemy machine-gun fire and some artillery retaliation near Battalion Headquarters.

'The first objective was the trench line running south-east in front of Niergnies, and by 6 a.m. this had been captured, with slight casualties. We had established connection with the units on our flanks, and the troops who were to take the second objective were in position. At 7.15 a.m. advanced Battalion Headquarters were established, to which signal communication with the troops on our first objective was established by telephone.

'D Company joined up in rear of the first objective, and, moving forward behind our barrage, reached the second with only 10 casualties. Up to this time the three companies had taken between them 200 prisoners.

'While returning from a reconnaissance of the front line, the Commanding Officer was struck in the knee by a splinter, which caused a severe bruise. Captain C. A. V. Porter, M.C., was slightly wounded in the face, but continued to do duty.

'At 8.15 a.m. the enemy launched his counter-attack with five tanks, supported by heavy artillery and machine-gun fire, though not by infantry. On the right of D Company, part of our second objective was still in the enemy's hands, while the troops on their left retired without warning, thus leaving them no alternative but to withdraw to the first objective, where the whole Battalion concentrated fire on the tanks, two of which were knocked out. The crew of the third gave themselves up, while the other two waddled off in a northerly direction.

'At 1.30 p.m. orders were issued for D Company to advance on the second objective again, as the troops on our left (63rd Division) were reported to have established themselves on the second objective, in advance of our flanks. In consequence it was not possible for our artillery to support our left.

'Zero for this attack was at 3 p.m., but just before starting Officer Commanding D Company observed enemy in positions which were supposed to be held by our troops ; but it was too late to alter the barrage, and he attempted to advance, despite heavy machine-gun fire. The Company struggled forward 500 yards, but received no support on either flank, and being unable to find any ground not exposed to machine-gun fire, retired to the first objective. In this operation the Company lost two officers, Lieutenant R. J. Anderson and 2nd Lieutenant M. W. Bing, and 66 other ranks, including the Company Sergeant-Major, and two out of three platoon sergeants.

'At 6 p.m. the 17th Royal Fusiliers, of the 6th Brigade, came up, and succeeded in taking Forenville, and as soon as it was dark our front-line companies pushed forward a small outpost line.

'Since 3 p.m. the enemy's machine-gun fire had been very constant, and this, with a good deal of heavy artillery and some gas shelling, continued until midnight. Then everything became unusually quiet, and our patrols reported that they suspected that the enemy was withdrawing. Shortly after we received orders that the 2nd Guards Brigade would pass through us in the morning, and that then the Battalion would be withdrawn.

'At 5 a.m. the first wave of the Guards Brigade formed up, and our Companies withdrew just before our artillery barrage opened at 5.20 a.m.

'At Nine Wood a short halt was made, and from there the Battalion moved back to rest in billets in the trenches just east of Flesquières.

'Our total casualties for the attack were :

	Killed.	*Wounded.*	*Missing.*
Officers . .	—	4	–
Other Ranks .	18	71	5

'We took about 200 prisoners.'

Our 1st Battalion were not again seriously engaged in the Great War.

On the same day, October 8, our 13th Battalion took part in the attack of the 37th Division, IV Corps, on the Masnières–Beaurevoir Line just north of Bel Aise. Their 'War Diary' tells us :

'Up to zero the night was quiet. At 4.30 a.m. our guns opened. By 5.10 a.m. the barrage had started forward. The barrage, although excellent, had not entirely broken the resistance, and D Company came under heavy fire, also they found the wire very little damaged, but rising to the occasion they poured quickly through the gaps, and deployed immediately on the other side, and had gained their objective by 7.30 a.m. The Division gained all their objectives, took many prisoners, the Battalion alone taking over 300.'

Our 4th Battalion were also engaged on October 8. The following account of the operation is taken from their War Records in the 'Chronicle':

'Orders came on the morning of the 7th to move forthwith to a position of readiness for further operations, which were to take place on the morning of the 8th. This fight consisted in the establishment of various posts in the neighbourhood of Marliches, forming part of the operations undertaken by the 66th and 38th Divisions; the latter to attack simultaneously north of Villers-Outreaux. The assembly was carried out with rapidity, owing to excellent guides provided for us.

'The operation was successful as far as we were concerned, and the posts established, but the advance on Marliches Farm was held up by machine-gun nests. At eleven o'clock the situation was very difficult, owing to machine-gun fire from Villers-Outreaux and continuous shelling of all the high ground, which appeared to be under direct observation from the enemy.

'At noon it was ascertained that all was quiet at Marliches Farm. The 25th Division having gone through our troops, at 3 p.m. we got orders to withdraw our posts to Vauxhall Quarry. During this fight Lieutenant Preece was killed, Lieutenants Munnion, Debnam, Crosby, and 2nd Lieutenant Austin were wounded; amongst the other ranks there were 12 killed and 40 wounded; we captured 2 officers, 111 other ranks, 1 field gun, and 49 machine guns.

'The Battalion accomplished a very difficult task successfully.

* * * * *

'The whole of the ground over which the Battalion advanced was under direct observation of the enemy, and there were a number of carefully constructed nests of machine guns, strongly manned and carefully sighted, to be overcome in the fighting.'

The enemy were now in full retreat all along their line.

From September 27 to October 10 we had taken 48,500 prisoners and 620 guns.

Our successes affected the position all the way to the east. The enemy had been putting up a stout resistance, and the progress of the Americans and the French Fourth Army had not been rapid, but now he began falling back all along his front. He withdrew to the Hunding Line running through Rethel and Sissonne, but we were by this time through the northern prolongation of that line, and he could not stay on it.

To turn now to the extreme left: on September 28 the British and Belgians attacked on a front of sixteen miles, from Voormezeele [1] to Dixmude.[2]

By the 30th they had gained ten miles. Our Second Army had taken 4,800 prisoners and 100 guns; the Belgians, 6,000 prisoners and 200 guns. The German retirement spread southwards, till, on October 14, they were back on the Douai Canal Line, in front of the left of the First Army. On that day the Allies advanced again, on a front reaching from Comines to near Dixmude. By evening they were within ten miles of Courtrai on the right, had taken Roulers, and were within two miles of Thourout on the left. Events followed each other rapidly, and by the 23rd the enemy had evacuated the Belgian coast, and was back on the line of the River Scheldt and the Oude-Schipdonck [3] Canal.

The Fourth, Third, and First Armies continued to follow up the enemy, but were not ready to attack him in his new line till October 17. The interval had not been without some severe fighting, but our 16th Battalion was the only one of our regiment to be engaged.

On October 11 the 98th Brigade, 33rd Division, were holding the line of the River Selle, while the enemy's front line was the Le Cateau–Solesmes railway, which was strongly wired and was some 500 yards from the river.

The account of this very glorious failure is taken from the 'Chronicle' of 1918:

[1] Map I. [2] Map VIII. [3] Not shown in Map.

'The 11th passed without incident, and in the evening a conference of Commanding Officers and Adjutants was held at Brigade Headquarters. At this conference it was learned that the Brigade had been ordered to make an attack across the River Selle to capture the line of the Le Cateau–Solesmes railway, and to consolidate on the high ground, 1,500 yards east of that railway. A mere glance at the map showed that even supposing the enemy were in the last stages of demoralisation such a task could not be undertaken lightly.

'As in the attack for the line of the Canal de l'Escaut, the advance would be made from high ground which fell at first gently and later rapidly until the river was reached, after which it rose sharply to the railway line, which, at this part, was alternately high embankment and deep cuttings, thence the ground rose gently, until its highest point was reached, some 1,500 yards east of the railway line. Intersecting these contours, i.e. running from west to east, were several ravines. The enemy had selected his position with much skill, and had wired the west side of the railway fairly thickly, with the help of forced civilian labour. Such was the position the Brigade were asked to take, and one felt that if success was to attend the operation all the qualities for which the Regiment is famous would be needed to the full. During the night 11th/12th two companies of the Worcestershire Regiment moved up, crossed the Selle River, and formed a covering party for the Royal Engineers, who put bridges across. The Royal Engineers also ran tapes from the bridges to the Le Cateau–Neuvilly Road. The work of the Royal Engineers was splendidly performed, in spite of the flooding of the northern portion of the river, which necessitated the hasty construction of bridges in places other than those first intended. The Battalion moved from its positions at Troisvilles at 01.00 hours on the 12th in a drizzling rain, which impeded movement, but, nevertheless, all were in position on the Neuvilly–Montay Road by 04.00 hours. At 05.00 hours the Battalion attacked in two columns, consisting of A Company with C Company in support as left column, and D Company with B Company in support as right column. The attack was to be made without a barrage, and in order that both columns might move simultaneously a message rocket was fired in a forward direction. This was the signal for the advance, and as soon as it was fired, both columns moved forward with the greatest dash. The enemy were standing to, awaiting attack, and opened a very heavy machine-gun fire immediately. In spite of this and the uncut wire the advance was pushed, and many splendid acts of gallantry were performed by Lewis-gun teams and by isolated parties of men who would not be denied.

'Rifleman Locket, finding the leading platoons of D Company held up by wire and machine guns, crawled underneath the wire, and, single-handed, rushed the railway embankment, capturing and dismantling 3 machine guns, killing their teams and capturing 5 prisoners. This splendid act enabled D Company to continue the advance, in spite of the fact that 2nd Lieutenant N. F. Surry, commanding, and 2nd Lieutenant F. G. Budd, M.M., the only other officer, had been killed and mortally wounded respectively in the initial stages of the attack. Without the slightest hesitation these splendid men continued the advance, though, owing to the loss of their officers, they were not certain when their objective had been reached. Seeing the situation, Captain W. C. Coates came forward and assumed command of D Company, as well as of B Company, and arranged consolidation.

'In the meantime a similar situation had arisen in the case of the left column. A Company were held up, and C Company were close upon them before they were aware of this. Captain Thomas set out to ascertain the situation, and he was able to find a place where the machine-gun fire was a little high, owing to the formation of the ground. With the assistance of some men he cut a lane through the wire at this place, and very soon both companies had passed through and the embankment was clear. By 09.00 hours it was established that the Battalion had entirely gained its objective, though the battalions on either flank had not been so fortunate. The lack of a reserve company was strongly felt at this moment, as the formation of defensive flanks was imperative without any delay. The left column sent for reinforcements of some sort, as they were entirely "in the air," and were so thin that they could do nothing. Accordingly the one remaining gun was sent to them. No information could be obtained as to the progress of the attack on the left, which it was feared had failed.

'The Commanding Officer [Pardoe] decided to move Battalion Headquarters forward to a quarry situated on the railway, in order to gain a better touch with the situation, which it was felt needed clearing up. Accordingly at 09.00

hours the Commanding Officer, Adjutant, and Intelligence Officer went forward from the ravine. At this time the enemy put down a very severe barrage, concentrating on the ravine in which Battalion Headquarters was situated, and on the bridges across the Selle. For fifteen minutes the barrage remained intense, and under the cover of this, enemy troops were moved up to positions level with, and even in rear of, our right column. He was assisted in this by the fact that a few yards north of our left flank there was a deep ravine running at right angles to the front. The first intimation received of this attack was on the arrival of the Commanding Officer and his party at the railway: they found large parties of the enemy working down and came face to face with them at about 20 yards' range. Heavy machine-gun and rifle fire was immediately opened, to which the Battalion Headquarters party replied as best they could with three revolvers and three rifles. Lieut.-Colonel Pardoe was hit severely after a few moments of this unequal duel, and one runner was killed. Fortunately, the Lewis gun which had been sent to Captain Thomas was intercepted, and with the aid of this the very determined attempt on the part of the enemy to cut off the whole battalion was checked, and they were held off with loss for about half an hour. These movements were seen by the troops in front, and accordingly the officers on the spot decided to withdraw and to take up positions on the railway embankment and to hold on there if possible.

'An unfortunate incident occurred at this juncture. A brigade on the left of the Battalion was conducting a relief, and these troops were seen moving in comparatively large bodies to the rear. This was mistaken for a general withdrawal on the British front, and our officers had some difficulty in rallying their tired and disorganised troops to meet a situation which was unfortunate and unforeseen. This incident, coupled with the very heavy shell fire which was being continued, caused remnants of the companies to move farther back than the railway, and reorganisation was not possible until the line of the Le Cateau–Neuvilly Road had been reached on the west bank of the Selle River.

'During these incidents a message had been sent back to Major Willis, who had been able to obtain two companies of the Worcestershire Regiment as reinforcements. Unfortunately, the damage had been done by the time these troops arrived, and to push these troops forward was merely to add to the disorganisation and congestion which already existed on the Le Cateau Road, which was for the moment the front line. Energetic measures were taken to re-form the remnants, and two companies were provisionally formed, A and C, under the command of Captain Thomas, and B and D under Captain Coates. These and 2nd Lieutenants Nayler and Jeffery were the only remaining officers with companies.

'The Battalion was later reinforced by the 1st Battalion Middlesex Regiment, and ordered to repeat the attack, zero hour being fixed at 17.00 hours. This was later altered to 17.50 hours. The attack was eventually cancelled, and the Battalion ordered to establish posts during the night in conjunction with the Middlesex Regiment and a detachment of Royal Engineers. Throughout this very trying period Captains Thomas and Coates were indefatigable. Their splendid reorganisation and the very clear and concise reports they were able to render were of inestimable value throughout the action. The Battalion was relieved by units of the 38th Division on the night 13th/14th, and moved to Troisvilles.

'The casualties in this action were;

Officers

Killed: 2nd Lieutenant N. F. Surry.
Died of Wounds: 2nd Lieutenant F. G. Budd.
Wounded: Lieut.-Colonel Pardoe.
Wounded and Missing: 2nd Lieutenant A. H. Villiers [prisoner of war].

Other Ranks

Killed	24
Died of Wounds	4
Wounded	76
Wounded and Missing . .	15

'This represents one-third of the numbers that accompanied the Battalion into action.'

After a few days' work on their communications, the Fourth, Third, and First Armies were ready for another blow, which was begun by the Fourth Army on October 17. The outline of the account of the final advance of the

Allies to victory has been taken chiefly from 'Sir Douglas Haig's Command,' and the quotation marks which follow show verbatim extracts from that work. By the 25th these three armies had advanced five to seven and a half miles on a twenty-six-mile front, and taken 20,000 prisoners and 475 guns. 'Their line ran from the Oise–Sambre Canal, north of Etreux, along the western outskirts of the Mormal Forest to south of Valenciennes.'[1]

The series of operations was opened by an attack by our Fourth Army, with the French First Army on its right. 'By the 19th the British had reached the Oise–Sambre Canal north of Oisy, and the French had filled in the angle between the canal and the British right.' The enemy fell back on a new line between Pouilly-sur-Serre[2] and Mont-d'Origny.[3]

On the 20th the Third and First Armies joined in north of Le Cateau, and carried the line of the river Selle.

By the end of October the enemy was in a bad way. The British were within seven or eight miles of Aulnoye, so the railway on which the whole of the German communications depended was under the fire of our heavy artillery.

Our 2nd Battalion took part in the attack of the Fourth Army on October 17, under Major H. F. E. Smith, D.S.O., Lieut.-Colonel E. G. St. Aubyn having gone to command a brigade. The following is the account of the action, taken from the 'Chronicle' of 1918:

'Early on October 17, at 1.30 a.m., we went to our assembly positions in the Bois de Busigny. The plan of attack was the 2nd Battalion, working in conjunction with the 1st Northamptons on our right and an American battalion on our left, was to follow close behind the attack of the 6th

[1] Map VIII. [2] Ten miles east of La Fère (Map V).
[3] Nine miles east of St. Quentin.

Division, and, when the latter had gained their objective, leap-frog through and carry on with the attack.

'The morning mist, together with the smoke barrage, made direction difficult to follow, and the Companies were for the moment disconnected. They, however, all got in touch again before we were due to pass through the 6th Division, and we continued to push forward in section artillery formation, A Company on the left, B on the right, D in support, and C in reserve. When the moment came to pass through the 6th Division we found that they were digging in some 800 to 1,000 yards short of their objective.

'At first little opposition was met with, but the shelling was fairly heavy. The day went well until the enclosed country north of La Vallée Mulâtre was reached. It was here that the enemy had a great number of well-concealed nests of machine guns in hedges, etc., which kept up a big volume of fire. One of D Company's platoons, working well, succeeded in outflanking two of these guns, but the remainder held up the attack. Consequently B and C Companies were ordered to work right round the left flank. While carrying out this movement, they had to deal with a sunken road to their left rear, which was still strongly held by the Germans, as the Americans were a little late in dealing with this obstacle. However, the obstacle was overcome, 30 prisoners taken, and later these two companies, together with one platoon of Americans, successfully rushed five enemy machine guns, which were firing from a railway embankment. Gallant as was this little affair, it did not ease the situation on the right. Accordingly A and D Companies made another attempt to move forward, with the help of three "whippet" tanks.

'This was again frustrated, partly by the enfilade fire, which was still very galling, and partly because the "whippets" were also soon placed *hors de combat* by anti-tank guns.

'Thus, unable to make progress, we held on to the ground already won and consolidated. It was very satisfactory that we had got farther than any battalion in the Division. During the night the 2nd Battalion Royal Scots pushed through us, but they too found that they could make but little headway, their flanks being in the air.

'An extremely interesting point about this fight was that we were engaged against the same enemy division that the Battalion had met at Nieuport in July 1917, and we actually took an officer prisoner who had been present at the battle of Nieuport. Time had gone full circle: [" The wheel," please! *Author*] the debt was paid. We took 100 prisoners, 14 guns, 12 trench-mortars, and many machine guns.

'Our losses in the fight were:

Officers

Killed: 2nd Lieutenants J. MacM. Hunter, A. C. Gant, W. S. Gibbs.

Died of Wounds: 2nd Lieutenant A. J. Stephen.

Wounded: Captain J. R. P. Maxwell; Lieutenant B. V. Cherry; 2nd Lieutenants T. O. S. White, T. Scatter, F. Tan, M.M.

Other Ranks

Killed	16
Died of Wounds	6
Wounded	135
Missing	16.'

On the same day our 4th Battalion had a very similar experience to that of the 16th Battalion on October 12, the terrain being almost identical, though the scene was some miles higher up the river Selle. The following account is an extract from their War Records:

'We had a quiet time until the 16th, when we moved up to take part in a major operation on the next day.

'This operation consisted in the crossing of the river Selle by the 50th Division, the 27th [American] Division being on our right, and the 1st King's Own Yorkshire Light Infantry on our left flank.

'C and D Companies were detailed to carry out the attack, with A Company in close support, and B in reserve. Lieut.-Colonel Brady and the Company Commanders reconnoitred the position, and selected sites on the river for portable bridges. There was some misunderstanding as regards the American barrage, which placed our point of assembly in danger, so Colonel Brady decided to assemble the Battalion 200 yards east of the Sunken Road.

'At about 4.30 a.m. on the morning of the 17th the Germans

put down a heavy barrage on St. Souplet, Captain Nutting, commanding B Company, being amongst the casualties, the other companies in the assembly area escaped without loss ; our barrage fell at 5.20 a.m., but owing to the American barrage, which fell at a line 200 yards west of the river, the attacking companies were unable to advance under the protection of our own barrage until the line of the railway had been reached, when the American barrage had worked forward in a line with our own.

'The crossing of the river was effected without great enemy hindrance, and bridging arrangements worked satisfactorily. A dense fog now came on, making it impossible to see anything at 50 yards' distance ; the mist did not clear until noon. At six o'clock the Battalion Headquarters and B Company, crossing the river, came at once under heavy machine-gun fire from the railway in the American area ; this nest of guns was located by sound, and silenced by B Company at 8.30 a.m.

'A message came in to say that the Battalion was within 600 yards of their objective ; they advanced in face of heavy machine-gun fire. The Officers Commanding C and D Companies, Captains Antrobus and Eden, also Lieutenants Stewart and Holgate, were wounded ; casualties were not heavy amongst the other ranks ; progress was slow owing to the fog, and the difficulty of keeping direction very great, the mist also prevented us locating the enemy machine guns. In spite of these obstacles the objective was gained at ten o'clock, and consolidation began along the line some 200 yards east of the road. An hour later the enemy delivered a strong counter-attack against the King's Own Yorkshire Light Infantry on our left, and, forcing them to withdraw, the left flank of the Battalion was thus exposed to the German machine-gun fire ; Colonel Brady therefore retired his left flank to the west of the road.

'About noon, under aeroplane direction, our artillery opened vigorously on the Germans, and most effectively stopped their attempting to advance. However, they kept up a heavy machine-gun fire on our position throughout the day, making movements very difficult. Eventually, owing to both flanks coming under heavy machine-gun fire, causing heavy casualties, the Battalion was ordered to move to the high ground at 3 p.m.

'At 4 p.m. news was received that the 7th Wiltshires, supported by the 3rd Battalion of the Royal Fusiliers, would move forward to re-occupy the position, and we were to stand fast unless required to deal with a counter-attack.

'It was then decided that there should be a forward move along the whole Divisional front, to capture the main objective, on the morning of the 18th.

'On the 18th our task was to move along the right flank of the Division, and maintain liaison with the 27th American Division, and give assistance if required to capture La Roue Farm. At 5 a.m. on October 18 we advanced with the Americans until the line of advance had cleared Le Quennelet Farm; here the Americans on the right flank of our Battalion lost direction, and swung half-left across the battle front, hanging up our advance for several hours; this accounts for the delay in the capturing of the objective.

'At 9 p.m. the Battalion withdrew. Having gone into action with 20 officers and 307 other ranks, our casualties were 7 officers and 117 other ranks [including 2nd Lieutenant H. I. Williams, killed in action]; we captured 110 prisoners, 2 field guns, and a large number of machine guns.

'The success of the Battalion in this operation was in a measure due to the fine work of Captain Wells, commanding A Company, who, at a critical moment, when the two company commanders were wounded, on his own initiative brought up his support Company by most successful and enterprising leadership, and led the attacking companies forward to their objective.'

The position, which had withstood the efforts of our 16th Battalion to capture it on October 12, having been taken by other troops while the 33rd Division was out of the line, this position formed the jumping-off line for a fresh attack by that Division on October 23. The Battalion was not in the fighting line on the first day. The story of their capture of the final objective of their Brigade is thus told in the 'Chronicle' of 1918:

'The situation at midnight on October 23/24 was that the 100th Brigade occupied outposts on the north-eastern edge of Vendegies Wood, a little in rear of the final objective of the

19th Brigade, which had not yet been carried. Orders were then received for the advance to be continued at 05.30 hours on the 24th, with a view to securing the line Poix-du-Nord–Englefontaine, which was the original task set for the 100th Brigade. The enemy resistance became much stiffer at this period, and by the evening of the 24th the objective had only been partially secured. The night 24th/25th was spent in endeavours to secure the whole line, but owing to the closeness of the country C Company lost their way, and the situation was much the same after this night's work as it was on the previous day.

'Accordingly a process of filtration was started by B and C Companies, with some success. In the meantime, a very bright little incident occurred on the front of A Company, who were holding their objective on the left of the line. A small post belonging to this Company was counter-attacked by about fifty of the enemy and driven in. Lieutenant Mather immediately made arrangements for a local counter-attack with the means at his disposal. He caused two flanking parties, each consisting of one N.C.O. and 4 men, to work round each side of the post. This move was so successful that the enemy decamped immediately, leaving two machine guns in our hands, and suffering some loss from the pursuit by fire which the flanking parties were able to open. For his good work on this occasion Sergeant Beresford received the Distinguished Conduct Medal.

'Later in the day B and C Companies were able to report their objectives gained, and this was the situation on the evening of the 25th, the Battalion being in touch along the whole front.

'Three days of splendid effort on the part of the men had brought about this result. The Battalion had advanced over ten kilometres of ground under fire for the whole distance, and fighting for a good portion of it. All ranks accordingly felt very satisfied with the operations, and looked forward to the relief which had been promised that evening. This, however, was not to be. Corps called for another effort, which entailed the complete capture of the village of Englefontaine and the advance of the line some 1,500 yards. Weary as they were, the Battalion responded most nobly to this last call, which, even if successful, would bring them almost to the limit of human endurance. Advance orders had been received at about 19.00 hours on October 25 that an attack was contemplated, and all commanding officers were ordered to be present at the Headquarters of the Battalion for the final verbal issue of orders by the Brigade Major at 20.00 hours. At about 22.00 hours a very dishevelled Brigade Major arrived. He was covered from head to foot in mud, and was cut about the head. He had started from Brigade Headquarters with orders rather later than was desirable from the point of view of the success of the operation, and on a very dark night was riding at a canter to the conference. He overtook and collided with an L.G.S. wagon. Horse and rider took a toss into the ditch, and to complete the discomfiture, the horse used the Brigade Major's head—fortunately protected by a steel helmet—as a stepping-stone to get back to the road. In spite of his shaken condition, however, the Brigade Major gave a clear account of the contemplated operations, the conference being completed by 23.00 hours on October 25, leaving two hours for final arrangements to be made, zero hour being fixed for 01.00 hours 26th.

'The dispositions of the Battalion at the time were as follows: the front line extended from the cross-roads south of the "R" [first] in Raucourt to the "A" in Englefontaine,[1] and was held from north to south by A, C, and B Companies respectively, with D Company in reserve in a quarry at about the "N" [first] in Englefontaine, Battalion Headquarters being at a farm-house about 200 yards south of the quarry. The operation which the Battalion were called upon to do was a flanking movement to the north of the village of Englefontaine, whilst the Glasgow Highlanders and 2nd Worcesters occupied themselves with the village itself. The 1st Queen's, about 200 strong, were ordered to assist the Battalion in the operation, the plan of which was as follows: at zero, plus 7, the Queen's were to move forward in two detachments, one along the small road running south-east from the left flank of A Company, whilst the other detachment advanced north-east along the main Bavai Road. These detachments were to meet on the small piece of road just east of the last "E" in Englefontaine, where they were to commence consolidation. Fourteen minutes after this movement started the Battalion were to move forward, mop up the ground which had been encircled by the Queen's, and eventually to consolidate along the

[1] These references apply to some other map.

line of the road running north from the main Bavai Road through the " O " in Raucourt.

'At zero, plus 7, the 1st Queen's commenced to move forward, and at zero plus 21—01.21 hours—we also commenced to move.

'Owing to the weakness of the Battalion and the necessity of getting touch during the night operation, D Company were ordered forward to take over a portion of the front from A and C Companies, thus thickening the front line a little ; and accordingly the order of battle was from north to south, A, D, C, and B Companies with no reserve, excepting the Battalion Headquarters Lewis-gun team with two guns.

'From the commencement the enemy surrendered freely, and, with the exception of D company, no resistance was encountered. D Company were unfortunate, losing two sections from two successive shells, and also encountering heavy machine-gun fire from a nest of guns. This caused D Company to lose direction, but the rapid advance of the companies on each flank soon caused this nest to surrender. Later inspection of the spot showed it to consist of no less than fifteen guns lined along a hedge. In view of this, D Company were lucky to get off with only seventeen casualties, including ten from the two shells mentioned above. The whole operation was completed with very few casualties, each battalion operating capturing at least two prisoners for every casualty sustained. By 08.00 hours October 26 all objectives had been gained ; but owing to the trouble experienced by D Company, the order of battle had now slightly altered ; it now read from north to south, A, C, D, and B Companies. The country was here thickly covered with fruit trees and hedges, and the whole morning was spent in cleaning up isolated machine-gun posts near to the Battalion front. Several small parties showed great enterprise in this, and during the morning 4 machine guns and a few prisoners were captured by stalking movements on the part of small parties. During the afternoon and evening the Battalion was relieved by the 17th Royal Welsh Fusiliers, the relief being completed without incident by 21.00 hours 26th. By midnight a weary but triumphant Battalion were resting in billets in Forest, caring nothing for the long-range shelling by which the village was harassed throughout the night.

'The casualties in the operations of October 22–26 were as follows :

Officers

Killed: 2nd Lieutenant D. R. Wilson, M.C.
Wounded: Major P. A. W. Laye (remaining at duty); Lieutenant F. J. Horth; 2nd Lieutenant G. H. Coe.

Other Ranks

Killed	13
Wounded	85
Missing	1
	99.'

Though nothing has been said of the operations of our allies to the east of the sphere of the British Expeditionary Force, they had all this time been progressing steadily, and the retreat of the enemy along his whole line had kept pace with that of the part covering the decisive point.

On October 31 the force under the King of the Belgians had again advanced, and had driven the enemy across the Scheldt. On November 1 the Americans pushed on again in the Argonne with the Fourth French Army on their left. The enemy opposite to them began falling back to the Meuse, and by November 4 their line ran from Stenay on the Meuse to Attigny on the Aisne.

On November 1 the First Army and part of the Third resumed the advance, and by the 3rd had taken Valenciennes.

'In the early morning of November 4 the Fourth, Third and First Armies attacked on a front of thirty miles from the Sambre to north of Valenciennes, the First French Army continuing the battle line for a further nine miles southward on our right, to the neighbourhood of Guise. On the whole of this front the Allies went forward, the French to a depth of one half to two miles and the British to a depth of from two to over five miles. Before dawn on November 5, British troops had reached the eastern edge of the Mormal Forest, from six to seven miles from their assembly positions. Despite the fact that on the First Army front the German withdrawal had already begun, on the first day over 10,000 prisoners were passed back by the British units engaged, and over 150 guns reported captured. The total captures by the British reached 19,000 prisoners and 450 guns, the increased proportion of guns to prisoners telling its own tale of German demoralisation. In addition the First French Army took 5,000 prisoners and many guns.' [' Sir Douglas Haig's Command.']

This was the end. The German resistance was over.

' On November 5, the day following our attack, the enemy retreated to a depth of from four to seven miles on a front of over ninety miles from Rethel to beyond Valenciennes. On November 6 the movement was continued on a front of 120 miles from the Meuse westwards, to a maximum depth of some nine or ten miles at the deepest part of the salient. So day by day the retreat continued, till on November 11 it had progressed to a depth of nearly forty miles on a front of 180 miles from east of the Meuse to Ghent.' [' Sir Douglas Haig's Command.']

Four of our battalions took part in the last week's fighting.

On November 4 the 2nd Battalion took part in the crossing of the Oise–Sambre Canal by the 1st Division between Petit-Cambresis and Catillon.

This action was a very interesting example of an opposed crossing by the use of floating bridges placed in position by the attacking troops.

The aeroplane photographs showed several footbridges in use by the enemy, but it was not thought advisable to use them, as they were certain to be well registered and, probably, prepared for destruction.

The 2nd Infantry Brigade, which was on the right of the 1st Division, attacked with the 2nd K.R.R.C. on the right, the 2nd Royal Sussex on the left, and the 1st Northants in reserve.

The country west of the canal was well adapted to the concealment of troops assembling for attack, as it was intersected by high and thick hedges, through which gaps were cut by night to allow the troops to move to their assembly positions about 300 yards from the canal bank, which was held by the enemy, who also had a few posts on the west bank.

The assembly of the attacking brigades and two field companies Royal Engineers of the 1st Division was carried out, and a certain amount of cover dug, without alarming the enemy.

At zero hour (05.45 hours) a heavy barrage came down on the line of the canal. At zero plus 3 minutes the barrage lifted and crept on till it reached the first objective, which was the line of the road from Petit-Cambresis to Chapelle-de-la-Brique, just across the canal from Catillon. Its farthest point was about 2,000 yards beyond the canal.

The 1st Brigade had an easy passage, four bridges being established 10 minutes after zero, and in another 10 minutes the two leading battalions of the Brigade were across.

The 2nd Brigade had more difficulty in placing their bridges, and during the consequent check they were heavily shelled, but, as the report of the 1st Division relates :

'The fine example of the Battalion Commander (2nd Royal Sussex) and of the Officer Commanding 409th Field Company, aided by their officers, however, was paralleled by the resolute bearing of all the troops—the infantry and Royal Engineers co-operating with the greatest determination—and in spite of machine-gun fire . . . the first bridge was in position by 25 minutes after zero.'

One company, 2nd K.R.R.C., had been ordered to cross independently on the right of the Brigade by one of the enemy's foot-bridges, or, failing it, by the use of Berthon boats. The bridge proved to be impassable, and the Berthon boats were too unwieldy to be brought up over the various intervening obstacles; the Company therefore rejoined the Battalion, and crossed with them. The Battalion crossed after the leading companies of the Royal Sussex, and then deployed on the right of that regiment for the attack on the first position.

Once the bridges were in position the enemy offered little resistance, and the first objective was quickly captured with many prisoners.

After the capture of the first objective there was a pause of an hour and a half for reorganisation, under a protective barrage. The advance was then resumed. In the attack on the second objective, in which three companies of the 2nd Battalion took part, the enemy surrendered freely. Our losses for the day were:

Officers

Killed: Lieutenant H. G. Oxley and 2nd Lieutenant S. Burroughes.
Wounded: 2nd Lieutenant W. E. Booth.

Other Ranks

Killed	10
Missing	3
Wounded	59

The next day the Battalion took part in the resumed advance, but, as the front narrowed, were squeezed out, and at 4 p.m. marched back to billets at Wassigny. They were not again engaged.

On November 4 our 13th Battalion took part in the

attack by the 111th Brigade on a line running north and south through the village of Louvignies-lez-Quesnoy. On the right of the Brigade the 13th K.R.R.C. were to take the first objective, and then, when the 10th Royal Fusiliers had passed through them, to be responsible for 'mopping up' the village of Louvignies.

At 05.30 hours the barrage opened, and at 05.34 hours the leading companies of the 13th K.R.R.C. and 13th Rifle Brigade advanced, the former closely followed by the 10th Royal Fusiliers. The enemy replied with a heavy barrage, which fortunately fell behind the attacking troops, and did little damage beyond interfering with the laying of wires between battalions and the brigade. Both battalions encountered strong opposition. Our 13th Battalion came under heavy machine-gun fire from the orchards and hedges on the western outskirts of Louvignies. In many cases, as soon as our men were within hand-to-hand fighting distance the enemy surrendered, but here and there more determined resistance was encountered, and had to be dealt with by the bayonet. About 70 dead Germans were counted on the front of C Company alone. Both battalions had reached their objective by the scheduled time, 07.15 hours.

The village was 'mopped up' by the supporting companies, B and D, and soon cleared of the enemy. One N.C.O. of B Company fought three Germans in a cellar, and killed all three, his weapon being a small hand-axe. About 7 officers and 270 other ranks were taken prisoners. The village was reported clear at 08.15 hours.

The Battalion spent the rest of the day consolidating the position they had won, and during the following night their division was relieved by the 5th Division and the Battalion moved into billets at Beaurain.

Their casualties were :

Officers

Wounded 8

Other Ranks

Killed, wounded, and missing 98

Their captures included 3 field guns, 12 trench-mortars, and 36 machine guns.

The share of our 4th Battalion in the final operations is thus described in their War Records, from the 'Chronicle' of 1918:

'The operations in which we were to take part on November 4 was [*sic*] for the Battalion to advance to the attack up the Laie-de-Mont-Carmel,[1] and having reached the line of our objective, to consolidate in depth. The 1st Battalion of the King's Own Yorkshire Light Infantry were to advance simultaneously by the Route-de-Fontaine,[1] and the 6th Battalion of the Royal Irish Fusiliers up the Route-de-Landrecies.[1]

'Zero was fixed at 6.15 a.m. We soon came in contact with the enemy, and a number of casualties were incurred in dislodging them from their position. Considerable assistance was received from an armoured car moving along the Route-de-Landrecies, and from this point onward, continuous touch was maintained with the enemy, and the Germans appeared to be fighting a rearguard action with their machine guns; the ground afforded ample cover for this form of warfare, and made a rapid advance difficult. It was not until 3.45 p.m. that our advance guard reached the eastern edge of the wood. After some skilful manœuvring on the part of D Company, the crest of the ridge on which the Germans were making a determined stand was captured just as dark was falling. We consolidated on the ridge, then held by the 1st King's Own Yorkshire Light Infantry, and with the 6th Royal Irish Fusiliers on our left.

'C and D Companies established themselves in an old German trench, with B Company in support, and A Company in reserve.

'At about midnight Brigade orders reached us with instructions that the Battalion would attack at 6.30 a.m. on the following day, our objective being the north bank of the Sambre River. A Battalion of the East Surrey Regiment,

[1] Not shown in Map.

part of the 18th Division, was to attack on our left, and the 6th Royal Irish Fusiliers on our right.

'The enemy shelled our line at intervals during the night, A Company suffering some casualties; our total casualties throughout the day were 3 officers and 30 other ranks, the 3 officers wounded being Lieutenant H. S. Bennett, 2nd Lieutenants F. Warren and F. G. Schofield.

'On Guy Fawkes' Day the Battalion advanced to the attack, as previously arranged, at 8.30 a.m.; A and B Companies held the river bank with a series of Lewis-gun posts, with the remainder of the Battalion in close support. The weather was extremely unkind, raining all day and the following night; our casualties during this fight were slight. During the night 2nd Lieutenant Fuller took out a patrol and returned with valuable information required by higher authority.

'On November 6 the 151st Infantry Brigade concentrated in the Hatchette Farm[1] area, and about midday orders came for the Battalion to march to billets in Noyelles. We reached our billets at 4 p.m.; fires were soon got going, and we dried ourselves as far as possible. We were not, however, allowed to remain in the place long, as, at 9 a.m. [? 9 p.m.], orders were received for the Brigade to march at 6 a.m. for St.-Remy-Chaussée, where we were to pass through with the 150th Infantry Brigade, and advance to attack the final objective, the Maubeuge–Avesnes Road.

'The Battalion marched at 6 a.m. on November 7, and arrived at St.-Remy-Chaussée at 8.40. On arrival it was discovered that the 19th Infantry Brigade had also established their Headquarters there, and we were told that a battalion of this brigade was pushing through the wood on the north side of the road. The Battalion then advanced as soon as possible on the south side of the road, suffering a number of casualties. On debouching from the road into an orchard, the advance guard met with stubborn opposition, and the Commanding Officer, Major G. A. Tryon, M.C., went forward to review the situation.

'Arrangements were then made to dislodge the enemy, which were successful, and the intermediate objective was captured at 11.15 a.m. Orders were then sent that no further advance would be made until instructions were sent to the Battalion to do so; the position was therefore consolidated

[1] Not shown in map.

and intermittently shelled by the Germans. C and D Companies sustained fairly heavy casualties.

'At 1 p.m. orders came to advance to the final objective.

'The country was difficult to work over, and the wood on the line of our advance was discovered to be dense with thick undergrowth. The German machine-gun fire was intense, and the resistance was stiffening.

'We had lost half of our fighting strength, and no touch could be obtained with the units on either flank; indeed, we were subjected to considerable machine-gun fire from each side, showing that flanking troops were held up.

'It was eventually decided to consolidate at 4 p.m. in a position slightly in rear, which appeared suitable.

'Touch was obtained with the D Company of the 1st King's Own Yorkshire Light Infantry, on the Doulers–Mont-Doulers Road, but no connection could be found with the unit on our left. During these operations the losses of the Battalion were: officers: Major G. A. Tryon, killed; 2nd Lieutenant [H.] Seymour (died of wounds); 2nd Lieutenant Austin, 90 other ranks, wounded.

'During the night two battalions of the Royal Welsh Fusiliers passed through our lines, and at 9 a.m. on November 8 orders came from the 151st Infantry Brigade that the advance would be continued to the final objective (Maubeuge–Avesnes Road).

'B Company, under the command of Captain Wells, M.C., formed the advance guard, with D Company, under 2nd Lieutenant W. Methven, and C Company, under Captain C. R. Truter, M.C., in close support, with A Company, under 2nd Lieutenant Fuller, in reserve.

'At 5.30 a.m., Lieut.-Colonel Brady, D.S.O., arrived at Battalion Headquarters, and took over command from Captain M. L. Buller.

'The attack was launched, and owing to the enemy machine-gun fire from both front and right flank, progress was not rapid; however, we continued to push ahead, and the position allotted as our objective was captured by 9.30 a.m. We suffered fairly heavy casualties during the advance, and the position was subject to fairly heavy shelling after capture, which resulted in further casualties during consolidation.

'At 2.30 p.m. the Battalion was relieved by the 2nd Royal Dublin Fusiliers, and marched back to billets to St.-Remy-

Chaussée. Our total casualties incurred during the fighting from November 4–8, both inclusive, were 8 officers and 173 other ranks.

'The greatest difficulty with which we had to contend on the 8th and 9th was the extreme fatigue of the men, due to our rapid advances and the great distance covered. It was with sincere regret that we learned on the 9th that 2nd Lieutenant Seymour had died from his wounds received on the 8th, and other officer casualties, in addition to Major G. A. Tryon, M.C., already mentioned, were Lieutenants F. E. G. Hayward, M.M., H. S. Bennett, 2nd Lieutenants F. Warren, A. J. Austin, F. J. Schofield, and Captain J. J. Edmond (R.A.M.C.) wounded.'

The 16th Battalion, since their fight on October 24 and 25, had spent their time clearing up the battlefield and reorganising. On November 4 they moved up into assembly positions east of the village of Hecq, preparatory to the attack on the Mormal Forest. The account of the action is taken from the 'Chronicle' of 1918 :

'The attack of the Battalion was due to commence at 05.00 hours on November 5, but at 02.00 hours sudden orders to advance were received. These orders were issued owing to the fact that at about midnight 4th/5th a German mounted orderly was captured, and on investigation he was found to have in his possession despatches ordering the immediate retirement of certain advanced elements of the enemy forces in the Forest.

'The Battalion got on the move immediately, and by 03.00 hours A Company, supported by B Company, had captured the small village of La-Tête-Noir with a few prisoners. Rain was falling steadily all the time, which made the whole operation most unpleasant. After this action touch was lost with the enemy until just before 10.00 hours, when he was again encountered near the village of Berlaimont. By 10.00 hours A Company, with B Company on their right, were clearing the village, and were commanding the crossings of the river Sambre. C Company were in support to this operation, and D Company in reserve. Touch was established with troops both on the right and left of the Battalion.

'The same evening the Battalion was relieved by the 1st Battalion Middlesex Regiment, and moved into Divisional Reserve at Sartbaras [Sart-Bara].

'The following day the Battalion moved to positions of readiness near the river Sambre. The front-line troops had already crossed the river, and information was received that Petit-Maubeuge had fallen into our hands. The Battalion was ordered to cross the river and get into touch with the right flank of the 2nd Worcestershire, and form a defensive flank facing Leval. This was done, and patrols were pushed out, and these cleared the village, which was held by the Battalion by 12.00 hours on the 6th.

'By this time, owing to the very rapid advance which was being carried out on a converging front, the situation was becoming a little confused. Information was received that units of the 50th Division (to whom the 4th Battalion was attached) were approaching the village of Leval from a south-west direction, and accordingly D Company were ordered to gain touch with this Division, which they succeeded in doing by 15.00 hours.

'Elements of the 19th Infantry Brigade passed through the Battalion, who were thus again relieved, and were quartered for the night in Leval, Battalion Headquarters remaining, however, at Sassegnies. Again, however, the respite of the Battalion was to be very short, as it became plainer each minute that the retirement of the enemy was rapidly becoming a rout.

'The Battalion was ordered to concentrate with the rest of the Brigade at Petit-Maubeuge at 07.45 hours on November 7, ready to push on with the pursuit. At this stage Lieut.-Colonel C. H. N. Seymour, D.S.O., who had been very ill from the commencement of the action, became too ill to carry on, and though he summoned his remaining vitality to protest to the Medical Officer, he had eventually to bow to that official's decision and be evacuated to C.C.S.[1] Major A. L. Y. Willis took command of the Battalion, who, in spite of the weather and the very trying days they had experienced, were in splendid fettle and were quite anxious to finish the war with as little delay as possible.

'On arrival at the concentration area near the brewery at Petit-Maubeuge, a brigade conference was held, during which

[1] Casualty Clearing Station.

the Brigadier informed the assembled officers that German delegates had gone to Paris to conclude an armistice. The Battalion then moved to Aulnoye, where hot tea was served to the men. Another conference was called at 14.00 hours, when verbal orders were issued to continue the advance with the eastern edge of the Bois-le-Roy as objective. On reaching the neighbourhood of Pot-de-Vin written orders were received in confirmation of the verbal instructions already issued. The Battalion continued the advance, but before the objective was reached information was received that owing to the shortening of the front our objective was already in the hands of the British troops. Accordingly, a weary battalion marched back in the rain to Petit-Maubeuge, where they were billeted, all being housed by about midnight on November 7/8.'

There they remained till the Armistice was signed.

CHAPTER XV

SIDE-SHOWS

MACEDONIA 1916–18[1]

WE left our 3rd and 4th Battalions in December 1915, when they had just joined the Allied army which was hurriedly digging and wiring a position covering Salonika.

The 4th Battalion remained in that theatre of war till the force was squeezed for reinforcements on the Western Front, in the perilous days of 1918, when it returned to France. The 3rd Battalion remained to the end.

For various reasons the Allied armies in Macedonia have never received the credit which is their due. No one wants to claim for them that they won the war because their opponents were the first to 'crack'; but let us consider what they did do. A fortnight after the commencement of their attack in September 1918, their opponents—a force of just about equal strength to their own—were making straight for home, and Bulgaria was suing for peace. With the Bulgar out of it, Franchet d'Espérey, Commander-in-Chief of the Allies, could afford to leave the Serb third of his force to go and clear their own country of the enemy, while with the other two-thirds of his force—French, British, and Greek—he could turn his attention to the Turk, who had no force at hand with which he could hope to prevent the immediate invasion of Thrace, the opening of the Dardanelles, or the occupation of Constantinople.

Allenby by the end of October had accounted for

[1] Map VII.

practically every Turkish soldier within reach of him, but he could reach no farther. It would be months before he could do the Turk any further harm. His campaign, no doubt, went a long way towards making the Turk want an armistice, but it was that of the army in Macedonia that made him want it in such a hurry.

The general public seems to have shut its eyes to these facts, and no one has ever taken the trouble to open them. Allenby's campaign has always been a popular one: Franchet d'Espérey's has escaped notice, at least in this country. One can excuse the 'man in the street.' He likes to read of cavalry charges in the Plain of Esdraelon and fighting round Damascus, while the Kosturino Pass and the river Maritza mean nothing to him; but those who ought to know better are just as blind. Here is a sample:

> 'Ignoring the facts that Lord Allenby's leadership resulted in the capitulation of Turkey, and was therefore largely responsible for the collapse of the Central Powers.' (From an article on Palestine in the *Quarterly Review* of July 1931, signed H. Charles Woods.)

Sir George Milne has been Chief of the Imperial General Staff for some years, and long may he remain so; but, although every schoolboy knows who took Jerusalem, few students outside the Staff College could say off-hand what British commander was the immediate danger to the Turks when they asked for an armistice.

Though rewarded in the end by such a crushing defeat of their enemy, the Allies in Macedonia had nearly three years of comparative inaction in a pestilential climate, with occasional spasms of none-too-successful operations, to be gone through before that could be achieved.

The original object of the expedition had been to go to

the rescue of Serbia. Too late to do this, and confronted by a victorious Bulgar Army, their immediate task, by the time our 3rd and 4th Battalions joined them, was to provide for their own security by digging in on a line covering Salonika.

The first Allied troops to arrive, one French division and one British from the Dardanelles, landed early in October, and were immediately pushed up-country to the help of the Serbs, for which purpose they were too late and too weak.

By the middle of November, 120,000 Allied troops had landed, two-thirds of which were French, and another British division arrived soon afterwards. Early in December the two divisions that had gone up-country arrived back, considerably the worse for wear. The Bulgars not coming on, the Allies improved on the hurried position they had first taken up by pushing forward, until early in the new year they were holding a line from the Gulf of Orfano to the neighbourhood of Monastir. The British held the right of the line, the French the left, the river Vardar being the boundary between the two.

General Sarrail was in command of the whole force, while the British force was commanded by Sir Bryan Mahon, who, after the first winter, was succeeded by Sir George Milne.

A difficult situation was caused by the fact that the Allies were occupying the country of a neutral Power, which had its own troops holding various points in front of and behind the Allies' line. For long it remained doubtful whether Greece would remain neutral, or join one side or the other. It would take far too much space to tell of all the ups and downs of the political situation. It is enough to say that the Greeks succeeded in remaining on the fence till the summer of 1917, when a good push brought them down on the side of M. Venizelos and the Allies.

Meanwhile, the Greek Army was a great source of danger and anxiety to the Allies, as most of their leaders were whole-heartedly on the side of the Central Powers. However, in May 1916 they overstepped the mark by the handing over of Fort Rupel to the Bulgar. The Allies then gave them the order to quit, and they were gradually withdrawn from Macedonia.

In the summer of 1916 the Allies were reinforced by an Italian contingent of about the strength of one division, but very weak in artillery.

That same summer also brought with it malaria in a particularly virulent form. Any troops that occupied low-lying ground were decimated by it, and the sick-rate became, and remained, a very much more serious consideration than in any other theatre of war outside the tropics.

The Serbian Army, the remains of which had been driven out of its own country by the combined attack of the Austrians and Bulgars in the autumn of 1915, had spent the winter reorganising, chiefly in Corfu, and in the spring of 1916 began to appear on the Macedonian front. By the end of July it had risen to a strength of over 150,000 men in six divisions.

The winter of 1915–16 and the spring and early summer passed off quietly; then both sides prepared to attack: the Central Powers presumably with the object of driving the Allies into the sea; the Allies with that of helping the Roumanians, who were on the point of coming into the war on their side.

Both sides got on the move about the middle of August, the Central Powers getting a slight start. Most of the fighting took place on the Allies' western wing, where

Serbs, French, and Italians gradually drove the enemy back and took Monastir.

The British force, on the right of the line from the Gulf of Orfano to the river Vardar, had advanced to the line of the river Struma and Lake Doiran without opposition at the end of July.

The fighting in the west went on for months, and it was not till the beginning of November that Monastir was taken. The Allies' new line ran only five kilometres to the north of that town, which remained under the enemy's shell-fire till September 1918.

When the British first arrived on the Struma line the 80th Brigade held the short length of the river between Lake Tahinos and the sea, our 3rd Battalion and the 2nd King's Shropshire Light Infantry holding the front line, beyond the river, with the 4th Rifle Brigade and our 4th Battalion in reserve behind it. For nearly two years there was no serious fighting on this part of the front, though there were frequent minor operations and perpetual patrol encounters in No Man's Land, which was here two and a half miles wide.

Space does not permit that many of these operations should be recorded, but an account of a few of them may be given as a sample of what went on at short intervals all the time our battalions were on this line.

On August 20, 1916, it was reported that the Bulgars were advancing with the object of seizing the section of the railway between Angista and Seres, and that they had already attacked some French troops near the latter place. It so happened that a party under Captain Hall, Royal Engineers, had gone out that very day to blow up some railway bridges over the Angista River. He reached one of the bridges at midnight the following night, and succeeded in destroying it before he was driven in.

A mobile column was sent out at 3 a.m. on the 23rd, under the command of Major A. F. C. Maclachlan, D.S.O., consisting of one troop of Yeomanry, one section 17th Field Company Royal Engineers, and 10 men from each battalion in the Brigade, mounted on mules, with orders to destroy as many of the road bridges over the Angista as possible.

The 3rd Battalion K.R.R.C. (Lieut.-Colonel W. J. Long, C.M.G.), with two 18-pounder guns, were to follow as far as Zdravik village as a support.

At 7 a.m. the Mobile Column reached Zdravik, and found it unoccupied by the enemy. The Battalion arrived half an hour later, halted there, and put out outposts.

The Mobile Column then pushed on to the river, and began destroying two bridges. While they were at work, at about 10.30 a.m., a force of the enemy, estimated at four battalions, was seen approaching the village of Rahova about 10,000 yards to the north.

Advancing within rifle range they deployed, and opened a heavy fire on the Mobile Column, but fortunately the shooting was bad. Captain G. S. Oxley's party of Muleteers of our 4th Battalion were the only sufferers, and they had only 1 rifleman and 1 sapper wounded. Our guns then opened on the Bulgars at 1,800 yards and, putting a shell into a company in close order, cooled their ardour. The two bridges were successfully destroyed, and the Mobile Column withdrew to Zdravik.

As the enemy were now showing an inclination to get round both flanks of the Zdravik position, it was decided not to try to blow up the Vulchista Bridge, three miles farther up the river, but to take that at Pasa Koprulu, near the mouth of the river.

The Mobile Column started off about 12.30 p.m., and Lieut.-Colonel Long began to prepare to withdraw from

Zdravik by first sending back his guns to a position two miles in rear. The Battalion followed at 3 p.m., and had gone about 1,000 yards when a long line of Bulgar infantry appeared on the position they had just left. The British guns opened on them with shrapnel, and they advanced no farther. By 3.30 p.m. the Pasa Koprulu bridge had been destroyed, and the Mounted Infantry rejoined the column, and took over the duties of rear-guard.

The Battalion got back to its own lines about 8 p.m., without a casualty, having marched over twenty miles.

As an illustration of how the political situation clashed with the tactical, it is of interest to record that the force in its retirement was accompanied by a small supply column of Greek troops, which had spent the night in the village. After going some way the officer in command of this party wanted to go back to the village, under the pretence that he had left his pony there. As it was pretty evident that all he wanted to do was to make a report to his friends the Bulgars, he was told that if he tried to drop behind the rear-guard he would be shot. In the end he did succeed in evading the rear-guard, and was seen no more.

Though the 80th Brigade had come in for no more important operations than those of which the day's work described above is a specimen, north of Lake Tahinos the rest of the 27th Division had been more seriously engaged. On one occasion two Bulgar regiments, of four battalions each, made a night attack on the 81st Brigade, commanded by Brigadier-General B. F. Widdrington (lately in command of our 4th Battalion), and were driven off with a loss of over 5,000 casualties.

On October 10 the Bulgar troops on the lower Struma were relieved by Turks.

On October 31 some operations were to be undertaken by the rest of the corps in the neighbourhood of Seres.

To assist these operations, the 80th Brigade had orders to keep the enemy opposite them busy.

With this object two battalions, 2nd King's Shropshire Light Infantry on the right, 3rd K.R.R.C. on the left, three companies each, left their trenches at 4 p.m. on the above date, to attack a mountain spur known as the Hog's Back. This spur was commanded at a distance of 700 yards by the enemy's main position, which was 400 or 500 feet above it. The enemy at once opened shell-fire on the advancing troops, but fortunately his barrage came down behind them, and he did not succeed in shortening enough to get into them till they had got into dead ground. He then bombarded our trench line, to occupy which two companies of our 4th Battalion had been sent up, with little result beyond the cutting of telephone wires.

At 4.30 p.m. the enemy opened rifle and machine-gun fire at 1,500 yards, but the plastering they got from our field artillery, greatly assisted by some monitors of the Navy, interfered with the accuracy of their fire, and they did little damage. A deserter who came in next day reported that he had never seen our infantry, as he and all his brother Turks had merely put their rifles over the parapet and fired without looking. The advance of the 3rd Battalion was also well covered by two of our machine guns, under Captain Bewicke-Copley.

At 6 p.m. the firing-line had reached a rocky crest within 200 yards of the enemy's trench. The two battalion Commanding Officers had established their headquarters on a knoll 300 yards behind the firing line, and our battalion signallers, under Sergeant Lizieri, had them connected with their Brigadier by telephone.

By 6.30 p.m. everything was ready for an assault on the trench, but as it was now nearly dark, and any further advance would have attained no useful object and would have led to casualties, of which so far there had been few, the Brigadier gave the order to withdraw.

The withdrawal began at 6.40 p.m., and was quite unmolested, though the enemy kept on firing and sending up flares most of the night.

Deserters reported that the enemy's losses had been considerable, whereas those of our 3rd Battalion amounted to 6 wounded, of whom 1 died; those of the King's Shropshire Light Infantry were 1 man killed, 1 officer and 5 men wounded.

Some months later a deserter reported that the Turkish soldiers had been told that they were to get a special decoration for defeating this attack. This may or may not have been true, but we may, anyhow, infer that the Turks thought that they had been the object of a heavy attack, the defeat of which was a great feat of arms. No better certificate could be given to the 80th Brigade to show that their operation had been a model of what a false attack should be. They had persuaded the enemy that he was in for a big thing, and had 'got away with it' at very slight loss to themselves. We may safely conclude that the Turks opposite them had no reserves to spare for their friends at Seres; where, it may be added, the British operations had been a complete success.

In the spring of 1917 General Sarrail, the French Commander-in-Chief of the Allied forces in Macedonia, made an attempt to break the Bulgarian line or, it should be said, that of the Central Powers, as all the time there was a considerable, though varying, force of Germans on the other side, and the chief command was always German.

After a failure in the Monastir area, in which the Serbs, French, and Italians took part, the British had a try between Lake Doiran and the river Vardar. A break through here would have opened the road up the Vardar into

Serbia and to the Kosturino Pass leading into Bulgaria, but the Bulgars' position was far too strong, and the British attack failed with heavy losses. The attack was then resumed by the French and Serbs, but all to no purpose, and Sarrail abandoned his efforts towards the end of May, after the Allies had lost 13,000 to 14,000 men. There followed a long period of inaction on both sides.

Our 3rd and 4th Battalions remained on the Struma line with little to break the monotony but occasional patrol encounters in No Man's Land. Precautions against malaria met with considerable success, and towards the end of the summer of 1917 the sick list began to decrease, but not before vast numbers had been invalided, and the greater part of the remainder were impregnated with the disease.

In June the Turks in the Struma valley were relieved by the Bulgars. The former, to celebrate their approaching departure, made an attack on the outpost line of our 3rd Battalion with one battalion in the small hours of June 17. They were driven off by artillery fire, but they left a rear-guard to cover the removal of their wounded, which fired on our patrols when they went out at daylight. Two Lance-Corporals of the Battalion were wounded, as was 2nd Lieutenant H. W. Searson, Essex Regiment, attached to the 3rd Battalion, who died of his wounds the same day. Captain A. E. C. S. Thurburn, of the same Regiment, had been killed in a patrol encounter the previous month. In July the 4th Battalion relieved the 3rd in the front line, where they had been for nearly a year. In November the 80th Brigade relieved the 82nd on the Struma above Lake Tahinos.

The difference of opinion between Venizelos and King Constantine—the former being determined to bring Greece into the war on the side of the Entente, the latter being equally determined to maintain a neutrality favourable to the Central Powers—had resulted, in the latter part of 1916, in the declaration of a Provisional Government of National Defence in Salonika, which at once began to create an army to take part with the Allies, while the rest of Greece remained faithful to the King and his policy. In June 1917 the Allies forced Constantine to abdicate, Venizelos became Prime Minister, and Greece was fairly in the war on the side of the Entente. It took a long time to get the Greek Army ready to take an active part, but in the summer of 1918 they took over the whole of the Struma front, which enabled General Milne very considerably to shorten his line, thereby greatly increasing his offensive power for the coming advance.

It is unnecessary to describe in detail the great battle by which, in the course of little more than a fortnight, Franchet d'Espérey, who had succeeded to the command of the Allied forces in June 1918, put Bulgaria out of the war, as our 3rd Battalion—the 4th had gone to France in the summer—was not engaged.

The main attack, begun on the morning of September 15, was made by the French and Serbs on the left wing of the Allies. It was successful from the start. To the British and Greeks fell the always unpleasant task of making a holding attack. It was aimed at that part of the line where a break would be most fatal to the enemy, but which, for that very reason, was most strongly held. It was delivered as such attacks should be, that is, with sufficient vigour to make the enemy mistake it for the main attack. It failed to break the enemy's line, though renewed again and again with the utmost gallantry; but its object had been achieved as not a man of the Bulgarian Army opposed to it could be spared to help to resist the Serbian advance.

General Milne's attacks had taken place on September

18 and 19; on the 21st the Bulgars, whose line of retreat was being threatened by the advance of the Serbs, showed signs of preparation for departure. Milne renewed his attack, and met with little resistance; the whole of the Bulgarian Army opposed to him was in full flight through the Kosturino Pass.

The 27th Division had been relieved by the Greeks on the Struma front towards the end of June, and the 3rd Battalion had started on their march to the Doiran–Vardar sector on the 25th of that month. On the night of July 8/9 they relieved some French troops in the front line.

On September 2 they were relieved and went into reserve. They took no part in the big attack, but on the night of the 20th/21st went up into the second line ready to take up the pursuit. They started to advance soon after midnight 21st/22nd, but on the morning of the 23rd they were squeezed out by the Greeks. By this time malaria and influenza had brought the fighting strength of the Battalion down to about 130 rank and file. A period of marching and camping on the lines of communication followed for the next few months, ending in a sea voyage from Salonika, which landed them in Constantinople on the night of February 2/3, 1919, but we need not follow them there, as the war is over.

North Russia [1]

Early in 1918 the Allies decided to send an expedition to North Russia. The whole story is full of complications, political and military, and anyone who wants to get a clear view of it should read 'The Murmansk Venture,' by Major-General Sir C. Maynard.

At the time when this decision was made, the situation

[1] Map IX.

of the Allies was a precarious one. The Germans had just made peace with the Bolshevik Government of Russia, and were sending division after division from the Eastern to the Western Front. Also the enemy's submarines were still a very serious menace, especially now that the American forces were beginning to cross the Atlantic in ever-increasing numbers.

It was thought that the despatch of an expedition to North Russia would help matters; firstly, by detaining a certain number of Germans in Russia; and, secondly, by preventing the Germans from securing the ice-free port of Murmansk, which, if used as a submarine base, would side-step the North Sea mine-fields and be a great threat to Atlantic shipping.

The Allied Expeditionary Force was only to be the nucleus of the force which was to be put into the field in North Russia. The main strength was to come from: (*a*) a Russian force which was to be raised among any Russians who might be found willing to join up and fight the Germans—to organise and equip which a strong military mission was to go out; (*b*) as many as could be collected of a force of about 50,000 Czechoslovaks, lately prisoners of war taken by the Russians from the Austrian Army, and strongly pro-Ally. These were, at the time, somewhere in Russia, and the Bolshevik Government had promised railway facilities for their journey to North Russia.

The enemy which this expedition was expected to encounter consisted of a German army in Finland of about 55,000, together with some 50,000 'White Finns,' i.e. anti-Communist Finns; the whole under General von der Goltz.

The Bolshevik Government were at first favourable to the expedition, but were not long in changing their minds. They probably realised that a Russian army raised to fight

Germans might, when it had done with the Germans, turn its attention to them.

By the time the expedition began to arrive the Bolsheviks had become actively hostile. So far from helping the Czechoslovaks on their road north, they attacked them *en route*, and turned them back and, whatever became of them, none of them ever turned up in North Russia.

The outcome of all this was that when the Armistice came, though the North Russia expedition had performed its allotted task of keeping the Germans out of the ports, its work was not over, as it was by that time busy fighting the Bolsheviks.

The operations of the first year may be left out of this history, as they have nothing to do with the annals of the King's Royal Rifle Corps, the detachment of our regiment not having arrived at Murmansk till April 1919.

The Company was formed at the Rifle Depot on April 5. It consisted of three platoons from the K.R.R.C. and one from the Rifle Brigade. It was commanded by Major V. Yeats-Brown, with Captain C. Smith as Adjutant and Quartermaster. The other officers were Captain G. Hayhurst-France, Lieutenants D. W. Gurney, D. Allhusen, S. C. F. de Salis, Hon. J. Jervis, all of the K.R.R.C., and Lieutenant J. S. W. Maclure, Rifle Brigade.

They reached Murmansk on April 17. At the time of the arrival of the Rifle Company at Murmansk the situation was as follows: General Maynard's fighting force consisted of one company Royal Marine Light Infantry, the Malmoot Company (Canadians from the Far West, locally known as the Bomb and Dagger Brigade), a Slavo-British force of from 200 to 300 men, under Lieut.-Colonel Geoffrey Moore, K.R.R.C., a battalion of Serbs, which had found its way through Russia from Odessa, a newly formed Russian regiment under Captain Daidoff, a band of about 200 ‘ partisans,’ under Colonel Krugliakoff, two companies of Italians, a small proportion of artillery, British and French, and an armoured train.

To these were now to be added the Rifle Company and a company of the Middlesex Regiment.

They were opposed by a Bolshevik force, of which the only thing definitely known about the numbers was that they were increasing.

The object of the enemy was to drive the Allies into the sea : that of the Allies was to evacuate the country as soon as possible, but before doing so to leave the Russian force, which they had been helping to raise, able to take care of itself.

With this latter end in view, General Maynard was anxious to enlarge the recruiting area for the Russian force by pushing on to the shores of Lake Onega, where he would find a more populous and altogether more civilised country than the wilderness of forest, lake, and marsh in which he had so far been operating.

The country being practically roadless, the operations of both sides were confined to the railway and a very short distance on either side of it. This railway had been hastily laid during the war. It was a gimcrack affair, and had suffered much from sabotage at the hands of the numerous friends of the Bolsheviks behind the Allied line, and it was only by the superhuman exertions of a corps of American railwaymen that it was kept open.

At the beginning of April 1919 the most advanced post of the Allies was at Segeja, on the railway, some 400 miles south of Murmansk, and half-way between the White Sea and Lake Onega. The Bolsheviks were facing them at Urosozero, twenty miles farther south.

The Officer Commanding at Segeja (Major ‘ Pete ’ Anderson, Malmoot Company) received information that the enemy was concentrating a large force preparatory to attacking his post. Deciding that his best method of defence would be to attack before the enemy could finish his preparations, he moved out on April 11 with his armoured train and a force of under 100 men. This bold course was completely successful. The Bolsheviks, though in greatly superior numbers, were driven out of Urosozero, leaving 50 dead and 40 prisoners behind them, as well as a large quantity of munitions of war. The Allied loss was 1 killed and 5 wounded.

This success was immediately followed by the capture of Vojmosalmi, fifty miles farther east, on a road (so-called) from Povynetz on Lake Onega to the White Sea, by Captain Daidoff and the new Russian battalion.

General Maynard then thought himself strong enough to push on to the shores of Lake Onega.

With the two newly arrived companies of British infantry, he could employ about 3,000 troops, of which 1,000 were British. He had to get leave from the War Office before he could advance, as his orders were to go no farther; but on April 29 the required sanction arrived.

The advance commenced on May 1 in three columns, the centre column on the railway, the left on the Povynetz Road, and the right, under Lieut.-Colonel Moore, a corresponding distance to the west. On May 3 Maselga was occupied after forty-eight hours' fighting.

On May 6 the Rifle Company detrained at Maselga, and joined the centre column, the other troops of which were the Malmoot Company, the Marines, and the Middlesex Company, the whole under Colonel Leckie, Canadian Infantry.

The column advanced again on May 7 and 8, and then halted for the railway to be repaired behind them. On the 11th the right column was attacked by the Bolsheviks and beat them off with a loss of 40 killed, 20 prisoners, and 3 machine guns.

On May 15 the advance was resumed, and the Rifle Company, with the Middlesex in support, had a brilliant little fight all to themselves. They captured a village, thenceforward known officially as 60th village, and took 2 machine guns and many prisoners. The enemy left 40 dead on the ground. Our losses were Lieutenants Allhusen and Gurney wounded (the latter very severely), and 8 other ranks wounded. The Middlesex, passing through, saw the enemy off the premises, inflicting more losses.

On the 19th the Company was engaged, when on reconnaissance in the woods, in what seems to have been something in the nature of an 'encounter battle,' and Lieutenant De Salis was wounded.

On the 21st Medvyejya Gora was taken by a combined attack of the right and centre columns. The left column had taken Povynetz on the 18th, so the force was well established on the shores of Lake Onega.

The Rifle Company spent the next month alternating the garrisoning of Medvyejya Gora with tours of outpost duty.

General Maynard's next move was the gaining of a footing on the Shunga Peninsula by Daidoff's Russians, the gradual occupation of which secured a useful recruiting-ground for the anti-Bolsheviks.

On the night of June 11/12 the Bolsheviks were turned out of Siding 10, five miles south of Medvyejya Gora, by the Middlesex Company and Rifle Brigade platoon, supported by the rest of the Rifle Company. The good shooting of two 4·5-inch howitzers left the infantry little to do.

Towards the end of June the weather became oppressively hot, and mosquitoes by night and horse-flies by day made life a torment.

The enemy was gradually pushed back in a series of small actions, and on the night of July 5/6 he was driven out of Kapaselga, leaving many prisoners behind him. The Rifle Company's share in this operation was some very fine work by patrols under Lieutenant W. M. Harrington and Sergeant F. Hammond, who, by fearlessly drawing the enemy's fire the previous night, accurately located all their front-line trenches. The consequence of this was that again the artillery bombardment (one 18-pounder and two 4·5-inch howitzers) made the task of the infantry a very easy one.

There followed a spell of outpost duty for the Rifle Company, during which their patrols seem to have done pretty well what they liked in No Man's Land.

At the end of July they were withdrawn to Medvyejya Gora for a rest. During July the enemy's defence hardened, and he made some counter-attacks, chiefly by the aid of Red Finns, all of which were beaten off with considerable loss.

On August 17 the Company took part in an attack on Siding 8 and a position beyond it, in which their task seems to have consisted principally in heartening up a company of native allies which was billed for the leading part, but suffered in the first act from a certain amount of stage fright.

A few days later the Company was relieved by some of the British reinforcements which had been sent from home to cover the withdrawal of our forces. The Company reached Murmansk on August 25, and remained there doing guards and other duties for a month. On September 23 they were broken up into a number of small detachments guarding bridges on the railway line between

Murmansk and Imandra, 100 miles farther south. There they remained while the evacuation proceeded, till they were picked up on the night of October 3/4 by the last train passing through to the north. They sailed for home next day, and so ended the services of the King's Royal Rifle Corps in the Great War.

FINIS

APPENDIX I

Past and Serving Officers, Non-Commissioned Officers, and Riflemen of the King's Royal Rifle Corps who gained the Victoria Cross in the Great War

Lieut.-Colonel A. D. Borton joined the King's Royal Rifle Corps in 1902, and served in the South African War. He retired in 1910 and rejoined on the outbreak of war. He was commanding the 2/22nd Battalion of the London Regiment in Allenby's campaign of 1917 when he gained the Victoria Cross :

'For most conspicuous bravery and leadership. Under most difficult conditions in darkness and in an unknown country, he deployed his battalion for attack, and at dawn led his attacking companies against a strongly held position. When the leading waves were checked by a withering machine-gun fire, Lieut.-Colonel Borton showed an utter contempt of danger, and moved freely up and down his lines under heavy fire. Reorganising his command, he led his men forward and captured the position. At a later stage of the fight he led a party of volunteers against a battery of field guns in action at point-blank range, capturing the guns and the detachments. His fearless leadership was an inspiring example to the whole brigade.'

Captain J. F. P. Butler joined the King's Royal Rifle Corps in 1907. He was in West Africa when the war broke out, and served in the Togoland and Cameroon Expeditions. He gained the Victoria Cross :

'For most conspicuous bravery in the Cameroons, West Africa, on November 17, 1914. With a party of 13 men he went into the thick bush, and at once attacked the enemy, in strength about 100, including several Europeans ; defeating them, and captured their machine gun and many loads of ammunition. On December 27, 1914, when on patrol duty with a few men, he swam the Ekam River, which was held by the enemy, alone, and in face of a brisk fire; completed his reconnaissance on the farther bank, and returned in safety. Two of his men were wounded while he was actually in the water.'

He died of wounds received in action on September 5, 1916.

Lieutenant J. H. S. Dimmer enlisted in the King's Royal Rifle Corps in 1902, and received a commission in the same regiment in 1908. He was serving in the 2nd Battalion in the First Battle of Ypres when he was awarded the Victoria Cross for gallant conduct, which is thus described in the 'Gazette':

'This officer served his machine gun during the attack, on November 12, at Klein Zillebeke, until he had been shot five times—three times by shrapnel and twice by bullets—and continued at his post until his gun was destroyed.'

He was killed in action as a Temporary Lieutenant-Colonel when commanding the 2/4th Royal Berkshire Regiment, on March 21, 1918.

No. 11941, Rifleman George Peachment, 2nd Battalion King's Royal Rifle Corps:

'For most conspicuous bravery near Hulluch on September 25, 1915. During very heavy fighting, when our front line was compelled to retire in order to reorganise, Rifleman Peachment, seeing his Company Commander, Captain Dubs, lying wounded, crawled to assist him. The enemy's fire was intense, but, though there was a shell-hole quite close, in which a few men had taken cover, Rifleman Peachment never thought of saving himself. He knelt in the open by his officer and tried to help him, but while doing this he was first wounded by a bomb and a minute later mortally wounded by a rifle bullet. He was one of the youngest men in his battalion, and gave this splendid example of courage and self-sacrifice.'

2815, Sergeant Alfred Gill, 1st Battalion:

'For most conspicuous bravery [July 7, 1916]. The enemy made a very strong counter-attack on the right flank of the Battalion, and rushed the bombing post, after killing all the company bombers. Sergeant Gill rallied the remnants of his platoon, none of whom were skilled bombers, and reorganised his defences, a most difficult and dangerous task, the trench being very shallow and much damaged. Soon afterwards the enemy nearly surrounded his men by creeping up through the thick undergrowth, and commenced sniping at about 20 yards' range. Although it was almost certain death, Sergeant Gill stood boldly up in order to direct the fire of his men. He was killed almost at once, but not before he had shown his men where the enemy were, and thus enabled them to hold up their advance. By his supreme devotion to duty and self-sacrifice he saved a very dangerous situation.'

A.2025, Rifleman W. Mariner, see page 91.

R.2794, Sergeant E. Cooper, see page 230.

R.15089, Acting-Corporal A. E. Shepherd, see page 248.

APPENDIX II

Casualties

The total casualties of the Regiment in the war amounted to not less than 145,000. Of these, 567 Officers, 74 Warrant Officers, 2,174 Non-commissioned Officers, 23 Buglers, and 9,986 Riflemen were killed, or died of wounds or from other causes.

The following is a complete list of officers of the Regiment killed and died from wounds or from other causes in the Great War, but does not include the names of officers from other Regiments attached to Battalions of the K.R.R.C. :

2 Abadie, Richard Nevile, D.S.O., Lieut.-Colonel, k. in a., 10/7/17.

1 Addy, Kenneth James Balguy, 2nd Lieutenant (temp.), k. in a., 23/10/15.

17 Aird, Allan Muir, 2nd Lieutenant (temp.), k. in a., 21/10/18 (attached 18th Battalion).

2 Amphlett-Morton, James Fairfax, 2nd Lieutenant, k. in a., 10/1/15.

1 Anderson, Charles Alexander Kenneth, 2nd Lieutenant, k. in a., 10/11/14.

21 Anderson, James Skelton, 2nd Lieutenant (temp.), d. of w., 10/10/16.

5 Anson, Nigel Fredrick Edward, M.C., 2nd Lieutenant, k. in a., 10/7/17 (attached 2nd Battalion).

7 Arnell, Reginald Brandt, 2nd Lieutenant (temp.), k. in a., 30/7/15.

Ash, Alfred William, 2nd Lieutenant, k. in a., 13/6/18 (attached 12th Battalion).

1 Ashwell, Alfred, 2nd Lieutenant (temp.), k. in a., 4/4/17 (attached 10th Battalion).

13 Atkinson, Fred, 2nd Lieutenant (temp.), k. in a., 23/4/17.

16 Atkinson, Richard Dermott, 2nd Lieutenant, k. in a., 16/7/16.

1 Austen-Cartmell, Arthur James, Lieutenant, k. in a., 1/6/16.

16 Averdieck, Godfrey Harold, Temp. 2nd Lieutenant, k. in a., 11/3/16.

17 Bailey, Alfred John, 2nd Lieutenant (temp.), k. in a., 3/9/16.

5 Bailey, Anthony Yorke, 2nd Lieutenant, k. in a., 27/7/16 (attached 1st Battalion).

4 Baines, Frederick Athelstan Fanshawe, 2nd Lieutenant, k. in a., 25/5/15.

21 Baker, Frank Vincent, 2nd Lieutenant (temp.), k. in a., 22/3/18.

4 Ballance, Leslie Arthur, Captain, k. in a., 28/9/16 (attached 2nd Battalion).

16 Balshaw, Newton Kesteven, Captain, k. in a., 13/4/18.

20 Banks, John Cook, M.C., Captain (temp.), k. in a., 1/5/17.

13 Barber, Graham Brooke, Lieutenant (temp.), k. in a., 25/8/18.

2 Barclay, Rafe Hedworth Myddleton, 2nd Lieutenant, k. in a., 14/9/14.

5 Barnes, Edward William, 2nd Lieutenant, d. of w., 10/7/17 (attached 2nd Battalion).

Barnes, Herbert George, 2nd Lieutenant (temp.), died, 31/8/17 (attached 7th Battalion).

1 Barnet, Henry Morton, 2nd Lieutenant (temp.), d. of w., 23/4/18 (in German hands).

Barnett, Reginald Walter, M.C., Lieutenant (temp. Major), k. in a., 12/8/18 (attached Staff, Divisional Headquarters).

1 Barrand, Sidney, Lieutenant (temp.), k. in a., 14/8/18.

Barrett, Arthur Edward, 2nd Lieutenant (temp.), k. in a., 22/8/17 (attached 8th Battalion).

7 Bartholomew, Guy Wollaston, Temp. Captain, k. in a., 25/8/16.

Bashford, Charles, 2nd Lieutenant, k. in a., 20/9/17 (attached 21st Battalion).

1 Battenberg, His Highness Prince Maurice Victor Donald, of, K.C.V.O., Lieutenant, k. in. a., 27/10/14.

Beaver, John Denistoun Campbell, 2nd Lieutenant, d. of w., 15/5/18 (attached 13th Battalion).

1 Beck, William, Lieutenant and Quartermaster, died, 18/4/18.

Beecheno, James Herbert, 2nd Lieutenant (temp.), d. of w., 25/10/18 (attached 13th Battalion).

10 Bell, Robert de Houghan Mark, Lieutenant (temp.), k. in a., 3/9/16.

9 Benson, Eric William, Temp. Lieut.-Colonel, k. in a., 15/9/16.

1 Bentall, Ernest Hammond, 2nd Lieutenant, k. in a., 3/10/15.

15 Benton, Frank, 2nd Lieutenant (temp.), k. in a., 15-17/9/16 (attached 21st Battalion).

5 Bernard, Arthur Basil, Lieutenant (Acting Captain), d. of w., 4/5/17 (in German hands) (attached 16th Battalion).

4 Bertie, Ninian Mark Kerr, 2nd Lieutenant, k. in a., 8/5/15.

2 Best, Edgar Harold, 2nd Lieutenant (temp.), d. of w., 18/9/18.

1 Bevan, Percival Johnstone, Lieutenant, k. in a., 10/3/15.

1 Bigge, The Hon. John Neville, Captain, k. in a., 15/5/15.

2 Bircham, Humphrey Francis William, D.S.O., Temp. Lieut.-Colonel, d. of w., 23/7/16.

7 Bird, Stanley Treadgold, 2nd Lieutenant (temp.), d. of w., 20/8/16.

6 Bird, William Ryder, 2nd Lieutenant (temp.), k. in a., 8/10/15 (attached 8th Battalion).

5 Bird, Wilfrid Stanley, Lieutenant, k. in a., 9/5/15 (attached 2nd Battalion).

7 Blackbourn, Edgar Singleton, 2nd Lieutenant (temp.), d. of w., 29/9/16.

10 Blake, Cecil Rodolph, Captain (temp.), k. in a., 4/4/17.

2 Blake, Maurice Frederic, Lieutenant, k. in a., 14/9/14.

8 Blane, James Pitcairn, Captain (temp.), d. of w., 23/11/15.

5 Blyth, James Charles, 2nd Lieutenant, k. in a., 13/4/17 (attached 1st Battalion).

2 Bond, Robert Harold, Lieutenant, k. in a., 14/9/14.

6 Boucher, Arthur Guy, 2nd Lieutenant, k. in a., 10/7/17 (attached 2nd Battalion).

Bourdillon, Tom Louis, M.C., Major (temp.), k. in a., 24/8/17 (attached 8th Battalion).

Bourke, Eustace George Walter, Captain, k. in a., 16/6/15 (attached 9th Battalion).

Bourne, Gerald Hugh Temple, Temp. 2nd Lieutenant, k. in a., 18/3/17 (and Royal Flying Corps, 4th Squadron).

Boyd, Gavin Haddow, 2nd Lieutenant (temp.), k. in a., 2/12/17 (attached 16th Battalion).

Brakenberry, William Horace, M.M., 2nd Lieutenant (temp.), d. of w., 23/10/18 (attached 13th Battalion).

Branker, Walter Robert, M.C., 2nd Lieutenant (temp.), k. in a., 5/10/18 (attached 11th Notts and Derby Regiments)

1 Brocklehurst, Archibald Henry, Captain, d. of w., 29/7/16.
20 Brooks, George William, 2nd Lieutenant (temp.), k. in a., 29/5/18.
11 Broster, Harold Broughton, 2nd Lieutenant (temp.), k. in a., 30/11/17.
Brown, Edward Dell, 2nd Lieutenant (temp.), k. in a., 16/8/17 (attached 12th Battalion).
16 Budd, Frederick George, M.C., 2nd Lieutenant (temp.), d. of w., 15/10/18.
6 Bulkeley-Hughes, George Montagu Warren, Temp. Lieutenant (Acting Captain), k. in a., 27/2/17 (attached 12th Battalion).
5 Bull, Alfred George, 2nd Lieutenant, k. in a., 6/8/18 (attached 8th Battalion).
10 Bull, John Lionel Robin, 2nd Lieutenant, k. in a., 30/11/17.
Bullen, Roy Evans, 2nd Lieutenant, d. of w., 29/4/16.
18 Bullivant, Eric Claud, 2nd Lieutenant, k. in a., 24/3/18.
Burroughes, Stephen, 2nd Lieutenant, k. in a., 4/11/18 (attached 2nd Battalion).
11 Bury, Edmond William, Captain (temp.), k. in a., 5/12/15.
13 Butcher, Norris de Gruchy, Lieutenant and Quartermaster, d. of w., 23/5/18.
17 Butcher, Arthur James Basil, 2nd Lieutenant, k. in a., 3/9/16.
7 Butler, The Hon. Brian Danvers, Temp. Lieutenant, k. in a., 18/8/16.
V.C. Butler, John Fitzhardinge Paul, D.S.O., Captain, d. of w., 5/9/16 (attached Gold Coast Regiment).
13 Cairns, Herbert, Temp. 2nd Lieutenant, k. in a., 4/10/17.
18 Calder, William Paul, Temp. 2nd Lieutenant, k. in a., 14/6/17.
13 Campbell, Charles, Temp. 2nd Lieutenant, d. of w., 10/1/18.
10 Capern, Henry James, Temp. 2nd Lieutenant, k. in a., 22/3/18 (attached 59th Trench Mortar Battery).
12 Carnegie, Theodore Arthur, Lieutenant, k. in a., 16/8/17.
7 Carter, Gerald Francis, 2nd Lieutenant (temp.), d. of w., 30/7/15.
1 Casey, James, Lieutenant, k. in a., 30/10/14.
1 Cassidy, Cyril Martin, 2nd Lieutenant, d. of w., 17/5/15.
2 Cathcart, Augustus Ernest, Captain, k. in a., 14/9/14.
8 Cayley, Francis Digby Edward, Temp. 2nd Lieutenant, k. in a., 29/9/15 (attached 1st Battalion).

8 Chambers, Robert Seymour Bennet, Temp. Lieutenant (Acting Captain), k. in a., 24/12/17.
9 Chaplin, Charles Slingsby, Lieut.-Colonel, k. in a., 30/7/15.
Charleston, Ebenezer, Temp. 2nd Lieutenant, k. in a., 20/9/17 (attached 11th Battalion).
12 Chaworth-Musters, Robert, M.C., Captain, died, 10/10/18 (attached 3rd Musketry Camp).
1 Chaworth-Musters, Patricius George, Lieutenant, d. of w., 12/1/15.
13 Chester-Master, Richard Chester, D.S.O., Brevet Major (Temp. Lieut.-Colonel), k. in a., 30/8/17.
13 Chidson, Laurence Drury, M.C., Temp. Lieutenant (Acting Captain), k. in a., 24/4/17.
13 Chinnery, Harry Broderick, Temp. Lieutenant, k. in a., 28/5/16.
18 Christmas, Edwin Cecil Russell, Temp. 2nd Lieutenant, d. of w., 7/10/16.
18 Clark, Douglas Scott Dalrymple, Captain, k. in a., 15/9/16 (and Trench Mortar Battery).
Claxton, Eric Abley, 2nd Lieutenant, d. of w., 31/7/17 (attached 18th Battalion).
11 Clifford, Herbert James, Temp. Lieutenant (Acting Captain), k. in a., 20/9/17.
Clinton, Walter Lawrence, Captain, died, 22/11/18.[1]
2 Clowes, Charles George Edric, Lieutenant, d. of w., 18/2/15.
15 Cobb, Kenneth Rhodes, Captain, k. in a., 1/7/15.
Coburn, Charles, 2nd Lieutenant, k. in a., 31/7/17 (attached 18th Battalion).
16 Coe, Sydney Urie Charles, Temp. 2nd Lieutenant, k. in a., 30/11/17.
2 Cockerell, Andrew Pepys, 2nd Lieutenant, k. in a., 15/8/16.
1 Collins, Charles, Lieutenant, d. of w., 28/7/16.
16 Cooban, Adrian Deighton, Temp. Major, k. in a., 16/7/16.
18 Cook, Percy Mellows, Temp. 2nd Lieut. k. in a., 4/10/16.
10 Coyle, Leonard Joseph, 2nd Lieutenant (temp.), k. in a., 23/11/16.
6 Craggs, John James, 2nd Lieutenant, k. in a., 17/2/17 (attached 1st Battalion).
16 Cram, Hubert Arthur, 2nd Lieutenant (temp.), d. of w., 16/4/18.
1 Crawhall, Fritz Portmore, 2nd Lieutenant, k. in a., 10/3/15.

[1] See pages 449, 450.

4 Croft-Smith, Edwin Spencer, 2nd Lieutenant, k. in a., 8/5/15.

12 Crooks, Edward Neilson, 2nd Lieutenant, k. in a., 22/3/18.

Cross, Samuel Allison, 2nd Lieutenant, k. in a., 14/1/18 (attached 2nd Battalion).

2 Crossman, William Ronald Morley, 2nd Lieutenant, k. in a., 2/11/14.

14 Cruikshanks, Ernest, Captain (temp.), k. in a., 17/10/15 (attached 9th Battalion).

Culme-Seymour, George, Captain (Adjutant Q.V. Rifles), k. in a., 7/5/15.

2 Cunningham, Alexander Pinman, 2nd Lieutenant (temp.), d. of w., 19/9/18.

18 Curwen, Cecil Neil, Temp. Lieutenant, k. in a., 15/9/16.

10 Davies, David Guy, M.C., Temp. Captain, k. in a., 4/4/17.

6 Davies, George Llewelyn, 2nd Lieutenant, k. in a., 15/3/15 (attached Rifle Brigade).

11 Davis, Henry Christopher, 2nd Lieutenant, k. in a., 4/4/17.

Davis, Mellville Allen Duff, M.C., 2nd Lieutenant (temp.), died, 29/5/18 (attached 9th Battalion).

8 Davis, William Jeffery, Captain and Adjutant, k. in a., 30/7/15.

2 Davison, Stuart, 2nd Lieutenant, k. in a., 14/9/14.

9 Daw, Reginald Samuel, Captain (temp.), d. of w., 25/9/16.

13 Dawe, Alfred Henry, Temp. 2nd Lieut., k. in a., 11/4/17.

17 Day, Percy Oliver James, 2nd Lieutenant (temp.), k. in a., 19/7/16.

2 Dean, Frank, 2nd Lieutenant, k. in a., 31/10/14.

16 Deedes, Herbert Philip, Temp. Captain, k. in a., 16/7/16.

16 Denniss, Kenneth George, Temp. 2nd Lieutenant, k. in a., 15/7/16.

9 Dent, Arthur Evelyn, Lieutenant (Acting Captain), k. in a., 9/4/17.

Denton-Cardew, Warnell de Montigny, Temp. 2nd Lieutenant, k. in a., 30/11/17 (attached 12th Battalion).

De Paravicini, John Marcus, Major, k. in a., 30/11/17 (attached 11th Battalion).

1 De Satgé, Frederick Gordon, Captain, k. in a., 15/9/16 (attached 7th Battalion).

16 Devitt, Herbert John, 2nd Lieutenant, k. in a., 12/9/18 (attached 13th Battalion).

2 Dick, Andrew Campbell, 2nd Lieutenant (temp.), d. of w., 23/10/18.

2 Dickenson, Aubrey Greville Newton, Lieutenant (temp.), d. of w., 1/7/16.

13 Dickens, Guy, Captain (temp.), d. of w., 17/7/16.

V.C. Dimmer, John Henry Stephen, M.C., Captain (temp. Lieut.-Colonel), k. in a., 21/3/18 (attached 2/4th Royal Berkshire Regiment).

12 Dove, Tom, M.C., Temp. Captain, k. in a., 16/8/17.

7 Dowling, Geoffrey Charles Walter, Temp. Captain, k. in a., 30/7/15.

9 Dowson, Humphrey, M.C., Temp. Captain, k. in a., 15/9/16.

6 Drummond, Nigel Felton, Lieutenant, killed, 20/12/16 (attached 1st Battalion).

9 Durnford, Richard Selby, Captain (temp.), k. in a., 31/7/15.

Eastman, William Viviash, Temp. 2nd Lieutenant, k. in a., 4/10/17 (attached 13th Battalion).

4 Eden, The Hon. William Alfred Morton, Lieutenant, k. in a., 1-2/3/15.

9 Edgar, George Geoffrey, Lieutenant (temp.), d. of w., 28/8/16.

2 Edwardes, Owen, 2nd Lieutenant, k. in a., 1/7/16.

Edwards, Lewis George, Temp. 2nd Lieutenant, k. in a., 20/9/17 (attached 11th Battalion).

8 Egerton, John Frederick, Temp. 2nd Lieutenant, d. of w., 3/4/16 (A.D.C.).

2 Egerton-Green, Charles Scroop, Lieutenant, k. in a., 1/7/16.

2 Eldridge, John Thomas, 2nd Lieutenant (temp.), k. in a., 18/9/18.

5 Eley, William Arthur Derrick, 2nd Lieutenant, k. in a., 17/2/17 (attached 1st Battalion).

6 Eminson, Robert Astley Franklin, 2nd Lieutenant, k. in a., 20/7/16 (attached Machine Gun Corps).

19 Erwood, Cecil Victor, Temp. 2nd Lieutenant, k. in a., 17/2/17 (attached 1st Battalion).

5 Everitt, John Wilson, 2nd Lieutenant, died, 12/4/18 (in German hands).

17 Ewen, Philip Keith Somerville, Lieutenant (temp.), k. in a., 3/9/16.

9 Exell, Noel Jardine, Captain (temp.), d. of w., 31/7/15.

6 Eyre, Charles Howard, Lieutenant, k. in a., 25/9/15 (attached 2nd Battalion).

9 Faber, Cecil Valdemar, 2nd Lieutenant (temp.), k. in a., 30/7/15.

7 Fairlie, Edward, Temp. Captain (Acting Major), k. in a., 30/3/18 (attached 17th Battalion).

5 Fardell, Gervase, M.C., Captain, k. in a., 29/9/18 (attached 1st Battalion).

7 Farmer, Charles George Edgar, Lieutenant (temp.), k. in a., 18/8/16.

6 Farmer, Henry Charles Maclean, 2nd Lieutenant, k. in a., 10/5/15 (attached 4th Battalion).

2 Farmer, James Inglesby, 2nd Lieutenant, k. in a., 9/5/15.

9 Farran, Charles, 2nd Lieutenant (temp.), k. in a., 24/8/16.

1 Fellowes, Hon. Robert, 2nd Lieutenant, k. in a., 10/3/15.

2 Fetherstonhaugh, Richard Collingwood, Lieutenant, d. of w., 14/5/15.

21 Feversham (Earl of), Charles William Reginald, Lieut.-Colonel, k. in a., 15/9/16.

5 Ffolkes, William Rupert Compton, 2nd Lieutenant, k. in a., 30/12/17 (attached 1st Battalion).

17 Fifield, Percival, P.V.F., Temp. 2nd Lieutenant, k. in a., 22/3/18.

15 Findlay, Arthur Bertram, Lieutenant, k. in a., 30/7/15 (attached 7th Battalion).

12 Fisher, Leslie Benito, Lieutenant (temp.), k. in a., 14/8/15.

Fleming, Ernest William, Temp. 2nd Lieutenant, k. in a., 4/11/18 (attached 13th Battalion).

2 Foljambe, Hubert Francis Fitzwilliam Brabazon, Major, k. in a., 14/9/14.

11 Forrest, Austin Lancelot, 2nd Lieutenant (temp.), k. in a., 3/9/16.

16 Forrest, Laurence Bernard, 2nd Lieutenant, k. in a., 20/5/17.

2 Forster, John, 2nd Lieutenant, k. in a., 14/9/14.

2 Fowler, George Glyn, Lieutenant, d. of w., 26/9/15.

3 Franks, John Fergusson, Captain and Adjutant, d. of w., 22/9/15.

2 Freeman, Frank Albert, 2nd Lieutenant, k. in a., 1/7/16.

Fryer, William Arthur, Temp. Lieutenant, k. in a., 3/10/18, (attached 4th Battalion).

2 Gant, Alfred Claude, Temp. 2nd Lieutenant, k. in a., 17/10/18.

Gantsman, Ernest, Temp. 2nd Lieutenant, k. in a., 10/11/17 (attached 9th Battalion).

16 Garrard, Reginald Herbert, Temp. 2nd Lieutenant, k. in a., 23/4/17.

9 Geen, William Purdon, 2nd Lieutenant, k. in a., 31/7/15.
Gibb, John Hardie, Temp. 2nd Lieutenant, k. in a., 31/7/17 (attached 18th Battalion).
2 Gibbs, Walter Septimus, Temp. 2nd Lieutenant, k. in a., 17/10/18.
11 Gilpin, Albert John, 2nd Lieutenant (temp.), k. in a., 17/9/16.
6 Glegg, Arthur Livingstone, 2nd Lieutenant, k. in a., 10/8/15 (attached 2nd Battalion).
6 Glegg, Walter Scott, 2nd Lieutenant, k. in a., 15/9/16 (attached 9th Battalion).
1 Godman, W. W. W., 2nd Lieutenant, k. in a., 24/1/15.
18 Goldby, William Charles, Temp. 2nd Lieutenant, k. in a., 22/8/18.
12 Goffey, John Graham, 2nd Lieutenant, k. in a., 3/9/16.
16 Gonner, Edward Maurice, Temp. Captain, k. in a., 23/4/17.
1 Goodwin, John, Temp. 2nd Lieutenant, k. in a., 29/11/17.
22 Goody, Gilbert Alexander, Temp. 2nd Lieutenant, d. of w., 6/11/16 (attached 16th Battalion).
9 Goody, Geoffrey Riddel, Temp. Lieutenant, killed, 14/7/18 (attached 10th Training Reserve Battalion).
12 Gordon, Peter, Temp. 2nd Lieutenant, k. in a., 24/8/18 (attached 18th Battalion).
6 Gore-Brown, Harold Thomas Thirlwall, 2nd Lieutenant, d. of w., 23/8/16 (attached 7th Battalion).
11 Gough, Harold Stuart, Lieutenant (temp)., k. in a., 17/6/16.
13 Gould, Gerald Oscar Alan, 2nd Lieutenant, d. of w., 25/6/16.
9 Gould, Patrick Wallace, 2nd Lieutenant (temp.), k. in a., 24/8/16.
Graham-Roe, Archibald Chaceley, Temp. 2nd Lieutenant, k. in a., 29/4/17 (attached 1st Battalion).
16 Grant, Edmund Henry, 2nd Lieutenant (temp.), d. of w., 2/8/16.
6 Grazebrook, Charles Alvery, Captain, k. in a., 10/3/15 (attached 1st Battalion).
2 Greenfield, Eric Frank, Temp. 2nd Lieutenant, killed, 13/2/17.
1 Grenville-Grey, Wilfred Hanbury, Lieutenant, d. of w., 16/5/15.
7 Grew, Hubert, 2nd Lieutenant, k. in a., 2/7/15.
1 Griffiths, George Richards, Temp. Lieutenant d. of w., 15/9/16.

9 Habershon, Philip Henry, 2nd Lieutenant (temp.), k. in a., 25/9/15.

Hain, Edward Sydney, Temp. 2nd Lieutenant, k. in a., 21/11/17 (attached 11th Battalion).

13 Hale, Frank Ernest, Temp. 2nd Lieutenant, k. in a., 25/8/18.

Hall, Henry Lewes, 2nd Lieutenant, k. in a., 30/11/17 (attached 10th Battalion).

1 Hambro, Percival, 2nd Lieutenant, d. of w., 23/3/18.

6 Hamilton, Vyvyan Lodwick, 2nd Lieutenant, k. in a., 14/6/17 (attached 18th Battalion).

Hancock, Frank Pine, 2nd Lieutenant, k. in a., 16/8/18 (attached 2nd Battalion).

Hardy, Richard Luard, Captain (temp.), k. in a., 24/8/17 (attached 8th Battalion).

1 Harman, Arthur, Captain and Quartermaster, k. in a., 26/6/15.

21 Harmon, Wilfred Baldwin, Temp. 2nd Lieutenant, k. in a., 1/8/17.

12 Harries, Frederick Ebenezer Melville, Temp. 2nd Lieutenant, k. in a., 26/2/17.

2 Harvie, Stuart McLaren, 2nd Lieutenant, d. of w., 1/6/18 (attached 6th Battalion).

20 Harvey, William Clayton, Temp. Lieutenant, k. in a., 14/7/16.

19 Hawke, Albert Edward Mountain Aysh, Temp. 2nd Lieutenant, d. of w., 11/9/16 (attached 2nd Battalion).

15 Hawkins, Gilbert William, Lieutenant (temp.), d. of w., 15/11/16 (attached 13th Battalion).

2 Hawley, Cyril Francis, Captain, k. in a., 2/11/14.

Haycroft, Frank Alexander, 2nd Lieutenant (temp.), k. in a., 10/8/17 (attached 10th Battalion).

5 Heberden, Arthur Clements, 2nd Lieutenant, k. in a., 10/7/17 (attached 2nd Battalion).

17 Hecht, Marcus Francis, Temp. Major, k. in a., 3/9/16.

6 Henderson, Donald, 2nd Lieutenant, k. in a., 11/1/15 (attached 1st Battalion).

8 Henriques, Philip Brydges Gutterlz, Temp. 2nd Lieutenant, d. of w., 24/7/15.

Herbertson, Andrew Hunter, Lieutenant, k. in a., 16/5/17 (attached 7th Battalion).

6 Herron, Alec Rowan, 2nd Lieutenant, k. in a., 10/3/15 (attached 1st Battalion).

21 Hervey, Thomas Percy Arthur, 2nd Lieutenant (temp.), k. in a., 15-17/9/16.

5 Hext, Thomas Madewood, 2nd Lieutenant, k. in a., 29/4/17 (attached 12th Battalion).

16 Hichens, James Bryan, Lieutenant (temp.), k. in a., 16/7/16.

6 Hill, Victor Baillie, M.C., Captain, d. of w., 15/1/18.

Hills, Walter Edward, Temp. 2nd Lieutenant, k. in a., 26/6/17 (attached 16th Battalion).

5 Hincks, Bertram, 2nd Lieutenant, k. in a., 18/12/16 (attached 10th Battalion).

12 Hoare, Archibald, Captain, d. of w., 27/11/17.

11 Hobbs, Reginald George, Temp. 2nd Lieutenant, k. in a., 20/9/17.

10 Hocken, Stephen Lotan, Temp. 2nd Lieutenant, k. in a., 3/9/16.

Hodges, Bernard, 2nd Lieutenant (temp.), d. of w., 16/4/18 (attached 16th Battalion).

6 Hodges, Harold Wardale, 2nd Lieutenant, k. in a., 9/5/15 (attached 2nd Battalion).

Hodgson, Charles Edward, D.C.M., 2nd Lieutenant (temp.), k. in a., 2/10/18 (attached 18th Battalion).

5 Hodson, Sydney, 2nd Lieutenant, k. in a., 21/3/18 (attached 9th Battalion).

18 Holbech, David, Temp. 2nd Lieutenant, k. in a., 8/4/17.

16 Holborow, Frederick Bernard, 2nd Lieutenant (temp.), k. in a., 16/4/18.

10 Hole, Michael, 2nd Lieutenant (temp.), k. in a., 19/9/17.

13 Holmes, Ernest Cameron, Temp. 2nd Lieutenant, k. in a., 14/11/16.

5 Holmes, Robert Bryan, 2nd Lieutenant, d. of w., 1/7/16 (attached 2nd Battalion).

5 Honey, Geoffrey Henry Le Sueur, Temp. 2nd Lieutenant, k. in a., 21/10/16 (attached 17th Battalion).

11 Hopkins, Arthur Martyn, 2nd Lieutenant (temp.), k. in a., 28/3/18.

10 Horner, William Arthur, Lieutenant (temp.), d. of w., 13/12/17.

10 Horsley, Ernest, 2nd Lieutenant (temp.), k. in a., 14/8/17 (attached 59th Trench Mortar Battery).

Hough, Geoffrey Goadsby, Temp. Lieutenant (Acting Captain), died, 8/9/18 (O.C., 214 P. of W. Coy.).

5 Howell, Edmund Lally, Temp. Captain, k. in a., 27/7/16 (attached 1st Battalion).

9 Howell, John, 2nd Lieutenant (temp.), k. in a., 25/9/15.

5 Hubbard, Archibald Charles, 2nd Lieutenant, k. in a., 8/11/17 (attached 2nd Battalion).

Hughes, Peter, Captain, k. in a., 25/3/18 (attached 11th Battalion).

Hughes, T. McKenny, Temp. Lieutenant, k. in a., 5/2/18 (attached Royal Flying Corps).

17 Hulks, Henry John, Captain (temp.), k. in a., 3/9/16.

13 Humphreys, Richard Grain, 2nd Lieutenant, k. in a., 28/9/17.

Hunter, James MacMillan, 2nd Lieutenant (temp.), k. in a., 17/10/18 (attached 2nd Battalion).

8 Huntington, George Waldeof, 2nd Lieutenant, k. in a., 24/8/16 (6th Battalion).

15 Ionides, Ambrose Constantine, Lieutenant (temp.), k. in a., 16/10/15 (attached 9th Battalion).

7 Jackman, Harold, M.C., Temp. 2nd Lieutenant (Acting Captain), k. in a., 21/3/18.

2 Jackson, Bertram Washington, Lieutenant, k. in a., 14/9/14.

6 James, Eric Samuel Pennant Kingsbury, Captain, k. in a., 17/3/15.

1 James, John Stephen Harvey, 2nd Lieutenant, k. in a., 16/5/15.

Jay, Frank Goldsmith, 2nd Lieutenant (temp.), k. in a., 29/9/18 (attached 18th Battalion).

20 Jenkins, John, M.C., Temp. Major (Acting Lieut.-Colonel), d. of w., 9/10/18 (attached 1st Monmouthshire Regiment).

Johnson, Harry Cecil, D.S.O., Brevet-Major, d. of w., 1/1/15 (Prisoner of War).

5 Johnson, Henry Earlam, 2nd Lieutenant, k. in a., 4/6/16.

11 Johnston, Benjamin, 2nd Lieutenant, died, 3/11/18 (in German hands).

2 Johnstone, Frederick John Lawrie, Lieutenant, d. of w., 29/8/16.

21 Jones, Philip Allsworth, Temp. 2nd Lieutenant, d. of w., 27/9/16.

Kay, Sir William Algernon Ireland, Bart., C.M.G., D.S.O., Brigadier-General, k. in a., 4/10/18 (and 3rd Infantry Brigade).

11 Kearton, Frank, Temp. 2nd Lieutenant, k. in a., 21/11/17.
Kelly, Henry John, Temp. 2nd Lieutenant, k. in a., 20/9/17 (attached 21st Battalion).
16 Kerr, Andrew Alan, 2nd Lieutenant, k. in a., 26/3/18.
Kidd, James Forrest, 2nd Lieutenant, died, 1/11/18 (and Royal Air Force).
King, Frank Maxfield, Major (temp.), k. in a., 22/3/18 (attached 9th Loyal North Lancashire Regiment).
4 King, Lucas Henry St. Aubyn, Lieutenant, k. in a., 8/5/15.
17 Kitchin, Ernest Harold, Captain (temp.), k. in a., 21/10/16 (15th Battalion).
16 Knight, Philip, 2nd Lieutenant (temp.), k. in a., 29/9/18.
Knowles, Richard Arthur Lees, M.C., Lieutenant, k. in a., 25/2/18 (attached 4th Battalion).
17 Lacey, Thomas Henry, Temp. 2nd Lieutenant, d. of w., 4/9/16.
4 Lagden, Ronald Owen, Captain, k. in a., 1-2/3/15.
12 Laird, James Duncan, 2nd Lieutenant (temp.), k. in a., 25/3/18.
9 Lambert, Jack Fellowes, 2nd Lieutenant, k. in a., 30/7/15.
Lambert, Montague Arthur, 2nd Lieutenant (temp.), k. in a., 2/10/18 (attached 18th Battalion).
13 Landale, Cyril, Captain (temp.), k. in a., 21/8/18.
18 Langford, John Joseph, Temp. 2nd Lieutenant, k. in a., 15/9/16.
18 Langford, Wallace George, Temp. 2nd Lieutenant, d. of w., 27/6/16.
2 Langton, Arthur Henry Brodie, Lieutenant, d. of w., 12/9/16.
6 Lawrence, Christopher Hal, 2nd Lieutenant, k. in a., 13/10/14 (attached 2nd Battalion).
6 Lawrence, Malcolm Eyton, Lieutenant, k. in a., 10/1/15 (attached 2nd Battalion).
18 Laycock, Joseph Harold, 2nd Lieutenant, k. in a., 7/10/16.
11 Leadbitter, Francis John Graham, Temp. 2nd Lieutenant, k. in a., 5/3/17.
8 Lee, Noel Esmond, Temp. Captain, k. in a., 24/8/17.
5 Leech, Geoffrey Charles Martyn, Temp. Lieutenant, d. of w., 9/4/17.
10 Leigh, John Egerton, Temp. Captain, k. in a., 4/4/17.
9 Le Mesurier, Haviland, 2nd Lieutenant (temp.), k. in a., 24/8/16.

18 Lester, John Beaumont, Captain (temp.), k. in a., 15/9/16.

1 Lever, Joseph, M.C., 2nd Lieutenant (temp.), d. of w., 1/10/18.

6 Levett, Richard William Byrd, 2nd Lieutenant, k. in a., 10/3/17 (attached 1st Battalion).

16 Levitt, Sydney Neville, 2nd Lieutenant (temp.), k. in a., 29/9/18.

16 Lewer, Richard Roy, Temp. Lieutenant, d. of w., 21/7/16.

7 Lewis, Lance Will, Temp. 2nd Lieutenant, k. in a., 9/8/16 (and Machine Gun Corps).

17 Lewis, Robert Frederick, Temp. 2nd Lieutenant, k. in a., 20/9/17 (and 117th Trench Mortar Battery).

6 Liddell, John Henry Tandy, Lieutenant, d. of w., 17/11/16 (attached 1st Battalion).

Lines, Herbert, Temp. 2nd Lieutenant, k. in a., 20/9/17 (attached 10th Battalion).

6 Loft, Percy Trotter, 2nd Lieutenant, k. in a., 24/3/18 (attached 18th Battalion).

7 Longbottom, Robert, Temp. 2nd Lieutenant, k. in a., 31/7/15.

6 Lonsdale, Arthur Carr Glyn, Lieutenant, k. in a., 10/3/15 (attached 2nd Battalion Royal Scots Fusiliers).

13 Low, John, 2nd Lieutenant, k. in a., 10/1/18.

5 Lowndes, Richard Forbes, 2nd Lieutenant, k. in a., 14/11/16 (attached 1st Battalion).

12 Loyd, Godfrey Beaumont, M.C., Captain, d. of w., 1/12/17.

12 Lycett Timothy, D.S.O., Lieutenant (temp. Captain), d. of w., 5/10/18.

3 Lyndall, Joseph Gwynne, Temp. 2nd Lieutenant, k. in a., 3/5/17.

5 Lynes, Wynne Parr, Captain, died, 8/10/16.

20 McDonald, Angus George, Temp. 2nd Lieutenant, died, 29/12/15.

5 Macdonald-Moreton, Norman Charles Henry, Temp. Captain, k. in a., 13/10/15.

MacIver, Kenneth Mackenzie, Lieutenant (temp.), killed, 30/10/18 (attached King's African Rifles).

Mackay, Terence Faulkner, 2nd Lieutenant (temp.), k. in a., 3/10/18 (attached 4th Battalion).

9 McKecknie, Alexander, 2nd Lieutenant (temp.), k. in a., 21/3/18.

4 Mackenzie, Mark Kincaid, Lieutenant, k. in a., 1/2/16.

McKenzie, Robert Andrew, Temp. 2nd Lieutenant, k. in a., 10/11/17 (attached 9th Battalion).
McKie, Eric, 2nd Lieutenant (temp.), k. in a., 24/3/18 (attached 11th Battalion).
Maclachlan, Alexander Fraser Campbell, C.M.G., D.S.O., Major (temp. Lieut.-Colonel, Commanding 12th Rifle Brigade), k. in a., 22/3/18.
2 McLure, David, 2nd Lieutenant (temp.), died, 8/3/18 (attached 4th Army Musketry School).
12 McMillan, Donald Cameron, Temp. 2nd Lieutenant, d. of w., 11/3/16.
3 Madeley, Sydney, 2nd Lieutenant, d. of w., 11/3/15.
11 Maggs, Eric William Bristowe, Temp. 2nd Lieutenant, k. in a., 20/8/18.
3 Makins, Geoffrey, M.V.O., Captain, d. of w., 23/8/15.
9 Mallalue, Maxwell, Captain, k. in a., 24/8/16.
Mann, Percy Charles, Temp. 2nd Lieutenant, k. in a., 31/7/17 (attached 17th Battalion).
8 Mansfield, Eric Oswald, Temp. 2nd Lieut., k. in a., 24/8/18.
Marlow, Albert Leopold Craddock, Temp. 2nd Lieutenant, d. of w., 4/4/17 (attached 10th Battalion).
12 Martin, William Gerald, Temp. Lieutenant (Acting Captain), k. in a., 14/1/17.
15 Mason, Gordon, Temp. 2nd Lieutenant, k. in a., 7/6/17 (attached 21st Battalion).
6 Mason, Peter, 2nd Lieutenant, k. in a., 17/2/17 (attached 1st Battalion).
18 Mathews, William Scott, Temp. Lieutenant, k. in a., 15/9/16.
10 Maude, John William Ashley, Temp. 2nd Lieutenant, k. in a., 24/8/15.
6 May, Herbert Cecil, 2nd Lieutenant, d. of w., 29/9/18 (attached 18th Battalion).
3 Maynard, John Wilmot, 2nd Lieutenant, k. in a., 24/4/15.
14 Meek, Hubert Kingsley, Temp. Captain, k. in a., 15/9/16.
13 Meikle, James Drysdale, Temp. 2nd Lieutenant, k. in a., 4/11/18.
6 Melville, William Woodfall, Lieutenant, k. in a., 9/5/15 (attached 2nd Battalion).
11 Meredith, Gerald, M.C., Temp. Captain, died, 27/3/18.
5 Messer, Allan Ernest, Captain, d. of w., 17/2/16 (attached 1st Battalion).

16 Middlecote, E. W. A. G., 2nd Lieutenant, k. in a., 3/10/18 (and Royal Air Force).

Mitchell, Norman Reid, Temp. 2nd Lieutenant, k. in a., 5/12/17 (attached 20th Battalion).

12 Molyneux, James Herbert, 2nd Lieutenant, k. in a., 16/8/17.

10 Moore, William Henry Hilme, Temp. Lieutenant, killed, 19/10/15.

Morrill, George Bertie, Temp. 2nd Lieutenant, k. in a., 23/10/18 (attached 13th Battalion).

2 Morris, Clive, Wilson, 2nd Lieutenant, k. in a., 9/5/15.

11 Morris, William Percy, Temp. Lieutenant, died, 28/12/18.

Morrison, E. A. A., Lieutenant, died, 13/11/18 (attached Royal Air Force).

5 Morrison, Kenneth Rae, 2nd Lieutenant, k. in a., 21/9/17 (attached 18th Battalion).

4 Morton, Daniel, 2nd Lieutenant, k. in a., 10/5/15.

2 Munro, Baillie Chisholm, M.C., 2nd Lieutenant, k. in a., 10/7/17.

12 Munsey, William Frederick, 2nd Lieutenant, k. in a., 16/8/17.

9 Murray, Charles William, Temp. 2nd Lieutenant, k. in a., 25/9/15.

20 Nainby, Whinfield Hamilton, Temp. 2nd Lieutenant, k. in a., 18/8/16.

20 Naish, Alfred Herbert, Temp. Lieutenant, k. in a., 13/7/16.

Nash, Llewellyn Charles, Lieutenant, d. of w., 29/9/15.

10 Newton, Charles Hercules Augustus Francis, Temp. Lieutenant, k. in a., 13/3/16.

5 Nivison, Robert Butler, Temp. 2nd Lieutenant, k. in a., 15-17/9/16 (attached 21st Battalion).

6 Noble, Norris Heatley, 2nd Lieutenant, d. of w., 15/8/16 (attached 1st Battalion).

6 Norbury, Francis Campbell, Captain, k. in a., 10/1/15 (attached 1st Battalion).

21 Norris, Ernest Arthur, 2nd Lieutenant, k. in a., 22/3/18 (attached 17th Battalion).

13 Norris, Gilbert Hume, Temp. Captain, d. of w., 9/3/18.

21 Norton, Frank Frederick, Temp. 2nd Lieutenant, k. in a., 20/9/17.

11 Orford, Stephen Mewburn, 2nd Lieutenant, k. in a., 25/6/16.

O'Rorke, Denis Clifford, M.C., Captain, k. in a., 24/3/18.

5 Orrey, Frederick William, Temp. 2nd Lieutenant, d. of w., 16/9/17 (attached 13th Battalion).

5 Osborne, Frederick William, 2nd Lieutenant, k. in a., 23/4/17 (attached 13th Battalion).
4 Oxley, Herman Grant, Temp. Lieutenant, k. in a., 4/11/18 (attached 2nd Battalion).
Paget, Desmond Otho, 2nd Lieutenant, k. in a., 21/3/18 (attached 7th Battalion).
9 Panes, Ernest Philip Morris, Temp. 2nd Lieutenant, k. in a., 25/9/15.
2 Parker, Cyril Edmund, 2nd Lieutenant, k. in a., 1/1/15.
1 Parker, Frederick Neville, 2nd Lieutenant, k. in a., 28/4/15.
17 Parry, Harold, Temp. 2nd Lieutenant, k. in a., 6/5/17.
6 Paul, Edgar Newton, Temp. Lieutenant (Acting Captain), k. in a., 28/12/17 (attached 12th Battalion).
12 Paul, Herbert James, Temp. 2nd Lieutenant, k. in a., 20/11/17.
6 Paul, Jeffery William Ensor, 2nd Lieutenant, k. in a., 27/7/16 (attached 1st Battalion).
Peacocke, Eric Forrester, 2nd Lieutenant, k. in a., 20/5/17 (attached 16th Battalion).
3 Pearse, John Francis Brice, Captain, k. in a., 29/4/15.
16 Pearson, Thomas Raleigh, 2nd Lieutenant, d. of w., 2/7/16.
9 Pemberton, Leigh, 2nd Lieutenant (temp.), k. in a., 25/9/15 (attached 9th Battalion Rifle Brigade).
13 Penhale, Thomas William, Temp. 2nd Lieutenant, d. of w., 15/4/17.
12 Perry, Stephen Ralph, Temp. Lieutenant, k. in a., 18/9/16.
20 Perry, William Claude, Temp. 2nd Lieutenant, d. of w., 13/7/16.
11 Pirret, James Kay, 2nd Lieutenant, k. in a., 4/4/17.
2 Pleydell-Bouverie, Jacob Edward, Lieutenant, d. of w., 1/11/14.
4 Poë, Charles Vernon Leslie, Captain, k. in a., 1-2/3/15.
Pollard, Ernest Madel, Temp. 2nd Lieutenant, d. of w., 16/8/17 (attached 12th Battalion).
11 Ponsonby, Cyril Thomas, Lieutenant, k. in a., 23/8/16.
6 Poole, Robert Evelyn Sandford, Lieutenant, k. in a., 4/11/18 (attached 13th Battalion).
15 Powell, George Alexander, Lieutenant, k. in a., 28/6/15.
17 Powles-Curtis, Arthur John, Temp. Captain, d. of w., 11/9/16.
6 Preece, Henry Raymond, Lieutenant, k. in a., 8/10/18 (attached 4th Battalion).

11 Priaulx, George Kendall, D.S.O., Major (temp. Lieut.-Colonel), k. in a., 24/3/18.

2 Purdon, George Hardress, 2nd Lieutenant, k. in a., 23/7/16.

7 Radcliffe, John Douglas Henderson, Captain, d. of w., 30/7/15.

12 Radford, Oswald Campbell, Temp. Captain, d. of w., 26/2/16.

7 Ramsay, Keith Winton, Temp. Lieutenant, k. in a., 3/5/16.

8 Rawes, Douglas, Lieutenant (temp.), d. of w., 16/8/15.

6 Rawson, Lionel Reginald, M.C., Lieutenant (Acting Captain), k. in a., 23/10/16.

18 Rayner, Percy Thomas, Temp. 2nd Lieutenant, k. in a., 26/8/18.

3 Reah, Kenneth Hudson, Temp. 2nd Lieutenant, died, 25/11/18.

Rebbeck, Edward William Wise, Temp. 2nd Lieutenant, killed, 24/4/16 (and Royal Flying Corps).

11 Rendall, George, 2nd Lieutenant, k. in a., 24/3/18.

9 Renton, Harry Noel Leslie, Temp. Lieutenant, k. in a., 30/7/15.

Rice, Arthur Henry, Lieutenant (temp.), k. in a., 20/9/17 (attached 17th Battalion).

11 Richardson, Frederick Edward John, 2nd Lieutenant (temp.), k. in a., 21/11/17.

9 Richmond, Harold Stedman, Temp. Captain, k. in a., 24/8/16.

18 Ridgway, William, 2nd Lieutenant, k. in a., 7/10/16.

6 Rixon, Theodore Meredith, M.C., Temp. Major (Acting Lieut.-Colonel), k. in a., 19/9/17 (attached 8th Battalion).

7 Robinson, Richmond Fothergill, (Temp. 2nd Lieutenant, k. in a., 30-31/7/15.

Robson, Gerald David, Lieutenant (temp.), k. in a., 24/8/17 (attached 9th Battalion).

17 Robson, William, Temp. 2nd Lieutenant, died, 30/10/18.

7 Roe, Albert John Havilland, 2nd Lieutenant (temp.), k. in a., 9/8/15.

8 Rogers, Robert Murray, 2nd Lieutenant, k. in a., 2/7/16.

7 Romer, Mark Leman Ritchie, Temp. Captain, d. of w., 20/9/16.

5 Rowley, The Hon. George Cecil, 2nd Lieutenant, k. in a., 17/2/17 (attached 1st Battalion).

19 Royden, Thomas Utting, Temp. 2nd Lieutenant, k. in a., 14/11/16 (attached 1st Battalion).

9 Runciman, Edmund Inglis, 2nd Lieutenant (temp. Lieutenant), k. in a., 22/10/15.

18 Rushworth, Henry, Temp. 2nd Lieutenant, k. in a., 11/8/18.

18 Ryan, John Stanley, Captain (temp.), k. in a., 25/6/16.

18 Sadd, Philip George, Temp. Major, k. in a., 15/9/16.

7 St. Aubyn, Francis Joseph, Temp. Lieutenant, k. in a., 10/4/17.

7 St. Aubyn, Morice Julian, M.C., Temp. Major, k. in a., 22/3/18.

2 St. Aubyn, The Hon. Piers Stewart, 2nd Lieutenant, k. in a., 31/10/14.

17 Saunders, Arthur Brain, Lieutenant (temp.), d. of w., 4/9/16.

Sawyer, Robert Fulwell, 2nd Lieutenant, d. of w., 24/8/17 (attached 17th Battalion).

6 Schwarz, Reginald Oscar, M.C., Captain (temp. Major), died, 18/11/18 (Staff Con. of Salvage).

12 Scott, Gilbert Ernest Josiah, Captain, k. in a., 25/3/18 (attached 19th Battalion).

13 Scott, James Robinson, Temp. 2nd Lieutenant, d. of w., 23/3/18.

2 Scudamore, John, 2nd Lieutenant, k. in a., 25/9/15.

13 Semple, William David, 2nd Lieutenant, k. in a., 29/6/16.

7 Seymour, Francis, Temp. Lieutenant, k. in a., 30/7/15.

4 Seymour, Harcourt, Temp. 2nd Lieutenant, d. of w., 9/11/18.

6 Shakerley, Eric Piers, Captain, k. in a., 10/3/15.

1 Shakerley, Geoffrey Charles, D.S.O., Major (temp. Lieut.-Colonel), k. in a., 15/5/15.

Shaw, Harold Joseph, Temp. 2nd Lieutenant, d. of w., 11/4/18 (attached 2nd Battalion).

7 Shaw, John William, Temp. 2nd Lieutenant, k. in a., 21/3/18.

6 Sheepshanks, William, 2nd Lieutenant, k. in a., 10/7/17 (attached 2nd Battalion).

4 Shennan, Douglas Francis Fairfax, Lieutenant, k. in a., 8/5/15.

6 Shepherd, Arthur Lindesay Moore, Lieutenant (temp.), died, 3/11/16 (and Royal Flying Corps) (in German hands).

2 Sherlock, Ronald Francis, Captain, k. in a., 23/7/16.

17 Sidney, Leicester Philip, 2nd Lieutenant, k. in a., 2/10/17 (and Royal Flying Corps).

13 Simonds, Charles Francis, Temp. Major, k. in a., 29/6/16.

8 Simpson, Henry Delafosse, Temp. Lieutenant, k. in a., 24/8/17.

6 Simpson, John Horace, 2nd Lieutenant, k. in a., 25/9/15 (attached 2nd Battalion).

18 Simpson, Rolf, 2nd Lieutenant (temp.), k. in a., 26/5/17.

24 Singlehurst, Reginald, Lieutenant (Acting Captain), k. in a., 21/3/18 (attached 9th Battalion).

1 Slater, Richard Henry, Temp. Captain, k. in a., 27/7/16.

Smith, Alexander Millar, Temp. 2nd Lieutenant, d. of w., 26/1/18 (attached 16th Battalion).

16 Smith, James Rockcliffe, M.C., Temp. Captain, k. in a., 20/5/17.

14 Snelgrove, Sidney Henry, Temp. Lieutenant, k. in a., 30/7/15 (attached 7th Battalion).

7 Somers-Smith, Richard William, 2nd Lieutenant, k. in a., 30/6/15.

3 Spanton, Thomas Henry, 2nd Lieutenant, k. in a., 1/7/15.

Spilling, Charles Nathaniel Jerald, Temp. 2nd Lieutenant, k. in a., 24/8/17 (attached 8th Battalion).

17 Spinney, Kenneth Trim, Temp. Lieutenant, k. in a., 3/9/16.

6 Spottiswoode, John, Captain, k. in a., 31/10/14 (attached 2nd Battalion).

22 Spreckley, Guy Lesingham, 2nd Lieutenant (temp.), k. in a., 23/4/17 (attached 7th Battalion).

5 Stearns, Patrick Chillingworth, 2nd Lieutenant, k. in a., 4/12/17 (attached 7th Battalion).

6 Stephen, Alan James, 2nd Lieutenant, d. of w., 18/10/18 (attached 2nd Battalion).

9 Stewart, Herbert, Temp. Lieutenant (acting Captain), k. in a., 9/4/17.

2 Stewart, John Cecil Grahame, 2nd Lieutenant, k. in a., 25/9/15.

6 Stokes, Robert John, 2nd Lieutenant, k. in a., 20/8/16 (attached 2nd Battalion).

Stone-Wootten, Frank, 2nd Lieutenant, k. in a., 21/9/17 (attached 18th Battalion).

16 Store, Albert Cash, Lieutenant, k. in a., 25/8/16 (attached 5th Battalion).

16 Surry, Norman Frederick, Temp. 2nd Lieutenant, k. in a., 12/10/18.

Tabor, John Morton, 2nd Lieutenant (temp.), k. in a., 21/9/17 (attached 18th Battalion).

9 Tanqueray, Andrew Alexander Truman, Temp. Captain, k. in a., 30/7/15.
10 Tate, Frederick Herman, Captain, k. in a., 11/8/17.
9 Tatham, John Savil, 2nd Lieutenant, k. in a., 9/2/17 (attached 6th King's Own Royal Lancashire Regiment).
13 Taylor, Frederick Cecil, Lieutenant (Acting Captain), k. in a., 22/8/18.
16 Taylor, Herbert, Temp. Captain, died, 11/10/15.
Taylor, Leslie Francis, M.C., Temp. Lieutenant, k. in a., 27/5/18 (and 8th Machine Gun Corps).
Tetlow, Joseph, Temp. Lieutenant, k. in a., 25/8/18 (attached 12th Battalion).
16 Thomas, Charles Alexander, Captain (temp.), k. in a., 23/8/16.
12 Thomas, Kenneth, Temp. Captain, k. in a., 3/6/16.
2 Thompson, George Samuel Rodie, 2nd Lieutenant, k. in a., 14/9/14.
Thornton-Smith, Arthur Donald, D.S.O., Temp. Lieutenant (Acting Captain), k. in a., 16/8/17 (attached 12th Battalion).
3 Thursby, Audley Delves, Temp. Captain, k. in a., 15/2/15.
3 Timmis, Richard Sutton, 2nd Lieutenant, d. of w., 10/5/15.
2 Tindall, Eric Vickers, 2nd Lieutenant, d. of w., 12/9/14.
8 Todd-Naylor, William Bryan, 2nd Lieutenant (temp.), k. in a., 24/8/16.
9 Toogood, Henry Duncan, Temp. 2nd Lieutenant, k. in a., 21/3/18.
1 Trench, The Hon. Frederick Sydney, Lieutenant, d. of w., 16/11/16.
Trowsdale, Charles Robert, 2nd Lieutenant, d. of w., 2/10/18 (attached 9th Battalion).
6 Tryon, George Arthur, M.C., Captain (Acting Lieut.-Colonel), k. in a., 7/11/18 (attached 4th Battalion).
Tufts, George Henry, Temp. 2nd Lieutenant, killed, 26/1/18 (and Royal Flying Corps).
11 Tunstall, James Charles Francis, 2nd Lieutenant (temp.), k. in a., 14/2/17.
2 Upton, The Hon. Eric Edward Montagu John, Captain, k. in a., 9/5/15.
9 Van Praagh, Ralp Bertram, Temp. 2nd Lieutenant, k. in a., 9/4/17.
6 Vigers, Robert Stanley Garrard, 2nd Lieutenant, d. of w., 5/4/17 (attached 10th Battalion).

5 Villiers, William Earle, Lieutenant (Acting Captain), k. in a., 10/11/17 (attached 9th Battalion).

7 Vincent, Frederick Charles, 2nd Lieutenant, k. in a., 21/3/18.

6 Wake, Charles, Baldwin Drury, 2nd Lieutenant, k. in a., 25/9/18 (attached 2nd Battalion).

7 Walford, Percy Frederick, Temp. 2nd Lieutenant, k. in a., 11/4/17.

2 Walker, Frank Benjamin, 2nd Lieutenant, k. in a., 23/7/16 (attached 6th Battalion).

5 Walley, Geoffrey Stephen, Lieutenant, d. of w., 20/8/16 (attached 2nd Battalion).

Wallington, Geoffrey Stafford, 2nd Lieutenant (temp. Captain), k. in a., 19/9/17 (attached to 10th Battalion).

19 Walsh, Frederick William, 2nd Lieutenant (temp.), d. of w., 11/7/16 (attached 17th Royal Welsh Fusiliers).

7 Walsham, Harold, Temp. 2nd Lieutenant, d. of w., 18/9/15.

18 Walton, Fred, Captain (temp.), k. in a., 15/9/16.

Walther, Kurt Albert, 2nd Lieutenant, k. in a., 4/11/18 (attached 13th Battalion).

Walton, Albert Bertie, M.M., 2nd Lieutenant, d. of w., 16/9/18 (attached 13th Battalion).

Ward, Kenneth Hilary Wodehouse, Captain, d. of w., 30/8/18. (*Spec. Employed.*)

8 Warham, Joseph, Temp. 2nd Lieutenant, d. of w., 7/5/17.

1 Waring, Edward Robert, 2nd Lieutenant, k. in a., 29/10/14.

21 Watson, Arthur Toward, Temp. Major, d. of w., 5/8/17.

8 Watson, Roger Wentworth, Temp. Lieutenant, k. in a., 30/7/15.

2 Webb, Evelyn Maxwell, Captain, k. in a., 23/7/16.

18 Webb, Thomas Richard Henry, Temp. 2nd Lieutenant, d. of w., 31/7/17.

13 Webster, Erwin Wentworth, Temp. Captain, k. in a., 9/4/17.

17 Welter, Leslie Dingman, 2nd Lieutenant, k. in a., 18/6/17.

1 West, Harold Douglas, 2nd Lieutenant, d. of w., 25/3/18.

Westerman, Harry, 2nd Lieutenant, k. in a., 11/8/18 (attached 21st Battalion).

1 Whall, Edwin Lionel, Haversham, 2nd Lieutenant (temp.), k. in a., 18-21/9/17.

12 White, Charles Douglas, 2nd Lieutenant, died, 10/5/16 (and Royal Flying Corps).

White, Wilfred Appleton, 2nd Lieutenant, k. in a., 3/10/18 (attached 4th Battalion).

7 Whitley, Charles, M.C., Temp. Captain, k. in a., 11/4/17.
4 Whitley, Herbert, 2nd Lieutenant, k. in a., 21/2/17.
13 Wiggett, Allan James, Temp. 2nd Lieutenant, d. of w., 15/3/16 (in German hands).
7 Wilberforce, W. R. S., 2nd Lieutenant, killed, 2/6/18 (and Royal Air Force).
Wilding, Horace Holden, 2nd Lieutenant, k. in a., 13/9/18 (attached 13th Battalion).
18 Willans, William Alan Jenne, Acting Captain, k. in a., 24/3/18.
7 Williams, Felix Roland, Temp. 2nd Lieutenant, k. in a., 10/4/17.
4 Williams, H. I., 2nd Lieutenant, k. in a., 18/10/18.
7 Williamson, George Hamilton, M.C., Captain (temp.), d. of w., 12/4/17.
7 Williamson, Kenneth Harper, Temp. 2nd Lieutenant, d. of w., 19/4/17.
6 Willmot, Robert Dyott, 2nd Lieutenant, k. in a., 17/2/18 (attached 2nd Battalion).
6 Wilson, Douglas Russell, 2nd Lieutenant, k. in a., 25/10/18.
15 Wilson, James Bannerman Gartly, Temp. 2nd Lieutenant, d. of w., 30/4/17 (attached 12th Battalion).
4 Wingfield, Cecil John Talbot Rhys, Captain, d. of w., 29/4/15.
18 Wingfield, Glanville Harry, 2nd Lieutenant, k. in a., 12/7/16.
Witt, Cecil, Temp. 2nd Lieutenant, k. in a., 28/2/18 (and Royal Flying Corps).
9 Wood, Thomas Anthony, Captain, died, 16/7/18.
Woodlock, Francis Joseph, Temp. 2nd Lieutenant, k. in a., 13/8/17 (attached 11th Battalion).
17 Woolmer, Stanley Herbert France, 2nd Lieutenant (temp.), k. in a., 3/9/16.
16 Wyand, Edward Herbert, Temp. Captain, k. in a., 30/1/16.
21 Yeaman, Denis John, Temp. 2nd Lieutenant, k. in a., 5-10/10/16.

It will be seen from the list at the beginning of this volume that of 145 officers serving in the four regular battalions of the Regiment on August 1, 1914, 43 were killed in action or died of wounds. Only 1 died from other causes. This was Captain W. L. Clinton, whose death was as much the result of active service as that of the other forty-three. Captain Clinton was taken prisoner at Nieuport in July 1917, and his escape from the prisoners of war camp at Graudenz, West Prussia (after many unsuccessful attempts), is thus described by a fellow captive :

' " On the outside of our buildings and fixed to the outside walls by strong iron brackets were the electric light cables. There were, I think, altogether four wires, and of these two ran just a little below the level of the second-floor windows, and the other two were on a level about 2 feet below. The lower pair were between 30 feet and 40 feet from the ground. They ran from one of the buildings in which we were housed right over the two fences which enclosed us from the outer world, and were then affixed by an iron bracket on to the wall of another building, which was used as a guard-room by our guard. The distance between the two buildings would be about 20 yards. About 7 p.m. on October 4 Clinton got out of a window on the second floor in our building ; he got his feet on to the lower wires, and he gripped the upper wires with his hands, and proceeded to work himself along the wires from our building over the barbed wire towards the guard room.

' " Needless to say, the wires sagged and swayed considerably during his passage. He was also spotted by the sentries. But he worked his way across to the guard house, and let himself down from there with a rope with which he had provided himself, and got clear away with a running start of about twenty seconds. The sentries made a mess of their job by failing to shoot when they first saw him—I fancy they thought that it was not possible that what they saw on the wires was a prisoner trying to escape."

' This was a truly magnificent feat, but Clinton never lived to reap the full fruits of his daring. After many vicissitudes, he received the truest friendship from the Poles, and, passing through Warsaw, Cracow, and Vienna, he eventually reached Belgrade on November 16, but on arriving at the hospital he was found to be suffering from pleurisy and pneumonia. He made a gallant struggle against fate, but his weakened constitution was unable to withstand the attack, and he passed away November 22 [1918].'

His fellow prisoner adds that Clinton's feat was described by an experienced eye-witness as ' the bravest thing he had ever seen.'

INDEX

C

M

Q

R

S

V

W

X

Y

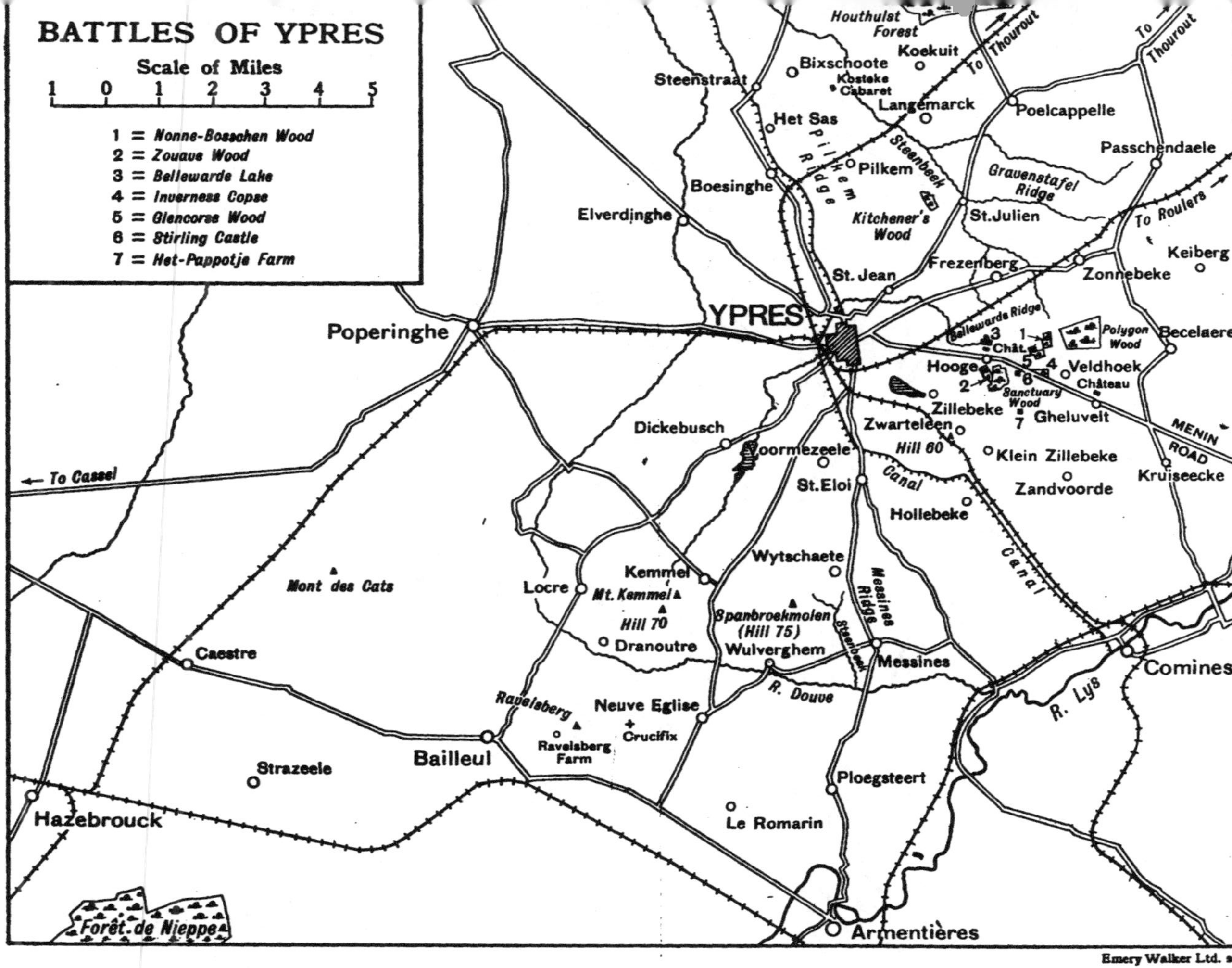
BATTLES OF YPRES
Scale of Miles
1 0 1 2 3 4 5
1 = Nonne-Bosschen Wood
2 = Zouave Wood
3 = Bellewarde Lake
4 = Inverness Copse
5 = Glencorse Wood
6 = Stirling Castle
7 = Het-Pappotje Farm
Houthulst Forest
Koekuit
To Thourout
To Thourout
Bixschoote
Kosteke Cabaret
Steenstraat
Langemarck
Poelcappelle
Het Sas
Pilkem Ridge
Steenbeek
Pilkem
Passchendaele
Gravenstafel Ridge
Boesinghe
Kitchener's Wood
St. Julien
To Roulers
Elverdinghe
Keiberg
St. Jean
Frezenberg
Zonnebeke
YPRES
Bellewarde Ridge
Polygon Wood
Becelaere
Poperinghe
Chât.
Hooge
Veldhoek
Château
Sanctuary Wood
Zillebeke
Gheluvelt
Zwarteleen
MENIN ROAD
Dickebusch
Voormezeele
Hill 60
Klein Zillebeke
Kruiseecke
To Cassel
St. Eloi
Canal
Zandvoorde
Hollebeke
Wytschaete
Canal
Kemmel
Messines Ridge
Mont des Cats
Locre
Mt. Kemmel
Spanbroekmolen (Hill 75)
Hill 70
Steenbeek
Caestre
Dranoutre
Wulverghem
Messines
Comines
R. Douve
R. Lys
Ravelsberg
Neuve Eglise
Crucifix
Ravelsberg Farm
Bailleul
Strazeele
Ploegsteert
Hazebrouck
Le Romarin
Forêt de Nieppe
Armentières
Emery Walker Ltd. sc.

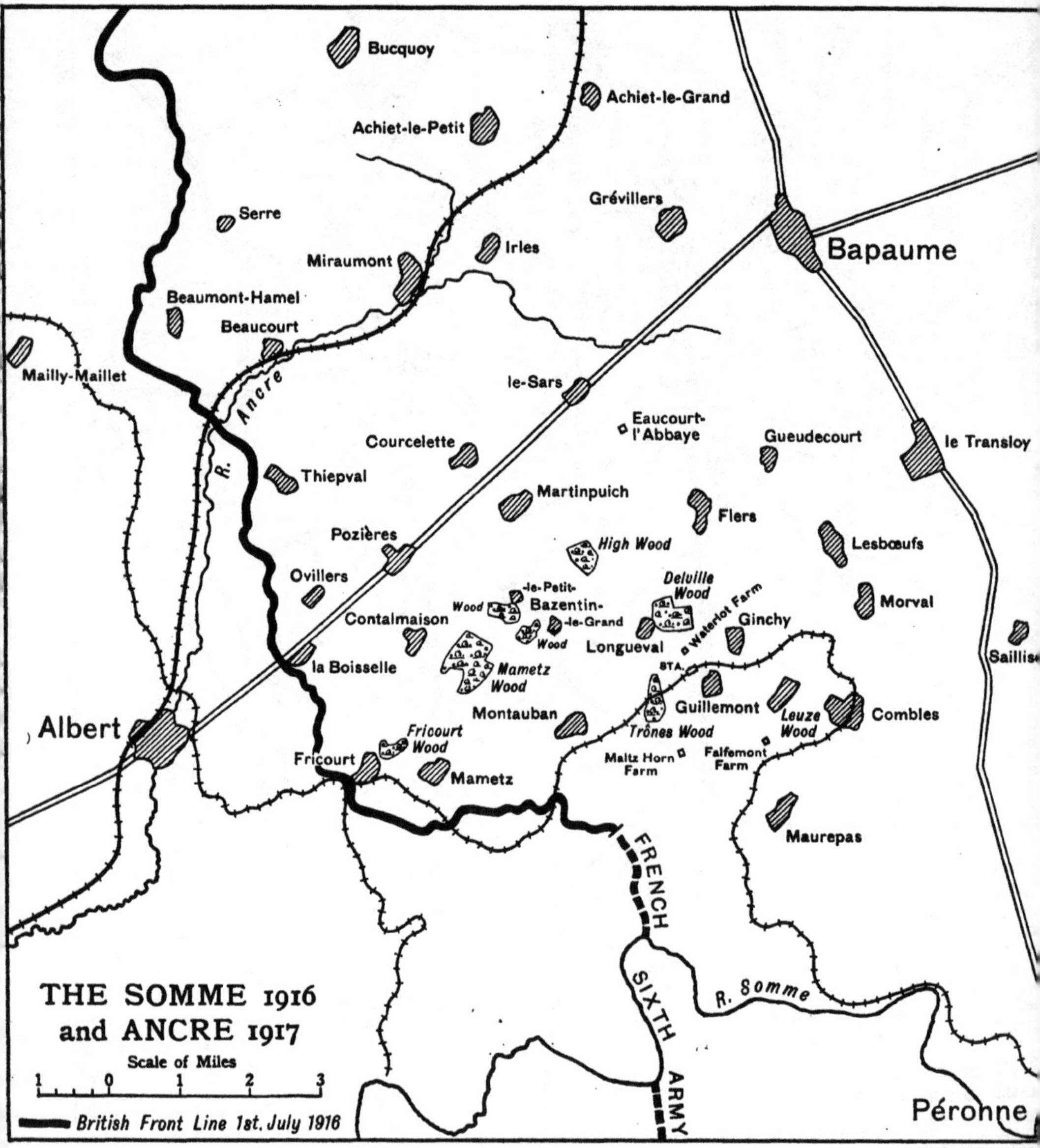

Emery Walker Ltd.

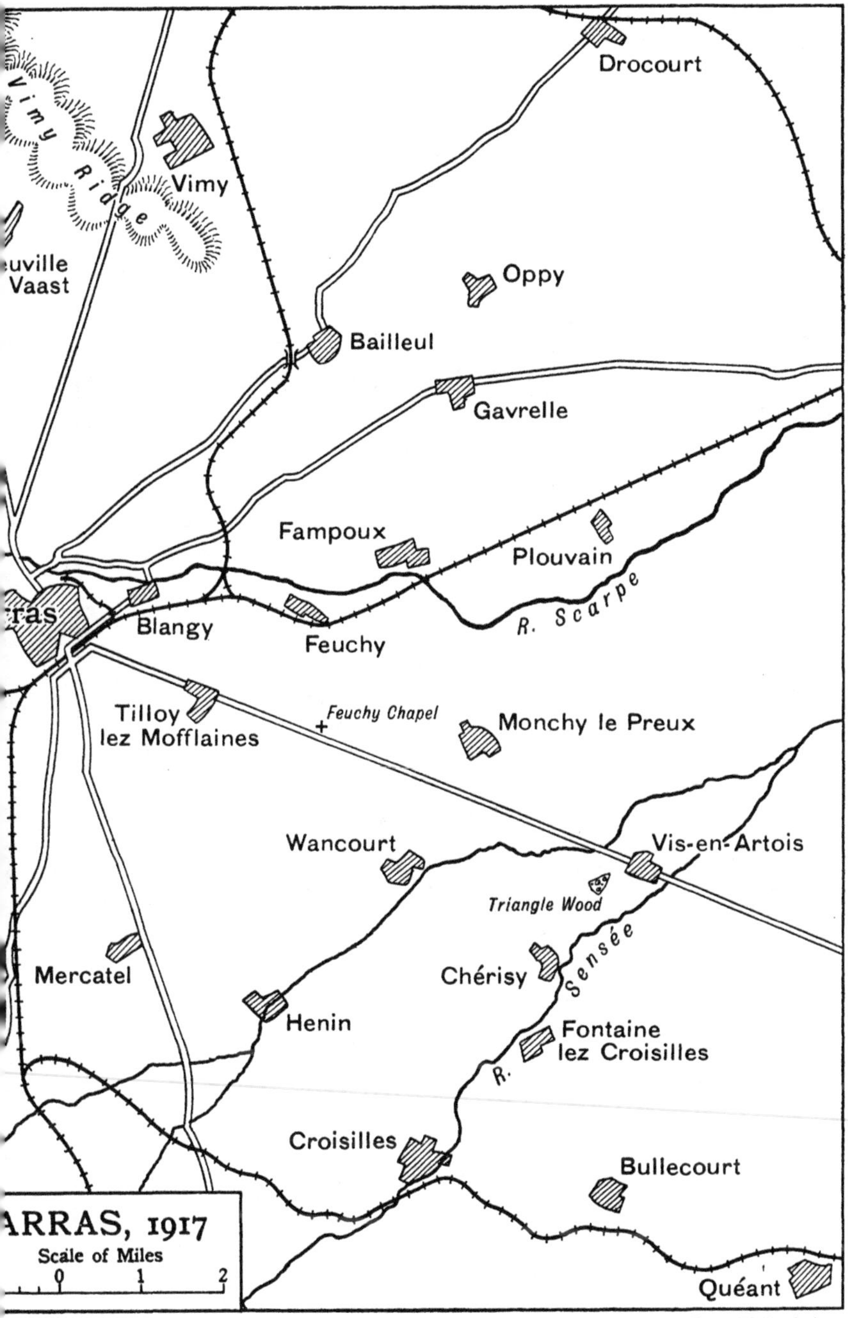

Emery Walker Ltd. sc.

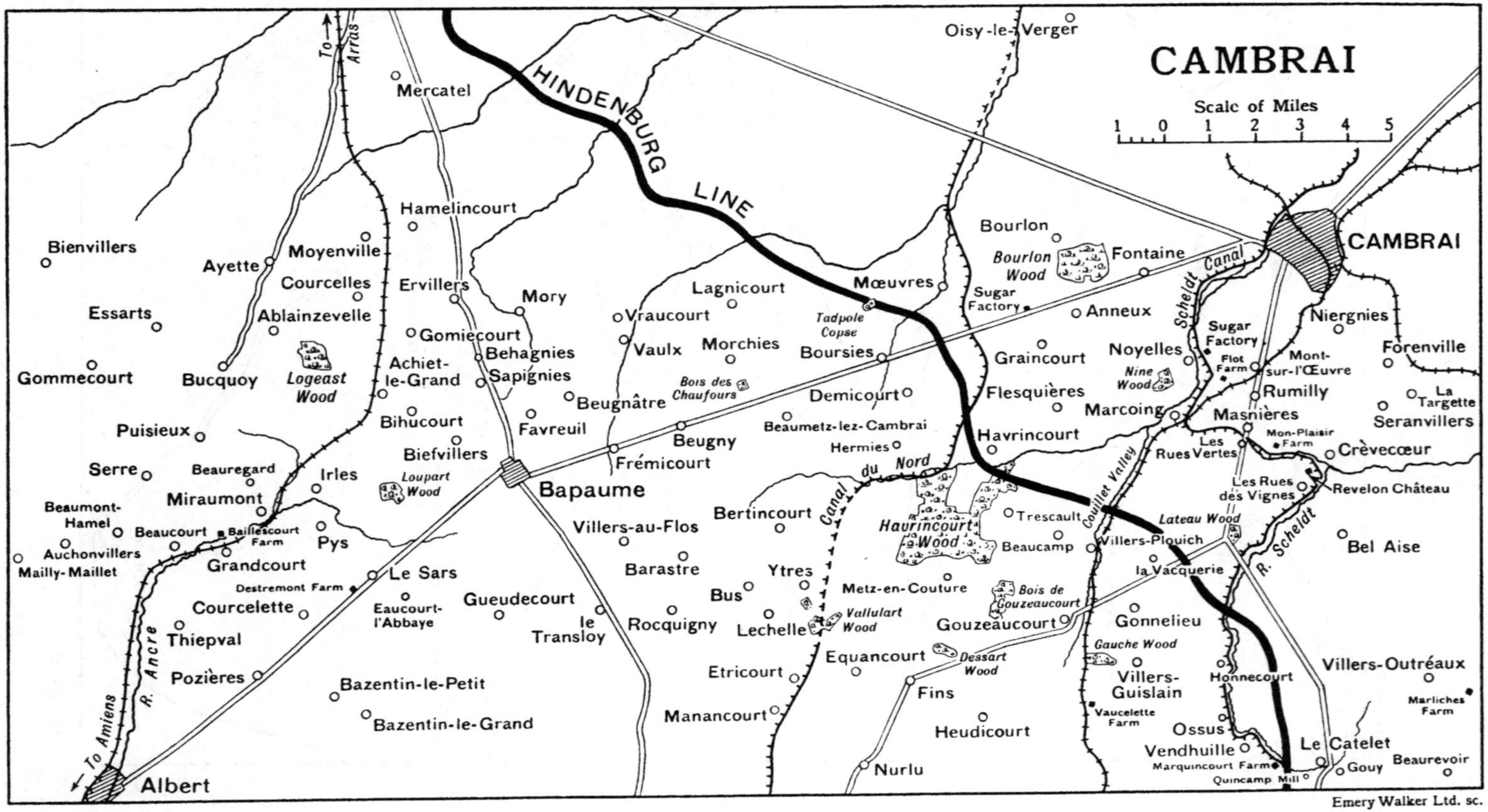

Emery Walker Ltd. sc.

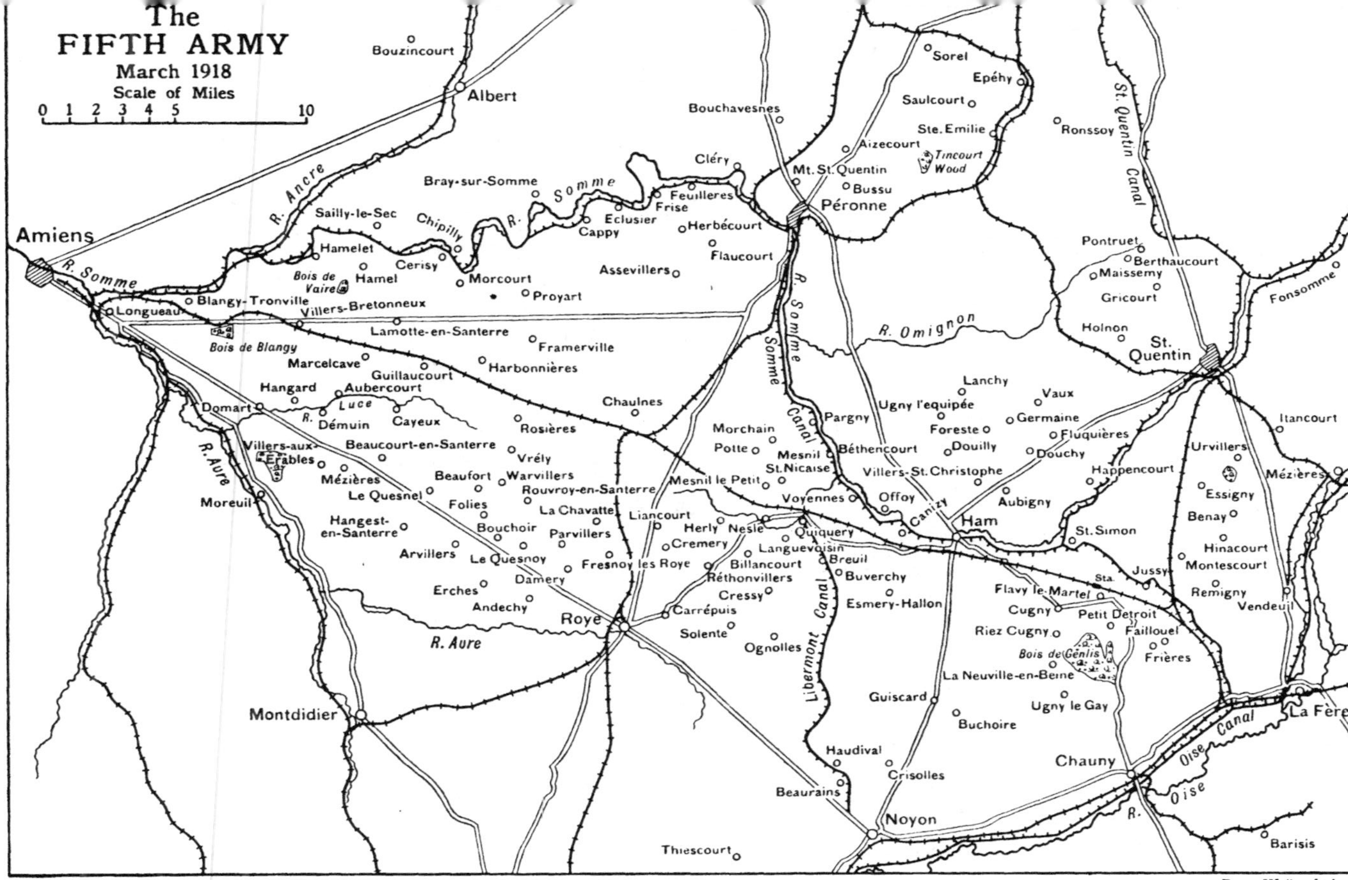

Emery Walker Ltd. sc.

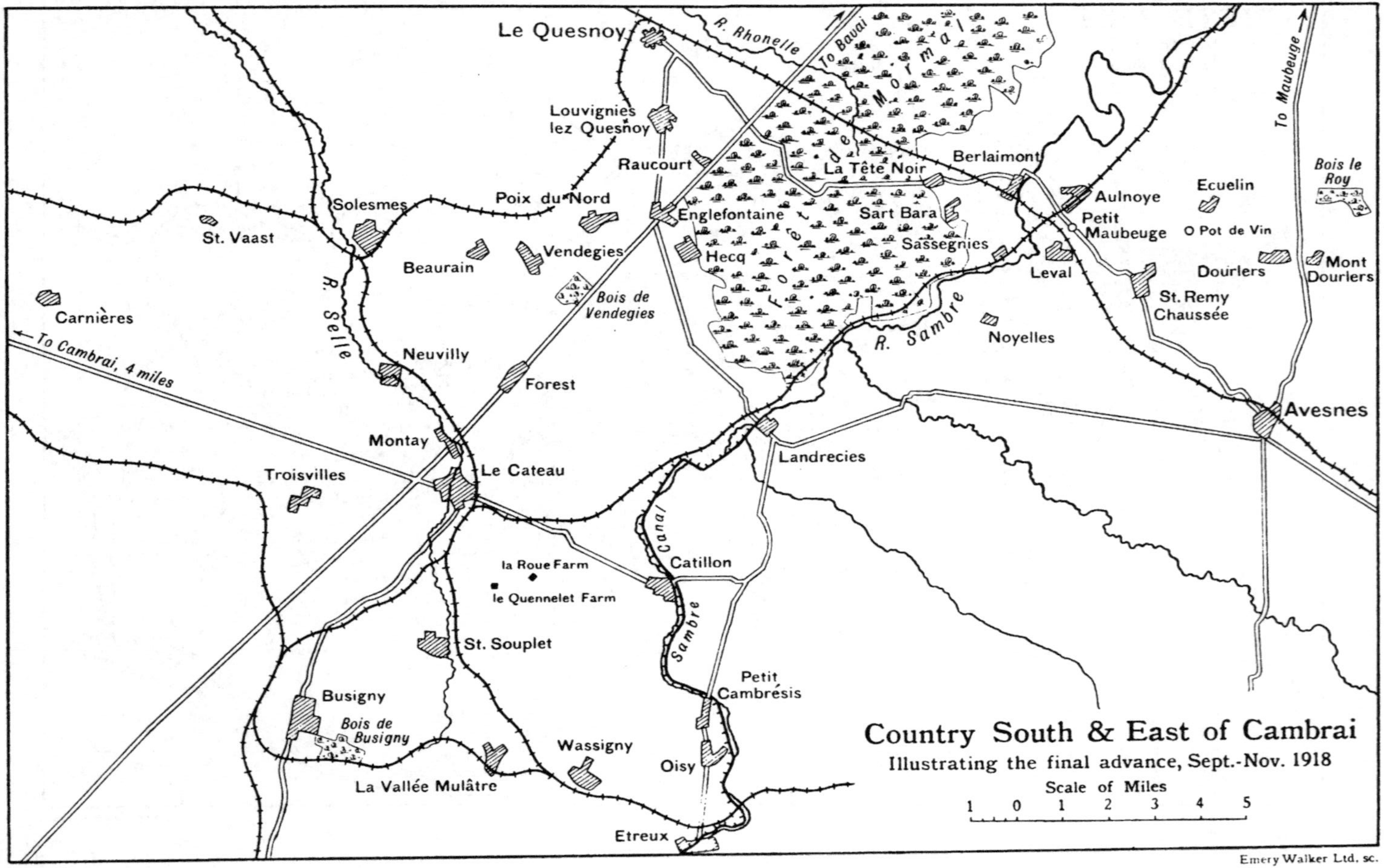

Country South & East of Cambrai
Illustrating the final advance, Sept.-Nov. 1918

Emery Walker Ltd. sc.

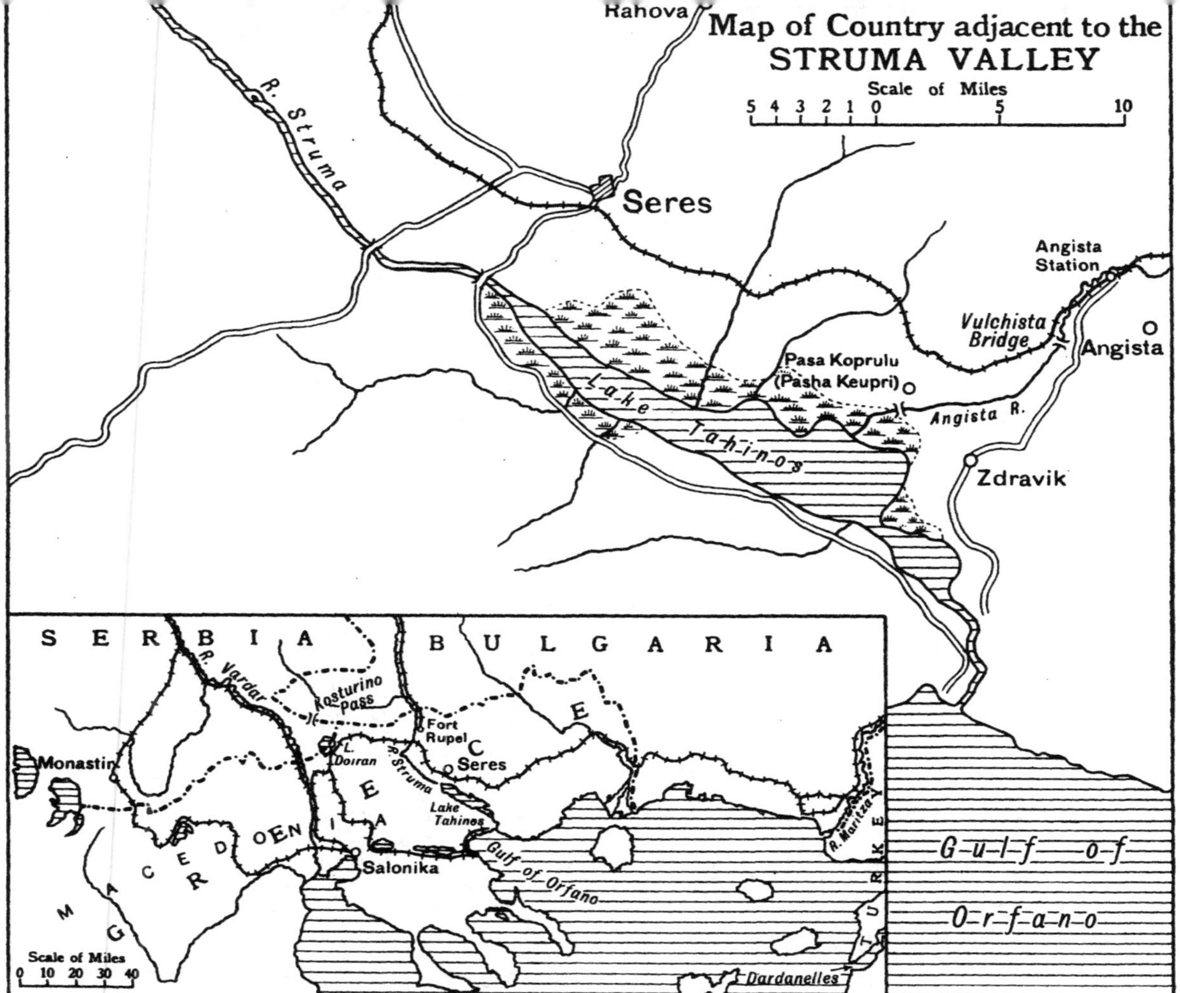

Emery Walker Ltd. sc.

MAP VIII

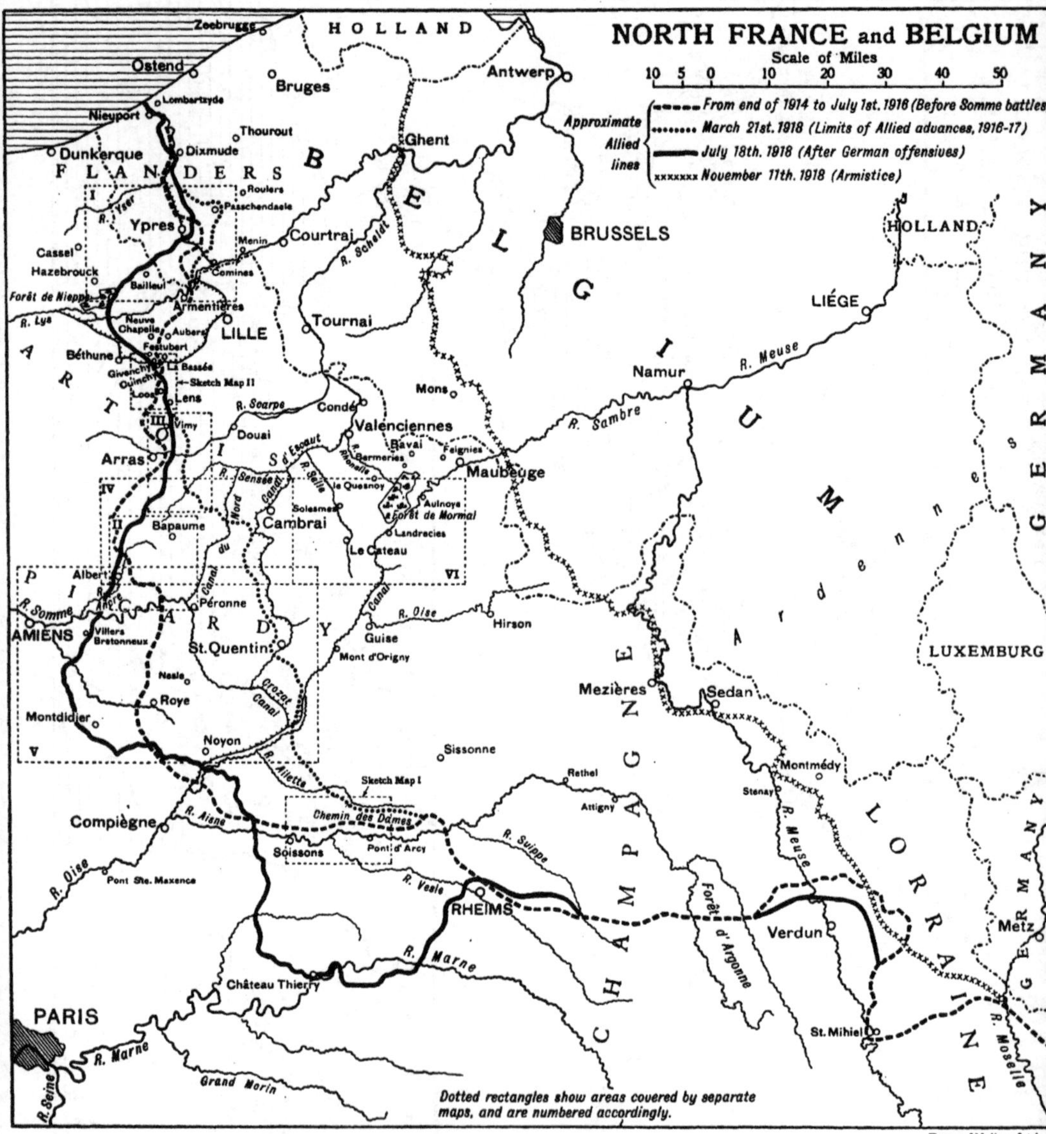

Emery Walker Ltd.

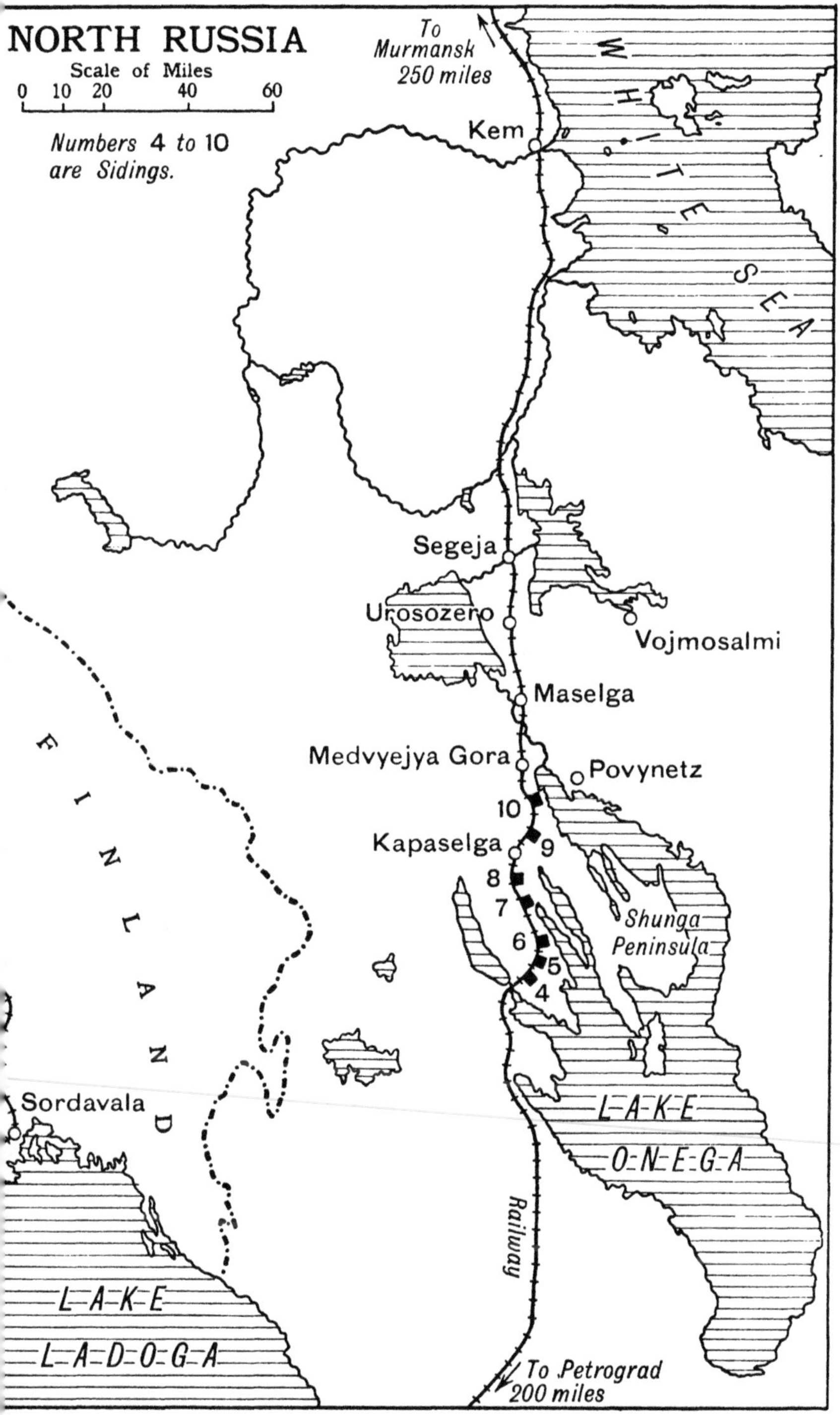

Emery Walker Ltd. sc.

Lightning Source UK Ltd.
Milton Keynes UK
UKHW021300100521
383454UK00002B/3

9 781843 424567